WELDING

Principles and Applications

FOURTH EDITION

STUDY GUIDE/LAB MANUAL

Larry Jeffus
Dewayne Roy

Delmar Publishers

an International Thomson Publishing company I(T)P®

Albany • Bonn • Boston • Cincinnati • Detroit • London • Madrid
Melbourne • Mexico City • New York • Pacific Grove • Paris • San Francisco
Singapore • Tokyo • Toronto • Washington

NOTICE TO THE READER

Publisher does not warrant or guarantee any of the products described herein or perform any independent analysis in connection with any of the product information contained herein. Publisher does not assume, and expressly disclaims, any obligation to obtain and include information other than that provided to it by the manufacturer.

The reader is expressly warned to consider and adopt all safety precautions that might be indicated by the activities herein and to avoid all potential hazards. By following the instructions contained herein, the reader willingly assumes all risks in connection with such instructions. The Publisher makes no representation or warranties of any kind, including but not limited to, the warranties of fitness for particular purpose or merchantability, nor are any such representations implied with respect to the material set forth herein, and the publisher takes no responsibility with respect to such material. The publisher shall not be liable for any special, consequential, or exemplary damages resulting, in whole or part, from the readers' use of, or reliance upon, this material.

Printed in the United States of America
10 9 8 7 6 5 4 3

For more information, contact Delmar, 3 Columbia Circle, PO Box 15015, Albany, NY 12212-0515; or find us on the World Wide Web at http://www.delmar.com

International Division List

Japan:
Thomson Learning
Palaceside Building 5F
1-1-1 Hitotsubashi, Chiyoda-ku
Tokyo 100 0003 Japan
Tel: 813 5218 6544
Fax: 813 5218 6551

Australia/New Zealand
Nelson/Thomson Learning
102 Dodds Street
South Melbourne, Victoria 3205
Australia
Tel: 61 39 685 4111
Fax: 61 39 685 4199

UK/Europe/Middle East:
Thomson Learning
Berkshire House
168-173 High Holborn
London
WC1V 7AA United Kingdom
Tel: 44 171 497 1422
Fax: 44 171 497 1426

Latin America:
Thomson Learning
Seneca, 53
Colonia Polanco
11560 Mexico D.F. Mexico
Tel: 525-281-2906
Fax: 525-281-2656

Canada:
Nelson/Thomson Learning
1120 Birchmount Road
Scarborough, Ontario
Canada M1K 5G4
Tel: 416-752-9100
Fax: 416-752-8102

Asia:
Thomson Learning
60 Albert Street, #15-01
Albert Complex
Singapore 189969
Tel: 65 336 6411
Fax: 65 336 7411

Library of Congress Cataloging-in-Publication Data

ISBN: 0-8273-8241-3

CONTENTS

SECTION 5 RELATED PROCESSES

SECTION 6 RELATED PROCESSES AND TECHNOLOGY

SECTION 7 OXYFUEL

INTRODUCTION

Many job opportunities exist for welders who have demonstrated their ability to make acceptable welds in various positions for the major welding processes. In addition to manual skills, the welder must have a basic understanding of the science of welding: how the weld is accomplished; why the various components of the welding setup interact as they do; and how the factors affecting the weld can be varied to obtain a better weld or to meet or overcome specific conditions.

To gain welding skills, the student performs the practices outlined in *WELDING: PRINCIPLES AND APPLICATIONS,* fourth edition. By performing welds in different positions on various types of material, the student will achieve proficiency in performing each major welding process. With practice, the student will gain enough skill and confidence in his or her abilities to complete certification tests for the various welding positions.

The other important part of becoming a good welder is to gain an understanding of the "why" of welding. Why do metals react as they do to heat? Why is one welding process preferred over another for a particular job? Why does the act of modifying one or more of the factors affecting a weld result in a better or different weld? The purpose of this guide is to help you answer these questions by developing a firm understanding of the theory of welding.

The *STUDY GUIDE/LAB MANUAL is* designed to focus your studies and assist in organizing your learning of welding principles. Once the reading assignments in the text have been completed, the instructor will ask you to complete the appropriate section in this guide. The sections consist of a combination of multiple choice questions, lists, matching items, identification, and completion questions. (Not all types of questions appear in each unit of the guide.) Do not guess at the answers to the questions. If you do not know the answer, leave the space blank. You can then see the topics that will need review again until you understand the information. Ask your instructor for help if you continue to have difficulty with any of the welding principles. You will be a better welder if you combine welding skills with a firm understanding of the *how* and *why* of welding.

Included with the *STUDY GUIDE/LAB MANUAL* is the Welding Symbols Wheel, a handy key to the symbols and abbreviations found on a welding print. Designed by Louis J. Siy, author of *Blueprint Reading for Welders,* 5E, the Wheel is a great reference tool for the welding booth or workstation.

CHAPTER 1: INTRODUCTION TO WELDING

PRACTICE 1-1

Name Louis Flores Date 4-5-00

Class Welding Instructor Hernandez Grade ____________

OBJECTIVE: After completing this practice, you should be able to identify items that are manufactured using various welding processes.

EQUIPMENT AND MATERIALS NEEDED FOR THIS PRACTICE

1. Paper and pencil.

INSTRUCTIONS

A. Answer the following questions by looking around your school, home, and community to identify items manufactured with the following welding process.

1. List 4 items that are manufactured using the oxyfuel welding, brazing or cutting process.

    Process Item

    a. ____________, ____

    b. ____________, ____

    c. ____________, ____

    d. ____________, ____

2. List 4 items that are manufactured using the shielding metal arc welding process.

    a. ____

    b. ____

    c. ____

    d. ____

3. List 4 items that are manufactured using the gas metal arc welding process.

    a. ____

    b. ____

    c. ____

    d. ____

4. List 4 items that are manufactured using the flux cored arc welding process.

    a. ____

    b. ____

    c. ____

    d. ____

5. List 4 items that are manufactured using the gas tungsten arc welding process.

   a. ____________________

   b. ____________________

   c. ____________________

   d. ____________________

PRACTICE 1-2

OBJECTIVE: After completing this practice, you should be able to identify various items found on control panels of different types of welding machinery.

EQUIPMENT AND MATERIALS NEEDED FOR THIS PRACTICE

1. Pencil and paper

INSTRUCTIONS

1. Using a separate sheet of paper, sketch the following types of welding machinery that are in your shop and identify the controls, switches and other items found on the main panel.

   a. Shielded metal arc welder
   b. Gas metal arc welder
   c. Flux cored arc welder
   d. Gas tungsten arc welder
   e. Plasma arc cutting machine

PRACTICE 1-3

OBJECTIVE: After completing this practice, you should be able to identify those jobs available in your local newspaper's employment section that require welding skills.

EQUIPMENT AND MATERIALS NEEDED FOR THIS PRACTICE

1. Pencil and paper

INSTRUCTIONS

1. Using your local newspaper, make a list of the jobs listed in the help wanted section that might require welding skills.

   a. ____________________

   b. ____________________

   c. ____________________

   d. ____________________

   e. ____________________

   f. ____________________

   g. ____________________

   h. ____________________

   i. ____________________

   j. ____________________

CHAPTER 1: INTRODUCTION TO WELDING QUIZ

Name Louis Flores Date 4-5-00

Class Welding Instructor Hernandez Grade ____________

Instructions: Carefully read Chapter 1 in the text and answer the following questions.

A. IDENTIFICATION

In the space provided identify the items shown on the illustration.

1. Identify the welding process shown.

____

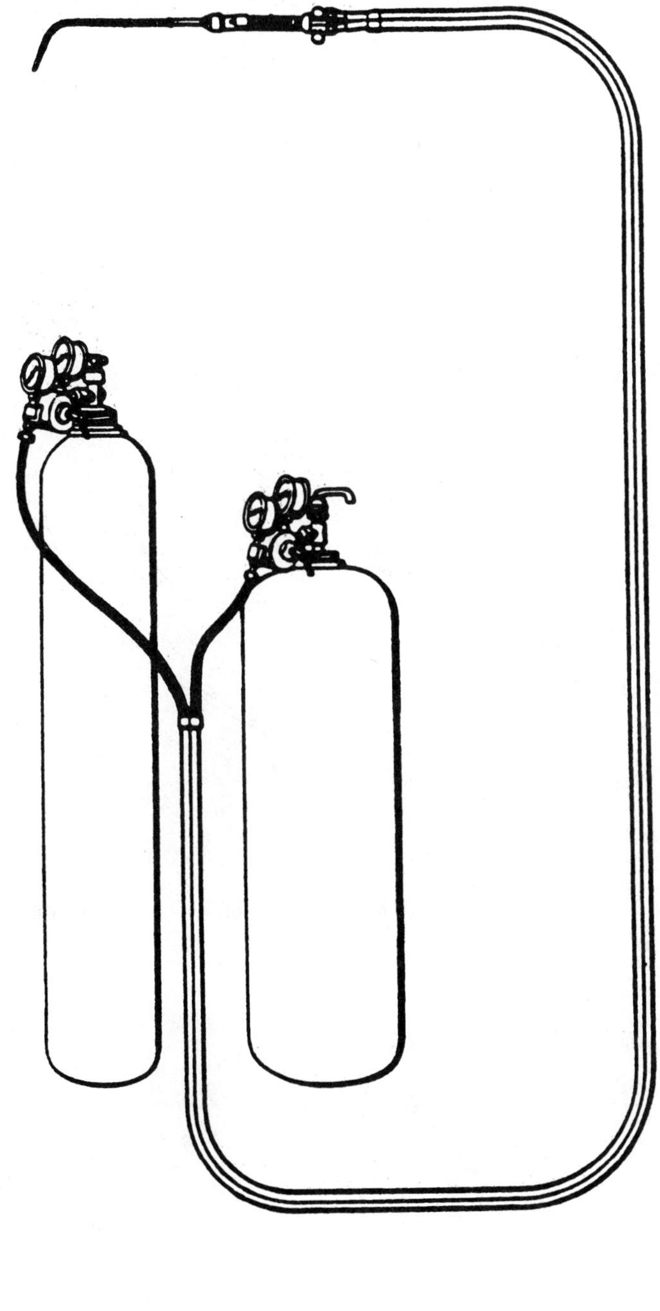

2. Identify the welding process shown.

____

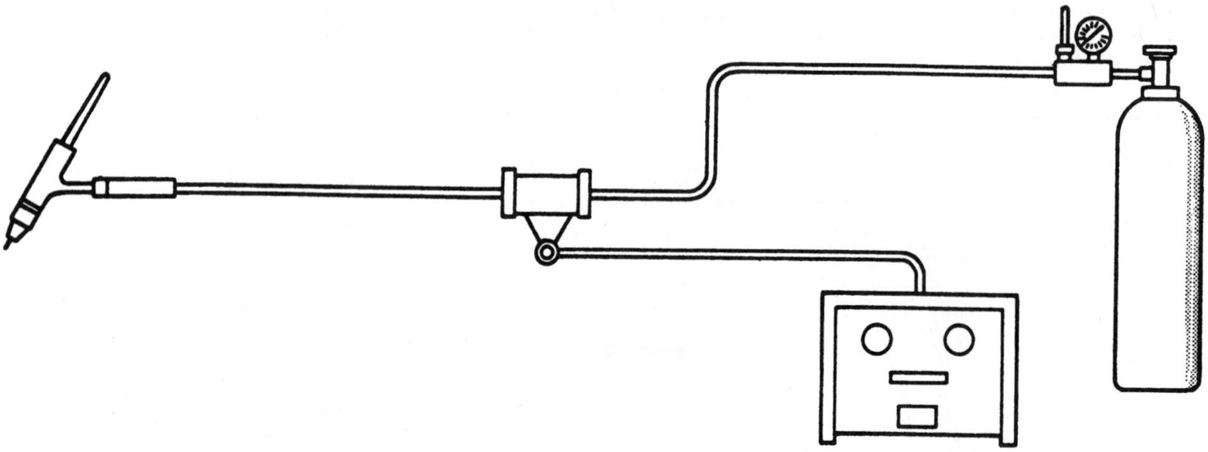

3. Identify the welding process shown.

____

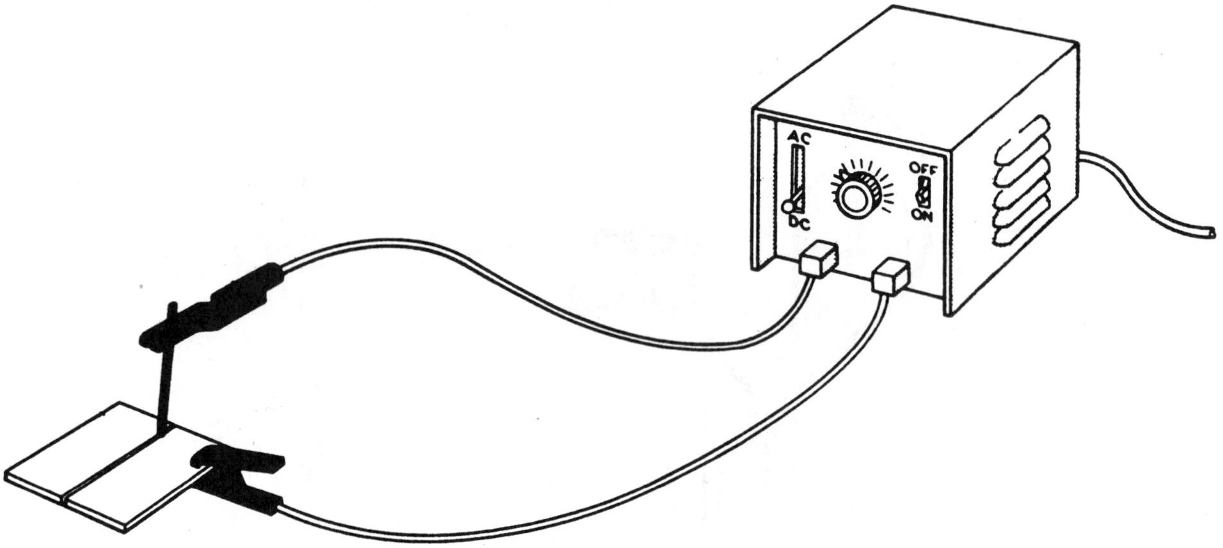

B. SHORT ANSWER

4. Using Table 1-1 on page 7 in the text give the full name for the following welding or allied process abbreviations.

   a. AB
   b. DS
   c. PEW
   d. MAC
   e. PAW
   f. FOW
   g. OFC-A
   h. SAW
   i. IW
   j. TW

5. What were the early work implements that were fastened together by individuals? ____________________.

6. When did forge welding become popular? ____________________.

7. What are four areas of modern employment that use welding?

   a. ____________________

   b. ____________________

   c. ____________________

   d. ____________________

8. What is the correct term for stick welding?

9. Convert 12 in. to mm

10. Convert 10°F to °Celsius

11. Convert 0°Kelvin to °C

12. Convert 50 sq ft to sq yd

13. Convert 8 yards to ft

14. Convert 40,000 meters to kilometers

15. Convert 460°Rankine to °F

C. ESSAY

16. Describe the type of jobs the following workers may do.

    a. welders
    b. tack welders
    c. welding operator
    d. welders' helper
    e. welder assemblers or welding fitters
    f. welding inspectors
    g. welding shop supervisor
    h. welding sales
    i. welding shop owner
    j. welding engineer

17. List and explain the various considerations that must be used when selecting the best joining process to be used for a particular welding job.

18. How does the American Welding Society define a weld?

19. What is welding?

D. DEFINITIONS

Define the following terms: qualification, certification, coalescence, OFC, OFW, TB, SMAW, GTAW, GMAW, FCAW, manual, semiautomatic, machine, automatic, automated, welder fitters.

____

____

____

____

____

CHAPTER 2: SAFETY IN WELDING; IMPORTANT SAFETY RULES FOR WELDERS

1. A welder will only weld with proper eye protection: One of the primary concerns in welding is the protection of the eyes.
2. Welders will always wear protective clothing: Protective clothing for your personal protection will be required for all welding.
3. Welders may only weld with proper ventilation: Welding fumes can be hazardous to the welding operator. Fumes will vary depending on the type of welding or cutting operation along with the type of filler metal, fluxes, coating, and the base metal being welded on.
4. Welders must never weld on any type of vessel or tank that has contained any type of flammable material: Welding or cutting should not be performed on drums, barrels, tanks, or other containers until they have been cleaned thoroughly, eliminating all flammable materials and all substances (such as detergents, solvents, greases, tars, or acids) which might produce flammable, toxic, or explosive vapors when heated.
5. Welders are not to lubricate pressure regulators: Do not use oil, grease, or any type of hydro-carbon product on any torch, regulator, or cylinder fitting. Oil and grease in the presence of oxygen may burn with explosive forces.
6. Welders must always use acetylene cylinders in the vertical (upright) position: Acetylene cylinders that have been lying on their side must stand upright for 15 or more minutes before they can be used safely.
7. Welders are not to use more than 15 psig acetylene working pressure: Acetylene becomes unstable at pressures higher than 15 psig and could explode at higher pressures.
8. Welders will always secure high pressure cylinders: Cylinders must be secured with a chain or other device so that they cannot be knocked over accidentally.
9. Welders are not to grind aluminum on a grinding stone designed for ferrous material. The stone will become glazed (the surface clogs with metal) and may explode due to frictional heat buildup.
10. Welders are always to keep a clean workstation: Always keep a safe clean work area.
11. Welders must always protect others from the welding arc's light: Welding curtains must always be used to protect other workers in an area that might be exposed to the welding light.
12. Welders must protect their hearing: Damage to your hearing caused by high sound levels may not be detected until later in life, and the resulting loss in hearing is non-recoverable. It will not get better with time. Each time you are exposed to high levels of sound your hearing will become worse.
13. Welders must always guard against problems caused by welding on used metal: Extreme caution must be taken to avoid the fumes produced when welding is done on dirty or used metal. Any chemicals that might be on the metal will become mixed with the welding fumes, and this combination can be extremely hazardous. All metal must be cleaned before welding to avoid this potential problem.
14. Welders must avoid electrical shock: Welding cables must never be spliced within 10 feet (3 m) of the electrode holder. All extension cords and equipment power cords must be in good repair. Never use equipment not properly grounded.
15. Welders must not carry flammable items: There is no safe place to carry butane lighters and matches while welding or cutting. They may catch fire or explode if they are subjected to welding heat or sparks. Butane lighters may explode with the force of 1/4 stick of dynamite. Matches can erupt into a ball of fire. Both butane lighters and matches must always be removed from the welder's pockets and placed a safe distance away before any work is started.
16. Welders must always be well informed about safe and proper equipment usage: Before operating any power equipment for the first time you must read the manufacturer's safety and operating instructions and should be assisted by someone with experience with the equipment. Be sure your hands are clear before the equipment is started. Always turn the power off and lock it off before working on any part of the equipment.

PRACTICE 2-1

Name____ Date ____________

Class ____________________ Instructor ____________________ Grade ____________

OBJECTIVE: After completing this practice, you should be able to identify violations of welding safety rules.

EQUIPMENT AND MATERIALS NEEDED FOR THIS PRACTICE

1. Paper and pencil.

INSTRUCTIONS

Carefully look at Figure 2-1 "Industrial Park Foul Ups" and identify as many of the 37 safety violations as you can.

1. ____________________
2. ____________________
3. ____________________
4. ____________________
5. ____________________
6. ____________________
7. ____________________
8. ____________________
9. ____________________
10. ____________________
11. ____________________
12. ____________________
13. ____________________
14. ____________________
15. ____________________
16. ____________________
17. ____________________
18. ____________________
19. ____________________
20. ____________________
21. ____________________
22. ____________________
23. ____________________
24. ____________________
25. ____________________
26. ____________________
27. ____________________
28. ____________________

29. ____________________
30. ____________________
31. ____________________
32. ____________________
33. ____________________
34. ____________________
35. ____________________
36. ____________________
37. ____________________

(Courtesy Smith Equipment, Division of Tescom Corporation, Watertown, South Dakota)

WELDING SAFETY QUIZ

Name____ Date __________

Class ____________________ Instructor ____________________ Grade __________

Instructions: Before working with any type of welding or cutting operation, you must be knowledgeable about the following. Carefully read and answer each question which can be found in Chapter 2 of the text.

A. SHORT ANSWER

Write a brief answer, in the space provided, that will answer the question or complete the statement.

1. Burns can be caused by ____________ light rays.
2. Arc welding produces ____________, ____________, and ____________ light.
3. ____________ protection must be worn in the welding shop at all times.
4. When grinding, chipping or when overhead work is being done, ____________ or a ____________ should be worn.
5. The two types of ear protection used in the welding shop are ____________ and ____________.
6. Welders should recognize that fumes of any type should not be ____________.
7. Forced ventilation is required when welding on metals that contain ____________, ____________, ____________, ____________, ____________, and ____________.
8. Acetylene cylinders that have been lying on their side must stand upright for ____________ or more minutes before they are used.
9. When moving cylinders, the ____________ should be replaced.
10. Highly combustible materials should be ____________ or more away from welding.
11. List the guidelines you should consider when selecting the following clothes for welding.

    a. Shirts

    ____

    b. Pants

    ____

    c. Boots

    ____

    d. Caps

    ____

B. IDENTIFICATION

In the space provided identify the items shown on the illustration.

A.

B.

C.

D.

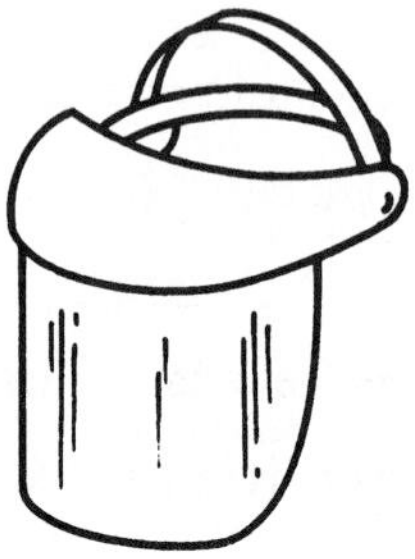

E.

F.

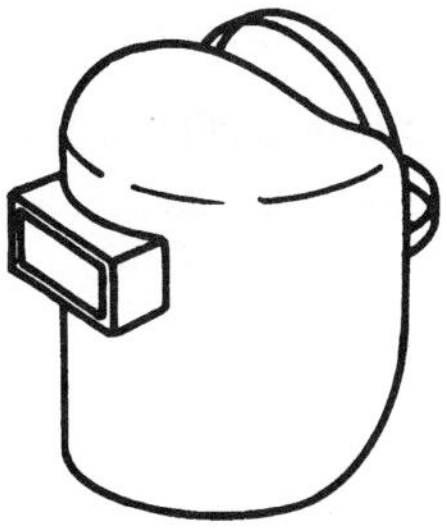

G.

12.Safety glasses with side shields

13.Full face shield

14.Goggles

15.Welding helmet

16.Air line respirator

17.Typical respirator

18.Belt-mounted respirator

C.ESSAY

Write complete answers for all of the following questions.

19. Describe first-, second-, and third-degree burns and the first aid that would be administered for each type of burn.

____

____

20. Why should eye burns be checked by a professional?

____

____

21. List the areas mentioned in this chapter that should not be used for cylinder storage.

____

____

22. What should be done with a leaking cylinder if the leak cannot be stopped?

23. Why must an acetylene cylinder that was stored horizontally be set in a vertical position for several minutes before it is used?

24. What is a MSDS?

25. Describe how a person should lift heavy objects.

26. What type of fire extinguishers are used in your shop? Where are they located?

27. Why is it so important to keep your work area clean?

28. How should a grinding stone be inspected for cracks?

29. What type of ventilation is used in your shop and is it adequate?

30. List three conditions that would require forced ventilation in a weld shop.

31. Describe how inert gases such as argon and carbon dioxide can be hazardous.

32. Explain how to avoid problems with electrical shock when arc welding.

33. Define the following terms: infrared light, ultraviolet light, forced ventilation, natural ventilation, valve protection cap, and acetone.

CHAPTER 3: SHIELDED METAL ARC EQUIPMENT, SETUP, AND OPERATION

PRACTICE 3-1

Name____ Date ____________

Class ____________________ Instructor ____________________ Grade ____________

OBJECTIVE: After completing this practice, you will be able to accurately calculate the amperage when the knob is at various settings.

EQUIPMENT AND MATERIALS FOR THIS PRACTICE

1. A pencil and paper
2. Amperage ranges as given for this practice (or from a machine in your shop).

INSTRUCTIONS

1. Estimate the amperage when the knob is at the 1/4, 1/2, and 3/4 settings.

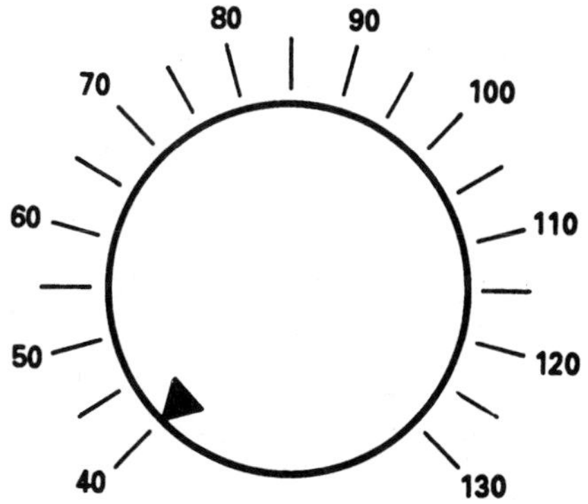

PRACTICE 3-2

OBJECTIVES: After completing this practice, you will be able to accurately calculate the amperages when the knob is set at 1, 4, 7, 9, 2.3, 5.7, and 8.5.

EQUIPMENT AND MATERIALS FOR THIS PRACTICE

1. A pencil and paper or a calculator
2. Amperage ranges as given for this practice (or from a machine in your shop).

INSTRUCTIONS

1. Calculate the amperages for each of the following knob settings: 1, 4, 7, 9, 2.3, 5.7, and 8.5.

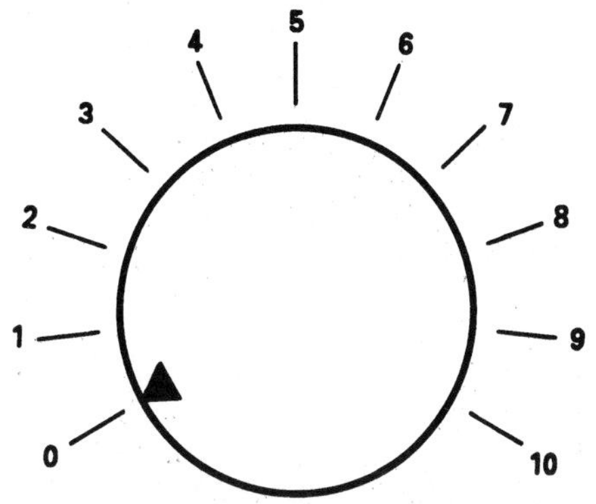

RANGE 75A TO 295

CHAPTER 3: SHIELDED METAL ARC EQUIPMENT, SETUP, AND OPERATION QUIZ

Name________________________________ Date ____________

Class ____________________ Instructor ____________________ Grade __________

Instructions: Read carefully Chapter 3 of the text. After reading, complete the following questions.

A. SHORT ANSWER

Write a brief answer, in the space provided, that will answer the question or complete the statement.

1. From the illustrations below, which one of the two is classified as straight polarity (DCSP).

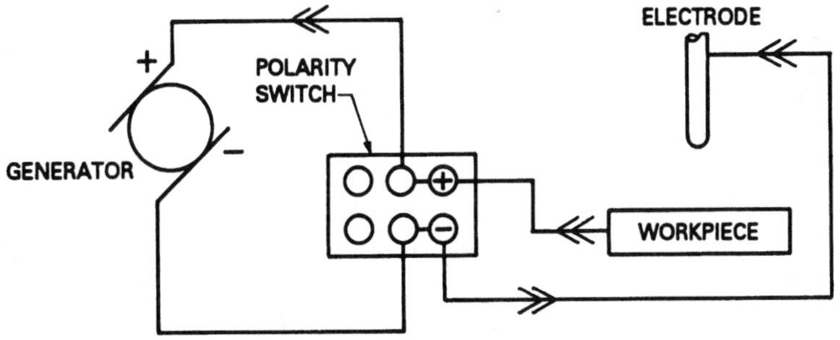

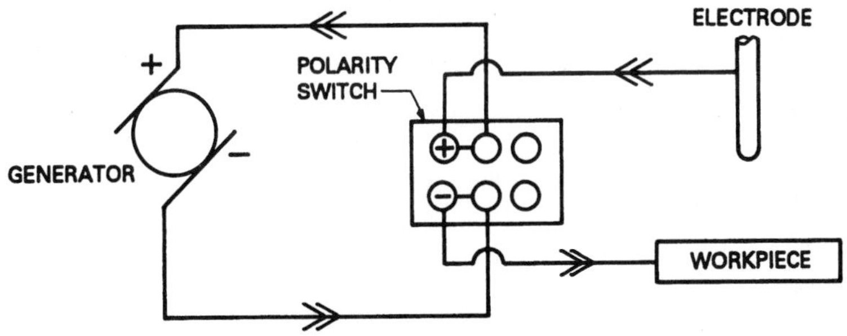

2. What is the minimum cable size that should be used if the length of the copper cable is 100 feet with a maximum of 200 amperes? Use the chart on the next page.

____

____

Copper Welding Lead Sizes

Length of Cable (ft)	(m)	100	150	200	250	300	350	400	450	500
50	15	2	2	2	2	1	1/0	1/0	2/0	2/0
75	23	2	2	1	1/0	2/0	2/0	3/0	3/0	4/0
100	30	2	1	1/0	2/0	3/0	4/0	4/0		
125	38	2	1/0	2/0	3/0	4/0				
150	46	1	2/0	3/0	4/0					
175	53	1/0	3/0	4/0						
200	61	1/0	3/0	4/0						
250	76	2/0	4/0							
300	91	3/0								
350	107	3/0								
400	122	4/0								

Aluminum Welding Lead Sizes

Length of Cable (ft)	(m)	100	150	200	250	300	350	400	450	500
50	15	2	2	1/0	2/0	2/0	3/0	4/0		
75	23	2	1/0	2/0	3/0	4/0				
100	30	1/0	2/0	4/0						
125	38	2/0	3/0							
150	46	2/0	3/0							
175	53	3/0								
200	61	4/0								
225	69	4/0								

(Column headings: Amperes)

3. What is the minimum cable size that should be used if the length of the aluminum welding cable is 100 feet with a maximum of 200 amperes? Use the same chart as question 2.

____

____

4. Why is a smaller cable sometimes spliced into the end of a large welding cable? What is the maximum length of the cable splice?

____

____

5. Name the item shown below.

____

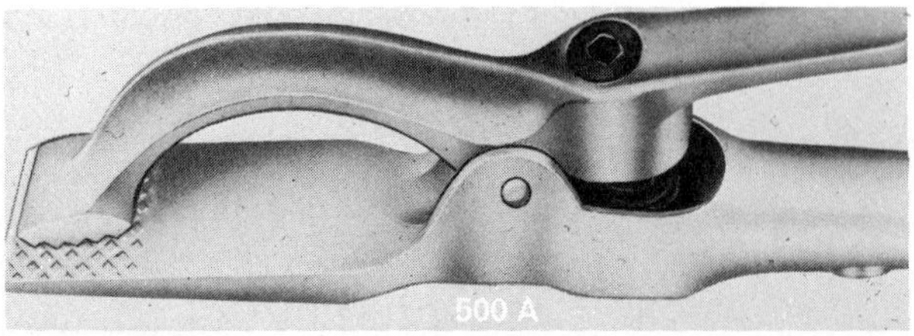

(Courtesy of Lenco, Inc.)

6. What can cause a properly sized electrode holder to overheat?

____

7. Name the item shown below.

____

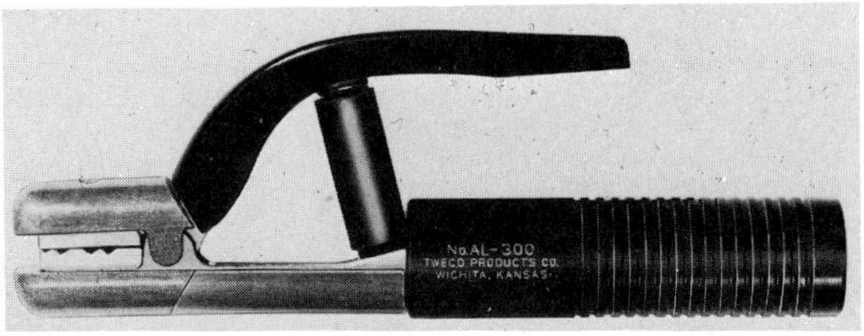

(Courtesy of Tweco Products Company.)

8. Why should you occasionally touch the work clamp?

B. MATCHING

Match the following terms in column B with the correct definition in column A.

Column A		Column B
____ 9. What is the measurement of electrical pressure?	a.	duty cycle
____ 10. What is the measurement of the amount of power in the arc?	b.	operating voltage
____ 11. What is the measurement of the electron flow?	c.	voltage
____ 12. What reduces the arc resistance, making it easier to hold a arc?	d.	arc stabilizers
____ 13. What is the voltage at the electrode before striking an arc?	e.	tap type
____ 14. What is the voltage at the arc during welding?	f.	step down transformer
____ 15. What takes high-voltage, low-amperage current and changes it into a	g.	amperage
low-voltage, high-amperage current?	h.	open circuit voltage
____ 16. What is the percentage of time a welding machine can be used continuously?	i.	wattage
____ 17. What type of welding machine allows the selection of higher current settings	j.	rectifiers
by tapping into the secondary coil at higher turn values?		
____ 18. What is used to change AC to DC?		

C. TRUE - FALSE

Write the letter T in the space to the left if the statement is true and F if the statement if false.

____ 19. The welding machine and its main power switch should be off while a person is installing or working on the cables.

____ 20. The welding cables should never be wrapped around arms, shoulders, wrists, or any other part of the body.

____ 21. Never dip a hot electrode holder in water to cool it off.

____ 22. The maximum safe open circuit voltage for welding machines is 80 volts.

D. SHORT ANSWER

Write a brief answer, in the space provided, that will answer the question or complete the statement.

23. What is the temperature of the SMAW arc in degrees F and degrees C?

____

24. List the parts of the SMAW process and electrode.

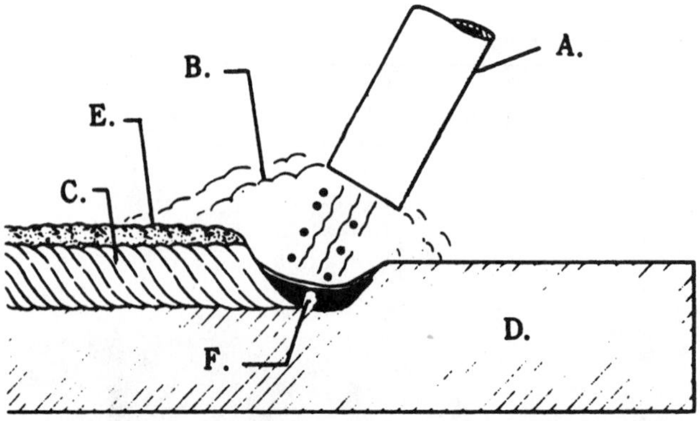

a. ______________________

b. ______________________

c. ______________________

d. ______________________

e. ______________________

f. ______________________

25. What is the minimum thickness of metal normally welded using the SMAW process?

a. 8 gauge
b. 10 gauge
c. 12 gauge
d. 16 gauge

26. What is the estimated amperage at which the following knob is set?
(10 to 120 ampere range)

a. 46 amperes
b. 54 amperes
c. 60 amperes

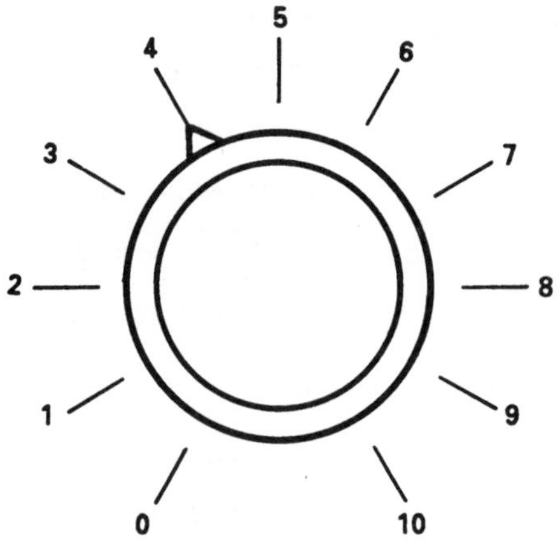

27. List three items that should be routinely checked each month on portable welding equipment.

____

____

____

28. Why are transformer and transformer-rectifier welding machines classified as the industry standard?

29. Why must a welding machine periodically be blown out with compressed air?

30. What are the 3 units used to measure welding current?

31. What type of welding power is produced by a constant current machine?

32. How does a transformer operate?

33. How does an inverter type welding power supply work?

34. What is the difference between a generator welder and an alternator welder?

CHAPTER 4: SHIELDED METAL ARC WELDING OF PLATE

Lens Filter Recommendation	
Shielded Metal Arc Welding Operation	Suggested Shade #
Shielded Metal Arc Welding, up to 5/32-in. electrodes	10
Shielded Metal Arc Welding, 3/16 to 1/4-in. electrodes	12

Welding Current Adjustment

The selection of the proper welding current depends on the electrode size, plate thickness, welding position and the welder's skill. Electrodes of the same size can be used with a higher current in the flat position than they can in the vertical or overhead position. Since several factors affect the current requirements, data provided by welding equipment and electrode manufacturers should be used. For initial settings, use the table below.

Electrode Size	Classification					
	E6010	E6011	E6012	E6013	E7016	E7018
3/32-in.	40–80	50–70	40–90	40–85	75–105	70–110
1/8-in.	70–130	85–125	75–130	70–120	100–150	90–165
5/32-in.	100–165	130–160	120–200	130–160	140–190	125–220

After setting the current on the welding machine, you must master the skill of starting the arc.

Two methods are used for starting any arc, the striking or brushing method, Figure 4-1, and the tapping method, Figure 4-2.

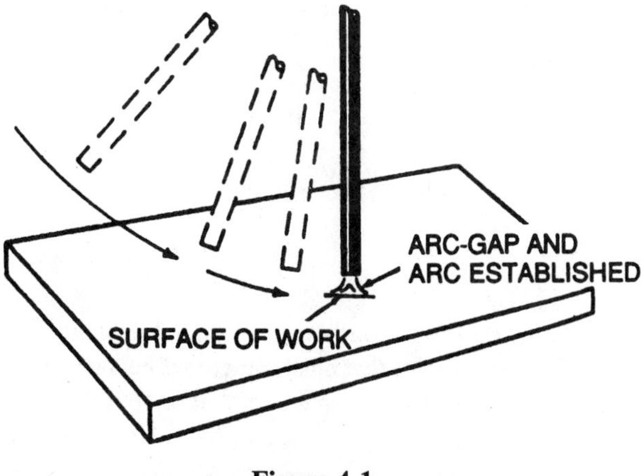

Figure 4-1

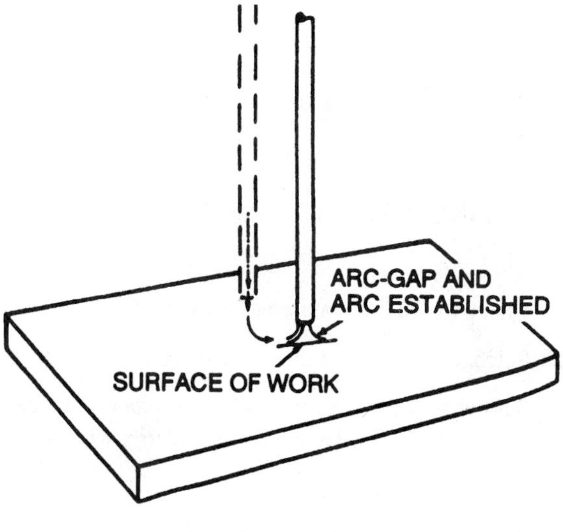

Figure 4-2

In the striking or brushing method, the electrode is brought to the surface of the work in a lateral motion similar to striking a match. As soon as the electrode touches the surface, the electrode is raised to establish the arc, Figure 4-1. The arc length or gap between the electrode and the work should be approximately equal to the diameter of the electrode. When the proper arc length is obtained, a sharp crackling sound is heard.

In the tapping method the electrode is held in a vertical position to the work and tapped, or bounced on the work surface, Figure 4-2. Upon contact, the electrode is raised approximately the diameter of the electrode to establish the proper arc length.

If the electrode is raised too slowly with either of the above arc starting methods, the electrode will adhere and stick to the base metal. If this occurs, the electrode can usually be freed by a quick sideways twist to snap the end of the electrode from the base metal. However, if twisting does not dislodge the electrode, turn off the welding machine, remove the holder from the electrode, and free the electrode from the base metal by bending it back and forth. When using this method use extreme caution because the electrode may be hot.

WORKSTATION CHECK LIST

OBJECTIVE: You will demonstrate your knowledge of inspecting a SMA welding station.

In the space provided to the right, place an (S) for Satisfactory if the item is in good working condition or an (R) for Repair if the site needs repair.

____ 1. Check to see that the power to the welding machine has been turned off (if not, turn it off before starting).

____ 2. Inspect your welding helmet for holes, cracks and proper head band adjustment.

____ 3. Inspect your filter lens for the correct shade, make sure the lens cover is clean and that there are not any light leaks around the lens.

____ 4. Make sure you are wearing proper clothing for welding: long sleeve shirt, leather gloves, safety glasses, leather shoes or boots, etc. Refer to Chapter 2 in the text if you have any questions about welding apparel.

5. Inspect the electrode lead and work lead for:

____ a. proper connections between the electrode holder and cable.

____ b. proper connections between the work lead and the ground clamp.

____ c. broken insulation, exposed wire over the full length of the electrode and work lead.

____ d. tight connections at both the electrode and work lugs on the welding machine.

____ 6. Proper ventilation. Refer to Chapter 2 in the text if you have questions about proper ventilation.

____ 7. Inspect the welding area for the safety of others that may be working around you. Check for holes in curtains, cracks in walls or even doors that are to be closed while you are welding. Always be concerned with the safety of others.

____ 8. Inspect for flammable materials in the work area such as paper, rags, wood, oil and other flammable liquids.

____ 9. Make sure you have pliers, wire brush, and a chipping hammer that are in good working condition.

OPERATING INSTRUCTIONS FOR SMAW EQUIPMENT

Step

1. Check to see that your work area is safe for welding.
2. Select the proper electrode for the work to be done.
3. Set the welding machine on the correct current and polarity for the electrode you have chosen. Some welding machines will have a switch for the polarity while others only have welding cables that must sometimes be disconnected from the positive and negative poles of the machine and then reconnected again. Remember that on reverse polarity the electrode is positive and the work (ground) is negative. When using straight polarity, the cables are the opposite, the electrode is negative and work (ground) is positive. If you are using an AC welding machine, there is no straight or reverse polarity, therefore, the AC welding machine does not have a positive or negative receptacle. See Chapter 3 of the text for AC welding current.
4. Connect the work clamp (ground) to the part that is to be welded. In some instances, you may wish to connect the clamp to a metal table on which the part to be welded can make direct contact.
5. Place the range selector switch in the desired position. Check the electrode amperage settings for the desired settings.

6. Place the amperage adjustment control to the desired setting.
7. Turn on the welding machine's power switch.
8. Place the electrode in the electrode holder.
9. Start welding.
10. Readjust the amperage adjustment control if necessary.

SMAW TROUBLESHOOTING

Welding Problem	How to Correct
Arc Blow	1. adjust electrode angle 2. move ground clamp 3. use AC current instead of DC 4. inspect the part to see if it has become magnetized and if so, demagnetize
Brittle Welds	1. use proper pre and post heat on the metal to be welded 2. use low-hydrogen electrodes 3. make sure parts being welded are not cooled too quickly, as in dipping in water
Cracks in Weld	1. reduce welding speed, use an electrode that has a more convex bead 2. use low-hydrogen electrodes 3. use pre and post heat on the weld
Distortion	1. reduce current 2. use chill plates 3. increase welding speed 4. clamp or fix parts being welded 5. weld thick sections first
Incomplete Penetration	1. increase amperage 2. use a larger root opening 3. decrease the electrode diameter 4. reduce the welding speed
Inferior Appearance	1. use correct electrode 2. use electrodes that have not been wet 3. use the correct polarity 4. increase or decrease current 5. manipulate the electrode differently
Porosity	1. use dry electrodes 2. do not weld on wet metal 3. clean paint, grease, oil, etc., from the metal being welded 4. shorten arc length 5. use low-hydrogen electrodes
Slag Inclusions	1. increase current 2. decrease welding speed 3. do not allow the welding pool to get ahead of the arc 4. change polarities 5. if welding multi-pass welds, always chip and wire brush between passes
Spatter	1. decrease current 2. shorten arc length 3. weld on dry metal with dry electrodes
Undercutting	1. decrease current 2. reduce welding speed 3. shorten arc length 4. change electrode angle

PRACTICE 4-1

Name____________________ Date __________ Electrode Used __________

Class ________________ Instructor ________________ Grade ________

OBJECTIVE: After completing this practice, you should be able to safely set up a Shielded Metal Arc Welding work station.

EQUIPMENT AND MATERIALS NEEDED FOR THIS PRACTICE

1. Properly set up and adjusted arc welding machine, proper safety protection (welding hood, safety glasses, wire brush, chipping hammer, leather gloves, pliers, long sleeve shirt, long pants, and leather boots or shoes). Refer to Chapter 2 in the text for more specific safety information.

INSTRUCTIONS

1. Demonstrate the use of proper general work clothing, special protective clothing, eye and ear protection to prevent burns and other possible injuries.
2. Explain what material specification data sheets are and what types of information they contain.
3. Describe the ventilation provided in the area.
4. Point out electrical safety provisions.
5. List proper work station clean-up procedures.

Comments

PRACTICE 4-2

OBJECTIVE: After completing this practice, you should be able to make a straight stringer bead in the flat position using an E6010 or E6011 series electrode and an E6012 or E6013 series electrode and an E7016 and E7018 series electrode.

EQUIPMENT AND MATERIALS NEEDED FOR THIS PRACTICE

1. Properly set up and adjusted arc welding machine, proper safety protection (welding hood, safety glasses, wire brush, chipping hammer, leather gloves, pliers, long sleeve shirt, long pants, and leather boots or shoes). Refer to Chapter 2 in the text for more specific safety information.
2. Arc welding electrodes with a 1/8-in. (3-mm) diameter.
3. One piece of mild steel plate, 6 in. (152 mm) long x 1/4 in. (6 mm) thick.

INSTRUCTIONS

1. Starting at one end of the plate, make a straight weld the full length of the plate. Watch the molten weld pool at the points, not the end of the electrode. As you become more skillful, it is easier to watch the molten weld pool.
2. Repeat the beads with all three (F) groups of electrodes until you have consistently good beads.
3. Cool, chip, and inspect the bead for defects after completing it.
4. Turn off the welding machine and clean up your work area when you are finished welding.

Comments

PRACTICE 4-3

OBJECTIVE: After completing this practice, you should be able to make stringer beads in the vertical up position using E6010 or E6011 electrodes, E6012 or E6013 electrodes, and E7016 or E7018 electrodes.

EQUIPMENT AND MATERIALS NEEDED FOR THIS PRACTICE

1. Properly set up and adjusted arc welding machine, proper safety protection (welding hood, safety glasses, wire brush, chipping hammer, leather gloves, pliers, long sleeve shirt, long pants, and leather boots or shoes). Refer to Chapter 2 in the text for more specific safety information.
2. Arc welding electrodes with a 1/8-in. (3-mm) diameter.
3. One piece of mild steel plate, 6 in. (152 mm) long x 1/4 in. (6 mm) thick.

INSTRUCTIONS

1. Start with the plate at a 45° angle. This technique is the same as that used to make a vertical weld. However, a lower level of skill is required at 45° and it is easier to develop your skill. After the welder masters the 45° angle, the angle is increased successively until a vertical position is reached.
2. Before the molten metal drips down the bead, the back of the molten weld pool will start to bulge. When this happens, increase the speed of travel and the weave pattern.
3. Cool, chip, and inspect each completed weld for defects.
4. Repeat the beads as necessary with all three (F) groups of electrodes until consistently good beads are obtained in this position.
5. Turn off the welding machine and clean up your work area when you are finished welding.

Comments

___

PRACTICE 4-4

Name________________________ Date __________ Electrode Used __________

Class ____________________ Instructor ____________________ Grade __________

OBJECTIVE: After completing this practice, you should be able to weld a square butt in the 2G position using E6010 or E6011 electrodes, E6012 or E6013 electrodes, and E7016 or E7018 electrodes.

EQUIPMENT AND MATERIALS NEEDED FOR THIS PRACTICE

1. Properly set up and adjusted arc welding machine, proper safety protection (welding hood, safety glasses, wire brush, chipping hammer, leather gloves, pliers, long sleeve shirt, long pants, and leather boots or shoes). Refer to Chapter 2 in the text for more specific safety information.
2. Arc welding electrodes having a 1/8-in. (3-mm) diameter.
3. Two or more pieces of mild steel plate, 6 in. (152 mm) long x 1/4 in. (6 mm) thick.

INSTRUCTIONS

1. Start practicing these welds with the plate at a slight angle.
2. Strike the arc on the bottom plate and build the molten weld pool until it bridges the gap. If the weld is started on the top plate, slag will be trapped in the root at the beginning of the weld because of incomplete initial penetration. The slag may cause the weld to crack when it is placed in service.
3. The "J" weave pattern is recommended in order to deposit metal on the lower plate so that it can support the bead. By pushing the electrode inward as you cross the gap between the plates, deeper penetration is achieved.
4. As you acquire more skill, gradually increase the plate angle until it is vertical and the weld is horizontal.
5. Cool, chip, and inspect the weld for uniformity and defects.
6. Repeat the welds with all three (F) groups of electrodes until you can consistently make welds free of defects.
7. Turn off the welding machine and clean up your work area when you are finished welding.

Comments

PRACTICE 4-5

OBJECTIVES: After completing this practice, you should be able to weld a lap joint in the 1F position using E6010 or E6011 electrodes, E6012 or E6013 electrodes, and E7016 or E7018 electrodes.

EQUIPMENT AND MATERIALS NEEDED FOR THIS PRACTICE

1. Properly set up and adjusted arc welding machine, proper safety protection (welding hood, safety glasses, wire brush, chipping hammer, leather gloves, pliers, long sleeve shirt, long pants, and leather boots or shoes). Refer to Chapter 2 in the text for more specific safety information.
2. Arc welding electrodes having a l/8-in. (3-mm) diameter.
3. Two or more pieces of mild steel plate, 6 in. (152 mm) long x l/4 in. (6 mm) thick.

INSTRUCTIONS

1. Hold the plates together tightly and with an overlap of not more than l/4 in. (6 mm).
2. Tack weld the plates together. A small tack weld may be added in the center to prevent distortion during welding.
3. Chip the tacks before you start to weld.

4. The "J", "C", or zigzag weave pattern works well on this joint.
5. Strike the arc and establish a molten pool directly in the joint.
6. Move the electrode out on the bottom plate and then onto the weld to the top edge of the top plate.
7. Follow the surface of the plates with the arc. Do not follow the trailing edge of the weld bead. Following the molten weld pool will not allow for good root fusion and will also cause slag to collect in the root. If slag does collect, a good weld is not possible. Stop the weld and chip the slag to remove it before the weld is completed.
8. Cool, chip, and inspect the weld for uniformity and defects.
9. Repeat the welds with all three (F) groups of electrodes until you can consistently make welds free of defects.
10. Turn off the welding machine and clean up your work area when you are finished welding.

Comments

PRACTICE 4-6

OBJECTIVE: After completing this practice, you should be able to weld a lap joint in the 2F position using E6010 or E6011 electrodes, E6012 or E6013 electrodes, and E7016 or E7018 electrodes.

EQUIPMENT AND MATERIALS NEEDED FOR THIS PRACTICE

1. Properly set up and adjusted arc welding machine, proper safety protection (welding hood, safety glasses, wire brush, chipping hammer, leather gloves, pliers, long sleeve shirt, long pants, and leather boots or shoes). Refer to Chapter 2 in the text for more specific safety information.
2. Arc welding electrodes having a l/8-in. (3-mm) diameter.
3. Two or more pieces of mild steel plate, 6 in. (152 mm) long x l/4 in. (6 mm) thick.

INSTRUCTIONS

1. The horizontal lap joint and the flat lap joint require nearly the same technique and skill to achieve a proper weld.
2. Use the "J", "C", or zigzag weave pattern to make the weld.
3. Do not allow slag to collect in the root. The fillet must be equally divided between both plates for good strength.
4. After completing the weld, cool, chip, and inspect the weld for uniformity and defects.
5. Repeat the welds using all three (F) groups of electrodes until you can consistently make welds free of defects.
6. Turn off the welding machine and clean up your work area when you are finished welding.

Comments

PRACTICE 4-7

OBJECTIVE: After completing this objective, you will be able to weld a tee joint in the 1F position using E6010 or E6011 electrodes, E6012 or E6013 electrodes, and E7016 or E7018 electrodes on carbon steel.

EQUIPMENT AND MATERIALS NEEDED FOR THIS PRACTICE

1. Properly set up and adjusted arc welding machine, proper safety protection (welding hood, safety glasses, wire brush, chipping hammer, leather gloves, pliers, long sleeve shirt, long pants, and leather boots or shoes). Refer to Chapter 2 in the text for more specific safety information.
2. Arc welding electrodes having a 1/8-in. (3-mm) diameter.

3. Two or more pieces of mild steel plate, 6 in. (152 mm) long x l/4 in. (6 mm) thick.

INSTRUCTIONS

1. After the plates are tack welded together, place them on the welding table so the weld bend will be in the flat position.
2. Start at one end and establish a molten weld pool on both plates.
3. Allow the molten weld pool to flow together before starting the weave pattern. Any of the weave patterns will work well on this joint.
4. To prevent slag inclusions, use a slightly higher than normal amperage setting.
5. When the 6-in. (152-mm)-long weld is completed, cool, chip, and inspect it for uniformity and soundness.
6. Repeat the welds as needed for all these groups of electrodes until you can consistently make welds free of defects.
7. Turn off the welding machine and clean up your work area when you are finished welding.

Comments

PRACTICE 4-8

OBJECTIVE: After completing this practice, you should be able to weld a tee joint in the 3F position using E6010 or E6011 electrodes, E6012 or E6013 electrodes, and E7016 or E7018 electrodes.

EQUIPMENT AND MATERIALS NEEDED FOR THIS PRACTICE

1. Properly set up and adjusted arc welding machine, proper safety protection (welding hood, safety glasses, wire brush, chipping hammer, leather gloves, pliers, long sleeve shirt, long pants, and leather boots or shoes). Refer to Chapter 2 in the text for more specific safety information.
2. Arc welding electrodes having a 1/8-in. (3-mm) diameter.
3. Two or more pieces of mild steel plate, 6 in. (152 mm) long x l/4 in. (6 mm) thick.

INSTRUCTIONS

1. Practice this weld with the plate at a 45° angle vertical up. This position will allow you to develop your skill for the vertical position.
2. Start the arc and molten weld pool deep in the root of the joint.
3. Build a shelf large enough to support the bead as it progresses up the joint. The square, "J" or "C" pattern can be used, but the "T" or stepped pattern will allow deeper root penetration.
4. For this weld, undercut is a problem on both sides of the weld. It can be controlled by holding the arc on the side long enough for filler metal to flow down and fill it.
5. Cool, chip, and inspect the weld for uniformity and defects.
6. Repeat the welds as necessary with all three (F) groups of electrodes until you can consistently make welds free of defects.
7. Turn off the welding machine and clean up your work area when you are finished welding.

Comments

CHAPTER 4: SHIELDED METAL ARC WELDING OF PLATE QUIZ

Name______________________________ Date __________

Class ________________ Instructor ________________ Grade __________

Instructions: Read carefully Chapter 4 of the text. After reading, complete the following questions.

A. TRUE-FALSE

Write the letter T, in the space to the left, if the statement is true and F if the statement if false.

____ 1. An increase in the amount of spatter can be caused from long arcing.

____ 2. A weld may have slag or gas inclusions because the molten weld pool is fluid for too long a period of time.

____ 3. If the ripples in a weld are pointed, the weld is cooling too slowly because of excessive heat.

____ 4. When setting your welding current, make sure to change the settings while the machine is under load.

____ 5. Several factors that can affect arc lengths are joint design, type of electrode, metal thickness, and current settings.

____ 6. A leading angle can be used to minimize penetration or to hold metal in place for vertical welds.

____ 7. As the welding electrode angle decreases toward the vertical position, the penetration will decrease.

____ 8. A circular welding pattern is recommended for welding on metal that has oil, dirt, or paint on it.

____ 9. Electrodes with rutile based fluxes produce excess spatter.

____ 10. If full plate penetration on 1/4-in. mild steel is required, the edges of the joint do not need beveling, just increase the current.

B. SHORT ANSWER

Write a brief answer, in the space provided, that will answer the question or complete the statement.

11. Name four factors that can prevent cold lap and slag inclusions.

a. ______________________________

b. ______________________________

c. ______________________________

d. ______________________________

12. List seven characteristics of a weld that can be controlled by the movement or weaving of the welding electrode.

a. ______________________________

b. ______________________________

c. ______________________________

d. ______________________________

e. ______________________________

f.______________________________

g. ______________________________

13. List two methods of striking the arc.

____

____

14. List the four welding positions.

____

____

C. MATCHING

In the space provided to the left, write the letter from column B that best answers the question or completes the statement in column A.

column A	column B
_____ 15. What is the rate that the weld metal is added to the weld?	a. root opening
_____ 16. What is a large piece of metal used to absorb excessive heat?	b. stringer bead
_____ 17. What is a straight weld bead on the surface of a plate, with little or no side-to-side electrode movement called?	c. direction of travel
_____ 18. What is the space between two plates to be welded called?	d. deposition rate
_____ 19. What is the electrode angle that is measured from the electrode to the surface of the metal?	e. chill plate

D. ESSAY

20. How much of the electrode end should be discolored if the current is set correctly?

____

____

21. What can happen to an electrode if it is overheated?

____

____

22. What three steps can a welder take to prevent a weld from overheating?

____

____

23. Approximately how long is a correct arc length?

____

____

24. Which weave pattern works well on a horizontal butt joint?

____

____

25. How can an arc be started at the exact point where the welder wants it to start?

____

____

26. How is deep penetration obtained on a flat butt joint?

____

____

27. What effect does a short arc length have on a weld?

____

____

28. How can a welder prevent slag inclusions on a flat butt joint?

____

____

29. For what is the figure-8 weave pattern used?

____

____

30. Why should welders hold on to a stable object when they are welding?

____

____

31. What indicates that a vertical weld bead is becoming too large?

____

____

32. Why should a welder start practicing vertical welds at a 45° angle?

____

____

33. How does a welder prevent slag from being trapped in the root of a flat lap welded joint?

____

____

CHAPTER 5: SHIELDED METAL ARC WELDING OF PIPE

JOINT PREPARATION FOR PIPE WELDING:

It is important that the bevel be at the correct angle, which is 37.5° for vertical up welds and 35° for vertical down welds, and that each end of the mating pipes meet squarely, Figure 5-1(a) and (b).

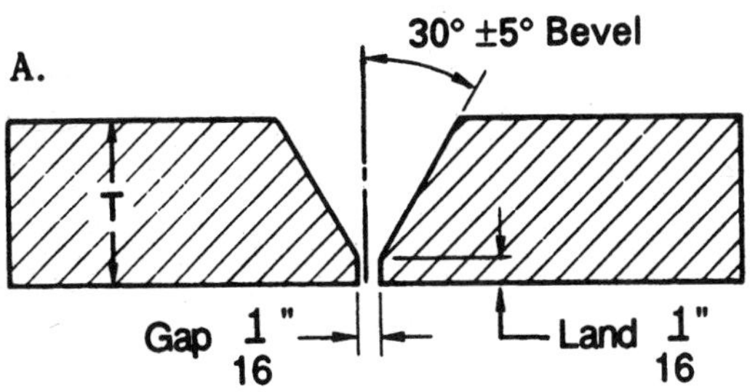

Figure 5-1 (A). Standard joint design for vertical down welding.

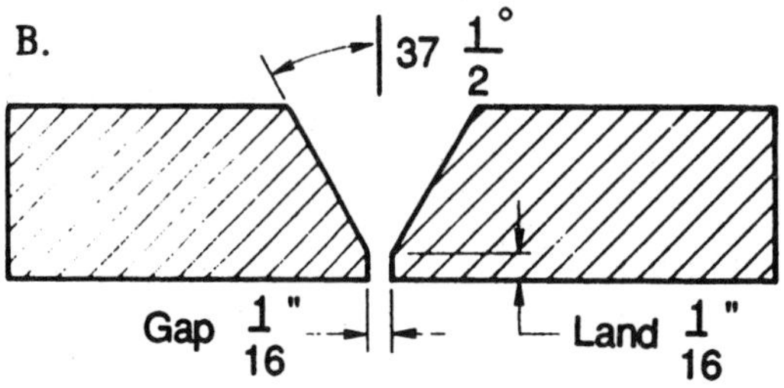

Figure 5-1(B). Standard joint design for vertical up and horizontal welding.

Weld bead sequencing for vertical down welding is shown in Figure 5-2.

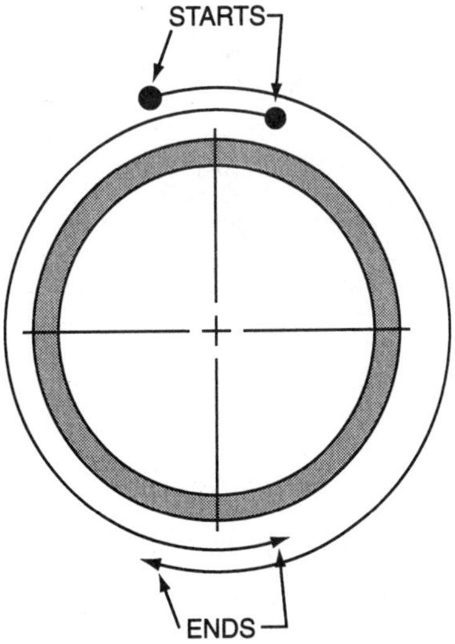

Figure 5-2

The above illustration is for EXX10-type electrodes, designed for welding circumferential pipe joints in the vertical down position. The number of passes required for welding pipe will vary with the diameter of the electrode, the thickness of the pipe, the welding position, the type of current being used and welding operators. The typical number of passes required to weld pipe using the vertical down technique is shown in Table 5-1.

Pipe Wall Thickness	Number of Passes
1/4"	3
5/16"	4
3/8"	5
1/2"	7

Table 5-1. Passes required for vertical down welding on pipe.

Weld bead sequencing for vertical up welding is shown in Figure 5-3.

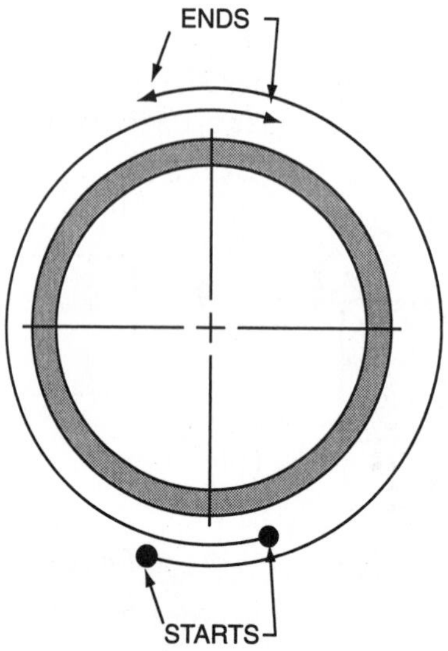

Figure 5-3

When welding carbon steel pipe, E6010 or E7010 electrodes are used for the first pass. All other passes normally are welded using an EXX18 (low-hydrogen) type electrode. The number of passes required for welding pipe will vary with the diameter of the electrode, the thickness of the pipe, the welding position, the type of current being used and welding operators. The typical number of passes required to weld pipe using the vertical up technique is shown in Table 5-2.

Pipe Wall Thickness	Number of Passes
1/4"	2
5/16"	2
3/8"	3
1/2"	3
5/8"	4
3/4"	6
1"	7

Table 5-2. Passes required for vertical up welding on pipe.

Weld bead sequencing for a horizontal butt weld on pipe is shown in Figure 5-4.

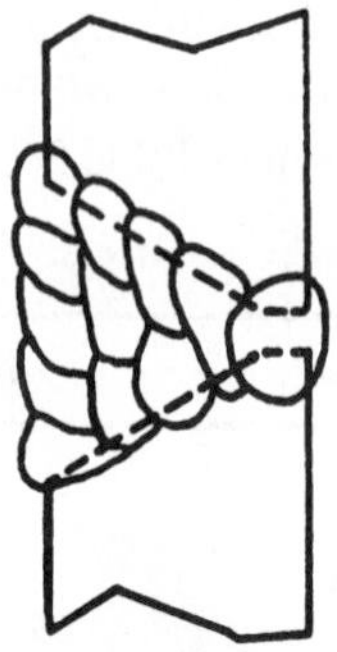

Figure 5-4

PRACTICE 5-1

Name________________________ Date __________ Electrode Used __________

Class ____________________ Instructor ____________________ Grade ________

OBJECTIVE: After completing this practice, you should be able to weld stringer beads on carbon steel pipe in the 1G position using E6010, E6011, and E7018 electrodes.

EQUIPMENT AND MATERIALS NEEDED FOR THIS PRACTICE

1. A properly set up and adjusted arc welding machine.
2. Proper safety protection (welding hood, safety glasses, wire brush, chipping hammer, leather gloves, long sleeve shirt, long pants, leather boots or shoes, and a pair of pliers). Refer to Chapter 2 in the text for more specific safety information.
3. E6010 or E6011 and E7018 arc welding electrodes, having a 1/8-in. (3-mm) diameter.
4. Schedule 40 mild steel pipe, 3 in. (76 mm) or larger in diameter.
5. A piece of soapstone.
6. A flexible straight edge.

INSTRUCTIONS

1. Be sure the pipe is clean and free of rust, grease, paint or other contaminants that will effect the weld.
2. Use your flexible straight edge and draw straight lines completely around the pipe with a spacing of 1/2-inch.
3. Place the pipe horizontally on the welding table in a vee block made of angle iron. The vee block will hold the pipe steady and allow it to be moved easily between each weld bead.
4. Strike an arc on the pipe at the 11 o'clock position.
5. Make a stringer bead over the 12 o'clock position, stopping at the 1 o'clock position.
6. Roll the pipe until the end of the weld is at the 11 o'clock position.
7. Clean the weld crater by chipping and wire brushing.
8. Strike the arc again and establish a molten weld pool at the leading edge of the weld crater.
9. With the molten weld pool reestablished, move the electrode back on the weld bead just short of the last full ripple. This action will both reestablish good fusion and keep the weld bead size uniform.
10. Now that the new weld bead is tied into the old weld, continue welding to the 1 o'clock position again.
11. Stop welding, roll the pipe, clean the crater, and resume welding.
12. Keep repeating this procedure until the weld is completely around the pipe.
13. Before the last weld is started, clean the end of the first weld so that the end and beginning beads can be tied together smoothly.
14. When you reach the beginning bead, swing your electrode around on both sides of the weld bead. The beginning of a weld bead is always high, narrow, and has little penetration. By swinging the weave pattern (the "C" Pattern is best) on both sides of the bead, you can make the bead width uniform. The added heat will give deeper penetration at the starting point.
15. Hold the arc in the crater for a moment until it is built up.
16. Cool, chip, and inspect the bead for defects.
17. Repeat the beads as needed until they are mastered.
18. Turn off the welding machine and clean up your work area when you are finished welding.

Comments

PRACTICE 5-2

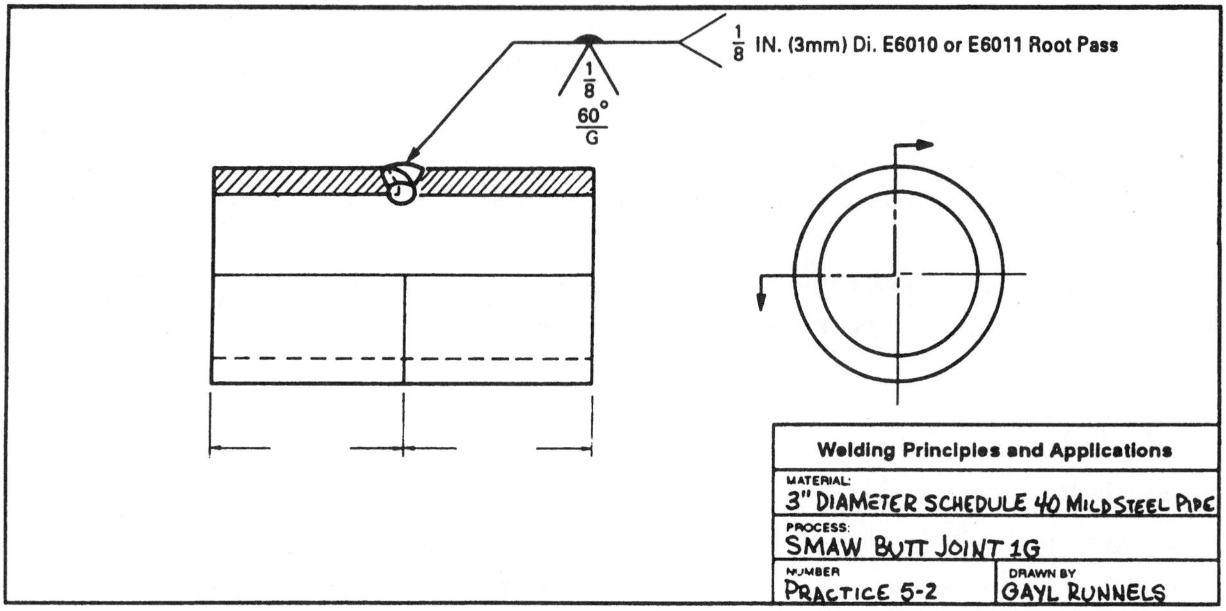

OBJECTIVE: After completing this practice, you should be able to weld carbon steel pipe in the 1G position for low-pressure, light service applications.

EQUIPMENT AND MATERIALS NEEDED FOR THIS PRACTICE

1. A properly set up and adjusted arc welding machine.
2. Proper safety protection (welding hood, safety glasses, wire brush, chipping hammer, leather gloves, long sleeve shirt, long pants, leather boots or shoes, and a pair of pliers). Refer to Chapter 2 in the text for more specific safety information.
3. E6010 or E6011 arc welding electrodes having a 1/8-in. (3-mm) diameter.
4. Two or more pieces of schedule 40 mild steel pipe, 3 in. (76 mm) or larger in diameter.

INSTRUCTIONS

1. Tack weld two pieces of pipe together.
2. Place the pipe horizontally in a vee block on the welding table.
3. Start the root pass at the 11 o'clock position.
4. Using a very short arc and high current setting, weld toward the 1 o'clock position.
5. Stop and roll the pipe, chip the slag, and repeat the weld until you have completed the root pass.
6. Clean the root pass by chipping and wire brushing. The root pass should not be ground this time.
7. Replace the pipe in the vee block on the table so that the hot pass can be done.
8. Turn up the machine amperage, enough to remelt the root weld surface, for the hot pass.
9. Use a step electrode pattern, moving forward each time the molten weld pool washes out the slag, and returning each time the molten weld pool is nearly all solid.

10. Weld from the 11 o'clock position to the 1 o'clock position before stopping, rolling, and chipping the weld.
11. Repeat this procedure until the hot pass is complete. The filler pass and cover pass may be the same pass on this joint.
12. Turn down the machine amperage.
13. Use a "T," "J," "C," or zigzag pattern for this weld.
14. Start the weld at the 10 o'clock position and stop at the 12 o'clock position.
15. Sweep the electrode so that the molten weld pool melts out any slag trapped by the hot pass.
16. Watch the back edge of the bead to see that the molten weld pool is filling the groove completely.
17. Turn, chip, and continue the bead until the weld is complete.
18. Repeat this weld until you can consistently make welds free of defects.
19. Turn off the welding machine and clean up your work area when you are finished welding.

Comments

PRACTICE 5-3

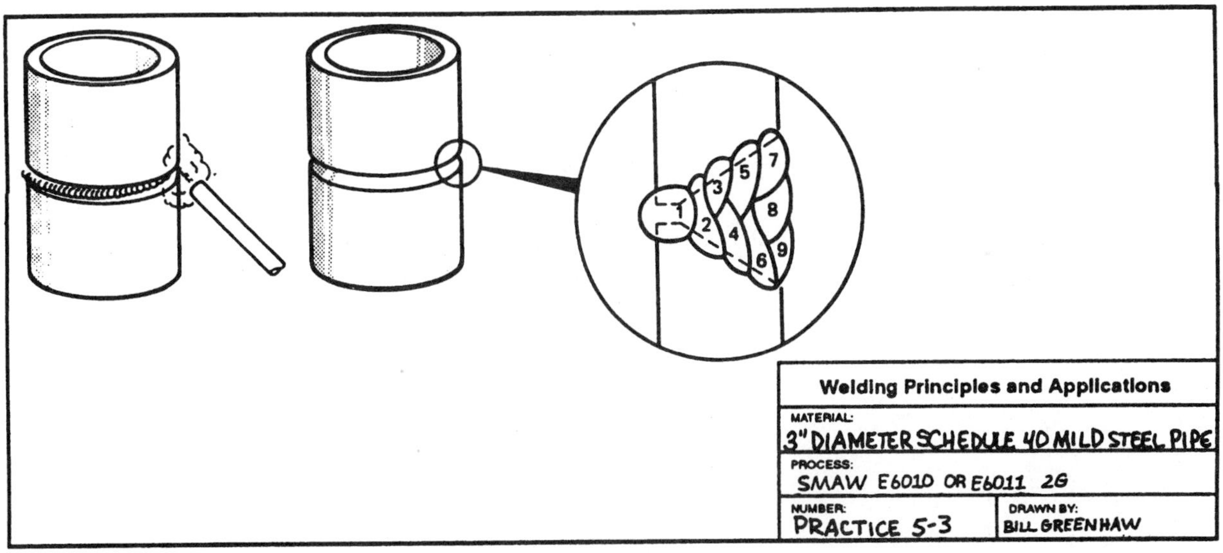

OBJECTIVE: After completing this practice, you should be able to weld carbon steel pipe in the 2G position using E6010 or E6011 electrodes.

EQUIPMENT AND MATERIALS NEEDED FOR THIS PRACTICE

1. A properly set up and adjusted arc welding machine
2. Proper safety protection (welding hood, safety glasses, wire brush, chipping hammer, leather gloves, long sleeve shirt, long pants, leather boots or shoes, and a pair of pliers). Refer to Chapter 2 in the text for more specific safety information.
3. E6010 or E6011 arc welding electrodes having a 1/8-in. (3-mm) diameter
4. Two or more pieces of schedule 40 mild steel pipe, 3 in. (76 mm) or larger in diameter.

INSTRUCTIONS

1. Place the pipe on the arc welding table.

2. Strike an arc and make a root weld that is as long as possible. If the root gap is close and uniform, a straight, forward movement can be used. For wider gaps, a step pattern must be used.
3. After completing and cleaning the root pass, make a hot pass. The hot pass need only burn the root pass clean. Undercut on the top pipe is acceptable.
4. The filler and cover passes should be stringer beads or small weave beads. By keeping the molten weld pool size small, control is easier.
5. Cool, chip, and inspect the completed weld for uniformity and defects.
6. Repeat this weld until you can consistently make welds free of defects.
7. Turn off the welding machine and clean up your work area when you are finished welding.

Comments

___

PRACTICE 5-4

Name____________________ Date __________ Electrode Used __________

Class ____________________ Instructor ____________________ Grade __________

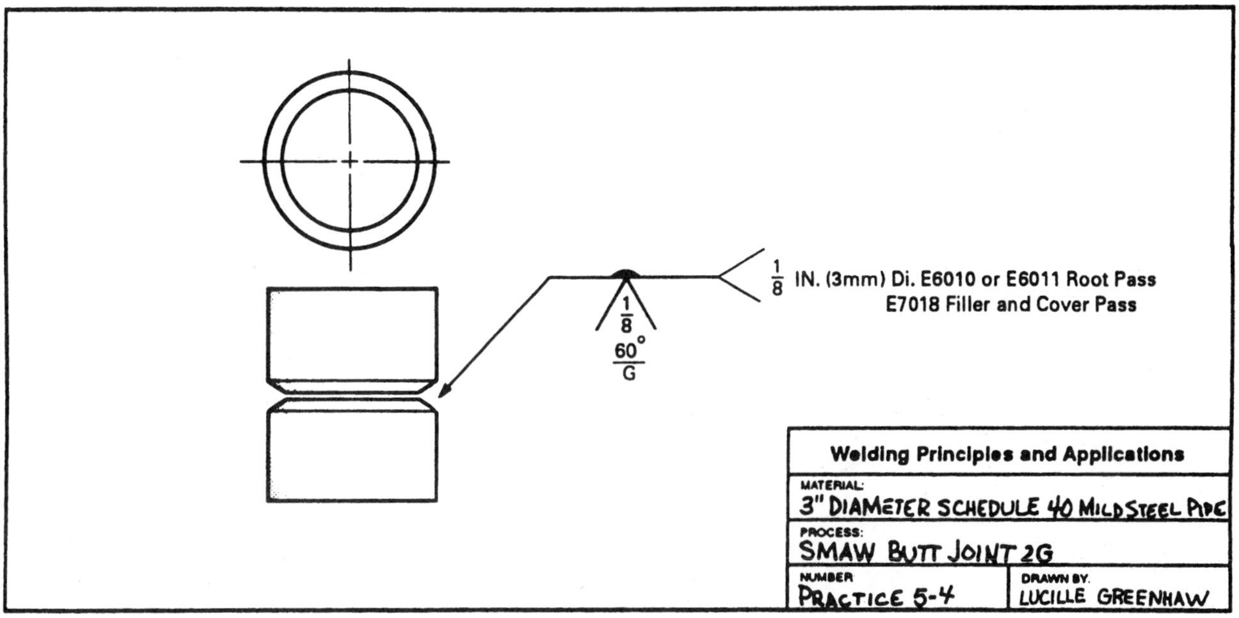

OBJECTIVE: After completing this practice, you should be able to weld carbon steel pipe in the 2G position using E6010 or E6011 for the root pass and E7018 electrodes for the filler and cover passes.

EQUIPMENT AND MATERIALS NEEDED FOR THIS PRACTICE

1. A properly set up and adjusted arc welding machine
2. Proper safety protection (welding hood, safety glasses, wire brush, chipping hammer, leather gloves, long sleeve shirt, long pants, leather boots or shoes, and a pair of pliers). Refer to Chapter 2 in the text for more specific safety information.
3. E6010 or E6011 and E7018 arc welding electrodes, having a 1/8-in. (3-mm) diameter.
4. Schedule 40 mild steel pipe, 3 in. (76 mm) or larger in diameter.

INSTRUCTIONS

1. Place the pipe vertically on the welding table.
2. Hold the electrode at a 90° angle to the pipe and with a slight trailing angle. The electrode should be held tightly into the joint. If a burnthrough occurs, quickly push the electrode back over the burnthrough while increasing the trailing angle. This action forces the weld metal back into the opening.
3. When the root pass is complete, chip the surface slag and then clean out the trapped slag by grinding or chipping, or use a hot pass.
4. Use E7018 electrodes for the filler and cover passes with a stringer pattern. The weave bead with this electrode and position tends to undercut the top and overlap the bottom edge.
5. After the weld is completed, visually inspect it for 100% penetration around 80% of the root length.
6. Check the weld for uniformity and visual defects on the cover pass.
7. Repeat the weld until you can consistently make welds free of defects.

8. Turn off the welding machine and clean up your work area when you are finished welding.

Comments

CHAPTER 5: SHIELDED METAL ARC WELDING OF PIPE QUIZ

Name____ Date ____________

Class ____________________ Instructor ____________________ Grade ____________

Instructions: Carefully read Chapter 5 in the text to complete the following questions.

A. SHORT ANSWER

Write a brief answer, in the space provided, that will answer the question or complete the statement.

1. How does the measurement of tubing differ from that of pipe?

____

____

____

2. The wall thickness of pipe is determined by its ________________.
3. What is the purpose of the hot pass?

____

____

____

4. List two methods for aligning and holding pipe ends in place for tacking and welding.

   a.______________________________________

   b. ______________________________________

5. List three ways pipe joints are beveled in preparation for welding.

   a.______________________________________

   b. ______________________________________

   c.______________________________________

6. What two weld positions use stringer beads almost exclusively?

   a.______________________________________

   b. ______________________________________

7. What are consumable inserts used for?

____

____

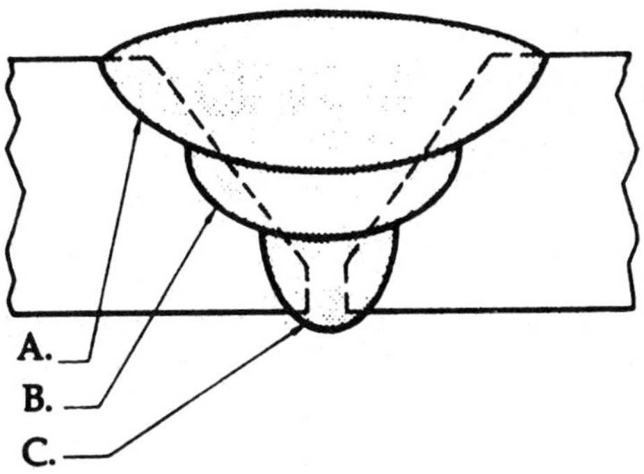

B.IDENTIFICATION

In the space provided identify the items shown on the illustration.

8.Correctly match the following from the illustration.

a.filler pass

b. cover pass

c.root pass

C. ESSAY

9. Why is reinforcement added to a weld bead?

10. What is the difference between pipe and tubing?

11. What is meant by the phrase *schedule of a pipe?*

12. List five advantages of welded pipe joints as compared to threaded pipe joints.

13. Why is root face needed on a pipe bevel?

14. Why is the slag cleaned from a bead before a new electrode is used to continue the weld bead?

15. What is the correct sequence for positioning the welds for a horizontal weld?

16. When making a pipe weld, why are the weld bead ends and beginnings overlapped?

17. When should a root pass be welded uphill and not downhill?

18. Why is the 6G position the most difficult pipe welding position?

19. Define the following terms: suck back, icicles, land, root gap, concave root surface, and root face.

CHAPTER 6: ADVANCED SHIELDED METAL ARC WELDING

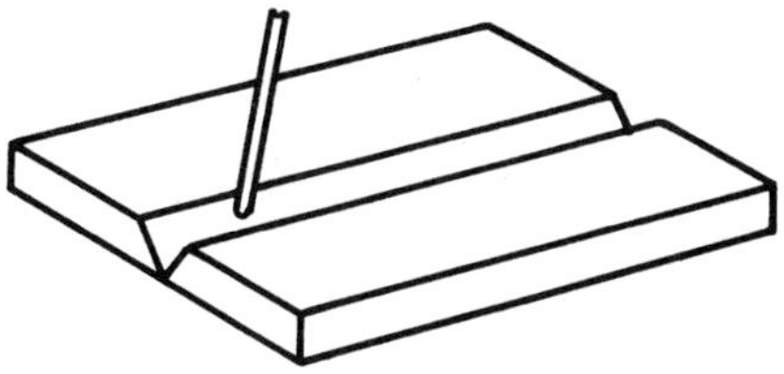

1G

1G Flat position—The welding position used to weld from the upper side of the joint; the face of the weld is approximately horizontal.

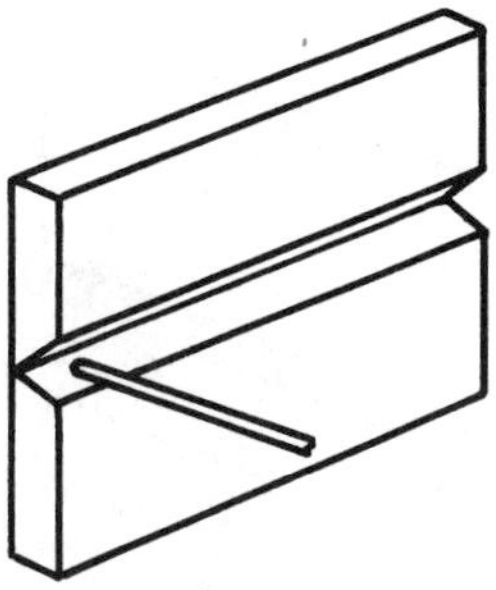

2G

2G Horizontal position—The position of welding in which the axis of the weld lies in an approximately horizontal plane and the face of the weld lies in an approximately vertical plane.

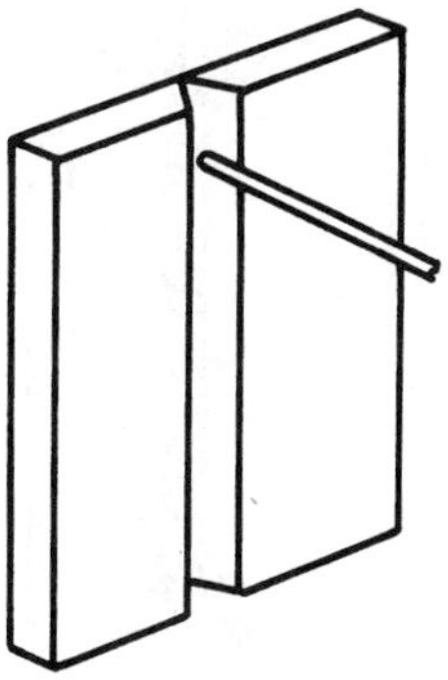

3G

3G Vertical position—The position of welding in which the axis of the weld is approximately vertical.

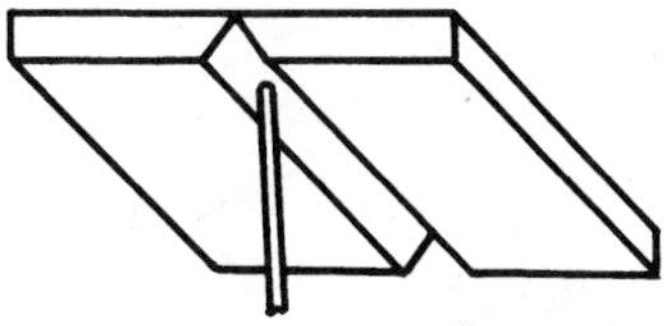

4G

4G Overhead position—The position in which welding is performed from the underside of the joint.

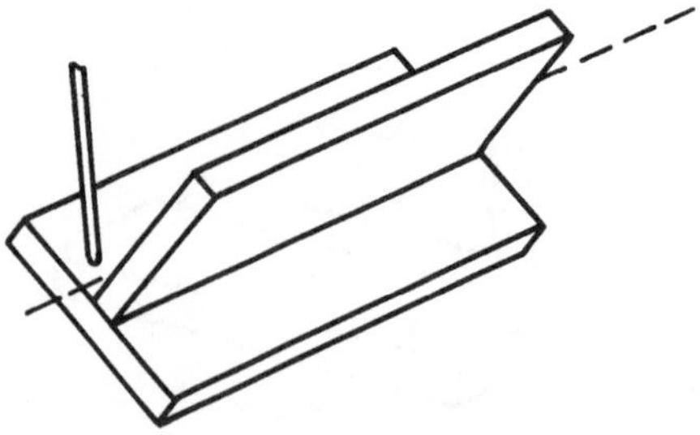

1F

1F Flat position—The welding position used to weld from the upper side of the joint; the face of the weld is approximately horizontal.

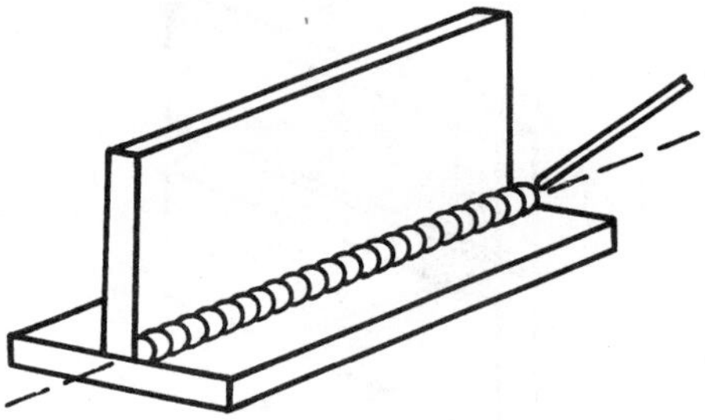

2F

2F Horizontal position—The position in which welding is performed on the upper side of an approximately horizontal surface and against an approximately vertical surface.

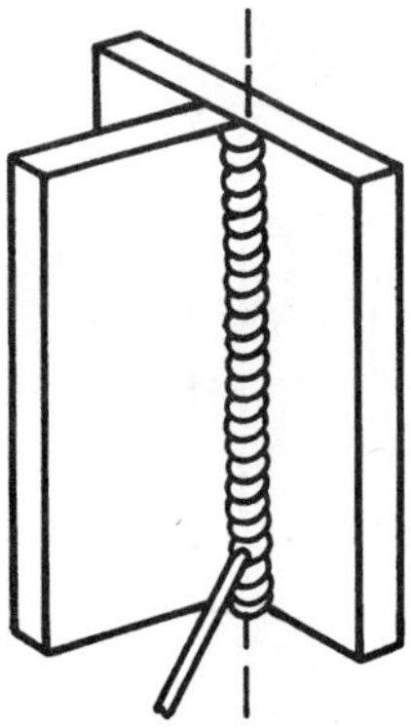

3F

3F Vertical position—The position of welding in which the axis of the weld is approximately vertical.

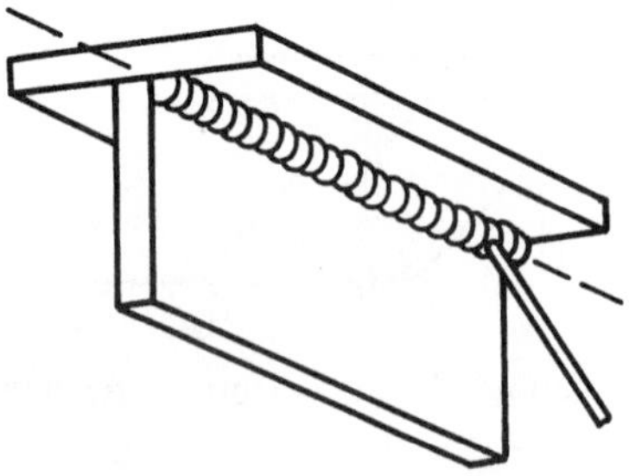

4F

4F Overhead position—The position is which welding is performed from the underside of the joint.

PRACTICE 6-1

Name______________________ Date ____________ Electrode Used ____________

Class ______________________ Instructor ______________________ Grade ____________

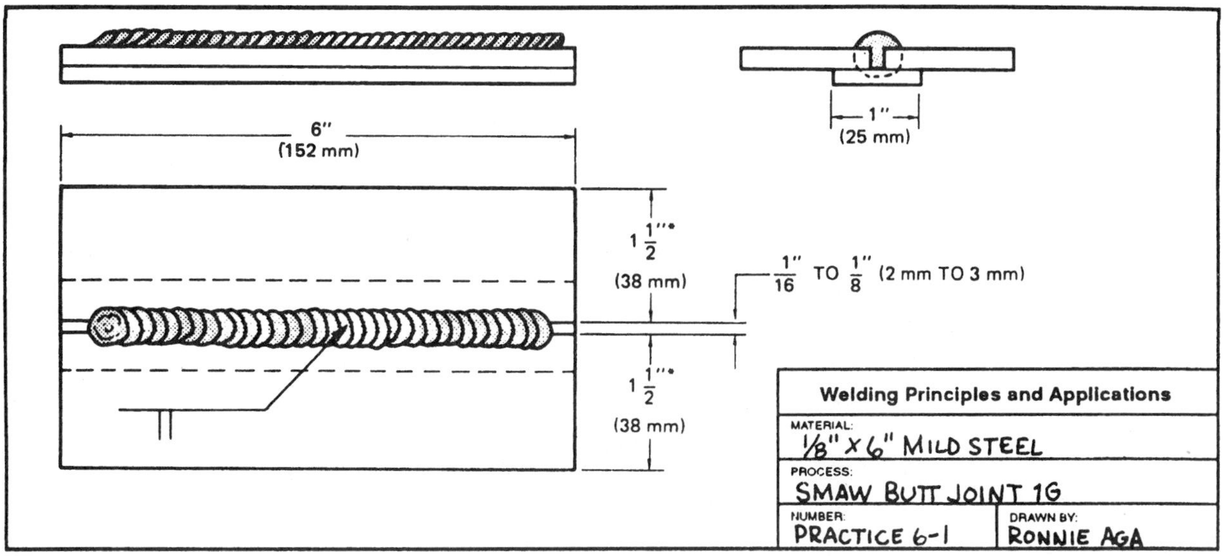

OBJECTIVE: After completing this practice, you should be able to weld a butt joint with a backing strip using E6010 or E6011 electrodes.

EQUIPMENT AND MATERIALS NEEDED FOR THIS PRACTICE

1. A properly set up and adjusted welding machine, proper safety protection (welding hood, safety glasses, wire brush, chipping hammer, leather gloves, pliers, long sleeve shirt, long pants and leather boots or shoes). Refer to Chapter 2 in the text for more specific safety information.
2. 1/8-in. (3 mm) diameter E6010 or E6011 arc welding electrodes
3. 3 pieces of mild steel plate, (2) 1/8 in. (3 mm) thick x 6 in. (152 mm) long, and one strip of mild steel, (1) 1/8 in. (3 mm) thick x 1 in. (25 mm) wide x 6 in. (152 mm) long.

INSTRUCTIONS

1. Tack weld the plates together with a 1/16-in. (2 mm) to 1/8-in. (3 mm) root opening, Figure 6-1. Be sure there are no gaps between the backing strip and plates when the pieces are tacked together. If there is a small gap between the backing strip and the plates, it can be removed by placing the assembled test plates on an anvil and striking the tack weld with a hammer. This will close up the gap by compressing the tack welds.
2. Chip and wire brush tack welds.
3. Adjust the welding current by welding on a scrap plate.
4. Use a straight step or "T" pattern for this root weld. Push the electrode into the root opening so that there is complete fusion with the backing strip and bottom edge of the plates. Failure to push the penetration deep into the joint will result in a cold lap at the root.
5. Watch the molten weld pool and keep its size as uniform as possible. As the molten weld pool increases in size, move the electrode out of the weld pool. When the weld pool begins to cool, bring the electrode back in to the molten weld pool. Use these weld pool indications to determine how far to move the electrode and when to return to the molten weld pool. After completing the weld, cut the plate and inspect the cross-section of the weld for complete fusion at the edges.

6. Chip and wire brush the weld and examine to see if you have complete fusion. Repeat the welds as necessary until you can consistently make welds free of defects.
7. Turn off the welding machine and clean up your work area when you are finished welding.

Comments

PRACTICE 6-2

Name____________________ Date __________ Electrode Used __________

Class ________________ Instructor ________________ Grade __________

OBJECTIVE: After completing this practice, you should be able to weld a multiple pass weld in a V-joint using E6010 or E6010 electrodes in the 1G, 2G, 3G, and 4G positions.

EQUIPMENT AND MATERIALS NEEDED FOR THIS PRACTICE

1. A properly set up and adjusted welding machine, proper safety protection (welding hood, safety glasses, wire brush, chipping hammer, leather gloves, pliers, long sleeve shirt, long pants and leather boots or shoes). Refer to Chapter 2 in the text for more specific safety information.
2. 1/8-in. (3 mm) diameter E6010 or E6011 arc welding electrodes
3. 2 pieces of mild steel plate, 6 in. (152 mm) long x 3/8 in. (9 mm) thick.

INSTRUCTIONS

1. Tack weld the plates together at the corner so that they form a V.
2. Chip and wire brush all tack welds.
3. Starting at one end, make a stringer bead along the entire length using the straight step or "T" weave pattern.
4. Thoroughly clean all the slag from the weld before making the next bead.
5. Continue making welds and cleaning them until the weld is 1 in. (25 mm) or more thick.
6. After the weld is completed, it can be visually inspected for uniformity. Repeat this weld until you can consistently make it defect free.
7. Turn off the welding machine and clean up your work area when you are finished welding.

Comments

____

PRACTICE 6-3

Name________________________ Date ____________ Electrode Used ____________

Class ____________________ Instructor ______________________ Grade ____________

OBJECTIVE: After completing this practice, you should be able to weld a multiple pass weld in a V-joint using E7018 electrodes in the 1G, 2G, 3G, and 4G positions.

EQUIPMENT AND MATERIALS NEEDED FOR THIS PRACTICE

1. A properly set up and adjusted welding machine, proper safety protection (welding hood, safety glasses, wire brush, chipping hammer, leather gloves, pliers, long sleeve shirt, long pants and leather boots or shoes). Refer to Chapter 2 in the text for more specific safety information.
2. 1/8-in. (3 mm) diameter E7018 arc welding electrodes
3. 2 pieces of mild steel plate, 6 in. (152 mm) long x 3/8 in. (9 mm) thick.

INSTRUCTIONS

1. Tack weld the plates together at the corner so that they form a V.
2. Chip and wire brush all tack welds.
3. Starting at one end, make a stringer bead along the entire length using the straight step or "T" weave pattern.
4. Thoroughly clean all the slag from the weld before making the next bead.
5. Continue making welds and cleaning them until the weld is 1 in. (25 mm) or more thick.
6. After the weld is completed, it can be visually inspected for uniformity. Repeat this weld until you can consistently make it defect free.
7. Turn off the welding machine and clean up your work area when you are finished welding.

Comments

PRACTICE 6-4

OBJECTIVE: After completing this practice, you should be able to make a cover weld using E7018 electrodes in the 1G, 2G, 3G, and 4G positions.

EQUIPMENT AND MATERIALS NEEDED FOR THIS PRACTICE

1. A properly set up and adjusted welding machine, proper safety protection (welding hood, safety glasses, wire brush, chipping hammer, leather gloves, pliers, long sleeve shirt, long pants and leather boots or shoes). Refer to Chapter 2 in the text for more specific safety information.
2. 1/8-in. (3 mm) diameter E7018 arc welding electrodes
3. A piece of mild steel plate, 6 in. (152 mm) long x 3/8 in. (9 mm) thick.

INSTRUCTIONS

1. Using a zigzag or weave pattern, start welding at one end of the plate and weld to the other end.
2. The weld bead should be about 5/16 in. (7 mm) wide having no more than 1/8 in. (3 mm) of uniform buildup.
3. The weld buildup should have a smooth transition at the toe, with the plate and the face somewhat convex.
4. After the weld is completely cooled, chip and inspect it for uniformity and defects. Repeat the welds as necessary until you can consistently make welds free of defects.

5. Turn off the welding machine and clean up your work area when you are finished welding.

Comments

PRACTICE 6-5

Name____________________ Date __________ Electrode Used __________

Class ________________ Instructor ________________ Grade __________

OBJECTIVE: After completing this practice, you should be able to weld a single V-groove joint with a backing strip using E6010 or E6011 electrodes for the root pass and E7018 electrodes for the filler and cover passes, following a WELDING PROCEDURE SPECIFICATION (WPS).

EQUIPMENT AND MATERIALS NEEDED FOR THIS PRACTICE

1. A properly set up and adjusted welding machine, proper safety protection (welding hood, safety glasses, wire brush, chipping hammer, leather gloves, pliers, long sleeve shirt, long pants and leather boots or shoes). Refer to Chapter 2 in the text for more specific safety information.
2. 1/8-in. (3 mm) diameter E6010 or E6011 and E7018 arc welding electrodes
3. 3 pieces of mild steel plate, (2) approximately 6 in. (152 mm) long x between 3/8 in. (10 mm) to 3/4 in. (20 mm) thick, and (1) approximately 8 in. (200 mm) long x 1 in. (25 mm) wide x 1/4 in. (6 mm) thick.

INSTRUCTIONS

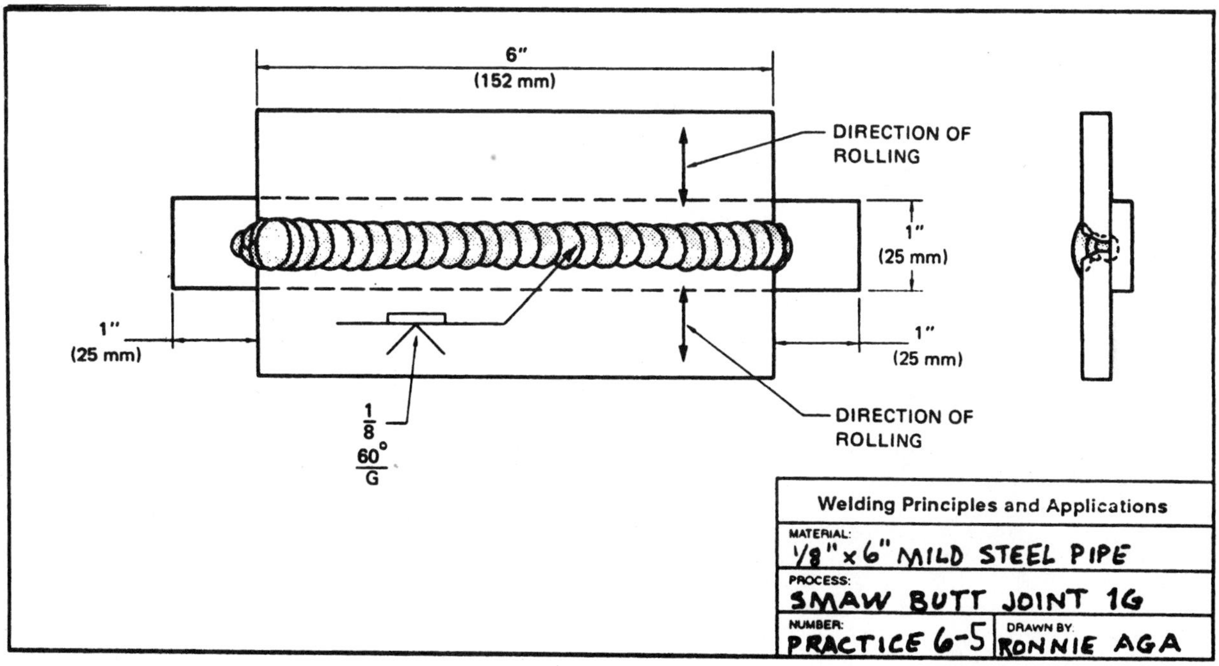

Remember to turn off the welding machine and clean up your work area when you are finished welding.

Comments

____

PRACTICE 6-6

Name____________________ Date __________ Electrode Used __________

Class ________________ Instructor ________________ Grade __________

OBJECTIVE: After completing this practice, you should be able to weld a single V-groove joint with an open root using E6010 or E6011 electrodes for the root pass and E7018 electrodes for the filler and cover passes, following a WELDING PROCEDURE SPECIFICATION (WPS).

EQUIPMENT AND MATERIALS NEEDED FOR THIS PRACTICE

1. A properly set up and adjusted welding machine, proper safety protection (welding hood, safety glasses, wire brush, chipping hammer, leather gloves, pliers, long sleeve shirt, long pants and leather boots or shoes). Refer to Chapter 2 in the text for more specific safety information.
2. 1/8-in. (3 mm) diameter E6010 or E6011 and E7018 arc welding electrodes
3. 2 pieces of mild steel plate, approximately 6 in. (152 mm) long x between 3/8 in. (10 mm) to 3/4 in. (20 mm) thick.

INSTRUCTIONS

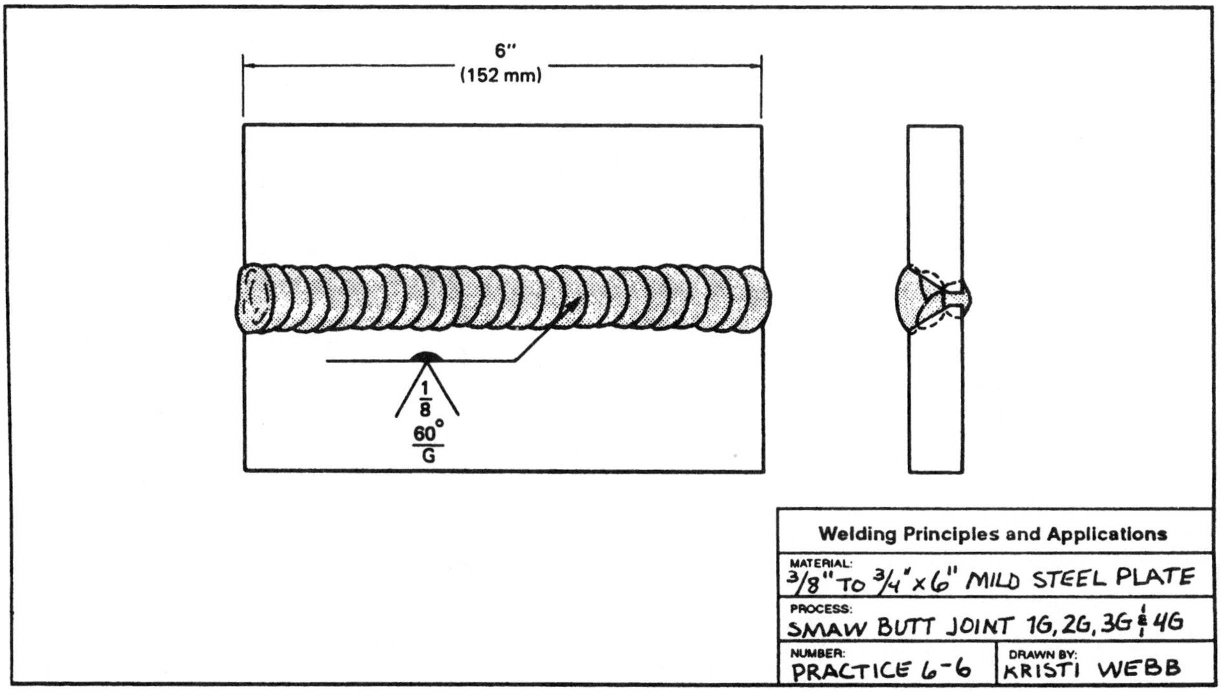

Remember to turn off the welding machine and clean up your work area when you are finished welding.

Comments

____

PRACTICE 6-7

Name________________________________ Date ____________ Electrode Used ______________

Class __________________________ Instructor _________________________ Grade ____________

OBJECTIVE: After completing this practice, you should be able to weld a single V-groove joint with a open root using E6010 or E6011 electrodes for the root pass and E7018 electrodes for the filler and cover passes, following a WELDING PROCEDURE SPECIFICATION (WPS).

EQUIPMENT AND MATERIALS NEEDED FOR THIS PRACTICE

1. A properly set up and adjusted welding machine, proper safety protection (welding hood, safety glasses, wire brush, chipping hammer, leather gloves, pliers, long sleeve shirt, long pants and leather boots or shoes). Refer to Chapter 2 in the text for more specific safety information.
2. 1/8-in. (3 mm) diameter E6010 or E6011 and E7018 arc welding electrodes
3. 2 pieces of mild steel schedule 40 pipe, approximately 6 in. (152 mm) long x between 3 in. (76 mm) to 4 in. (102 mm) diameter.

INSTRUCTIONS

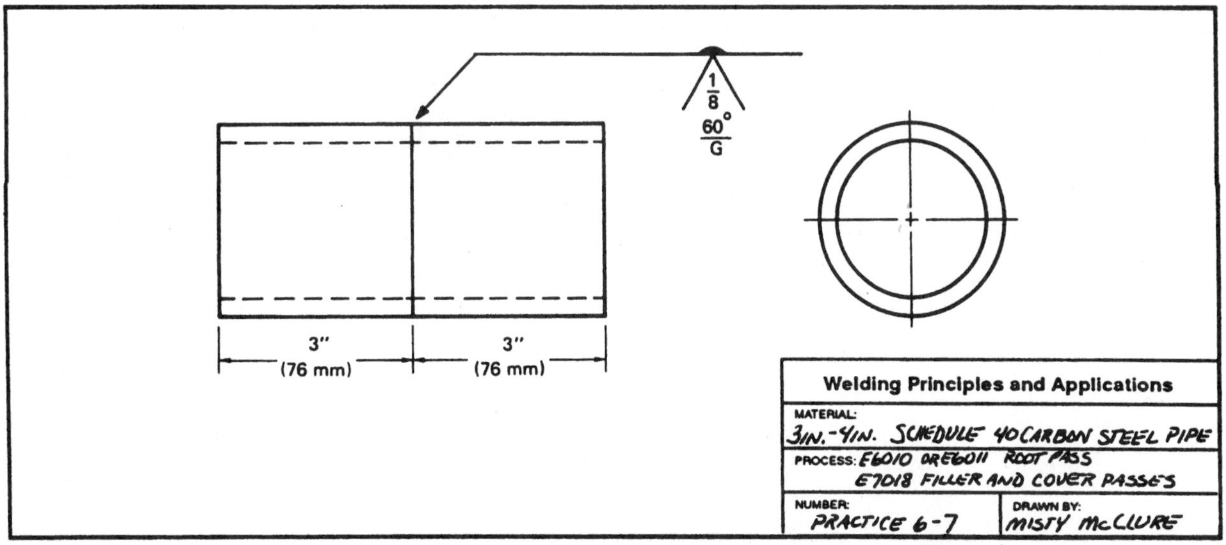

Remember to turn off the welding machine and clean up your work area when you are finished welding.

Comments

____

CHAPTER 6: ADVANCED SHIELDED METAL ARC WELDING QUIZ

Name____ Date ____________

Class ____________________ Instructor ____________________ Grade ____________

Instructions: Carefully read Chapter 6 of the text. After reading, complete the following questions.

A. TRUE - FALSE

Write the letter T, in the space to the left, if the statement is true and the letter F if the statement if false.

____ 1. Hot passes are to be used on noncritical, noncode welds only.

____ 2. Slag does not have to be removed between filler weld passes.

____ 3. All that is required of a filler weld is that it have complete penetration.

____ 4. The lap joint is normally prepared with a groove for added strength.

____ 5. Slag should always be chipped and the weld crater should be cleaned each time before restarting a weld.

____ 6. Starting and stopping weld beads in corners should be avoided.

____ 7. When welding on plates that are 3/8-inch thick or thicker, it is necessary to prepare the plates before welding.

____ 8. For high-quality welds, a hot pass should be used on the root pass to clean it.

____ 9. Taking a certification test according to specifications always qualifies a welder for any agency's testing procedures.

____ 10. The electrode angle can be changed to control penetration and burnthrough.

B. IDENTIFICATION

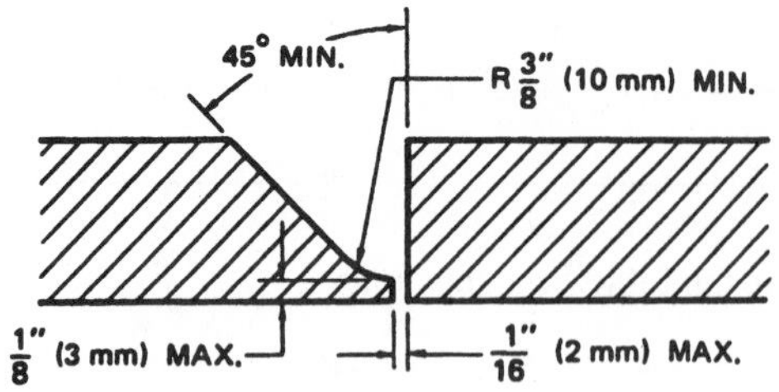

A.

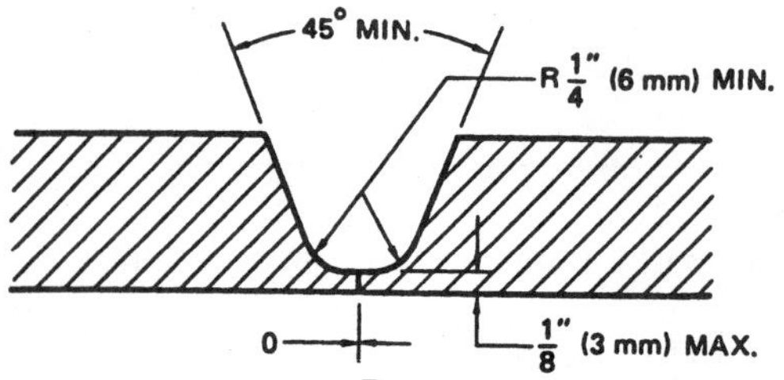

B.

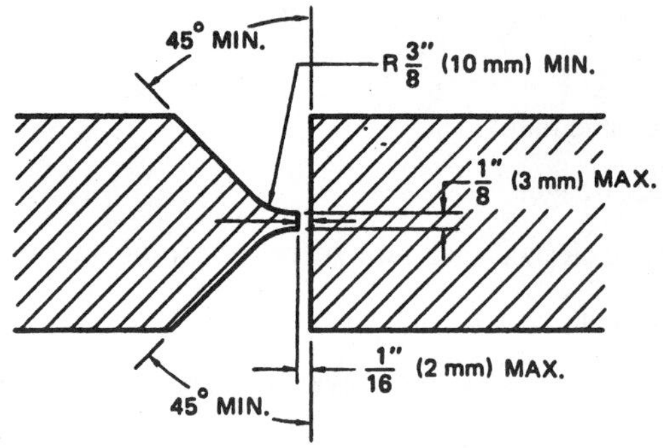

C.

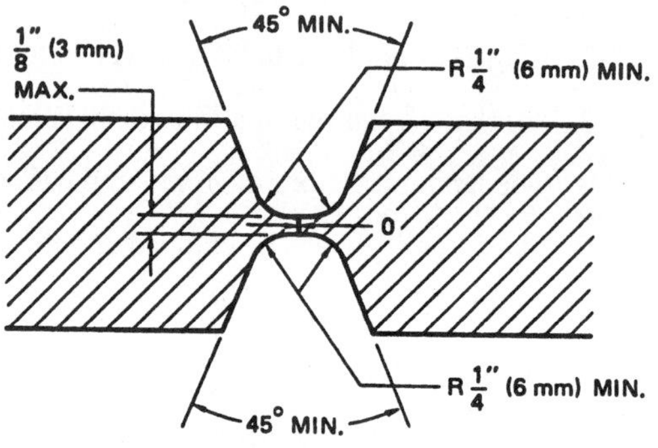

D.

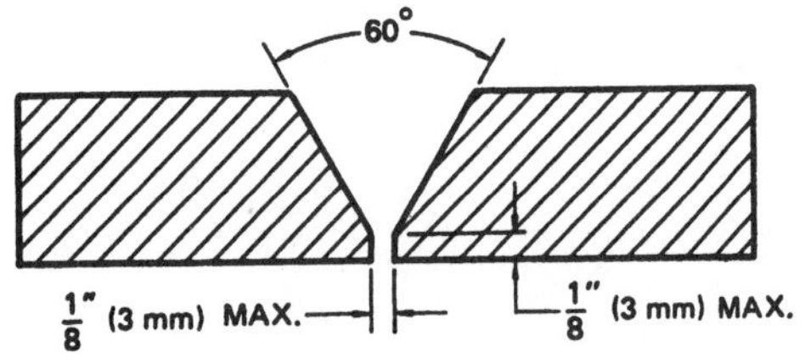

E.

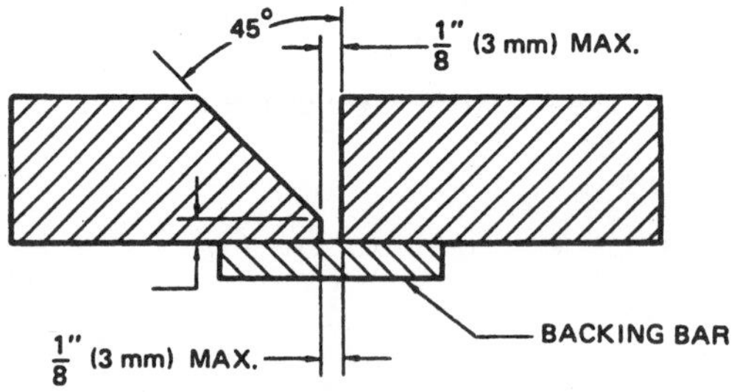

F.

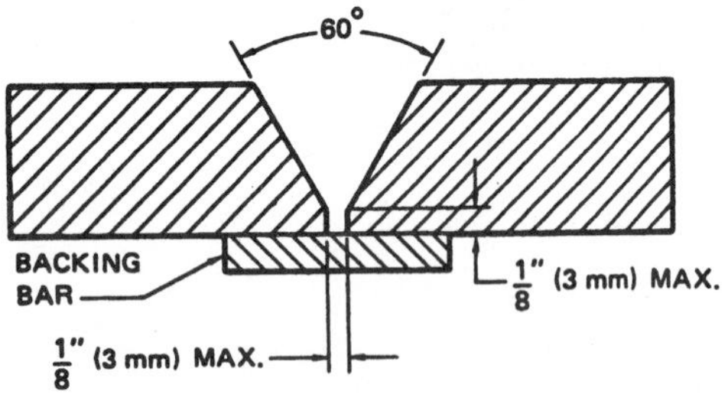

G.

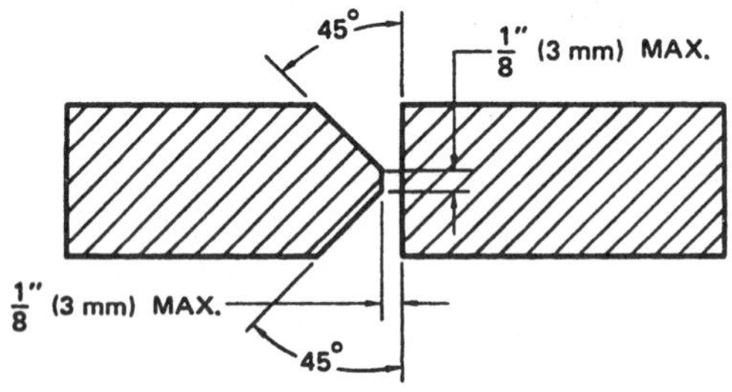

H.

11. ________________
12. ________________
13. ________________
14. ________________
15. ________________
16. ________________
17. ________________
18. ________________

C. MATCHING

In the space provided to the left, write the letter from column B that best answers the question or completes the statement in column A.

column A	column B
____ 19. What is the first weld bead of a multiple pass weld called?	a. filler passes
____ 20. What is last weld bead on a multipass weld called?	b. key hole
____ 21. What is the process of cutting a groove in the back side of a joint that has been welded called?	c. wagon tracks
	d. interpass temperature
____ 22. What is used to slow the cooling rate and reduce hardening?	e. root pass
____ 23. This process helps to reduce cracking, hardness, distortion and stresses.	f. concave
____ 24. What is the temperature of the plate during welding called?	g. back gouging
____ 25. Failure to clean a convex root weld will result in this type of discontinuity.	h. coverpass
____ 26. After the root pass is completed and it has been cleaned by grinding or with a hot pass, the groove is filled with weld metal. What are these weld beads called?	i. preheating
	j. postheating
____ 27. Which weld surface is more easily cleaned by chipping, wire brushing, or grinding?	
____ 28. What must be maintained to ensure 100% joint penetration?	

D. ESSAY

29. When should a root weld be ground?

____

____

30. Describe how to prepare a guided bend test specimen.

____

____

31. What are the maximum defects allowable on a guided bend specimen in order for the specimen to pass?

____

____

32. For what reason is a hot pass used?

____

____

33. On an open root weld, how can burnthrough be controlled?

____

____

34. When should a root weld be ground?

____

____

35. Why is thick plate prepared for welding?

36. What is the reason for back gouging some welds?

37. List four agencies that issue welding codes or standards.

38. Describe how to prepare a guided bend test specimen.

39. How is a weld bead restarted without causing excessive buildup and loss of penetration?

40. Why should some plates be preheated before welding?

41. What are the maximum defects allowable on a guided bend specimen in order for the specimen to pass?

42. Define the following terms: solidify, burnthrough, key hole, molten weld pool, root pass, hot pass, cover pass, and back gouge.

CHAPTER 7: FLAME CUTTING

EYE PROTECTION FOR FLAME CUTTING

A general guide for the selection of eye and face protection equipment is listed below.

TYPE OF CUTTING OPERATION	HAZARD	SUGGESTED SHADE NUMBER
Light cutting up to 1 inch	Sparks, harmful rays, molten metal, flying particles	3 or 4
Medium cutting, 1–6 inches		4 or 5
Heavy cutting, over 6 inches		5 or 6

Metal Thickness in (mm)	Center Orifice Size No. Drill Size	Tip Cleaner No.*	Oxygen Pressure lb/in² (kPa)	Acetylene lb/in² (kPa)
1/8 (3)	60	7	10 (70)	3 (20)
1/4 (6)	60	7	15 (100)	3 (20)
3/8 (10)	55	11	20 (140)	3 (20)
1/2 (13)	55	11	25 (170)	4 (30)
3/4 (19)	55	11	30 (200)	4 (30)
1 (25)	53	12	35 (240)	4 (30)
2 (51)	49	13	45 (310)	5 (35)
3 (76)	49	13	50 (340)	5 (35)
4 (102)	49	13	55 (380)	5 (35)
5 (127)	45	**	60 (410)	5 (35)

*The tip cleaner number when counted from the small end toward the large end in a standard tip cleaner set

**Larger than normally included in a standard tip cleaner set

PRACTICE 7-1

Name____ Date ____________

Class __________________ Instructor __________________ Grade ____________

OBJECTIVE: After completing this practice, you should be able to safely set up a cutting torch.

EQUIPMENT AND MATERIAL NEEDED FOR THIS PRACTICE

1. The following equipment and materials will be needed for this practice: oxygen and fuel gas cylinders, security chain or strap, a place or object to secure cylinders, fuel and oxygen regulators, reverse flow valve or flashback arrestor, torch and tip, proper fitting wrench, leak-detecting solution, and tip cleaner.
2. Proper safety protection (welding hood, safety glasses, wire brush, chipping hammer, leather gloves, pliers, long sleeve shirt, long pants, and leather boots or shoes). Refer to Chapter 2 in the text for more specific safety information.

INSTRUCTIONS

1. The oxygen and acetylene cylinders must be securely chained to a cart or wall before the safety caps are removed.
2. After removing the safety caps, stand to one side and crack (open and quickly close) the cylinder valves, being sure there are no sources of possible ignition that may start a fire. Cracking the cylinder valves is done to blow out any dirt that may be in the valves.
3. Visually inspect all of the parts for any damage, needed repair or cleaning.
4. Attach the regulators to the cylinder valves and tighten them securely with a wrench.
5. Attach a reverse flow valve or flashback arrestor, if the torch does not have them built in, to the hose connection on the regulator or to the hose connection on the torch body, depending on the type of reverse flow valve in the set. Occasionally, test each reverse flow valve by blowing through it to make sure it works properly.
6. If the torch you will be using is a combination-type torch, attach the cutting head at this time.
7. Last, install a cutting tip on the torch.
8. Before the cylinder valves are opened, back out the pressure regulating screws so that when the valves are opened the gauges will show zero pounds working pressure.
9. Stand to one side of the regulators as the cylinder valves are opened slowly.
10. The oxygen valve is opened all the way until it becomes tight, but don't over tighten, and the acetylene valve is opened no more than one-half turn.
11. Open one torch valve and then turn the regulating screw in slowly until 2 psig to 4 psig (14 kPag to 30 kPag) shows on the working pressure gauge. Allow the gas to escape so that the line is completely purged.
12. If you are using a combination welding and cutting torch, the oxygen valve nearest the hose connection must be opened before the flame adjusting valve or cutting lever will work.
13. Close the torch valve and repeat the purging process with the other gas.
14. Be sure there are no sources of possible ignition that may result in a fire.
15. With both torch valves closed, spray a leak-detecting solution on all connections including the cylinder valves. Tighten any connection that shows bubbles.

PRACTICE 7-2

OBJECTIVE: After completing this practice, you should have the ability and knowledge to clean a cutting tip properly.

EQUIPMENT AND MATERIAL NEEDED FOR THIS PRACTICE

1. The following equipment and materials will be needed for this practice: oxygen and fuel gas cylinders, security chain or strap, a place or object to secure cylinders, fuel and oxygen regulators, reverse flow valve or flashback arrestor, torch and tip, proper fitting wrench, leak-detecting solution, and tip cleaner.
2. Proper safety protection (welding hood, safety glasses, wire brush, chipping hammer, leather gloves, pliers, long sleeve shirt, long pants, and leather boots or shoes). Refer to Chapter 2 in the text for more specific safety information.

INSTRUCTIONS

1. Turn on a small amount of oxygen. This procedure is done to blow out any dirt loosened during the cleaning.
2. The end of the tip is first filed flat, using the file provided in the tip cleaning set.
3. Try several sizes of tip cleaners in a preheat hole until the correct size cleaner is determined. It should easily go all the way into the tip.
4. Push the cleaner in and out of each preheat hole several times. Tip cleaners are small, round files. Excessive use of them will greatly increase the orifice (hole) size.
5. Next, depress the cutting lever and, by trial and error, select the correct size tip cleaner for the center cutting orifice.

NOTE: **A tip cleaner should never be forced. If the tip needs additional care, refer back to the section on tip care in Chapter 4.**

PRACTICE 7-3

OBJECTIVE: After completing this practice, you should be able to light and extinguish a torch safely.

EQUIPMENT AND MATERIAL NEEDED FOR THIS PRACTICE

1. The following equipment and materials will be needed for this practice: oxygen and fuel gas cylinders, security chain or strap, a place or object to secure cylinders, fuel and oxygen regulators, reverse flow valve or flashback arrestor, torch and tip, proper fitting wrench, leak-detecting solution, and tip cleaner.
2. Proper safety protection (welding hood, safety glasses, wire brush, chipping hammer, leather gloves, pliers, long sleeve shirt, long pants, and leather boots or shoes). Refer to Chapter 2 in the text for more specific safety information.

INSTRUCTIONS

1. Set the regulator working pressure for the tip size. If you don't know the correct pressure for the tip, start with the fuel set at 5 psig (35 kPag) and the oxygen set at 25 psig (170 kPag).
2. Point the torch tip upward and away from any equipment or other students.
3. Turn on just the acetylene valve and use only a sparklighter to ignite the acetylene. The torch may not stay lit. If this happens, close the valve slightly and try to relight the torch.
4. If the flame is small, it will produce heavy black soot and smoke. In this case, turn the flame up to stop the soot and smoke. The welder need not be concerned if the flame jumps slightly away from the torch tip.
5. With the acetylene flame burning smoke free, slowly open the oxygen valve and by using only the oxygen valve, adjust the flame to a neutral setting.
6. When the cutting oxygen lever is depressed, the flame may become slightly carbonizing. This may occur because of a drop in line pressure due to the high flow of oxygen through the cutting orifice.
7. With the cutting lever depressed, readjust the preheat flame to a neutral setting. The flame will become slightly oxidizing when the cutting lever is released. Since an oxidizing flame is hotter than a neutral flame, the metal being cut

will be preheated faster. When the cut is started by depressing the lever, the flame automatically returns to the neutral setting and does not oxidize the top of the plate.

8. Extinguish the flame by turning off the acetylene and then the oxygen.

CAUTION **Sometimes with large cutting tips the tip will POP when the acetylene is turned off first. If that happens, turn the oxygen off first.**

PRACTICE 7-4

OBJECTIVE: After completing this practice, you should be able to safely set the working pressure on a regulator using oxygen and acetylene.

EQUIPMENT AND MATERIALS NEEDED FOR THIS PRACTICE

1. The following equipment and materials will be needed for this practice: oxygen and fuel gas cylinders, security chain or strap, a place or object to secure cylinders, fuel and oxygen regulators, reverse flow valve or flashback arrestor, torch and tip, proper fitting wrench, leak-detecting solution, and tip cleaner.
2. Proper safety protection (welding hood, safety glasses, wire brush, chipping hammer, leather gloves, pliers, long sleeve shirt, long pants, and leather boots or shoes). Refer to Chapter 2 in the text for more specific safety information.

INSTRUCTIONS

Setting the working pressure of the regulators can be done by following a table, or it can be set by watching the flame.

1. To set the regulator by watching the flame, first set the acetylene pressure at 2 psig to 4 psig (14 kPag to 30 kPag) and then light the acetylene flame.
2. Open the acetylene torch valve one to two turns and reduce the regulator pressure by backing out the setscrew until the flame starts to smoke.
3. Increase the pressure until the smoke stops and then increase it just a little more. This is the maximum fuel gas pressure the tip needs. With a larger tip and a longer hose, the pressure must be set higher. This is the best setting, and it is the safest one to use. With this lowest possible setting, there is less chance of a leak. If the hoses are damaged, the resulting fire will be much smaller than a fire burning from a hose with a higher pressure. There is also less chance of a leak with the lower pressure.
4. With the acetylene adjusted so that the flame just stops smoking, slowly open the torch oxygen valve.
5. Adjust the torch to a neutral flame. When the cutting lever is depressed, the flame will become carbonizing, not having enough oxygen pressure.
6. While holding the cutting lever down, increase the oxygen regulator pressure slightly. Readjust the flame, as needed, to a neutral setting by using the oxygen valve on the torch.
7. Increase the pressure slowly and readjust the flame as you watch the length of the clear cutting stream in the center of the flame. The center stream will stay fairly long until a pressure is reached that causes turbulence disrupting the cutting stream. This turbulence will cause the flame to shorten in length considerably.
8. With the cutting lever still depressed, reduce the oxygen pressure until the flame lengthens once again. This is the maximum oxygen pressure that this tip can use without causing turbulence in the cutting stream. This turbulence will cause a very inferior cut. The lower pressure also will keep the sparks from being blown a longer distance from the work.

PRACTICE 7-5

Name_______________________________ Date ____________

Class ______________ Instructor ______________ Grade ____________

OBJECTIVE: After completing this practice, you should be able to make a quality straight cut on a 1/4-in. (6-mm) steel plate.

EQUIPMENT AND MATERIAL NEEDED FOR THIS PRACTICE

1. Properly set up and adjusted oxyfuel cutting equipment, proper safety protection (welding hood, safety glasses, wire brush, chipping hammer, leather gloves, pliers, long sleeve shirt, long pants, and leather boots or shoes). Refer to Chapter 2 in the text for more specific safety information.
2. A straight edge
3. A piece of soapstone
4. A piece of mild steel plate, 6 in. (152 mm) long x 1/4 in. (6 mm) thick

INSTRUCTIONS

1. Using a straight edge and soapstone, make several straight lines 1/2 in. (13 mm) apart. Starting at one end, make a cut along the entire length of plate.
2. The strip must fall free, be slag free, and be within ±3/32 in. (2 mm) of a straight line and ±5° of being square.
3. Repeat this procedure until the cut is mastered.
4. Turn off the gas cylinders, regulators and clean up your work area when you are finished cutting.

PRACTICE 7-6

OBJECTIVE: After completing this practice, you should be able to make a quality straight cut on a 1/2-in. (13-mm) steel plate.

EQUIPMENT AND MATERIAL NEEDED FOR THIS PRACTICE

1. Properly set up and adjusted oxyfuel cutting equipment, proper safety protection (welding hood, safety glasses, wire brush, chipping hammer, leather gloves, pliers, long sleeve shirt, long pants, and leather boots or shoes). Refer to Chapter 2 in the text for more specific safety information.
2. A straight edge
3. A piece of soapstone
4. A piece of mild steel plate, 6 in. (152 mm) long x 1/2 in. (6 mm) thick

INSTRUCTIONS

1. Using a straight edge and soapstone, make several straight lines 1/2 in. (13 mm) apart. Starting at one end, make a cut along the entire length of plate.
2. The strip must fall free, be slag free, and be within ±3/32 in. (2 mm) of a straight line and ±5° of being square.
3. Repeat this procedure until the cut is mastered.
4. Turn off the gas cylinders, regulators and clean up your work area when you are finished cutting.

NOTE: Remember that starting a cut in thick plate will take longer and the cutting speed will be slower.

PRACTICE 7-7

OBJECTIVE: After completing this practice, you should be able to bevel 3/8-inch plate.

EQUIPMENT AND MATERIAL NEEDED FOR THIS PRACTICE

1. Properly set up and adjusted oxyfuel cutting equipment, proper safety protection (welding hood, safety glasses, wire brush, chipping hammer, leather gloves, pliers, long sleeve shirt, long pants, and leather boots or shoes). Refer to Chapter 2 in the text for more specific safety information.
2. A piece of soapstone
3. A straight edge
13. A piece of mild steel plate, 6 in. (152 mm) long x 3/8 in. (10 mm) thick

INSTRUCTIONS

1. Using a straight edge and soapstone, mark the plate in strips 1/2 in. (13 mm) wide.
3. Set the tip for beveling and cut a bevel. The bevel should be within ±3/32 in. (2 mm) of a straight line and ±5° of a 45° angle. There may be some soft slag, but no hard slag, on the beveled plate.
4. Repeat this practice until the cut is mastered.
5. Turn off the gas cylinders, regulators and clean up your work area when you are finished cutting.

PRACTICE 7-8

Name____ Date ______________

Class ______________________ Instructor ______________________ Grade ______________

OBJECTIVE: After completing this practice, you should be able to cut 1/4-in. to 3/8-in. (6-mm to 10-mm) carbon steel in both the vertical up and down position.

EQUIPMENT AND MATERIAL NEEDED FOR THIS PRACTICE

1. Properly set up and adjusted oxyfuel cutting equipment, proper safety protection (welding hood, safety glasses, wire brush, chipping hammer, leather gloves, pliers, long sleeve shirt, long pants, and leather boots or shoes). Refer to Chapter 2 in the text for more specific safety information.
2. A piece of soapstone
3. A straight edge
4. A piece of mild steel plate, 6 in. (152 mm) long x 1/4 in. (6 mm) to 3/8 in. (10 mm) thick, marked in strips 1/2 in. (13 mm) wide 1/4-in. and 3/8-in. (6-mm and 10-mm) carbon steel plate 6 inches long

INSTRUCTIONS

1. Using a straight edge and soapstone, make several straight lines 1/2 inch (13 mm) apart on the steel plate.
2. Place the plate in a vertical position.
3. Start your first cut at the top of the plate and travel downward. Then, starting at the bottom, make the next cut upward. Make sure that the sparks do not cause a safety hazard and that the metal being cut off will not fall on any person or object.
4. The cut must be free of hard slag and within $\pm 3/32$ in. (2 mm) of a straight line and $\pm 5°$ of being square.
5. Repeat these cuts until they are mastered.
6. Turn off the gas cylinders, regulators and clean up your work area when you are finished cutting.

CHAPTER 7: FLAME CUTTING QUIZ

Name________________________________ Date ____________

Class ____________ Instructor ____________ Grade ____________

Instructions: Read carefully Chapter 7 of the text. After reading, complete the following questions.

A. SHORT ANSWER

Write a brief answer, in the space provided, that will answer the question or complete the statement.

1. List the parts of the oxyfuel cutting torch.

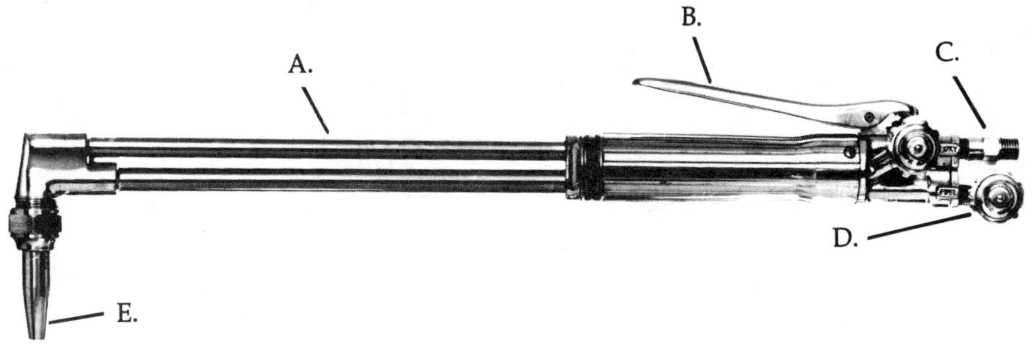

(Courtesy of Victor Equipment Company.)

a.____________________

b. ____________________

c.____________________

d. ____________________

e.____________________

2. List five fuel gases that are used for flame cutting.

a.____________________

b. ____________________

c.____________________

d. ____________________

e.____________________

3. What fuel gas is most frequently used?

____

4. Explain the differences between a combination torch set and a cutting torch.

____

5. What could happen if acetylene was used in a tip with more than eight preheat holes, or in a two-piece tip?

____

____

____

____

6. From the illustrations shown below, which torch is classified as an injector mixing torch?

____

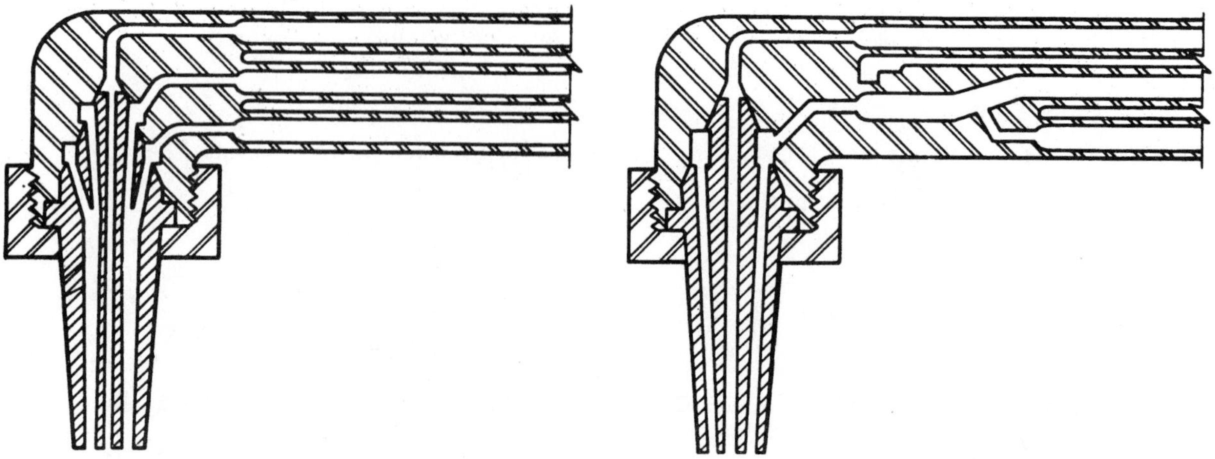

A. B.

7. Define coupling distance.

____

____

____

____

8. What are the two major methods for controlling distortion while making a cut?

____

____

9. Why is a slight forward torch angle used when cutting a straight line? Why not on patterns?

____

____

____

____

B. TRUE-FALSE

Write the letter T, in the space to the left, if the statement is true and the letter F if the statement if false.

_____ 10. Most hand torches can cut metal up to seven inches thick.

_____ 11. It is possible to cut steel that is four feet thick.

_____ 12. Acetylene is the most frequently used fuel gas.

_____ 13. Acetylene should be used in a two-piece cutting tip.

_____ 14. Acetylene cutting tips should be one piece with 1 to 6 preheat holes.

_____ 15. There is less chance of a flashback with low pressure regulator settings than with high pressure settings.

_____ 16. The oxyfuel gas cutting torch works as a result of the metal being rapidly melted.

_____ 17. Hard slag is easier than soft slag to remove.

_____ 18. Distortion is not a problem if the correct fuel gas is used.

_____ 19. By looking at the drag lines in a cut, you can determine whether the cut was made correctly or incorrectly.

C. IDENTIFICATION

In the space provided identify the items shown on the illustration.

_____ 20. Travel speed too fast

_____ 21. Preheat flames too high above the surface

_____ 22. Travel speed too slow

_____ 23. Cutting oxygen pressure too high

_____ 24. Correct cut

_____ 25. Preheat flames too close to the surface

A.

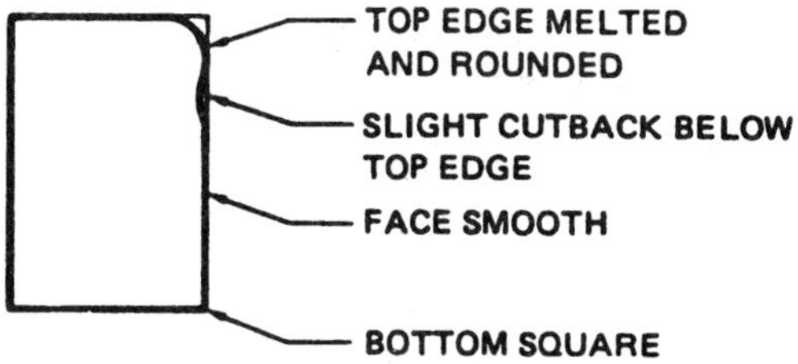

B.

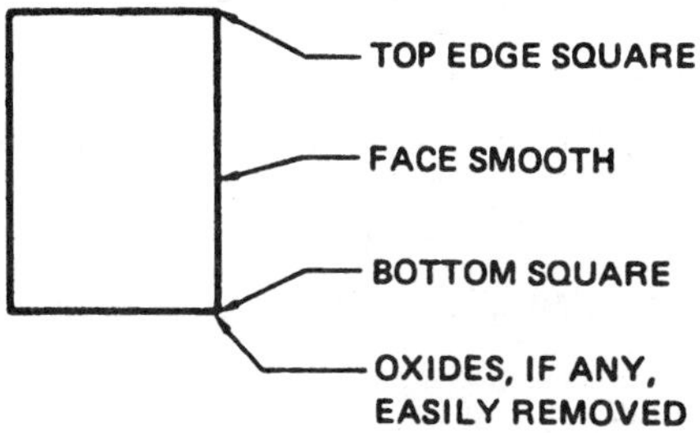

C.

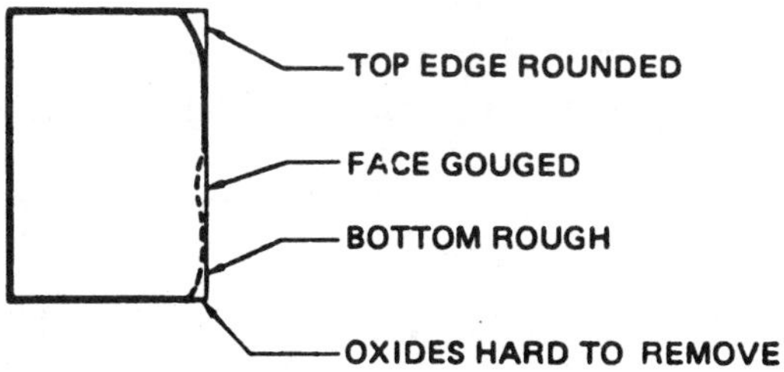

D.

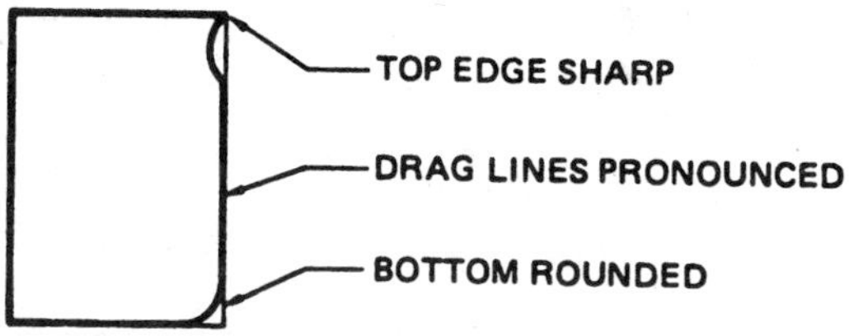

E.

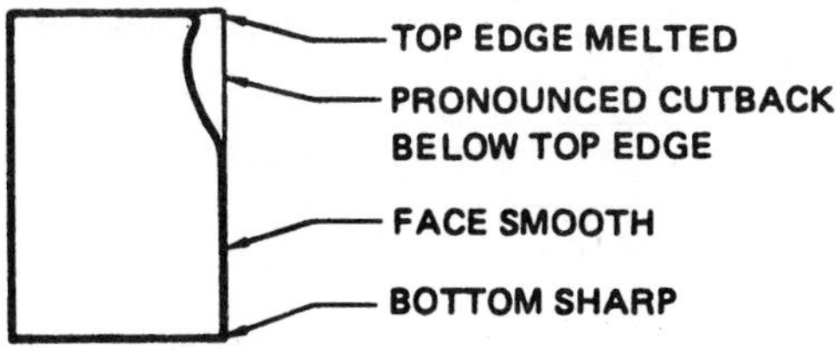

F.

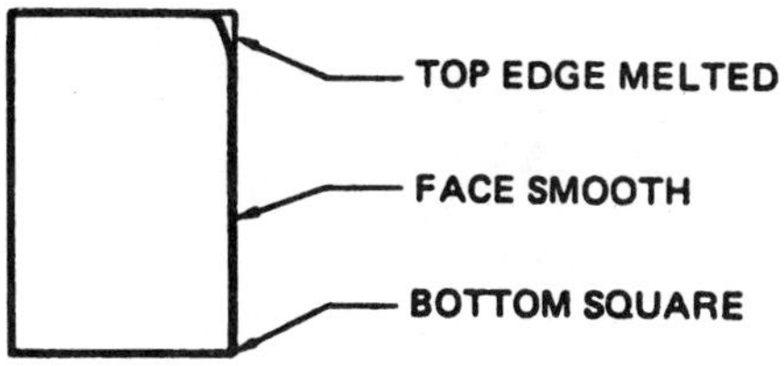

D. ESSAY

Provide complete answers for all of the following questions.

26. List the advantages of a combination welding and cutting torch.

27. When does a welder need to use more preheat flames?

28. How are MPS and propane two-piece tips different from each other? Why?

29. How is a tip removed from the torch head if it is stuck even after the nut has been removed?

30. How is a tip seal checked for a leak?

31. Why is the oxygen turned on while a welder is cleaning a tip?

32. Without using a chart, how can a welder correctly set the gas pressures?

33. If a metal is to be cut by the oxyfuel gas cutting process, what property must the metal have?

34. Define the following terms: kindling temperature, kerf, slag, oxide, MPS gases, hand cutting, and psig (kPsg).

CHAPTER 8: PLASMA ARC CUTTING

PRACTICE 8-1

Name____ Date ______________

Base Metal __________________________________ Thickness __________

Class ____________________ Instructor ____________________ Grade ____________

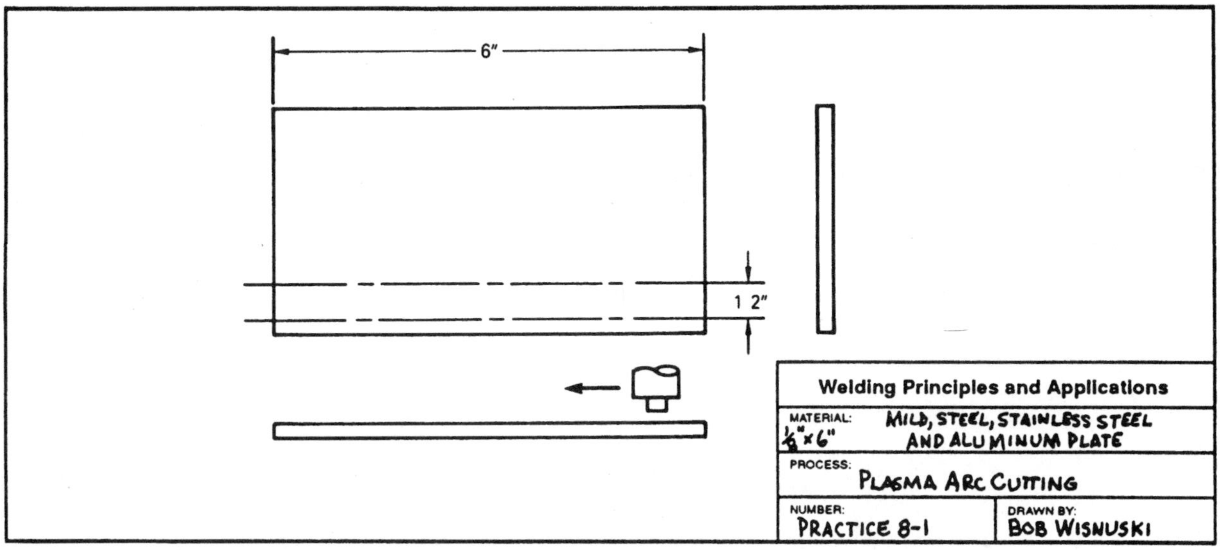

OBJECTIVE: After completing this practice, you should be able to safely set up and operate a PAC machine to make straight cuts on thin gauge metals in the flat position.

EQUIPMENT AND MATERIALS NEEDED FOR THIS PRACTICE

1. A properly set up and adjusted PAC machine
2. Proper safety protection (welding hood, safety glasses, leather gloves, pliers, long sleeve shirt, long pants, and leather boots or shoes). Refer to Chapter 2 in the text for more specific safety information.
3. One or more pieces of mild steel, stainless steel and aluminum, 6 in. (152 mm) long and 16 gauge and 1/8 in. (3 mm) thick.

INSTRUCTIONS

1. Starting at one end of the piece of metal that is 1/ 8 in. (3 mm) thick, hold the torch as close as possible to a 90° angle.
2. Lower your hood and establish a plasma cutting stream.
3. Move the torch in a straight line down the plate toward the other end.
4. If the width of the kerf changes, speed up or slow down the travel rate to keep the kerf the same size for the entire length of the plate.
5. Repeat the cut using both thicknesses of all three types of metals until you can make consistently smooth cuts that are within ±3/32 in. (2.3 mm) of a straight line and ± 5° of being square.

Comments

____

PRACTICE 8-2

Name______________________________ Date ____________

Base Metal ____________________________ Thickness__________

Class ________________ Instructor ________________ Grade ____________

OBJECTIVE: After completing this practice, you should be able to safely set up and operate a PAC machine to make straight cuts on thick plate in the flat position.

EQUIPMENT AND MATERIALS NEEDED FOR THIS PRACTICE

1. A properly set up and adjusted PAC machine
2. Proper safety protection (welding hood, safety glasses, leather gloves, pliers, long sleeve shirt, long pants, and leather boots or shoes). Refer to Chapter 2 in the text for more specific safety information.
3. One or more pieces of mild steel, stainless steel and aluminum, 6 in. (152 mm) long and 1/4 in. (6 mm) and 1/2 in. (13 mm) thick

INSTRUCTIONS

1. Starting at one end of the piece of metal that is 1/8 in. (3 mm) thick, hold the torch as close as possible to a 90° angle.
2. Lower your hood and establish a plasma cutting stream.
3. Move the torch in a straight line down the plate toward the other end.
4. If the width of the kerf changes, speed up or slow down the travel rate to keep the kerf the same size for the entire length of the plate.
5. Repeat the cut using both thicknesses of all three types of metals until you can make consistently smooth cuts that are within ±3/32 in. (2.3 mm) of a straight line and ±5° of being square.

Comments

____

PRACTICE 8-3

Name____ Date ____________

Base Metal ____ Thickness__________

Class ______________________ Instructor ______________________ Grade ____________

OBJECTIVE: After completing this practice, you should be able to safely set up and operate a PAC machine to cut 1/2-in. (13-mm) and 1-in. (25 mm) holes in various types and thicknesses of sheet metal and plates.

EQUIPMENT AND MATERIALS NEEDED FOR THIS PRACTICE

1. A properly set up and adjusted PAC machine
2. Proper safety protection (welding hood, safety glasses, leather gloves, pliers, long sleeve shirt, long pants, and leather boots or shoes). Refer to Chapter 2 in the text for more specific safety information.
3. One or more pieces of mild steel, stainless steel and aluminum, 16 gauge, 1/8 in. (3 mm), 1/4 in. (6 mm) and 1/2 in. (13 mm) thick

INSTRUCTIONS

1. Starting with the piece of metal that is 1/8 in. (3 mm) thick, hold the torch as close as possible to a 90° angle.
2. Lower your hood and establish a plasma cutting stream.
3. Move the torch in an outward spiral until the hole is the desired size.
4. Repeat the hole cutting process until both sizes of holes are made using all the thicknesses of all three types of metals until you can make consistently smooth cuts that are within ±3/32 in. (2.3 mm) of being round and ±5° of being square.

Comments

____

PRACTICE 8-4

Name____ Date ____________

Base Metal _______________________________________ Thickness ________

Class ______________________ Instructor ____________________ Grade ____________

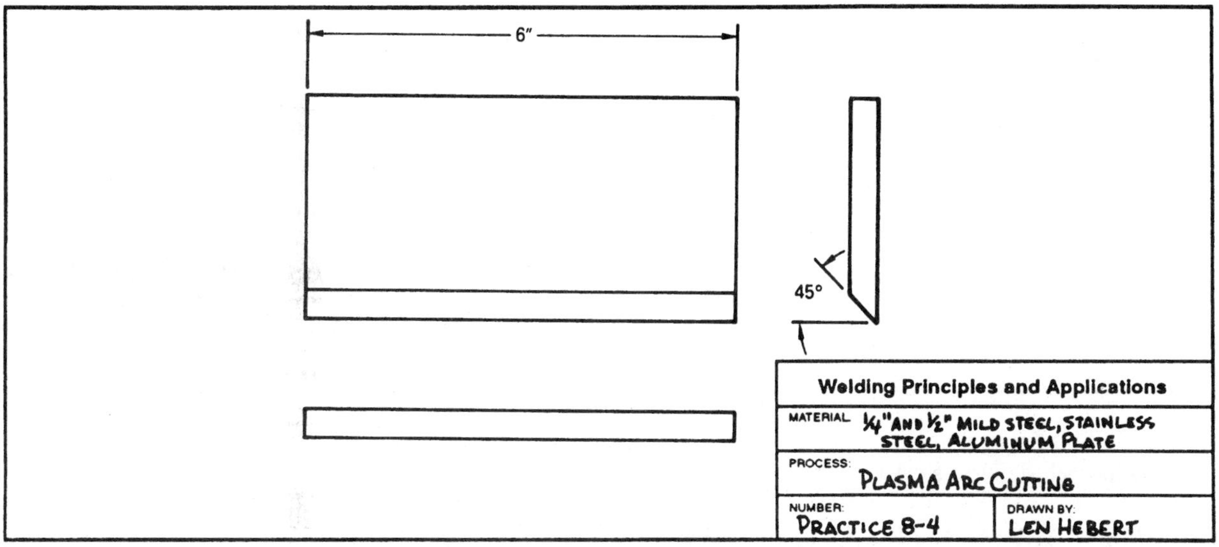

OBJECTIVE: After completing this practice, you should be able to safely set up and operate a PAC machine to bevel plate.

EQUIPMENT AND MATERIALS NEEDED FOR THIS PRACTICE

1. A properly set up and adjusted PAC machine
2. Proper safety protection (welding hood, safety glasses, leather gloves, pliers, long sleeve shirt, long pants, and leather boots or shoes). Refer to Chapter 2 in the text for more specific safety information.
3. One or more pieces of mild steel, stainless steel and aluminum, 6 in. (152 mm) long and 1/4 in. (6 mm) and 1/2 in. (13 mm) thick. You will cut a 45° bevel down the length of the plate.

INSTRUCTIONS

1. Starting at one end of the piece of metal that is 1/4 in. (6 mm) thick, hold the torch as close as possible to a 45° angle.
2. Lower your hood and establish a plasma cutting stream.
3. Move the torch in a straight line down the plate toward the other end.
4. Repeat the cut using both thicknesses of all three types of metals until you can make consistently smooth cuts that are within ±3/32 in. (2.3 mm) of a straight line and ±5° of a 45° angle.

Comments

____

PRACTICE 8-5

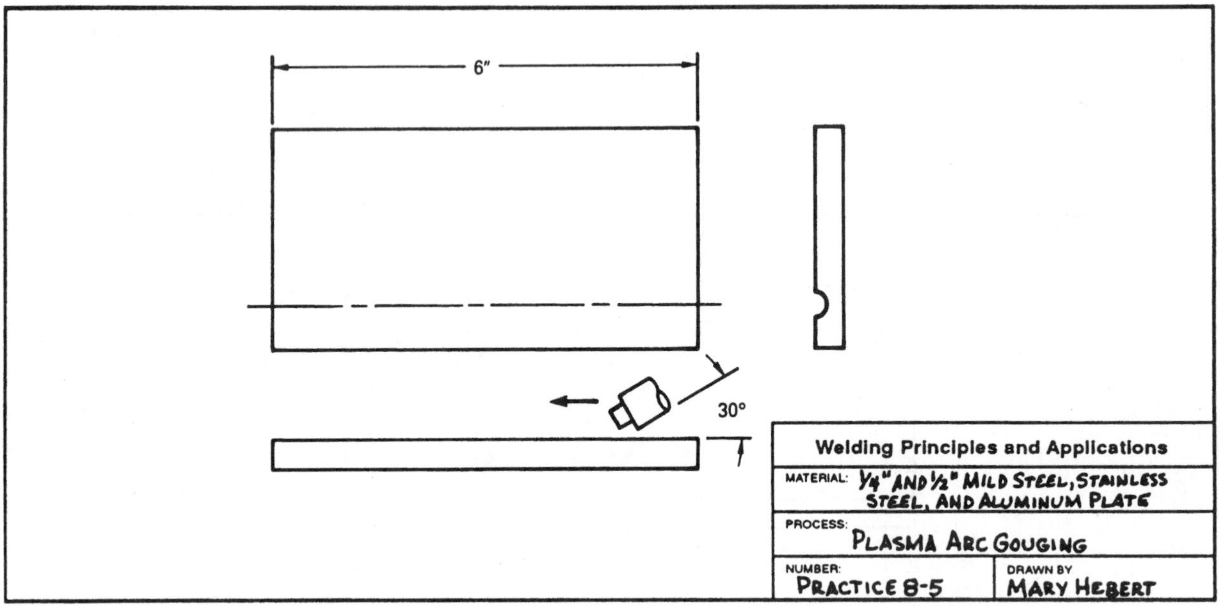

OBJECTIVE: After completing this practice, you should be able to safely set up and operate a PAC machine to make a U-groove in steel, stainless steel and aluminum.

EQUIPMENT AND MATERIALS NEEDED FOR THIS PRACTICE

1. A properly set up and adjusted PAC machine
2. Proper safety protection (welding hood, safety glasses, leather gloves, pliers, long sleeve shirt, long pants, and leather boots or shoes). Refer to Chapter 2 in the text for more specific safety information.
3. One or more pieces of mild steel, stainless steel and aluminum, 6 in. (152 mm) long and 1/4 in. (6 mm) or 1/2 in. (13 mm) thick

INSTRUCTIONS

1. Starting at one end of the piece of metal, hold the torch as close as possible to a 30° angle.
2. Lower your hood and establish a plasma cutting stream.
3. Move the torch in a straight line down the plate toward the other end.
4. If the width of the U-groove changes, speed up or slow down the travel rate to keep the groove the same width and depth for the entire length of the plate.
5. Repeat the gouging of the U-groove using all three types of metals until you can make consistently smooth grooves that are within ±3/32 in. (2.3 mm) of a straight line and uniform in width and depth.

Comments

____

CHAPTER 8 PLASMA ARC CUTTING QUIZ

Name______________________________________ Date ____________

Class ____________________ Instructor ____________________ Grade ____________

Instructions: Read carefully Chapter 8 of the text. After reading, complete the following questions.

A. MATCHING

In the space provided to the left, write the letter from column B that best answers the question or completes the statement in column A.

	column A		column B
____	1. What is the state of matter that is found in the region of an electrical discharge?	a.	cup
____	2. What is the spacing between the electrode tip and the nozzle tip?	b.	plasma
____	3. The nozzle is sometimes called the ________________.	c.	dross
____	4. What is the space left in the metal as the metal is removed during a cut?	d.	electrode setback
____	5. What is the metal compound that resolidifies and attaches itself to the bottom of a cut?	e.	kerf

B. IDENTIFICATION

In the space provided identify the items shown on the illustration.

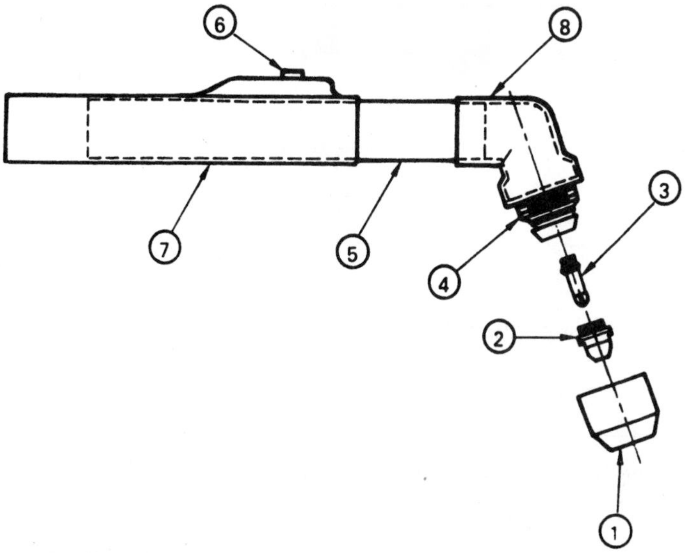

(Courtesy of Lincoln Electric, Cleveland, OH.)

6. Identify the replaceable torch components.

1. ______________________________________
2. ______________________________________
3. ______________________________________
4. ______________________________________
5. ______________________________________
6. ______________________________________

7. ______________________________

8. ______________________________

C. TRUE-FALSE

Write the letter T, in the space to the left, if the statement is true and the letter F if the statement if false.

_____ 7. A plasma is present in any electrical discharge.

_____ 8. Because of the high temperature of a plasma arc, distortion of metal is greater than that of an oxyfuel cut.

_____ 9. Only aluminum, stainless steel, and carbon steel can be cut with the plasma process.

_____ 10. The nozzle standoff distance is critical to producing quality plasma cuts.

_____ 11. Eye protection is not required when using PAC process.

D. SHORT ANSWER

Write a brief answer, in the space provided, that will answer the question or complete the statement.

12. What is the function of a water shroud nozzle?

____

____

13. List eight factors that can affect the width of a PAC kerf.

a. ______________________________

b. ______________________________

c. ______________________________

d. ______________________________

e. ______________________________

f. ______________________________

g. ______________________________

h. ______________________________

14. Why do all plasma cuts have a slight bevel?

____

____

15. List seven factors for controlling dross when making a plasma arc cut.

a. ______________________________

b. ______________________________

c. ______________________________

d. ______________________________

e. ______________________________

f. ______________________________

g. ______________________________

16. Define the term *plasma arc.*

____

____

17. Why are some plasma arc torches water cooled?

____

____

18. List the purpose of four of the wires, hoses, and/or cables that attach the PAC torch to the power supply.

____

____

19. Why is there less distortion when parts are cut using a plasma torch as compared to a standard oxyfuel torch?

____

____

20. What effect do the higher cutting speeds have on the hardness zone formed along the cut edge?

____

____

21. Why must plates be preheated before they are cut using oxyfuel?

____

____

22. Why were aluminum, stainless steel, and copper the metals most often cut using plasma?

____

____

23. How can nonconductive materials be cut with the PAC process?

____

____

24. Explain how the plasma cut is started.

____

____

25. Explain the nontransfer arc method of cutting.

____

____

26. Why are some plasma torches designed to swirl the plasma gas?

____

____

27. List four of the effects on the cut that changing the PAC gas(es) will have.

____

____

28. List six things that can affect the formation of dross on the bottom of a PAC plate.

____

____

29. Why are dyes added to the water in a PAC water table?

30. Why are most manual cutting machines limited to 100 amperes or less?

31. Why must the power be off before working on any part of the plasma arc torch, machine, cables, etc.?

32. Explain each of the following special safety concerns as they apply to plasma arc cutting:

A. electrical shock—

B. moisture—

C. noise—

D. light—

E. fumes—

F. gases—

G. sparks—

33. Define the following terms: plasma arc gouging, water tables, stack cutting, water injection, pilot arc, nontransfer, high frequency alternating current, kerf, dross, heat affected zone, travel speed, water shroud, gas lens, electrode tip, nozzle insulator, nozzle tip, nozzle guide, nozzle, electrode setback, and cup.

CHAPTER 9: RELATED CUTTING PROCESSES

Air Carbon Arc Electrode Current Recommendations									
	Electrode Diameter								
Current	5/32	3/16	1/4	5/16	3/8	1/2	5/8	3/4	FLAT
Min DC	90	200	300	350	450	800	1000	1250	300
Max DC	150	250	400	450	600	1000	1250	1600	500
Min AC	—	200	300	325	350	500	—	—	—
Max AC	—	250	400	425	450	600	—	—	—

Air Carbon Arc Cutting Electrode Recommendations			
Metal	Electrode	Current	Polarity
Steel	DC	DC	DCRP
Cast Iron:			
Gray, Ductile,	DC	DC	DCRP
Malleable	DC	DC	DCSP
Copper Alloys	DC	DC	DCSP
	DC	DC	—
Nickel Alloys	AC	AC or DC	DCSP

PRACTICE 9-1

Name____ Date ____________

Class ____________________ Instructor ____________________ Grade ____________

OBJECTIVE: After completing this practice, you should be able to safely set up and operate an air carbon arc cutting torch to make a V-groove gouge on carbon steel plate.

EQUIPMENT AND MATERIALS NEEDED FOR THIS PRACTICE

1. An air carbon arc cutting torch and welding power supply that has been safely set up in accordance to the manufacturer's specific instructions in the owner's manual.
2. Proper safety protection equipment (safety glasses, welding helmet, leather gloves, pliers, long sleeve shirt, long pants, and leather boots or shoes). Refer to Chapter 2 and Chapter 9 in the text for more specific safety information.

INSTRUCTIONS

1. Adjust the air pressure to approximately 80 psi.
2. Set the amperage within the range for the diameter electrode you are using by referring to the box the electrodes came in or referring to Table 9-3.
3. Check to see that the stream of sparks will not start a fire or cause any damage to anyone or anything in the area.
4. Make sure the area is safe and turn on the welder.
5. Using a suitable dry leather glove to avoid electrical shock, insert the electrode in the torch jaws so that about 6 inches is extending outward. Be sure not to touch the electrode to any metal parts because it may short out.
6. Turn on the air at the torch head.
7. Lower your arc welding helmet.
8. Slowly bring the electrode down at about a 30° angle so it will make contact with the plate near the starting edge. Be prepared for a loud sharp sound when the arc starts.
9. Once the arc is struck, move the electrode in a straight line down the plate toward the other end. Keep the speed and angle of the torch constant.
10. When you reach the other end, lift the torch so the arc will stop.
11. Raise your helmet and stop the air.
12. Remove the remaining electrode from the torch so it will not accidently touch anything.
13. When the metal is cool, chip or brush any slag or dross off of the plate. This material should remove easily. The groove must be within ±1/8 in. (3 mm) of being straight and within ±3/32 in. (2.3 mm) of uniformity in width and depth.
14. Repeat this cut until it can be made within these tolerances.
15. Turn off the welding machine and clean up your work area when you are finished welding.

PRACTICE 9-2

OBJECTIVE: After completing this practice, you should be able to safely set up and operate an air carbon arc cutting torch to make a J-groove along the edge of a plate.

EQUIPMENT AND MATERIALS NEEDED FOR THIS PRACTICE

1. An air carbon arc cutting torch and welding power supply that has been safely set up in accordance to the manufacturer's specific instructions in the owner's manual.
2. Proper safety protection equipment (safety glasses, welding helmet, leather gloves, pliers, long sleeve shirt, long pants, and leather boots or shoes). Refer to Chapter 2 and Chapter 9 in the text for more specific safety information.

INSTRUCTIONS

1. Adjust the air pressure to approximately 80 psi.
2. Set the amperage within the range for the diameter electrode you are using.
3. Check to see that the stream of sparks will not start a fire or cause any damage to anyone or anything in the area.
4. Make sure the area is safe and turn on the welder.
5. Using a suitable dry leather glove to avoid electrical shock, insert the electrode in the torch jaws so that about 6 inches is extending outward. Be sure not to touch the electrode to any metal parts because it may short out.
6. Turn on the air at the torch head.
7. Lower your arc welding helmet.
8. Slowly bring the electrode down at about a 30° angle so it will make contact with the plate near the starting edge.
9. Once the arc is struck, move the electrode in a straight line down the edge of the plate toward the other end. Keep the speed and angle of the torch constant.
10. When you reach the other end, lift the torch so the arc will stop.
11. Raise your helmet and stop the air.
12. Remove the remaining electrode from the torch so it will not accidently touch anything.
13. When the metal is cool, chip or brush any slag or dross off of the plate. This material should remove easily. The groove must be within ±1/8 in. (3 mm) of being straight and within ±3/32 in. (2.3 mm) of uniformity in width and depth.
14. Repeat this cut until it can be made within these tolerances.
15. Turn off the welding machine and clean up your work area when you are finished welding.

PRACTICE 9-3

Name____________________ Date __________ Electrode Used __________

Class ________________ Instructor ________________ Grade __________

OBJECTIVE: After completing this practice, you should be able to make a U-groove along the root face of a weld joint on a plate.

EQUIPMENT AND MATERIALS NEEDED FOR THIS PRACTICE

1. An air carbon arc cutting torch and welding power supply that has been safely set up in accordance to the manufacturer's specific instructions in the owner's manual.
2. Proper safety protection equipment (safety glasses, welding helmet, leather gloves, pliers, long sleeve shirt, long pants, and leather boots or shoes). Refer to Chapter 2 and Chapter 9 in the text for more specific safety information.
3. Two plates 6 inches in length.

INSTRUCTIONS

1. Adjust the air pressure to approximately 80 psi.
2. Set the amperage within the range for the diameter electrode you are using by referring to the box the electrodes came in or referring to Table 9-3.
3. Check to see that the stream of sparks will not start a fire or cause any damage to anyone or anything in the area.
4. Make sure the area is safe and turn on the welder.
5. Using a suitable dry leather glove to avoid electrical shock, insert the electrode in the torch jaws so that about 6 inches is extending outward. Be sure not to touch the electrode to any metal parts because it may short out.
6. Turn on the air at the torch head.
7. Lower your arc welding helmet.
8. Start the arc at the joint between the 2 plates.
9. Once the arc is struck, move the electrode in a straight line down the edge of the plate toward the other end. Watch the bottom of the cut to see that it is deep enough. If there is a line along the bottom of the groove, it needs to be deeper. Once the groove depth is determined keep the speed and angle of the torch constant.
10. When you reach the other end, break the arc off.
11. Raise your helmet and stop the air.
12. Remove the remaining electrode from the torch so it will not accidently touch anything.
13. When the metal is cool, chip or brush any slag or dross off of the plate. This material should remove easily. The groove must be within ±1/8 in. (3 mm) of being straight, but it may vary in depth so that all of the unfused root of the weld has been removed.
14. Repeat this cut until it can be made within these tolerances.
15. Turn off the welding machine and clean up your work area when you are finished welding.

PRACTICE 9-4

OBJECTIVE: After completing this practice, you should be able to make a U-groove to remove a weld from a plate.

EQUIPMENT AND MATERIALS NEEDED FOR THIS PRACTICE

1. An air carbon arc cutting torch and welding power supply that has been safely set up in accordance to the manufacturer's specific instructions in the owner's manual.
2. Proper safety protection equipment (safety glasses, welding helmet, leather gloves, pliers, long sleeve shirt, long pants, and leather boots or shoes). Refer to Chapter 2 and Chapter 9 in the text for more specific safety information.
3. Two steel plates that have been welded together, minimum length 6 inches.

INSTRUCTIONS

1. Adjust the air pressure to approximately 80 psi.
2. Set the amperage within the range for the diameter electrode you are using by referring to the box the electrodes came in or referring to Table 9-3.
3. Check to see that the stream of sparks will not start a fire or cause any damage to anyone or anything in the area.
4. Make sure the area is safe and turn on the welder.
5. Using a suitable dry leather glove to avoid electrical shock, insert the electrode in the torch jaws so that about 6 inches (152 mm) is extending outward. Be sure not to touch the electrode to any metal parts because it may short out.
6. Turn on the air at the torch head.
7. Lower your arc welding helmet.
8. Start the arc on the weld.
9. Once the arc is struck, move the electrode in a straight line down the weld toward the other end. Watch the bottom of the cut to see that it is deep enough. If there is not a line along the bottom of the groove, it needs to be deeper. Once the groove depth is determined, keep the speed and angle of the torch constant.
10. When you reach the other end, break the arc off.
11. Raise your helmet and stop the air.
12. Remove the remaining electrode from the torch so it will not accidently touch anything.
13. When the metal is cool, chip or brush any slag or dross off of the plate. This material should remove easily. The groove must be within $\pm 1/8$ inch (3 mm) of being straight, but it may vary in depth so that all of the weld metal has been removed.
14. Repeat this cut until it can be made within these tolerances.
15. Turn off the welding machine and clean up your work area when you are finished welding.

CHAPTER 9: RELATED CUTTING PROCESSES QUIZ

Name____ Date ______________

Class ____________________ Instructor ____________________ Grade ______________

Instructions: Read carefully Chapter 9 of the text. After reading, complete the following questions.

A. SHORT ANSWER

Write a brief answer, in the space provided, that will answer the question or complete the statement.

1. List six advantages of laser cutting.
   a.____
   b. ____
   c.____
   d. ____
   e.____
   f.____
2. List three advantages of using a laser to drill a hole.
   a.____
   b. ____
   c.____
3. What are the four major differences between an air carbon arc torch and a shielded metal arc welding electrode holder?
   a.____
   b. ____
   c.____
   d. ____
4. What are the three shapes of air carbon arc electrodes?
   a.____
   b. ____
   c.____
5. List four metals that can be cut using the air carbon arc process.
   a.____
   b. ____
   c.____
   d. ____

B. TRUE-FALSE

Write the letter T, in the space to the left, if the statement is true and the letter F if the statement if false.

____ 6. Cast iron is a metal that cannot be carbon arc gouged.

____ 7. Lasers are not to be used on thin materials because of the high concentration of heat.

____ 8. Oxyfuel cutting can only be performed on metals that can be rapidly oxidized by the cutting stream of oxygen.

_____ 9. An oxygen lance can be used to cut concrete.

_____ 10. The water jet cutting process uses yttrium aluminum garnet to improve the cutting surface on hard materials such as tungsten carbide and ceramics.

C. ESSAY

Provide complete answers for all of the following questions.

11. List 4 things that manufacturers use lasers to do.

____

____

12. List 3 materials that can be used to produce a laser light.

____

____

13. What are the two major types or divisions of lasers?

____

____

14. List 4 gases or mixtures of gases that can be used to produce laser light.

____

____

15. What surface condition stops the laser's ability to penetrate it?

____

____

16. What does the phrase "threshold of the surface temperature" mean in relation to lasers?

____

____

17. Explain how a laser is used to drill a hole through thick materials.

____

____

18. What is the power range of most lasers?

____

____

19. Why was early carbon arc cutting limited to vertical and overhead positions?

____

____

20. What are the major differences between an electrode holder and an air carbon arc torch?

____

____

21. What is the purpose of the following air carbon arc electrodes?

    A. round— ____________________

    B. flat— ____________________

22. Why are some air carbon arc electrodes able to be joined together?

    ____

    ____

23. Why will a small diameter hose have an adverse effect on air flowing to the air carbon arc torch?

    ____

    ____

24. What might become a hazard to your health without proper safety precautions, including adequate ventilation, when air carbon arc cutting?

    ____

    ____

25. Why would air carbon arc "washing" be used?

    ____

    ____

26. List and explain 6 air carbon arc safety considerations.

    ____

    ____

27. How are most oxygen lances "started" for cutting?

    ____

    ____

28. When water jet cutting, what will cause the kerf to be wider?

    ____

    ____

29. Define the following terms: monochromatic, synchronized wave form, YAG, photo energy, exothermic gases, graphite, gouging, and washing.

    ____

    ____

    ____

    ____

    ____

    ____

    ____

    ____

    ____

CHAPTER 10: GAS METAL ARC WELDING EQUIPMENT SETUP AND OPERATION QUIZ

Name____ Date ____________

Class ____________________ Instructor ____________________ Grade ____________

Instructions: Carefully read Chapter 10 of the text. After reading, complete the following questions.

A. MATCHING

In the space provided to the left, write the letter from column B that best answers the question or completes the statement in column A.

column A	column B
____ 1. What is the short period at the end of the weld when the wire feed stops but the current does not?	a. deposition rate
____ 2. What is the welding technique that uses a push angle?	b. electrode extension
____ 3. What is the distance from the contact tube to the arc measured along the wire?	c. burn-back time
____ 4. What is the measure of the amount of weld metal deposited?	d. wire melting rate
____ 5. What is the rate at which the wire is being consumed by the arc?	e. forehand welding

Correctly match the following terms to the illustrations below.

A

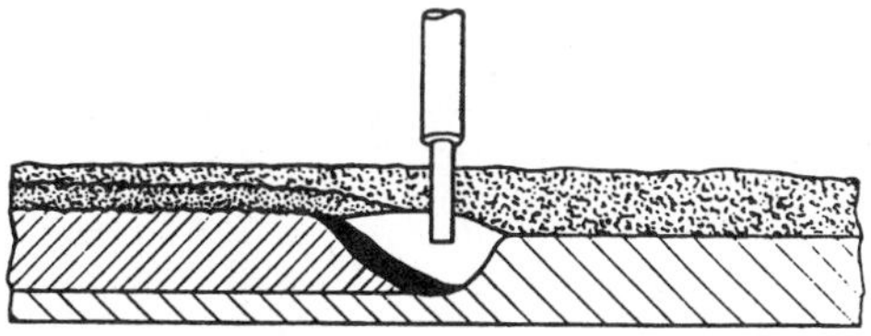

B

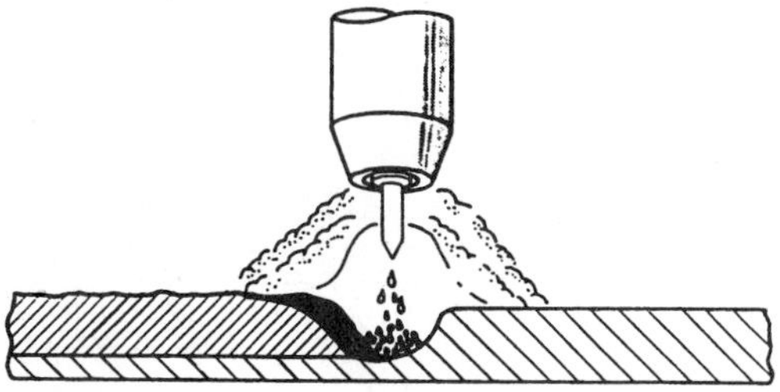

C

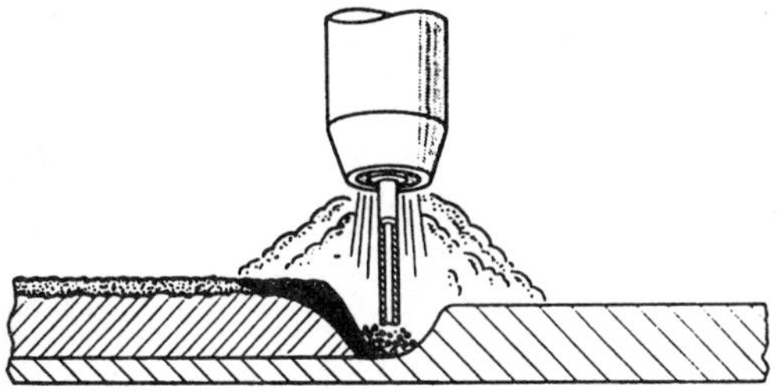

____ 6. GMAW

____ 7. SAW

____ 8. FCAW

B. TRUE-FALSE

Write the letter T, in the space to the left, if the statement is true and the letter F if the statement if false.

_____ 9. GMA can be used to make high-quality arc spot welds.

_____ 10. The main limitation of flux cored arc welding is that only ferrous metals can be welded.

_____ 11. Knurled V-groove feed rollers are best suited for soft wires such as aluminum.

_____ 12. Changes in gun angle, electrode extension, and weave pattern cannot be made without stopping the weld.

_____ 13. The short-circuiting process is too cold to be effective for making quality welds in sections much thicker than 1/4-inch (6 mm) metal.

_____ 14. Carbon-dioxide is an oxidizing gas which restricts its applications to welding carbon steel.

_____ 15. The wire feed speed setting also determines the current.

_____ 16. Both flux cored arc welding, (FCAW) and submerged arc welding (SAW) use a different power source than the GMAW process.

_____ 17. The major disadvantage of FCAW is its low deposition rate.

_____ 18. The addition of scavengers in some of the FCAW wires is used to remove sulfur from the weld metal.

C. IDENTIFICATION

In the space provided identify the items shown on the illustration. Identify the major parts of the GMA welding equipment.

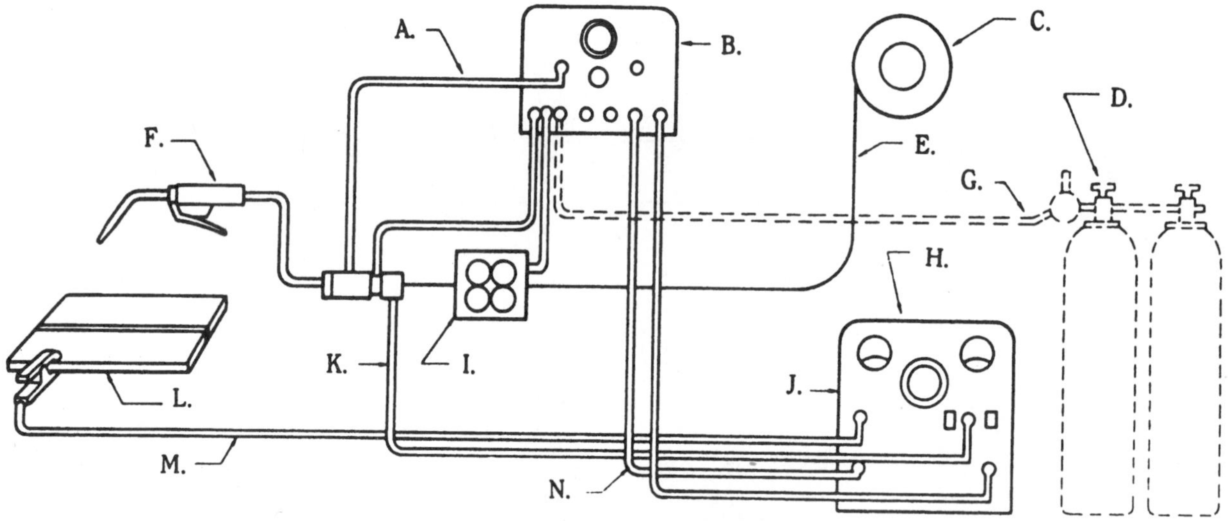

19. _____ welding machine
20. _____ wire feed drive motor
21. _____ wire
22. _____ gun
23. _____ gas out
24. _____ wire feed and current control
25. _____ work cable
26. _____ shielding gas
27. _____ voltage control
28. _____ wire reel
29. _____ gun cable
30. _____ gas in
31. _____ work
32. _____ contractor control

D. SHORT ANSWER

Write a brief answer, in the space provided, that will answer the question or complete the statement.

33. List three methods of transferring filler metal with the GMAW process.

a.____

b. ____

c.____

34. List five types of electrode (wire) feed units.

a.____

b. ____

c.____

d. ____

e.____

35. List three types of feed rollers used in the GMAW process.

a.____

b. ____

c.____

36. List five factors that can control the GMAW weld pool.

a.____

b. ____

c.____

d. ____

e.____

37. List three advantages of the GMA spot welding process.

a.____

b. ____

c.____

38. Constant voltage power supplies are available as ______________ or ______________ .

E. ESSAY

Provide complete answers for all of the following questions.

39. What effect does changing the inductance have on a GMA weld?

____

____

40. What effect does changing the slope have on a GMA weld?

____

____

41. Explain the short-circuiting arc weld cycle.

42. Why does changing the gun angle affect the weld?

43. Why does changing the electrode extension length affect the weld?

44. What groove shape should be used on feed rollers for aluminum electrode wire? Why?

45. What type of conduit liner is needed for aluminum electrode wire? Why?

46. How does a linear electrode feed change the wire speed?

47. How does pulsed power help to control weld bead size?

CHAPTER 11: GAS METAL ARC WELDING

Arc Welding Operation	Suggested Shade Number
Gas Metal Arc Welding Non-ferrous	11
Gas Metal Arc Welding Ferrous	12

Troubleshooting for GMAW

Problem	**Correction**
Arc Blow	1. Change gun angle. 2. Move ground clamp. 3. Use backup bars, brass or copper. 4. Demagnetize part.
Cracked Welds	1. Check filler wire compatibility with base metal 2. Use pre- & postheat on weldment. 3. Use a convex weld bead. 4. Check design of root opening. 5. Change welding speed. 6. Change shielding gas.
Dirty Welds	1. Decrease gun angle. 2. Hold gun nozzle closer to work. 3. Increase gas flow. 4. Clean weld joint area, .gas flow. 5. Check for draft that may be blowing shielding gas away. 6. Check gun nozzle for damaged or worn parts. 7. Center contact tip in gun nozzle. 8. Clean filler wire before it enters wire drive. 9. Check cables and gun for air or water leaks. 10. Keep unused filler wire in shipping containers.
Wide Weld Bead	1. Increase welding speed. 2. Reduce current. 3. Use a different welding technique. 4. Shorten arc length
Incomplete Penetration	1. Increase current. 2. Reduce welding speed. 3. Shorten arc length. 4. Increase root opening 5. Change gun angle.

Problem	Correction
Irregular Arc Start	1. Use wire cutters to cut off the end of the filler wire before starting new weld. 2. Check ground. 3. Check contact tip. 4. Check polarity. 5. Check for drafts. 6. Increase gas flow.
Irregular Wirefeed Burn-back	1. Check contact tip. 2. Check wire feed speed. 3. Increase drive roll pressure. 4. Check voltage. 5. Check polarity. 6. Check wire spool for kinks or bends. 7. Clean or replace worn conduit liner.
Welding Cables Overheating	1. Check for loose cable connections. 2. Use larger cables. 3. Use shorter cables. 4. Decrease welding time.
Porosity	1. Check for drafts. 2. Check shielding gas. 3. Increase gas flow. 4. Decrease gun angle. 5. Hold nozzle close to work. 6. Do not weld if metal is wet. 7. Clean weld joint area. 8. Center contact tip with gun nozzle. 9. Check gun nozzle for damage. 10. Check gun and cables for air or water leaks.
Spatter	1. Change gun angle. 2. Shorten arc length. 3. Decrease wire speed. 4. Check for draft.
Undercutting	1. Reduce current. 2. Change gun angle. 3. Use different welding technique. 4. Reduce welding speed. 5. Shorten arc length.
Incomplete Fusion	1. Increase current. 2. Change welding technique. 3. Shorten arc length. 4. Check joint preparation. 5. Clean weld joint area.
Unstable Arc	1. Clean weld area. 2. Check contact tip. 3. Check for loose cable connections.

SHIELDING GASES AND GAS MIXTURES USED FOR GAS METAL ARC WELDING

Shielding Gas	Chemical Behavior	Uses and Usage Notes
1. Argon	Inert	Welding virtually all metals except steel
2. Helium	Inert	Al and Cu alloys for greater heat and to minimize porosity
3. Ar & He (20–80 to 50–50%)	Inert	Al and Cu alloys for greater heat and to minimize porosity, but with quieter, more readily controlled arc action
4. N_2	Reducing	On Cu, very powerful arc
5. Ar + 25–30% N_2	Reducing	On Cu, powerful but smoother operating more readily controlled arc than with N_2.
6. Ar + 1–2% O_2	Oxidizing	Stainless and alloy steels, also for some deoxidized copper alloys
7. Ar + 3–5% O_2	Oxidizing	Plain carbon, alloy, and stainless steels (generally requires highly deoxidized wire)
8. Ar + 3–5% O_2	Oxidizing	Various steels using deoxidized wire
9. Ar + 20–30% O_2	Oxidizing	Various steels, chiefly with short-circuiting arc
10. Ar + 5% O_2 + 15% CO_2	Oxidizing	Various steels using deoxidized wire
11. CO_2	Oxidizing	Plain-carbon and low-alloy steels, deoxidized wire essential
12. CO_2 + 3–10% O_2	Oxidizing	Various steels using deoxidized wire
13. CO_2 + 20% O_2	Oxidizing	Steels

GENERALLY RECOMMENDED FILLER METALS AND SHIELDING GASES FOR GAS METAL ARC WELDING VARIOUS BASE METALS

Base Metal Type	Shielding Gas Composition	Specific Alloy to Be Welded	Filler Metal Type Electrode
Aluminum & its alloys	Pure argon or helium-argon (75–25)	1100	1100 or 4043
		2219	4145 or 2319
		3003, 3004	319
		5050	4043
		5052	4043 or 5554
		5154, 5254	5554 or 5154
		5083, 5084, 5486	5554 or 5154
		6061	5556 or 5356
		7039	4043 or 5556
			5556, 5356, or 5183
Magnesium alloys	Pure argon	AZ31B, 61A, 81A ZE10XA ZK20XA	AZ61A
		AZ31B, 61A, 63A 80A, 81A, 91C, 92A AM80A, 100A ZE10XA XK20XA	AZ92A
Copper	Helium-argon mixture (75–25; pure argon on thin sections	Deoxidized copper	Deoxidized copper Silicon-0.25% Tin-0.75% Mn-0.15%
Copper-nickel alloy	Pure argon	Cu-Ni alloy: 70–30 90–10	Titanium deoxidized 70–30 Cu-Ni 70–30 or 90–10
Bronzes	Pure argon	Manganese bronze	Aluminum bronze
		Aluminum bronze	Aluminum bronze
		Nickel-aluminum bronze	Aluminum bronze
	Argon + 5% O_2	Tin bronze	Phosphor bronze
Nickel and nickel alloys	Helium-argon mixture (75–25) or pure argon	Nickel Nickel-copper (Monel) Nickel–Chromium (Inconel)	Similar to base metal, titanium deoxidized (see supplier)
Plain low-carbon steel	CO_2; argon + 10 to 30% CO_2; or argon + 2 to 5% O_2	Hot or cold rolled sheet or plate ASTM A7, A36 A285, A373, or equivalent	Deoxidized plain carbon steel
Low-alloy carbon steel	Argon + 1–2% O_2 or argon + 10–30% CO_2	Hot or cold rolled sheet of various grades	Deoxidized low-alloy steel
Stainless steel	Argon + 1–5% O_2	302, 304, 321, 347, 309, 310 316, etc.	Electrode to match base alloy

TYPICAL SHIELDING GAS FLOW RATES* FOR GAS METAL ARC WELDING VARIOUS MATERIALS

	Spray-Type Arc — 1/16 in. dia. filler wire				
Materials	Argon	Helium	Argon-Helium (25–75)	Argon-Oxygen (1–5% O_2)	CO_2
Aluminum	50	100	80	—	—
Magnesium	50	100	80	—	—
Plain C Steel	—	—	—	40	40
Low-alloy steel	—	—	—	40	40
Stainless steel	40	—	—	40	—
Nickel	50	100	80	—	—
Ni-Cu alloy	50	100	80	—	—
Ni-Cr-Fe alloy	50	100	80	—	—
Copper	50	100	80	—	—
Cu-Ni alloy (70-30)	50	100	80	—	—
Si bronze	40	80	60	—	—
Al bronze	50	100	80	—	—
Phos. bronze	40	80	80	40	—

	Short Circuiting Arc — 0.035 dia filler wire			
Materials	Argon	Argon-Oxygen (1–5% O_2)	Argon-CO_2 (75–25)	CO_2
Aluminum	35	—	—	—
Magnesium	35	—	—	—
Plain C Steel	25	25	25	35
Low-alloy steel	25	25	25	35
Stainless steel	25	25	—	35
Nickel	35	—	—	—
Ni-Cu alloy	35	—	—	—
Ni-Cr-Fe alloy	35	—	—	—
Copper	30	—	—	—
Cu-Ni alloy (70–30)	30	—	—	—
Si bronze	25	25	—	—
Al bronze	25	—	—	—
Phos. bronze	25	25	—	—

*All rates are in cubic feet per hour and are plus or minus 40%. The lower rates would be most suitable for indoor work and moderate amperage welding. The higher rates would be more suitable for high current, maximum speed, and outdoor welding.

OPERATING INSTRUCTIONS FOR GMAW

1. Set Polarity

   Making sure the machine is turned off, connect the electrode cable to either the positive stud for reverse polarity or to the negative stud for straight polarity. Check with your instructor for the correct polarity. Some machines have a polarity switch instead of changing cables; this makes the changing of the polarity much easier.

2. To Start the Welder

   Place the "power switch" to the "on" position. On some machines, you will also have to place the "power switch" on the wire feeder to the "on" position.

3. Open the Shielding Gas Valve.

   Slowly open the flowmeter valve, simultaneously squeezing the gun trigger until the flowmeter reads approximately 15 to 20 cubic feet per hour.

4. Voltage.

   Set the voltage by either increasing or decreasing the voltage control knob on the machine. Open circuit voltage should be approximately 2 volts higher than the desired welding voltage.

5. Amperage (Wire Speed Control).

   Most amperage (wire speed control) adjustment knobs are calibrated in inches per minute. Set the control knob to the desired wire speed. If you are not sure of what setting you need, place the adjustment knob in the 9 to 10 o'clock position and then fine tune the amperage while making a sample weld.

6. The final setting for both voltage and amperage must be made while welding.

PRACTICE 11-1

Name____ Date ____________

Class ____________________ Instructor ____________________ Grade ____________

OBJECTIVE: After completing this practice, you should be able to safely set up the GMAW equipment.

EQUIPMENT AND MATERIALS NEEDED FOR THIS PRACTICE

1. GMAW power source
2. Welding gun
3. Electrode feed unit
4. Electrode supply
5. Shielding gas supply
6. Shielding gas regulator
7. Electrode conduit
8. Power and work leads
9. Shielding gas hoses
10. Assorted hand tools (see instructor)

INSTRUCTIONS

1. Be sure the power to the machine is off. If the shielding gas supply is a cylinder, it must be chained securely in place before the valve protection cap is removed. Standing to one side of the cylinder, quickly crack the valve to blow out any dirt in the valve before the flowmeter regulator is attached. Attach the correct hose from the regulator to the "gas-in" connection on the electrode feed unit or machine.
2. Install the reel of electrode (welding wire) on the holder and secure it.
3. Check the roller size to ensure that it matches the wire size.
4. The conduit liner size should be checked to be sure that it is compatible with the wire size.
5. Connect the conduit to the feed unit. The conduit or an extension should be aligned with the groove in the roller and set as close to the roller as possible without touching. Misalignment at this point can contribute to a bird's nest. Bird nesting of the electrode wire results when the feed roller pushes the wire into a tangled ball because the wire would not go through the outfeed side conduit. It appears to look like a bird's nest.
6. Be sure the power is off before attaching the welding cables. The electrode and work leads should be attached to the proper terminals. The electrode lead should be attached to electrode or positive (+). If necessary, it is also attached to the power cable part of the gun lead. The work lead should be attached to work or negative (-).
7. The shielding "gas-out" side of the solenoid is then attached to the gun lead. If a separate splice is required from the gun switch circuit to the feed unit, it should be connected at this time.
8. Check to see that the welding contractor circuit is connected from the feed unit to the power source. The welding gun should be permanently attached to the main lead cable and conduit.
9. There should be a gas diffuser attached to the end of the conduit liner to ensure proper alignment.
10. A contact tube (tip) of the correct size to match the electrode wire size being used should be installed.
11. A shielding gas nozzle is attached to complete the assembly.
12. Recheck all fittings and connections for tightness. Loose fittings can leak; loose connections can cause added resistance, reducing the welding efficiency.
13. Some manufacturers include detailed setup instructions with their equipment.

PRACTICE 11-2

OBJECTIVE: After completing this practice, you should be able to safely thread the GMAW wire into the equipment.

EQUIPMENT AND MATERIALS NEEDED FOR THIS PRACTICE

1. GMAW power source
2. Welding gun
3. Electrode feed unit
4. Electrode supply
5. Shielding gas supply
6. Shielding gas regulator
7. Electrode conduit
8. Power and work leads
9. Shielding gas hoses
10. Assorted hand tools (see instructor)

INSTRUCTIONS

1. Check to see that the unit is assembled correctly according to the manufacturer's specifications.
2. Switch on the power and check the gun switch circuit by depressing the switch. The power source relays, feed relays, gas solenoid, and feed motor should all activate.
3. Cut the end of the electrode wire free. Hold it tightly so that it does not unwind. The wire has a natural curve that is known as its cast. The cast is measured by the diameter of the circle that the wire would make if it were loosely laid on a flat surface. The cast helps the wire make a good electrical contact as it passes through the contact tube. However, the cast can be a problem when threading the system.
4. To make threading easier, straighten about 12 in. (305 mm) of the end of the wire and cut any kinks off.
5. Separate the wire feed rollers and push the wire first through the guides, then between the rollers, and finally into the conduit liner.
6. Reset the rollers so there is a slight amount of compression on the wire.
7. Set the wire feed speed control to a slow speed.
8. Hold the welding gun so that the electrode conduit and cable are as straight as possible.
9. Press the gun switch. The wire should start feeding into the liner. Watch to make certain that the wire feeds smoothly and release the gun switch as soon as the end comes through the contact tube.

   CAUTION **If the wire stops feeding before it reaches the end of the contact tube, stop and check the system. If no obvious problem can be found, mark the wire with tape and remove it from the gun. It then can be held next to the system to determine the location of the problem.**

10. With the wire feed running, adjust the feed roller compression so that the wire reel can be stopped easily by a slight pressure. Too light a roller pressure will cause the wire to feed erratically. Too high a pressure can turn a minor problem into a major disaster. If the wire jams at a high roller pressure, the feed rollers keep feeding the wire, causing it to bird nest and possibly short out. With a light pressure, the wire can stop, preventing bird nesting. This is very important with soft wires. The other advantage of a light pressure is that the feed will stop if something like clothing or gas hoses are caught in the reel.
11. With the feed running, adjust the spool drag so that the reel stops when the feed stops. The reel should not coast to a stop because the wire can be snagged easily. Also, when the feed restarts, a jolt occurs when the slack in the wire is taken up. This jolt can be enough to momentarily stop the wire, possibly causing a discontinuity in the weld.

12. When the test runs are completed, the wire can either be rewound or cut off. Some wire feed units have a retract button. This allows the feed driver to reverse and retract the wire automatically. To rewind the wire on units without this retract feature, release the rollers and turn them backward by hand. If the machine will not allow the feed rollers to be released without upsetting the tension, you must cut the wire.

    CAUTION **Do not discard pieces of wire on the floor. They present a hazard to safe movement around the machine. In addition, a small piece of wire can work its way into a filter screen on the welding power source. If the piece of wire shorts out inside the machine, it could become charged with high voltage which may cause injury or death. Always wind the wire tightly into a ball or cut it into short lengths before discarding it in the proper waste container.**

PRACTICE 11-3

Name______________________________ Date ____________

Class ______________ Instructor ______________ Grade ____________

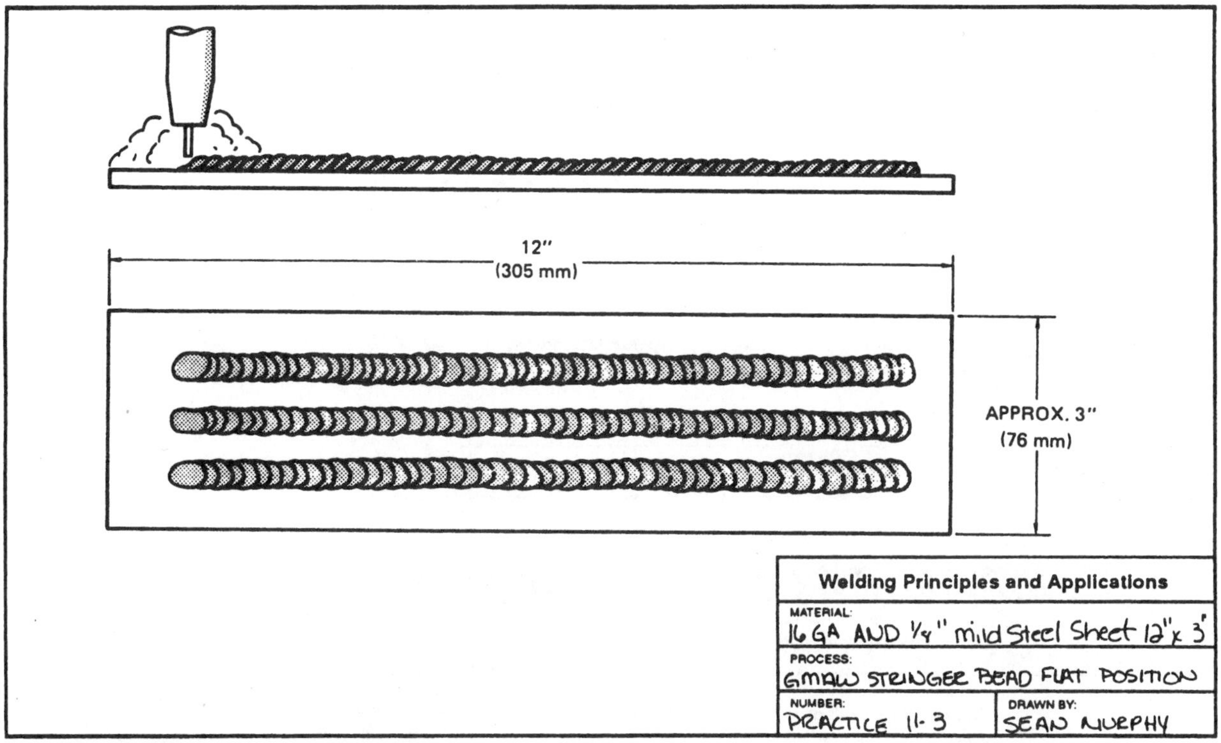

OBJECTIVE: After completing this practice, you should be able to make stringer beads on the 1/8-inch and 16 gauge carbon steel using the short-circuiting metal transfer method in the flat position.

EQUIPMENT AND MATERIALS NEEDED FOR THIS PRACTICE

1. A properly set up and adjusted GMA welding machine.
2. Proper safety protection (welding hood, safety glasses, leather gloves, wire cutting pliers, long sleeve shirt, long pants, leather shoes or boots). Refer to Chapter 2 in the text for more specific safety information.
3. 035-in. and/or .045-in. (0.9-mm and/or 1.2-mm)-diameter wire.
4. Two or more pieces of mild steel sheet, 12 in. (305 mm) long and 16 gauge and 1/8 in. (3 mm) thick.

INSTRUCTIONS

1. Starting at one end of the plate and using either a pushing or dragging technique, make a weld bead along the entire 12-in. (305-mm) length of the metal.
2. After the weld is complete, check its appearance. Make any needed changes to correct the weld.
3. Repeat the weld and make additional adjustments.
4. After the machine is set, start to work on improving the straightness and uniformity of the weld. Keeping the bead straight and uniform can be hard because of the limited visibility due to the small amount of light and the size of the molten weld pool. The welder's view is further restricted by the shielding gas nozzle. Even with limited visibility, it is possible to make a satisfactory weld by watching the edge of the molten weld pool, the sparks, and the weld bead produced. Watching the leading edge of the molten weld pool (forehand welding, push technique) will show you the molten weld pool fusion and width. Watching the trailing edge of the molten weld pool (backhand welding, drag

technique) will show you the amount of buildup and the relative heat input. The quantity and size of sparks produced can indicate the relative location of the filler wire in the molten weld pool. The number of sparks will increase as the wire strikes the solid metal ahead of the molten weld pool. The gun itself will begin to vibrate or bump as the wire momentarily pushes against the cooler, unmelted base metal before it melts. Changes in weld width, buildup, and proper joint tracking can be seen by watching the bead as it appears from behind the shielding gas nozzle.

5. Repeat each type of bead as needed until consistently good beads are obtained.
6. Turn off the welding machine, shielding gas and clean up your work area when you are finished welding.

PRACTICE 11-4

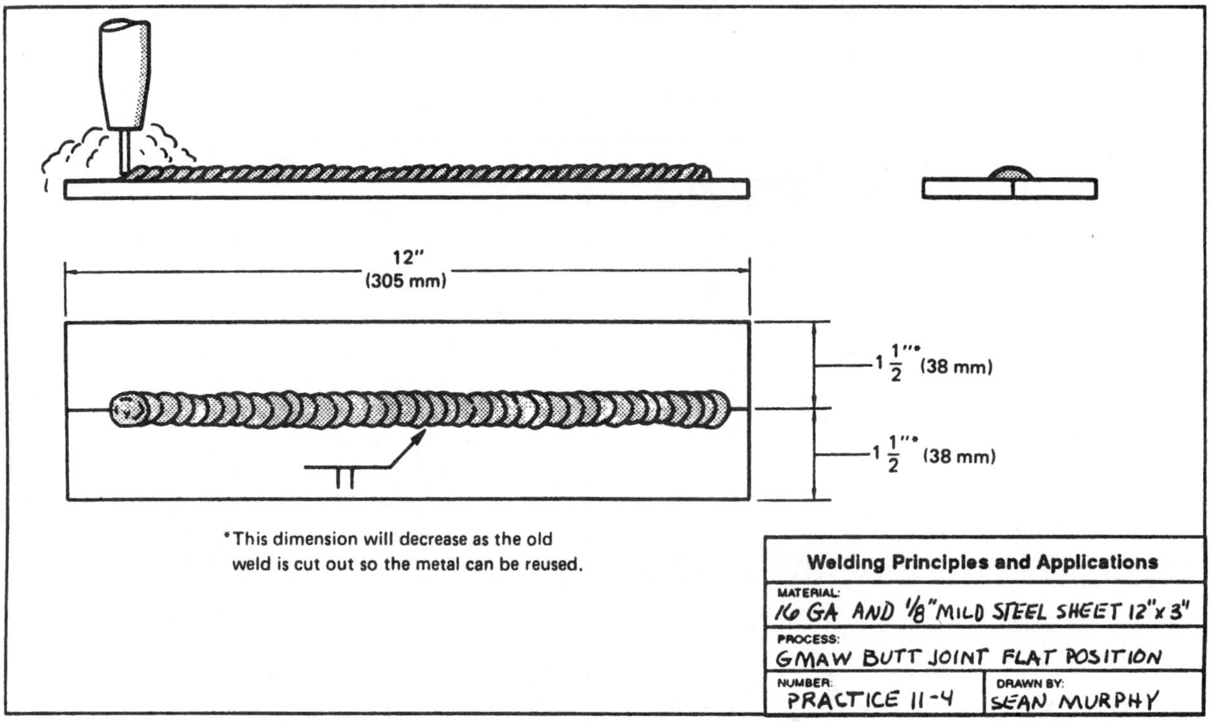

OBJECTIVE: After completing this practice, you should be able to weld a butt lap and tee joint in the flat position using 1/8-in. and 16 gauge carbon steel.

EQUIPMENT AND MATERIAL NEEDED FOR THIS PRACTICE

1. A properly set up and adjusted GMA welding machine.
2. Proper safety protection (welding hood, safety glasses, leather gloves, wire cutting pliers, long sleeve shirt, long pants, leather shoes or boots). Refer to Chapter 2 in the text for more specific safety information.
3. 035-in. and/or .045-in. (0.9-mm and/or 1.2-mm)-diameter wire.
4. Two or more pieces of mild steel sheet, 12 in. (305 mm) long and 16 gauge and 1/8 in. (3 mm) thick.

INSTRUCTIONS

1. Tack weld the sheets together and place them flat on the welding table.
2. Starting at one end, run a bead along the joint. Watch the molten weld pool and bead for signs that a change in technique may be required.
3. Make any needed changes as the weld progresses. By the time the weld is complete, you should be making the weld nearly perfect.

4. Using the same technique that was established in the last weld, make another weld. This time, the entire 12 in. (305-mm) of weld should be flawless.
5. Repeat each type of joint with both thicknesses of metal as needed until consistently good beads are obtained.
6. Turn off the welding machine, shielding gas and clean up your work area when you are finished welding.

PRACTICE 11-5

OBJECTIVE: After completing this practice, you should be able to make stringer beads on sheet steel at a 45° angle vertical up position.

EQUIPMENT AND MATERIALS NEEDED FOR THIS PRACTICE

1. A properly set up and adjusted GMA welding machine.
2. Proper safety protection (welding hood, safety glasses, leather gloves, wire cutting pliers, long sleeve shirt, long pants, leather shoes or boots). Refer to Chapter 2 in the text for more specific safety information.
3. 035-in. and/or .045-in. (0.9-mm and/or 1.2-mm)-diameter wire.
4. Two or more pieces of mild steel sheet, 12 in. (305 mm) long and 16 gauge and 1/8 in. (3 mm) thick.

INSTRUCTIONS

1. Place the steel sheet on the welding table at a 45° inclined angle.
2. Start at the bottom of the plate and hold the welding gun at a slight angle to the plate.
3. Brace yourself, lower your hood, and begin to weld.
4. Depending upon the machine settings and type of shielding gas used, you will make a weave pattern.
5. If the molten weld pool is large and fluid (hot), use a "C" or "J" weave pattern to allow a longer time for the molten weld pool to cool.
6. Do not make the weave so long or fast that the wire is allowed to strike the metal ahead of the molten weld pool. If this happens, spatter increases and a spot or zone of incomplete fusion may occur.
7. If the molten weld pool is small and controllable, use a small "C," zigzag, or "J" weave pattern to control the width and buildup of the weld. A slower travel speed can also be used.
8. Watch for complete fusion along the leading edge of the molten weld pool.
9. A weld that is high and has little or no fusion is too "cold." Changing the welding technique will not correct this problem. The welder must stop welding and make the needed adjustments.
10. As the weld progresses up the plate, the back or trailing edge of the molten weld pool will cool, forming a shelf to support the molten metal. Watch the shelf to be sure that molten metal does not run over, forming a drip. When it appears that the metal may flow over the shelf, either increase the weave lengths or stop and start the current for brief moments to allow the weld to cool. Stopping for brief moments will not allow the shielding gas to be lost.
11. Continue to weld along the entire 12-in. (305-mm) length of plate.
12. Repeat this weld as needed until a straight and uniform weld bead is produced.
13. Turn off the welding machine, shielding gas and clean up your work area when you are finished welding.

PRACTICE 11-6

OBJECTIVE: After completing this practice, you should be able to make stringer beads on sheet steel in the vertical up position.

EQUIPMENT AND MATERIALS NEEDED FOR THIS PRACTICE

1. A properly set up and adjusted GMA welding machine.
2. Proper safety protection (welding hood, safety glasses, leather gloves, wire cutting pliers, long sleeve shirt, long pants, leather shoes or boots). Refer to Chapter 2 in the text for more specific safety information.
3. 035-in. and/or .045-in. (0.9-mm and/or 1.2-mm)-diameter wire.
4. Two or more pieces of mild steel sheet, 12 in. (305 mm) long and 16 gauge and 1/8 in. (3 mm) thick.

INSTRUCTIONS

1. Place the steel sheet on the welding table at a 90° angle, vertical up position.
2. Start at the bottom of the plate and hold the welding gun at a slight angle to the plate.
3. Brace yourself, lower your hood, and begin to weld.
4. Depending upon the machine settings and type of shielding gas used, you will make a weave pattern.
5. If the molten weld pool is large and fluid (hot), use a "C" or "J" weave pattern to allow a longer time for the molten weld pool to cool.
6. Do not make the weave so long or fast that the wire is allowed to strike the metal ahead of the molten weld pool. If this happens, spatter increases and a spot or zone of incomplete fusion may occur.
7. If the molten weld pool is small and controllable, use a small "C," zigzag, or "J" weave pattern to control the width and buildup of the weld. A slower travel speed can also be used.
8. Watch for complete fusion along the leading edge of the molten weld pool.
9. A weld that is high and has little or no fusion is too "cold." Changing the welding technique will not correct this problem. The welder must stop welding and make the needed adjustments.
10. As the weld progresses up the plate, the back or trailing edge of the molten weld pool will cool, forming a shelf to support the molten metal. Watch the shelf to be sure that molten metal does not run over, forming a drip. When it appears that the metal may flow over the shelf, either increase the weave lengths or stop and start the current for brief moments to allow the weld to cool. Stopping for brief moments will not allow the shielding gas to be lost.
11. Continue to weld along the entire 12-in. (305-mm) length of plate.
12. Repeat this weld as needed until a straight and uniform weld bead is produced.
13. Turn off the welding machine, shielding gas and clean up your work area when you are finished welding.

PRACTICE 11-7

OBJECTIVE: After completing this practice, you should be able to make butt, lap, and tee joints in the vertical up position at a 45° angle.

EQUIPMENT AND MATERIALS NEEDED FOR THIS PRACTICE

1. A properly set up and adjusted GMA welding machine.
2. Proper safety protection (welding hood, safety glasses, leather gloves, wire cutting pliers, long sleeve shirt, long pants, leather shoes or boots). Refer to Chapter 2 in the text for more specific safety information.
3. 035-in. and/or .045-in. (0.9-mm and/or 1.2-mm)-diameter wire.
4. Two or more pieces of mild steel sheet, 12 in. (305 mm) long and 16 gauge and 1/8 in. (3 mm) thick.

INSTRUCTIONS

1. Tack weld the metal pieces of the butt, lap, and tee joints together and brace them on the welding table at a 45° inclined angle.
2. Start at the bottom of the plate and hold the welding gun at a slight angle to the plate.
3. Brace yourself, lower your hood, and begin to weld.
4. Depending upon the machine settings and type of shielding gas used, you will make a weave pattern.
5. If the molten weld pool is large and fluid (hot), use a "C" or "J" weave pattern to allow a longer time for the molten weld pool to cool.
6. Do not make the weave so long or fast that the wire is allowed to strike the metal ahead of the molten weld pool. If this happens, spatter increases and a spot or zone of incomplete fusion may occur.
7. If the molten weld pool is small and controllable, use a small "C," zigzag, or "J" weave pattern to control the width and buildup of the weld. A slower travel speed can also be used.
8. Watch for complete fusion along the leading edge of the molten weld pool.
9. A weld that is high and has little or no fusion is too "cold." Changing the welding technique will not correct this problem. The welder must stop welding and make the needed adjustments.
10. As the weld progresses up the plate, the back or trailing edge of the molten weld pool will cool, forming a shelf to support the molten metal. Watch the shelf to be sure that molten metal does not run over, forming a drip. When it appears that the metal may flow over the shelf, either increase the weave lengths or stop and start the current for brief moments to allow the weld to cool. Stopping for brief moments will not allow the shielding gas to be lost.
11. Continue to weld along the entire 12-in. (305-mm) length of plate.
12. Repeat this weld as needed until a straight and uniform weld bead is produced.
13. Turn off the welding machine, shielding gas and clean up your work area when you are finished welding.

PRACTICE 11-8

OBJECTIVE: After completing this practice, you should be able to weld a butt, lap, and tee joint on 1/16" and 1/8" carbon steel with 100% penetration in the vertical up position.

EQUIPMENT AND MATERIALS NEEDED FOR THIS PRACTICE

1. A properly set up and adjusted GMA welding machine.
2. Proper safety protection (welding hood, safety glasses, leather gloves, wire cutting pliers, long sleeve shirt, long pants, leather shoes or boots). Refer to Chapter 2 in the text for more specific safety information.
3. 035-in. and/or .045-in. (0.9-mm and/or 1.2-mm)-diameter wire.

4. Two or more pieces of mild steel sheet, 12 in. (305 mm) long and 16 gauge and 1/8 in. (3 mm) thick.

INSTRUCTIONS

1. Tack weld the metal pieces of the butt, lap, and tee joints together.
2. Increase the current slightly for the 100% penetration.
3. Place your plates on the welding table in a vertical position.
4. Start your weld at the bottom of each joint and hold the welding gun at a slight upward angle.
5. Brace yourself, lower your hood, and begin to weld.
6. Use a weave pattern but do not make the weave so long or fast that the wire is allowed to strike the metal ahead of the molten pool.
7. Weld the entire 12 inch (305mm) length of the plate.
8. Repeat this weld as needed until each welded joint is uniform and defect free.
9. Turn off the welding machine, shielding gas and clean up your work area when you are finished welding.

PRACTICE 11-9

OBJECTIVE: After completing this practice, you should be able to make stringer beads on sheet steel in the vertical down position.

EQUIPMENT AND MATERIALS NEEDED FOR THIS PRACTICE

1. A properly set up and adjusted GMA welding machine.
2. Proper safety protection (welding hood, safety glasses, leather gloves, wire cutting pliers, long sleeve shirt, long pants, leather shoes or boots). Refer to Chapter 2 in the text for more specific safety information.
3. 035-in. and/or .045-in. (0.9-mm and/or 1.2-mm)-diameter wire.
4. Two or more pieces of mild steel sheet, 12 in. (305 mm) long and 16 gauge and 1/8 in. (3 mm) thick.

INSTRUCTIONS

1. Place the sheet steel on the welding table at a 90° angle, vertical down position.
2. Start at the bottom of the plate and hold the welding gun at a slight angle to the plate.
3. Brace yourself, lower your hood, and begin to weld.
4. Depending upon the machine settings and type of shielding gas used, you will make a weave pattern.
5. If the molten weld pool is large and fluid (hot), use a "C" or "J" weave pattern to allow a longer time for the molten weld pool to cool.
6. Do not make the weave so long or fast that the wire is allowed to strike the metal ahead of the molten weld pool. If this happens, spatter increases and a spot or zone of incomplete fusion may occur.
7. If the molten weld pool is small and controllable, use a small "C," zigzag, or "J" weave pattern to control the width and buildup of the weld. A slower travel speed can also be used.
8. Watch for complete fusion along the leading edge of the molten weld pool.
9. A weld that is high and has little or no fusion is too "cold." Changing the welding technique will not correct this problem. The welder must stop welding and make the needed adjustments.
10. As the weld progresses up the plate, the back or trailing edge of the molten weld pool will cool, forming a shelf to support the molten metal. Watch the shelf to be sure that molten metal does not run over, forming a drip. When it appears that the metal may flow over the shelf, either increase the weave lengths or stop and start the current for brief moments to allow the weld to cool. Stopping for brief moments will not allow the shielding gas to be lost.

11. Continue to weld along the entire 12-in. (305-mm) length of plate.
12. Repeat this weld as needed until a straight and uniform weld bead is produced.
13. Turn off the welding machine, shielding gas and clean up your work area when you are finished welding.

PRACTICE 11-10

OBJECTIVE: After completing this practice, you should be able to make butt, lap, and tee joints in the vertical down position.

EQUIPMENT AND MATERIALS NEEDED FOR THIS PRACTICE

1. A properly set up and adjusted GMA welding machine.
2. Proper safety protection (welding hood, safety glasses, leather gloves, wire cutting pliers, long sleeve shirt, long pants, leather shoes or boots). Refer to Chapter 2 in the text for more specific safety information.
3. 035-in. and/or .045-in. (0.9-mm and/or 1.2-mm)-diameter wire.
4. Two or more pieces of mild steel sheet, 12 in. (305 mm) long and 16 gauge and 1/8 in. (3 mm) thick.

INSTRUCTIONS

1. Tack weld the metal pieces of the butt, lap, and tee joints together and brace them on the welding table at a 90° angle, for vertical down welding.
2. Start at the top of the plate, holding the welding gun with a slight dragging angle.
3. Brace yourself, lower your hood, and begin to weld.
4. Depending upon the machine settings and type of shielding gas used, you will make a weave pattern.
5. If the molten weld pool is large and fluid (hot), use a "C" or "J" weave pattern to allow a longer time for the molten weld pool to cool.
6. Do not make the weave so long or fast that the wire is allowed to strike the metal ahead of the molten weld pool. If this happens, spatter increases and a spot or zone of incomplete fusion may occur.
7. If the molten weld pool is small and controllable, use a small "C," zigzag, or "J" weave pattern to control the width and buildup of the weld. A slower travel speed can also be used.
8. Watch for complete fusion along the leading edge of the molten weld pool.
9. A weld that is high and has little or no fusion is too "cold." Changing the welding technique will not correct this problem. The welder must stop welding and make the needed adjustments.
10. As the weld progresses up the plate, the back or trailing edge of the molten weld pool will cool, forming a shelf to support the molten metal. Watch the shelf to be sure that molten metal does not run over, forming a drip. When it appears that the metal may flow over the shelf, either increase the weave lengths or stop and start the current for brief moments to allow the weld to cool. Stopping for brief moments will not allow the shielding gas to be lost.
11. Continue to weld along the entire 12-in. (305-mm) length of plate.
12. Repeat this weld as needed until a straight and uniform weld bead is produced.
13. Turn off the welding machine, shielding gas and clean up your work area when you are finished welding.

PRACTICE 11-12

OBJECTIVE: After completing this practice, you should be able to make horizontal stringer beads on plate with a reclined angle.

EQUIPMENT AND MATERIALS NEEDED FOR THIS PRACTICE

1. A properly set up and adjusted GMA welding machine.
2. Proper safety protection (welding hood, safety glasses, leather gloves, wire cutting pliers, long sleeve shirt, long pants, leather shoes or boots). Refer to Chapter 2 in the text for more specific safety information.
3. 035-in. and/or .045-in. (0.9-mm and/or 1.2-mm)-diameter wire.
4. Two or more pieces of mild steel sheet, 12 in. (305 mm) long and 16 gauge and 1/8 in. (3 mm) thick.

INSTRUCTIONS

1. Place the carbon steel on the welding table with a 45° reclined angle.
2. Start at one end of the plate with the gun pointed in a slightly upward direction.
3. You may use a pushing or a dragging leading or a trailing gun angle, depending upon the current setting and penetration desired.
4. Undercutting along the top edge and overlap along the bottom edge are problems with both gun angles. Careful attention must be paid to the manipulation "weave" technique used to overcome these problems. The most successful weave patterns are the "C" and "J" patterns. The "J" pattern is the most frequently used. The "J" pattern allows weld metal to be deposited along a shelf created by the previous weave. The length of the "J" can be changed to control the weld bead size.
5. Smaller weld beads are easier to control than large ones.
6. The weld must be straight and uniform and have complete fusion.
7. Repeat these welds until you have established the rhythm and technique that work well for you.
8. Turn off the welding machine, shielding gas and clean up your work area when you are finished welding.

PRACTICE 11-13

OBJECTIVE: After completing this practice, you should be able to make stringer beads in the horizontal position on carbon steel plate.

EQUIPMENT AND MATERIALS NEEDED FOR THIS PRACTICE

1. A properly set up and adjusted GMA welding machine.
2. Proper safety protection (welding hood, safety glasses, leather gloves, wire cutting pliers, long sleeve shirt, long pants, leather shoes or boots). Refer to Chapter 2 in the text for more specific safety information.
3. 035-in. and/or .045-in. (0.9-mm and/or 1.2-mm)-diameter wire.
4. Two or more pieces of mild steel sheet, 12 in. (305 mm) long and 16 gauge and 1/8 in. (3 mm) thick.

INSTRUCTIONS

1. Place the carbon steel plate in a horizontal position on the welding table.
2. Start at one end of the plate with the gun pointed in a slightly upward direction.
3. You may use a pushing or a dragging leading or a trailing gun angle, depending upon the current setting and penetration desired.
4. Undercutting along the top edge and overlap along the bottom edge are problems with both gun angles. Careful at-

tention must be paid to the manipulation "weave" technique used to overcome these problems. The most successful weave patterns are the "C" and "J" patterns. The "J" pattern is the most frequently used. The "J" pattern allows weld metal to be deposited along a shelf created by the previous weave. The length of the "J" can be changed to control the weld bead size.

5. Smaller weld beads are easier to control than large ones.
6. The weld must be straight and uniform and have complete fusion.
7. Repeat these welds until you have established the rhythm and technique that work well for you.
8. Turn off the welding machine, sheilding gas and clean up your work area when you are finished welding.

PRACTICE 11-14

OBJECTIVE: After completing this practice, you should be able to weld a butt, lap, and tee joint in the horizontal position on carbon steel plate.

EQUIPMENT AND MATERIALS NEEDED FOR THIS PRACTICE

1. A properly set up and adjusted GMA welding machine.
2. Proper safety protection (welding hood, safety glasses, leather gloves, wire cutting pliers, long sleeve shirt, long pants, leather shoes or boots). Refer to Chapter 2 in the text for more specific safety information.
3. 035-in. and/or .045-in. (0.9-mm and/or 1.2-mm)-diameter wire.
4. Two or more pieces of mild steel sheet, 12 in. (305 mm) long and 16 gauge and 1/8 in. (3 mm) thick.

INSTRUCTIONS

1. Tack weld the metal pieces of the butt, lap, and tee joints together and brace them on the welding table in the horizontal position.
2. Start at one end of the plate with the gun pointed in a slightly upward direction.
3. You may use a pushing or a dragging leading or a trailing gun angle, depending upon the current setting and penetration desired.
4. Undercutting along the top edge and overlap along the bottom edge are problems with both gun angles. Careful attention must be paid to the manipulation "weave" technique used to overcome these problems. The most successful weave patterns are the "C" and "J" patterns. The "J" pattern is the most frequently used. The "J" pattern allows weld metal to be deposited along a shelf created by the previous weave. The length of the "J" can be changed to control the weld bead size.
5. Smaller weld beads are easier to control than large ones.
6. The weld must be straight and uniform and have complete fusion.
7. Repeat these welds until you have established the rhythm and technique that work well for you.
8. Turn off the welding machine, shielding gas and clean up your work area when you are finished welding.

PRACTICE 11-15

OBJECTIVE: After completing this practice, you should be able to weld stringer beads in the overhead position on both 1/16" and 1/8" low carbon steel.

EQUIPMENT AND MATERIALS NEEDED FOR THIS PRACTICE

1. A properly set up and adjusted GMA welding machine.
2. Proper safety protection (welding hood, safety glasses, leather gloves, wire cutting pliers, long sleeve shirt, long pants, leather shoes or boots). Refer to Chapter 2 in the text for more specific safety information.
3. 035-in. and/or .045-in. (0.9-mm and/or 1.2-mm)-diameter wire.
4. Two or more pieces of mild steel sheet, 12 in. (305 mm) long and 16 gauge and 1/8 in. (3 mm) thick.

INSTRUCTIONS

1. In the overhead position, the molten weld pool should be kept small. This can be achieved by using lower current settings, traveling faster, or by pushing the molten weld pool.
2. When welding overhead, extra personal protection is required to reduce the danger of burns. Leather sleeves or leather jackets should be worn.
3. Make several short weld beads using various techniques to establish the method that is most successful and most comfortable for you. After each weld, stop and evaluate it before making a change.
4. When you have decided on the technique to be used, make a welded stringer bead that is 12 in. (305 mm) long.
5. Repeat the weld until it can be made straight, uniform, and free from any visual defects.
6. Turn off the welding machine, shielding gas and clean up your work area when you are finished welding.

PRACTICE 11-16

OBJECTIVE: After completing this practice, you should be able to weld a butt, lap, and tee joint in the overhead position.

EQUIPMENT AND MATERIALS NEEDED FOR THIS PRACTICE

1. A properly set up and adjusted GMA welding machine.
2. Proper safety protection (welding hood, safety glasses, leather gloves, wire cutting pliers, long sleeve shirt, long pants, leather shoes or boots). Refer to Chapter 2 in the text for more specific safety information.
3. 035-in. and/or .045-in. (0.9-mm and/or 1.2-mm)-diameter wire.
4. Two or more pieces of mild steel sheet, 12 in. (305 mm) long and 16 gauge and 1/8 in. (3 mm) thick.

INSTRUCTIONS

1. Tack weld the pieces of metal together and secure them in the overhead position.
2. When welding overhead, extra personal protection is required to reduce the danger of burns. Leather sleeves or leather jackets should be worn.
3. Make several short weld beads using various techniques to establish the method that is most successful and most comfortable for you. After each weld, stop and evaluate it before making a change.
4. When you have decided on the technique to be used, make a welded stringer bead that is 12 in. (305 mm) long.
5. Repeat the weld until it can be made straight, uniform, and free from any visual defects.
6. Turn off the welding machine, shielding gas and clean up your work area when you are finished welding.

PRACTICE 11-17

OBJECTIVE: After completing this practice, you should be able to weld a butt, lap, and tee joint in the overhead position with 100% penetration.

EQUIPMENT AND MATERIALS NEEDED FOR THIS PRACTICE

1. A properly set up and adjusted GMA welding machine.
2. Proper safety protection (welding hood, safety glasses, leather gloves, wire cutting pliers, long sleeve shirt, long pants, leather shoes or boots). Refer to Chapter 2 in the text for more specific safety information.
3. 035-in. and/or .045-in. (0.9-mm and/or 1.2-mm)-diameter wire.
4. Two or more pieces of mild steel sheet, 12 in. (305 mm) long and 16 gauge and 1/8 in. (3 mm) thick.

INSTRUCTIONS

1. Tack weld the pieces of metal together and secure them in the overhead position.
2. When welding overhead, extra personal protection is required to reduce the danger of burns. Leather sleeves or leather jackets should be worn.
3. Make several short weld beads using various techniques to establish the method that is most successful and most comfortable for you. After each weld, stop and evaluate it before making a change.
4. When you have decided on the technique to be used, make a welded stringer bead that is 12 in. (305 mm) long.
5. Repeat the weld until it can be made straight, uniform, and free from any visual defects.
6. Turn off the welding machine, shielding gas and clean up your work area when you are finished welding.

PRACTICE 11-18

Name____ Date ____________

Class ____________________ Instructor ____________________ Grade ____________

OBJECTIVE: After completing this practice, you should be able to make butt, lap, and tee joints on 1/4-in. (6mm) plate in the 1G and 1F position using the axial spray transfer method.

EQUIPMENT AND MATERIALS NEEDED FOR THIS PRACTICE

1. A properly set up and adjusted GMA welding machine.
2. Proper safety protection (welding hood, safety glasses, leather gloves, wire cutting pliers, long sleeve shirt, long pants, leather shoes or boots). Refer to Chapter 2 in the text for more specific safety information.
3. Two or more pieces of carbon steel plate, 12-in. (305mm) long X 1/4-in. (6mm) thick.
4. Shielding gas that will enable you to do spray transfer welding.

INSTRUCTIONS

1. Tack weld the metal together and place the assembly in the flat position on the welding table.
2. Start at one end and make a uniform weld along the entire 12-in. (305-mm) length of the joint.
3. Watch the sides of the fillet weld for signs of undercutting.
4. Repeat the weld until it can be made straight, uniform, and free from any visual defects.
5. Turn off the welding machine, shielding gas and clean up your work area when you are finished welding.

CHAPTER 11: GAS METAL ARC WELDING QUIZ

Name____ Date ______________

Class ______________________ Instructor ______________________ Grade ______________

Instructions: Carefully read Chapter 11 in the text and complete the following questions.

A. IDENTIFICATION

In the space provided identify the items shown on the illustration.

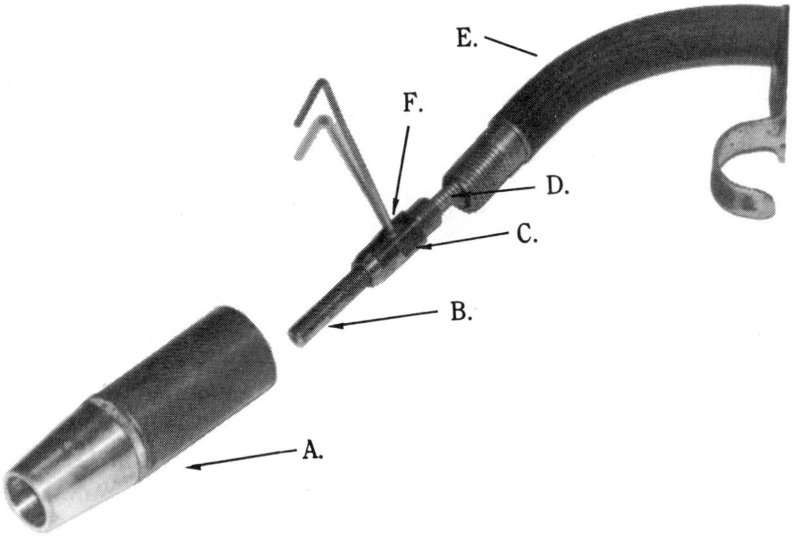

1. List the parts of the GMA welding gun.

A. ____________ D. ____________

B. ____________ E. ____________

C. ____________ F. ____________

B. MATCHING

In the space provided to the left, write the letter next to the term that identifies the part shown in the illustration.

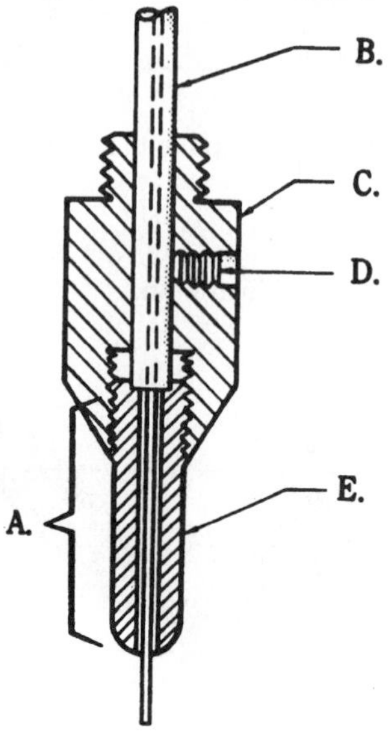

2. Match the following terms with the illustration above.

_____ gas diffuser

_____ contact tube (tip)

_____ the wire picks up the welding current in this area.

_____ conduit liner

_____ liner setscrew

3. Match the following terms with the illustration below.

_____ 1. single J

_____ 2. single U

_____ 3. double V

_____ 4. double bevel

_____ 5. double U

_____ 6. double J

_____ 7. single V

_____ 8. single bevel

C. SHORT ANSWER

Write a brief statement that will answer the question.

4. What problem(s) results from a failure to keep the wire in the correct spot on the pool?

5. How tight should the feed roller tension be set?

6. How can a welder locate a problem in feeding the wire through the conduit?

7. Changes in the wire feed speed have what effect on the weld bead?

8. What changes in the weld were observed with changes in shielding gas mixtures?

9. When can brief stops and starts be used?

10. Explain how to make a vertical up weld.

11. How can vertical down welds be made to ensure 100% fusion?

12. What changes in the weld bead occurred when the gun angle changed?

13. What changes in the weld bead were noticed when the contact tube-to-work distance changed?

14. Define the following terms: flow rate, wire feed speed, feed rollers, cast, and conduit liner.

CHAPTER 12: FLUX CORED ARC WELDING EQUIPMENT SETUP, AND OPERATION QUIZ

Name____ Date ____________

Class ____________________ Instructor ____________________ Grade ____________

Instructions: Carefully read Chapter 12 in the text and answer the following questions.

A. MATCHING

1. Match the following terms with the illustration below.

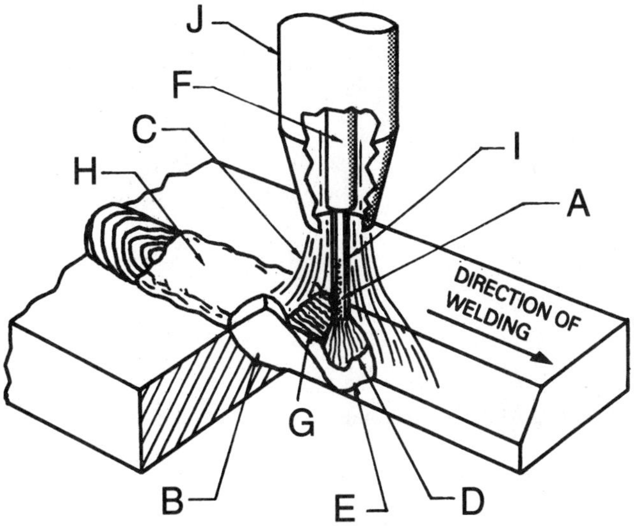

____ 1. Solidified Slag

____ 2. Tubular Electrode

____ 3. Weld Pool

____ 4. Shielding Gas

____ 5. Weld Metal

____ 6. Molten Slag

____ 7. Wire Guide & Contact Tube

____ 8. Gas Nozzle

____ 9. Powdered Metal Flux & Slag Forming Materials

____ 10. Arc & Metal Transfer

2. Match the following terms with the illustration below.

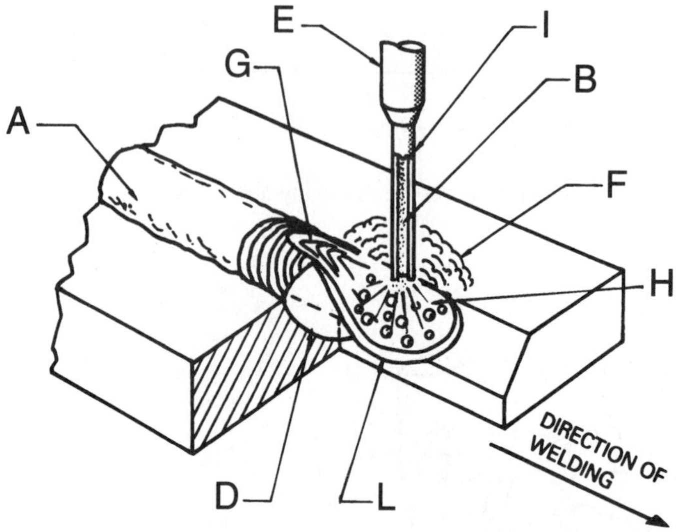

_____ 1. Weld Pool

_____ 2. Solidified Slag

_____ 3. Wire Guide and Contact Tube

_____ 4. Arc & Metal Transfer

_____ 5. Powdered Metal,Vapor Forming Materials, Deoxidizers and Scavengers

_____ 6. Weld Metal

_____ 7. Tubular Electrode

_____ 8. Molten Slag

_____ 9. Arc Shield Composed of Vaporized and Slag Forming Compounds

B. TRUE-FALSE

Write the letter T, in the space to the left, if the statement is true and the letter F if the statement if false.

_____ 3. One of the primary advantages of the FCAW process is that when the FCAW power source is correctly set, all welds will be quality welds.

_____ 4. The flux inside the welding wire can improve strength, corrosion properties and the appearance of the finished weld.

_____ 5. One of the purposes of the flux inside the welding wire is to slow down the weld's cooling rate which improves its physical properties.

_____ 6. The welding power supply is the same constant-current-voltage type that is required for SMAW.

_____ 7. Water cooled FCAW guns are the most common welding guns used in industry.

_____ 8. Excessive pressure on the electrode feed system can distort the electrode wire diameter and cause welding problems.

_____ 9. All FCA welding filler metal can be used with any shielding gas or mixture of shielding gas.

_____ 10. When using the FCAW process on thicker sections of steel, the bevel angle must be increased to a 50° angle.

_____ 11. The addition of deoxidizers and other fluxing agents allows high-quality welds to be made on plates with light surface oxides or mill scale.

_____ 12. Large diameter FCAW electrode wire is more expensive per pound than the same type in a smaller diameter.

C. SHORT ANSWER

Write a brief answer, in the space provided, that will answer the question or complete the statement.

13. Is there any problem with using a shielding gas on a FCAW electrode?

____

____

14. Comparing FCAW to GTAW, is the quality of the weld as good if the base material is 6061 T6 aluminum using 4043 filler?

____

____

15. What elements can be placed in the flux to improve the hardness of weld?

____

____

16. Why are 2 sets of feed rollers recommended when using the FCAW process?

____

____

17. What is the primary purpose of the flux used in the FCAW process?

____

____

D. ESSAY

Provide complete answers for all of the following questions.

18. What effect on the weld does electrode extension have?

____

____

19. What effect on the weld does gun angle have?

____

____

20. List five things that the electrode flux provides to the weld.

____

____

21. List three useful things that a slag covering helps with.

____

____

22. Why do some guns have hand-protecting shields?

____

____

23. Why is it often possible to make welds without having to bevel the edge of the plate?

24. What is meant when it's said that a plate can be welded in the "as cut" condition?

25. How is the flux packed inside the FCA welding wire?

26. What are the two elements used as the basis for most FCAW fluxes?

27. Why are some FCA welding filler electrodes not recommended for multiple pass welds?

28. List three limitations to the FCAW process.

29. Why is it important to remove the slag from a weld bead before the parts are painted?

CHAPTER 13: FLUX CORED ARC WELDING

ELECTRODE		WELDING POWER			SHIELDING GAS		BASE METAL	
Type	Size	Amps	Wire Feed Speed IPM (cm/min)	Volts	Type	Flow	Type	Thickness
E70T-1	0.035 in. (0.9 mm)	130 to 150	288 to 380 (732 to 975)	22 to 25	none	n/a	Low-Carbon Steel	1/4 in. to 1/2 in. (6 mm to 13 mm)
E70T-1	0.045 in. (1.2 mm)	150 to 210	200 to 300 (508 to 762)	28 to 29	none	n/a	Low-Carbon Steel	1/4 in. to 1/2 in. (6 mm to 13 mm)
E70T-5	0.035 in. (0.9 mm)	130 to 200	288 to 576 (732 to 1463)	20 to 28	75% Argon 25% CO_2	30 cfh	Low-Carbon Steel	1/4 in. to 1/2 in. (6 mm to 13 mm)
E70T-5	0.045 in. (1.2 mm)	150 to 250	200 to 400 (508 to 1016)	23 to 29	75% Argon 25% CO_2	35 cfh	Low-Carbon Steel	1/4 in. to 1/2 in. (6 mm to 13 mm)

Table 13-1 FCA welding parameters that can be used if specific settings are not available from the electrode manufacturer.

ELECTRODE		WELDING POWER			SHIELDING GAS		BASE METAL	
Type	Size	Amps	Wire Feed Speed IPM (cm/min)	Volts	Type	Flow	Type	Thickness
E70T-1	0.035 in. (0.9 mm)	130 to 150	288 to 380 (732 to 975)	22 to 25	none	n/a	Low-Carbon Steel	1/2 in. to 3/4 in. (13 mm to 19 mm)
E70T-1	0.045 in. (1.2 mm)	150 to 210	200 to 300 (508 to 762)	28 to 29	none	n/a	Low-Carbon Steel	1/2 in. to 3/4 in. (13 mm to 19 mm)
E70T-1	0.052 in. (1.4 mm)	150 to 300	150 to 350 (381 to 889)	25 to 33	none	n/a	Low-Carbon Steel	1/2 in. to 3/4 in. (13 mm to 19 mm)
E70T-1	1/16 in. (1.6 mm)	200 to 400	150 to 300 (381 to 762)	27 to 33	none	n/a	Low-Carbon Steel	1/2 in. to 3/4 in. (13 mm to 19 mm)
E70T-5	0.035 in. (0.9 mm)	130 to 200	288 to 576 (732 to 1463)	20 to 28	75% Argon 25% CO_2	30 cfh	Low-Carbon Steel	1/2 in. to 3/4 in. (13 mm to 19 mm)
E70T-5	0.045 in. (1.2 mm)	150 to 250	200 to 400 (508 to 1016)	23 to 29	75% Argon 25% CO_2	35 cfh	Low-Carbon Steel	1/2 in. to 3/4 in. (13 mm to 19 mm)
E70T-5	0.052 in. (1.4 mm)	150 to 300	150 to 350 (381 to 889)	21 to 32	75% Argon 25% CO_2	35 cfh	Low-Carbon Steel	1/2 in. to 3/4 in. (13 mm to 19 mm)
E70T-5	1/16 in. (1.6 mm)	180 to 400	145 to 350 (368 to 889)	21 to 34	75% Argon 25% CO_2	40 cfh	Low-Carbon Steel	1/2 in. to 3/4 in. (13 mm to 19 mm)

Table 13-2 FCA welding parameters that can be used if specific settings are not available from the electrode manufacturer.

ELECTRODE		WELDING POWER			SHIELDING GAS		BASE METAL	
Type	Size	Amps	Wire Feed Speed IPM (cm/min)	Volts	Type	Flow	Type	Thickness
E70T-1	0.030 in. (0.8 mm)	40 to 145	90 to 340 (228 to 864)	20 to 27	none	n/a	Low-Carbon Steel	16-Gauge to 18-Gauge
E70T-1	0.035 in. (0.9 mm)	130 to 200	288 to 576 (732 to 1463)	20 to 28	none	n/a	Low-Carbon Steel	16-Gauge to 18-Gauge
E70T-5	0.035 in. (0.9 mm)	90 to 200	190 to 576 (483 to 1463)	16 to 29	75% Argon 25% CO_2	35 cfh	Low-Carbon Steel	16-Gauge to 18-Gauge

Table 13-3 FCA welding parameters that can be used if specific settings are not available from the electrode manufacturer.

PRACTICE 13-1

Name______________________________ Date ____________

Class ______________ Instructor ______________ Grade ____________

OBJECTIVE:

After completing this practice, you should be able to safely set up FCAW equipment.

EQUIPMENT AND MATERIALS NEEDED FOR THIS PRACTICE

1. Semiautomatic welding power source approved for FCA welding
2. Welding gun
3. Electrode feed unit, electrode supply
4. Shielding gas supply, shielding gas flowmeter regulator
5. Electrode conduit, power and work leads
6. Shielding gas hoses (if required)
7. Assorted hand tools, spare parts, and any other required materials.

INSTRUCTIONS

NOTE: **Some manufacturers include detailed setup instructions with their equipment. If such instructions are available for your equipment, follow them. However, if no instructions are available, then follow the instructions listed below.**

1. If the shielding gas is to be used and it comes from a cylinder, the cylinder must be chained securely in place before the valve protection cap is removed. Stand to one side of the cylinder and quickly crack the valve to blow out any dirt in the valve before the flowmeter regulator is attached. Attach the correct hose from the regulator to the "gas-in" connection on the electrode feed unit or machine.
2. Install the reel of electrode (welding wire) on the holder and secure it. Check the feed roller size to ensure that it matches the wire size. The conduit liner size should be checked to be sure that it is compatible with the wire size. Connect the conduit to the feed unit. The conduit or an extension should be aligned with the groove in the roller and set as close to the roller as possible without touching. Misalignment at this point can contribute to a bird's nest.
3. Be sure the power is off before attaching the welding cables. The electrode and work leads should be attached to the proper terminals. The electrode lead should be attached to electrode or positive (+). If necessary, it is also attached to the power cable part of the gun lead. The work lead should be attached to work or negative (-).
4. The shielding "gas-out" side of the solenoid is then also attached to the gun lead. If a separate splice is required from the gun switch circuit to the feed unit, it should be connected at this time. Check to see that the welding contractor circuit is connected from the feed unit to the power source.
5. The welding cable liner or wire conduit must be securely attached to the gas diffuses and contact tube (tip). The contact tube must be the correct size to match the electrode wire size being used. If a shielding gas is to be used, a gas nozzle would be attached to complete the assembly. If a gas nozzle is not needed for a shielding gas, it may still be installed. Because it's easy for a student to touch the work with the contact tube during welding, an electrical short may occur. This short out of the contact tube will immediately destroy the tube. Although the gas nozzle may interfere with some visibility, it may be worth the trouble for a new welder.

PRACTICE 13-2

OBJECTIVE:

After completing this practice, you should be able to thread FCAW wire.

EQUIPMENT AND MATERIALS NEEDED FOR THIS PRACTICE

1. Semiautomatic welding power source approved for FCA welding
2. Welding gun
3. Electrode feed unit, electrode supply
4. Shielding gas supply, shielding gas flowmeter regulator
5. Electrode conduit, power and work leads
6. Shielding gas hoses (if required)
7. Assorted hand tools, spare parts, and any other required materials.

INSTRUCTIONS

NOTE: **Some manufacturers include detailed setup instructions with their equipment. If such instructions are available for your equipment, follow them. However, if no instructions are available, then follow the instructions listed below.**

1. Check to see that the unit is assembled correctly according to the manufacturer's specifications. Switch on the power and check the gun switch circuit by depressing the switch. The power source relays, feed relays, gas solenoid, and feed motor should all activate.
2. Cut off the end of the electrode wire if it's bent. When you are working with the wire, be sure to hold it tightly. The wire will become tangled if it's released. The wire has a natural curl called cast. Straighten out about 12 in. (300 mm) of the curl to make threading easier.
3. Separate the wire feed rollers and push the wire first through the guides, then between the rollers, and finally into the conduit liner. Reset the rollers so there is a slight amount of compression on the wire. Set the wire feed speed control to a slow speed. Hold the welding gun so that the electrode conduit and cable are as straight as possible.
4. Press the gun switch. The wire should start feeding into the liner. Watch to make certain that the wire feeds smoothly and release the gun switch as soon as the end comes through the contact tube. If the wire stops feeding before it reaches the end of the contact tube, stop and check the system. If no obvious problem can be found, mark the wire with tape and remove it from the gun. It then can be held next to the system to determine the location of the problem.
5. With the wire feed running, adjust the feed roller compression so that the wire reel can be stopped easily by a slight pressure. Too light a roller pressure will cause the wire to feed erratically. Too high a pressure can crush some wires causing some flux to be dropped inside the wire liner. If this happens, you will have a continual problem with the wire not feeding smoothly or jamming.
6. With the feed running, adjust the spool drag so that the reel stops when the feed stops. The reel should not coast to a stop because the wire can be snagged easily. Also, when the feed restarts, a jolt occurs when the slack in the wire is taken up. This jolt can be enough to momentarily stop the wire, possibly causing a discontinuity in the weld.

   When the test runs are completed, the wire can either be rewound or cut off. Some wire feed units have a retract button. This allows the feed driver to reverse and retract the wire automatically. To rewind the wire on units without this retract feature, release the rollers and turn them backward by hand. If the machine will not allow the feed rollers to be released without upsetting the tension, you must cut the wire. Some wire reels have covers to prevent the collection of dust, dirt and metal filings on the wire.

PRACTICE 13-3

Name____ Date ______________

Class ____________________ Instructor ____________________ Grade ______________

OBJECTIVE:

After completing this practice, you should be able to make a stringer bead weld in the flat position.

EQUIPMENT AND MATERIALS NEEDED FOR THIS PRACTICE

1. A properly set up and adjusted FCA welding machine
2. Table 13-1
3. Proper safety protection
4. 0.035-in. and/or 0.045-in. (0.9 mm and/or 1.2 mm) diameter E70T-1 and/or E70T-5 electrodes
5. One or more pieces of mild steel plate, 12 in. (305 mm) long and 1/4 in. (6 mm).

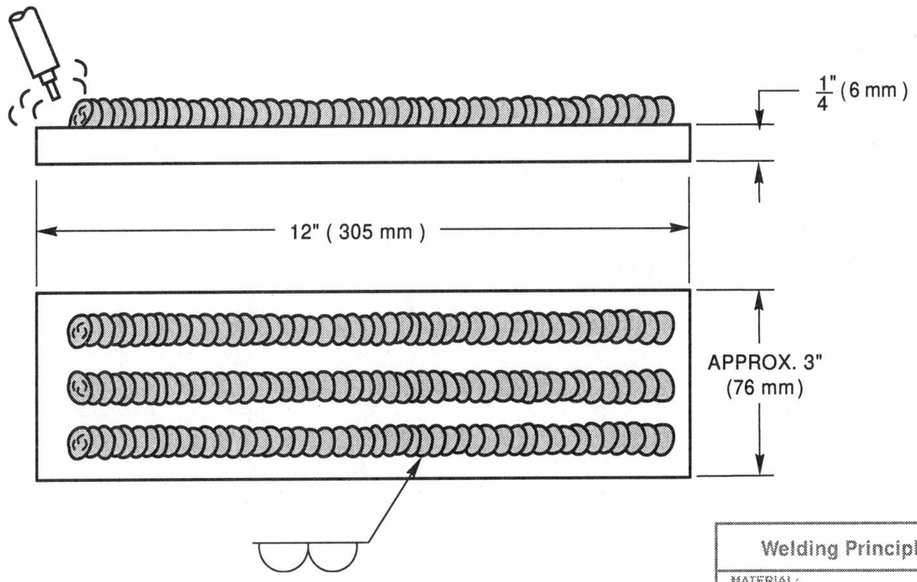

Welding Principles and Applications	
MATERIAL: 1/4" (6 mm) MILD STEEL PLATE 12" x 3" (305mm x 76mm)	
PROCESS: FCAW STRINGER BEAD FLAT POSITION	
NUMBER: PRACTICE 13-3	DRAWN BY: JESSICA ALVAREZ

INSTRUCTIONS

1. Starting at one end of the plate and using a dragging technique, make a weld bead along the entire 12-in. (305-mm) length of the metal.
2. After the weld is complete, check its appearance. Make any needed changes to correct the weld.
3. Repeat the weld and make additional adjustments.
4. After the machine is set, start to work on improving the straightness and uniformity of the weld.
5. Use weave patterns of different widths and straight stringers without weaving.
6. Repeat with both classifications of electrodes as needed until beads can be made straight, uniform, and free from any visual defects.
7. Turn off the welding machine, shielding gas and clean up your work area when you are finished welding.

PRACTICE 13-4

OBJECTIVE:

After completing this practice, you should be able to make a groove weld in the flat position.

EQUIPMENT AND MATERIALS NEEDED FOR THIS PRACTICE

1. A properly set up and adjusted FCA welding machine
2. Table 13-1
3. Proper safety protection
4. 0.035-in. and/or 0.045-in. (0.9 mm and/or 1.2 mm) diameter E70T-1 and/or E70T-5 electrodes
5. One or more pieces of mild steel plate, 12 in. (305 mm) long and 1/4 in. (6 mm).

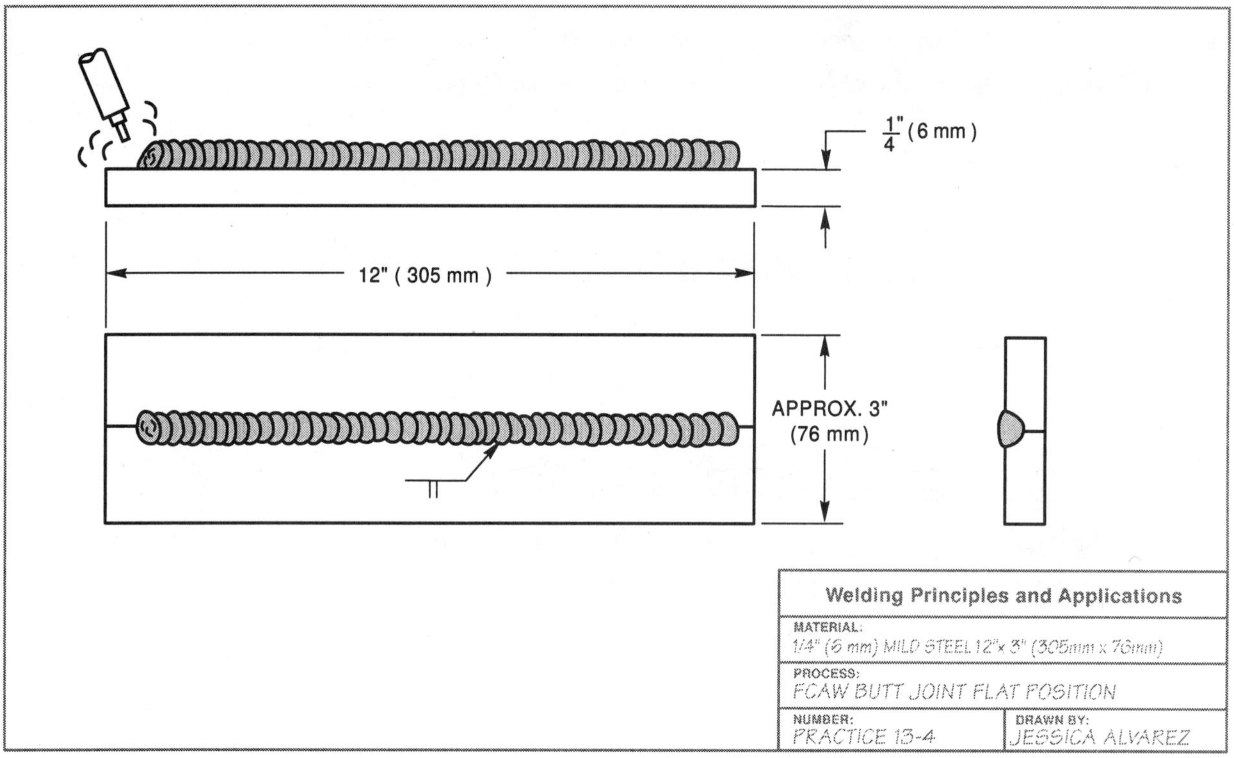

INSTRUCTIONS

1. Tack weld the plates together and place them in position to be welded.
2. Starting at one end, run a bead along the joint. Watch the molten weld pool and bead for signs that a change in technique may be required.
3. Make any needed changes as the weld progresses in order to produce a uniform weld.
4. Repeat with both classifications of electrodes as needed until consistently defect-free welds can be made in the 1/4 in. (6 mm) thick plate.
5. Turn off the welding machine, shielding gas and clean up your work area when you are finished welding.

PRACTICE 13-5

Name____ Date ______________

Class __________________ Instructor __________________ Grade ______________

OBJECTIVE: After completing this practice, you should be able to make a groove butt weld in the flat position.

EQUIPMENT AND MATERIALS NEEDED FOR THIS PRACTICE

1. A properly set up and adjusted FCA welding machine
2. Table 13-1
3. Proper safety protection
4. 0.035-in. and/or 0.045-in. (0.9 mm and/or 1.2 mm) diameter E70T-1 and/or E70T-5 electrodes
5. One or more pieces of mild steel plate, 12 in. (305 mm) long and 3/8 in. (9.5 mm) thick beveled plate
6. One piece of mild steel strap 14 in. (355 mm) long 1 in. (25 mm) wide and 1/4 in. (6 mm) thick for a backing strip.

INSTRUCTIONS

1. Tack weld the backing strip to the plates. There should be approximately 1/8 in. (3 mm) root gap between the plates. The beveled surface can be made with or without a root face.
2. Place the test plates in position at a comfortable height and location. Be sure that you will have complete and free movement along the full length of the weld joint. It's often a good idea to make a practice pass along the joint with the welding gun without power to make sure nothing will interfere with your making the weld. Be sure the welding cable is free and will not get caught on anything during the weld.
3. Start the weld outside of the groove on the backing strip tab. This is done so that the arc is smooth and the molten weld pool size is established at the beginning of the groove. Continue the weld out on to the tab at the outer end of the groove. This is to insure that the end of the groove is completely filled with weld.
4. Repeat with both classifications of electrodes as needed until consistently defect-free welds can be made.
5. Turn off the welding machine, shielding gas and clean up your work area when you are finished welding.

PRACTICE 13-6

Name________________________________ Date ____________

Class ________________ Instructor ________________ Grade ____________

OBJECTIVE:

After completing this practice, you should be able to make a groove butt weld in the flat position.

EQUIPMENT AND MATERIALS NEEDED FOR THIS PRACTICE

1. A properly set up and adjusted FCA welding machine
2. Table 13-2
3. Proper safety protection
4. 0.035-in. and/or through 1/16 in. (0.9 mm and/or through 1.6 mm) diameter E70T-1 and/or E70T-5 electrodes
5. 7 in. (178 mm) long and 3/4 in. (19 mm) or thicker beveled plate
6. one piece of mild steel strap 14 in. (355 mm) long 1 in. (25 mm) wide and 1/4 in. (6 mm) thick for a backing strip

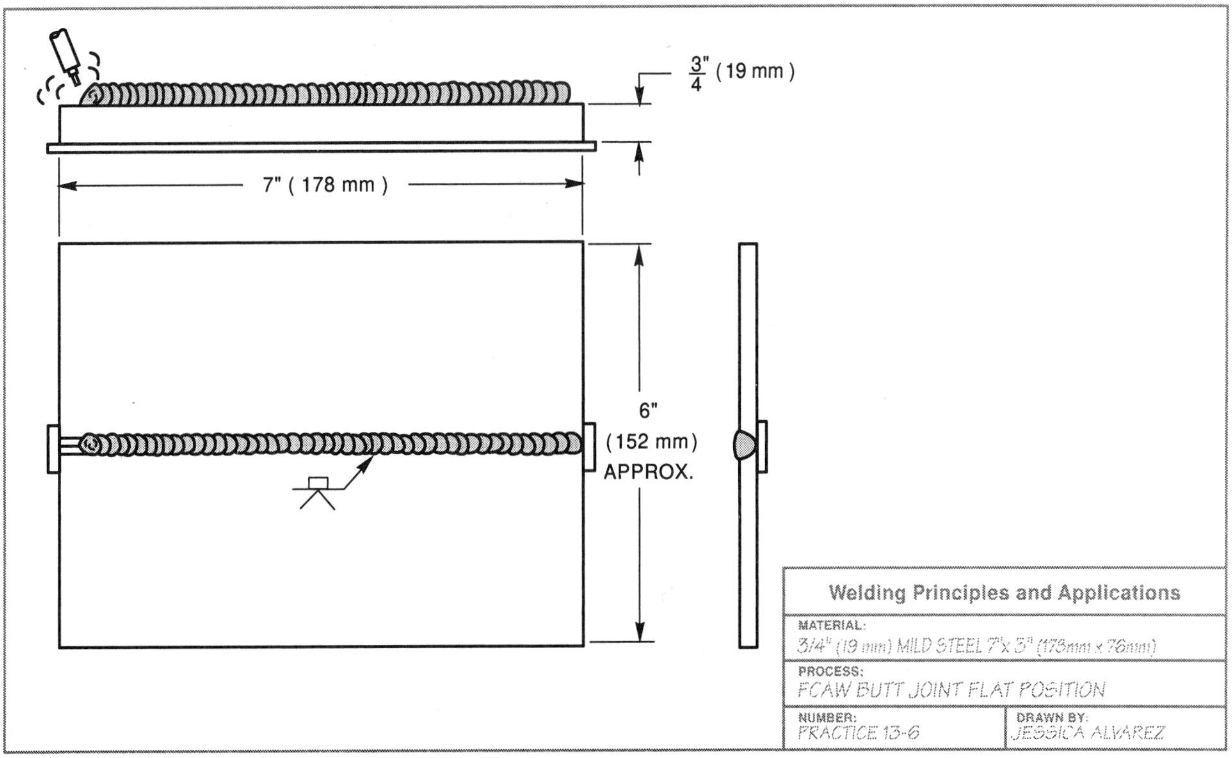

INSTRUCTIONS

1. Tack weld the backing strip to the plates. There should be approximately 1/8 in. (3 mm) root gap between the plates. The beveled surface can be made with or without a root face.
2. Place the test plates in position at a comfortable height and location. Be sure that you will have complete and free movement along the full length of the weld joint. It's often a good idea to make a practice pass along the joint with the welding gun without power to make sure nothing will interfere with your making the weld. Be sure the welding cable is free and will not get caught on anything during the weld.

3. Start the weld outside of the groove on the backing strip tab. This is done so that the arc is smooth and the molten weld pool size is established at the beginning of the groove. Continue the weld out on to the tab at the outer end of the groove. This is to insure that the end of the groove is completely filled with weld.
4. Repeat with both classifications of electrodes as needed until consistently defect-free welds can be made.
5. Turn off the welding machine, shielding gas and clean up your work area when you are finished welding.

PRACTICE 13-7

Name____ Date ____________

Class ______________________ Instructor ______________________ Grade ____________

OBJECTIVE:

After completing this practice, you should be able to make fillet welds in both lap and tee joints in the flat position.

EQUIPMENT AND MATERIALS NEEDED FOR THIS PRACTICE

1. A properly set up and adjusted FCA welding machine
2. Table 13-1
3. Proper safety protection
4. 0.035-in. and/or 0.045-in. (0.9 mm and/or 1.2 mm) diameter E70T-1 and/or E70T-5 electrodes
5. One or more pieces of mild steel plate, 12 in. (305 mm) long and 3/8 in. (9.5 mm)

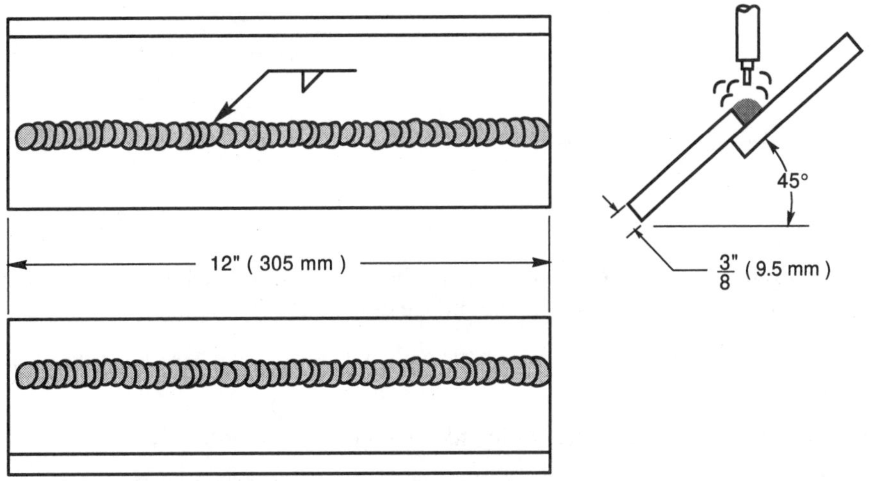

Welding Principles and Applications	
MATERIAL: 3/8" (9.5 mm) MILD STEEL PLATE 12" x 3" (305mm x 76mm)	
PROCESS: FCAW LAP JOINT FLAT POSITION	
NUMBER: PRACTICE 13-7	DRAWN BY: TRACI AGA

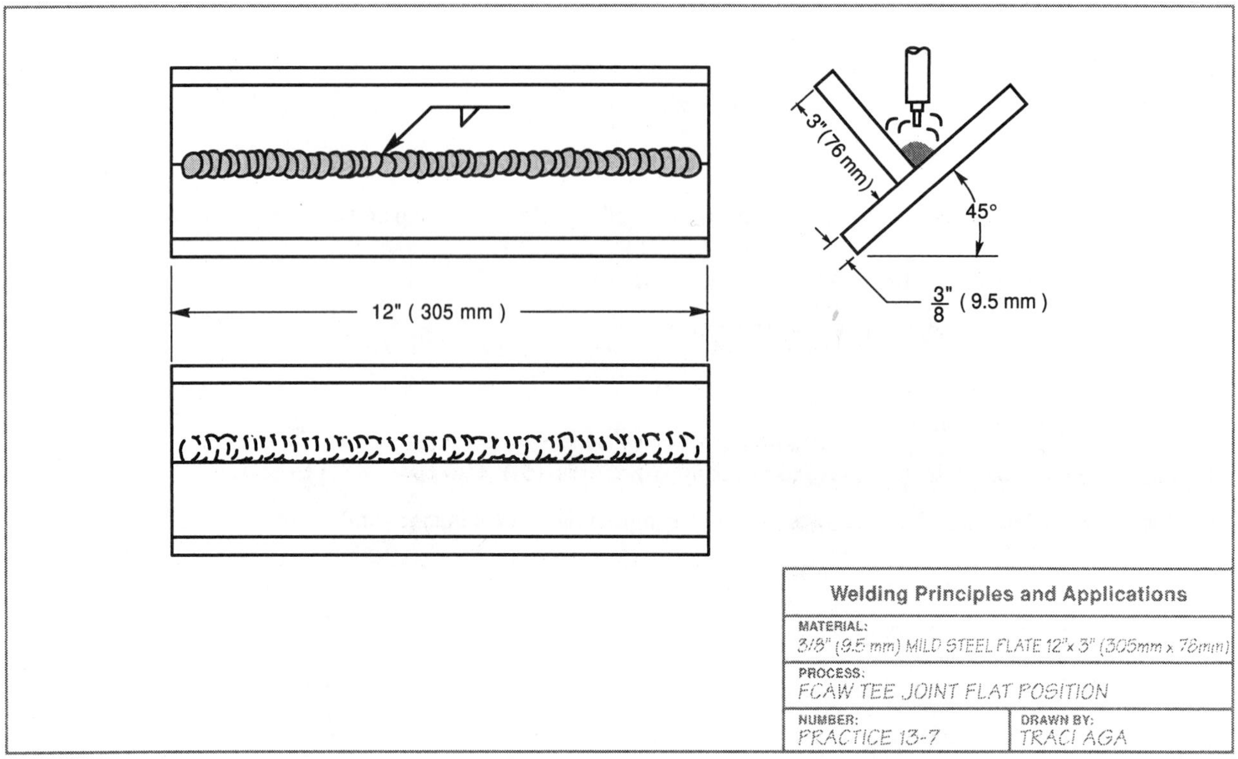

INSTRUCTIONS

1. Tack weld the plates together and place them in position to be welded. When making the lap or tee joints in the flat position, the plates must be at a 45° angle so that the surface of the weld will be flat.
2. Starting at one end, run a bead along the joint. Watch the molten weld pool and bead for signs that a change in technique may be required.
3. Make any needed changes as the weld progresses in order to produce a uniform weld.
4. Repeat with both classifications of electrodes as needed until consistently defect-free welds can be made.
5. Turn off the welding machine, shielding gas and clean up your work area when you are finished welding.

PRACTICE 13-8

Name______________________________ Date ____________

Class ____________________ Instructor ____________________ Grade ____________

OBJECTIVE:

After completing this practice, you should be able to make a fillet weld in a tee joint in the flat position.

EQUIPMENT AND MATERIALS NEEDED FOR THIS PRACTICE

1. A properly set up and adjusted FCA welding machine
2. Table 13-2
3. Proper safety protection
4. 0.035-in. and/or through 1/16 in. (0.9 mm and/or through 1.6 mm) diameter E70T-1 and/or E70T-5 electrodes
5. One or more pieces of mild steel plate, 7 in. (178 mm) long and 3/4 in. (19 mm)

INSTRUCTIONS

1. Tack weld the plates together and place them in position to be welded. When making the lap or tee joints in the flat position, the plates must be at a 45° angle so that the surface of the weld will be flat.
2. Starting at one end, run a bead along the joint. Watch the molten weld pool and bead for signs that a change in technique may be required.
3. Make any needed changes as the weld progresses in order to produce a uniform weld.
4. Repeat with both classifications of electrodes as needed until consistently defect-free welds can be made.
5. Turn off the welding machine, shielding gas and clean up your work area when you are finished welding.

PRACTICE 13-9

Name______________________________ Date ____________

Class ____________ Instructor ____________ Grade ____________

OBJECTIVE:

After completing this practice, you should be able to make a groove butt weld in the vertical position.

EQUIPMENT AND MATERIALS NEEDED FOR THIS PRACTICE

1. A properly set up and adjusted FCA welding machine
2. Table 13-1
3. Proper safety protection
4. 0.035-in. and/or 0.045-in. (0.9 mm and/or 1.2 mm) diameter E70T-1 and/or E70T-5 electrodes
5. One or more pieces of mild steel plate, 12 in. (305 mm) long and 1/4 in. (6 mm) thick beveled plate.

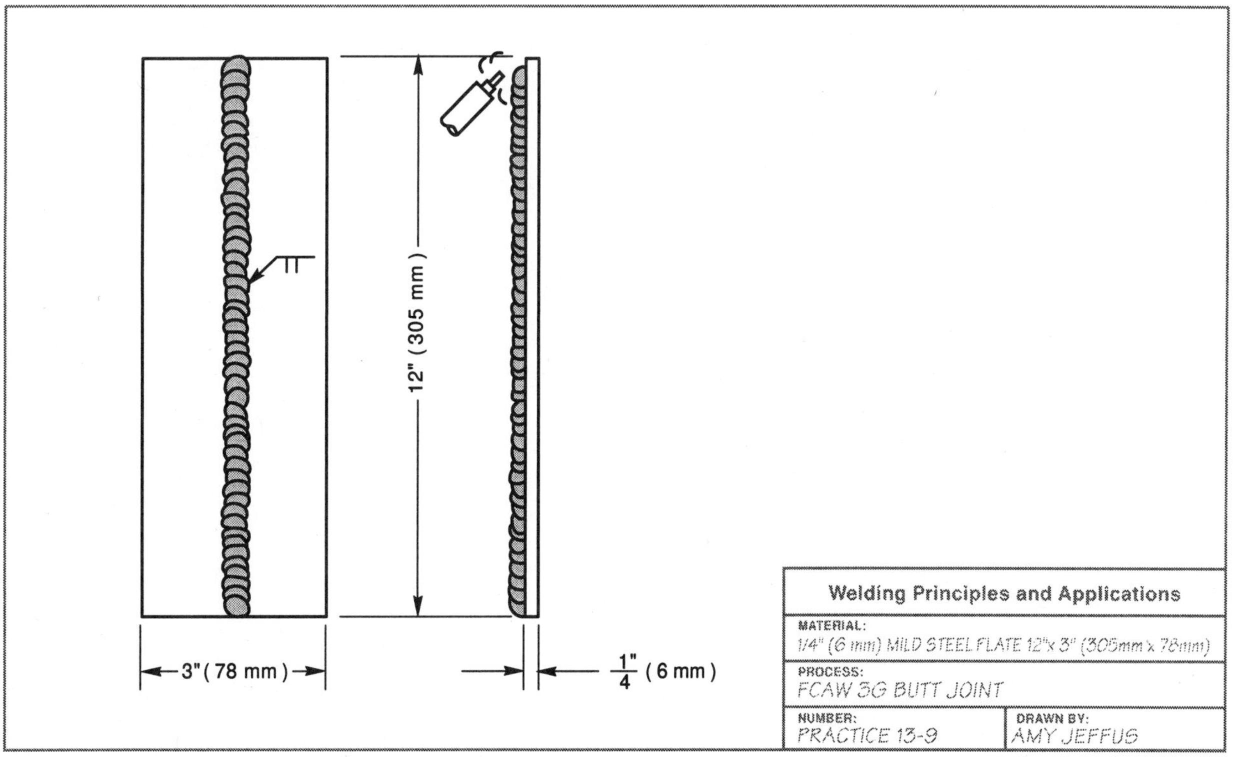

INSTRUCTIONS

1. Tack weld the plates together and place them in position to be welded.
2. Starting at one end, run a bead along the joint. Watch the molten weld pool and bead for signs that a change in technique may be required.
3. Make any needed changes as the weld progresses in order to produce a uniform weld.
4. Repeat with both classifications of electrodes as needed until consistently defect-free welds can be made in the 1/4 in. (6 mm) thick plate.
5. Turn off the welding machine, shielding gas and clean up your work area when you are finished welding.

PRACTICE 13-10

Name______________________________________ Date ____________

Class ____________________ Instructor ____________________ Grade ____________

OBJECTIVE: After completing this practice, you should be able to make a groove butt weld in the vertical up position.

EQUIPMENT AND MATERIALS NEEDED FOR THIS PRACTICE

1. A properly set up and adjusted FCA welding machine
2. Table 13-1
3. Proper safety protection
4. 0.035-in. and/or 0.045-in. (0.9 mm and/or 1.2 mm) diameter E70T-1 and/or E70T-5 electrodes
5. One or more pieces of mild steel plate, 12 in. (305 mm) long and 3/8 in. (9.5 mm) thick beveled plate
6. One piece of mild steel strap 14 in. (355 mm) long 1 in. (25 mm) wide and 1/4 in. (6 mm) thick for a backing strip

INSTRUCTIONS

1. Tack weld the backing strip to the plates. There should be approximately 1/8 in. (3 mm) root gap between the plates. The beveled surface can be made with or without a root face.
2. Place the test plates in position at a comfortable height and location. Be sure that you will have complete and free movement along the full length of the weld joint. It's often a good idea to make a practice pass along the joint with the welding gun without power to make sure nothing will interfere with your making the weld. Be sure the welding cable is free and will not get caught on anything during the weld.
3. Start the weld outside of the groove on the backing strip tab. This is done so that the arc is smooth and the molten weld pool size is established at the beginning of the groove. Continue the weld out on to the tab at the outer end of the groove. This is to insure that the end of the groove is completely filled with weld.
4. Repeat with both classifications of electrodes as needed until consistently defect-free welds can be made in the 1/4 in. (6 mm) thick plate.
5. Turn off the welding machine, shielding gas and clean up your work area when you are finished welding.

PRACTICE 13-11

Name____ Date ____________

Class ________________ Instructor ________________ Grade ____________

OBJECTIVE:

After completing this practice, you should be able to make fillet welds in both lap and tee joints in the horizontal position.

EQUIPMENT AND MATERIALS NEEDED FOR THIS PRACTICE

1. A properly set up and adjusted FCA welding machine
2. Table 13-1
3. Proper safety protection
4. 0.035-in. and/or 0.045-in. (0.9 mm and/or 1.2 mm) diameter E70T-1 and/or E70T-5 electrodes
5. One or more pieces of mild steel plate, 12 in. (305 mm) long and 3/8 in. (9.5 mm) thick beveled plate,

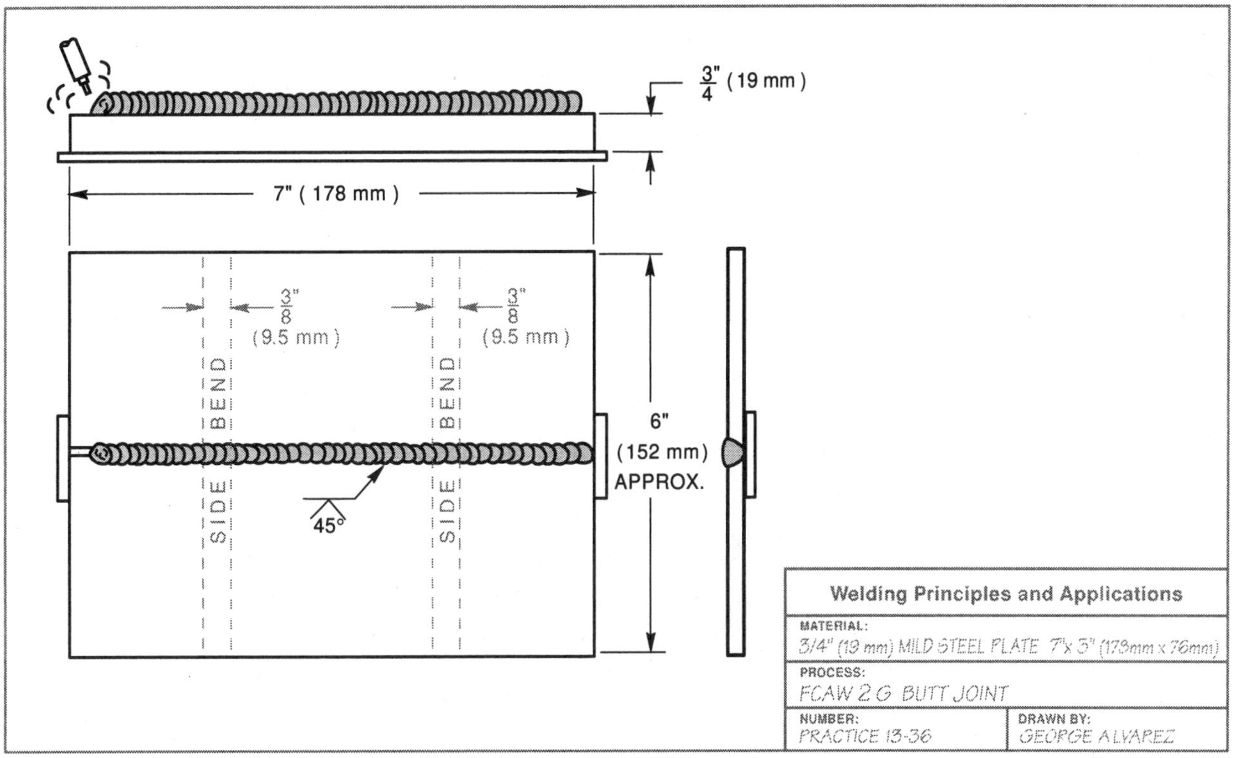

INSTRUCTIONS

1. Tack weld the plates together and place them in position.
2. Place the test plates in position at a comfortable height and location. Be sure that you will have complete and free movement along the full length of the weld joint. It's often a good idea to make a practice pass along the joint with the welding gun without power to make sure nothing will interfere with your making the weld. Be sure the welding cable is free and will not get caught on anything during the weld.
3. Start at one end and weld toward the other end. Keeping all of the weld beads small will help control their contour. Too large a root pass can trap slag under overlap which can occur along the lower edge of the weld.
4. Clean each pass thoroughly before the weld bead is started.

5. Repeat with both classifications of electrodes as needed until beads can be made straight, uniform, and free from any visual defects.
6. Turn off the welding machine, shielding gas and clean up your work area when you are finished welding.

PRACTICE 13-12

Name____ Date ____________

Class ____________________ Instructor ____________________ Grade ____________

OBJECTIVE: After completing this practice, you should be able to make a fillet weld in a tee joint in the horizontal position.

EQUIPMENT AND MATERIALS NEEDED FOR THIS PRACTICE

1. A properly set up and adjusted FCA welding machine
2. Table 13-2
3. Proper safety protection
4. 0.035-in. and/or through 1/16 in. (0.9 mm and/or through 1.6 mm) diameter E70T-1 and/or E70T-5 electrodes
5. 7 in. (178 mm) long and 3/4 in. (19 mm) or thicker beveled plate

INSTRUCTIONS

1. Tack weld the plates into position.
2. Place the test plates in position at a comfortable height and location. Be sure that you will have complete and free movement along the full length of the weld joint. It's often a good idea to make a practice pass along the joint with the welding gun without power to make sure nothing will interfere with your making the weld. Be sure the welding cable is free and will not get caught on anything during the weld.
3. Start at one end and weld toward the other end. Keeping all of the weld beads small will help control their contour. Too large a root pass can trap slag under overlap which can occur along the lower edge of the weld.
4. Repeat with both classifications of electrodes as needed until beads can be made straight, uniform, and free from any visual defects.
5. Turn off the welding machine, shielding gas and clean up your work area when you are finished welding.

PRACTICE 13-13

Name______________________________ Date ____________

Class ____________ Instructor ____________ Grade ____________

OBJECTIVE:

After completing this practice, you should be able to make a stringer bead weld on a plate in a 45° horizontal angle.

EQUIPMENT AND MATERIALS NEEDED FOR THIS PRACTICE

1. A properly set up and adjusted FCA welding machine
2. Table 13-1
3. Proper safety protection
4. 0.035-in. and/or 0.045-in. (0.9 mm and/or 1.2 mm) diameter E70T-1 and/or E70T-5 electrodes
5. One or more pieces of mild steel plate, 12 in. (305 mm) long and 1/4 in. (6 mm)

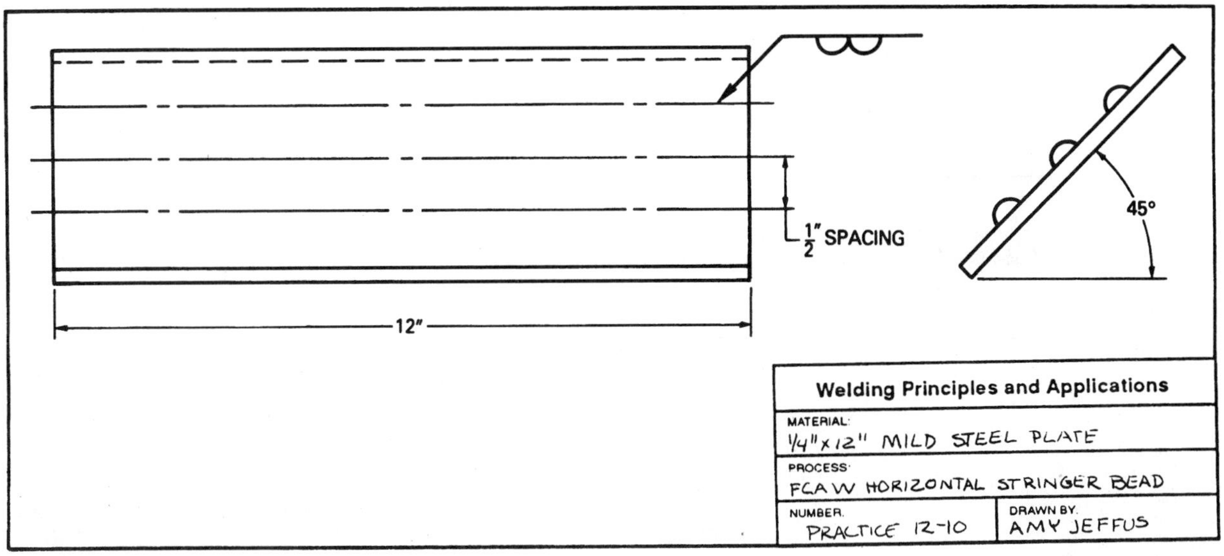

INSTRUCTIONS

1. Starting at one end of the plate and using a dragging technique, make a weld bead along the entire 12-in. (305-mm) length of the metal.
2. After the weld is complete, check its appearance. Make any needed changes to correct the weld.
3. Increase the plate angle gradually as you develop skill until you are making satisfactory horizontal welds across the vertical face of the plate.
6. Repeat with both classifications of electrodes as needed until beads can be made straight, uniform, and free from any visual defects on a plate that is in the vertical position.
7. Turn off the welding machine, shielding gas and clean up your work area when you are finished welding.

PRACTICE 13-14

OBJECTIVE:

After completing this practice, you should be able to make a groove butt weld in the horizontal position.

EQUIPMENT AND MATERIALS NEEDED FOR THIS PRACTICE

1. A properly set up and adjusted FCA welding machine
2. Table 13-1
3. Proper safety protection
4. 0.035-in. and/or 0.045-in. (0.9 mm and/or 1.2 mm) diameter E70T-1 and/or E70T-5 electrodes
5. One or more pieces of mild steel plate, 12 in. (305 mm) long and 1/4 in. (6 mm).

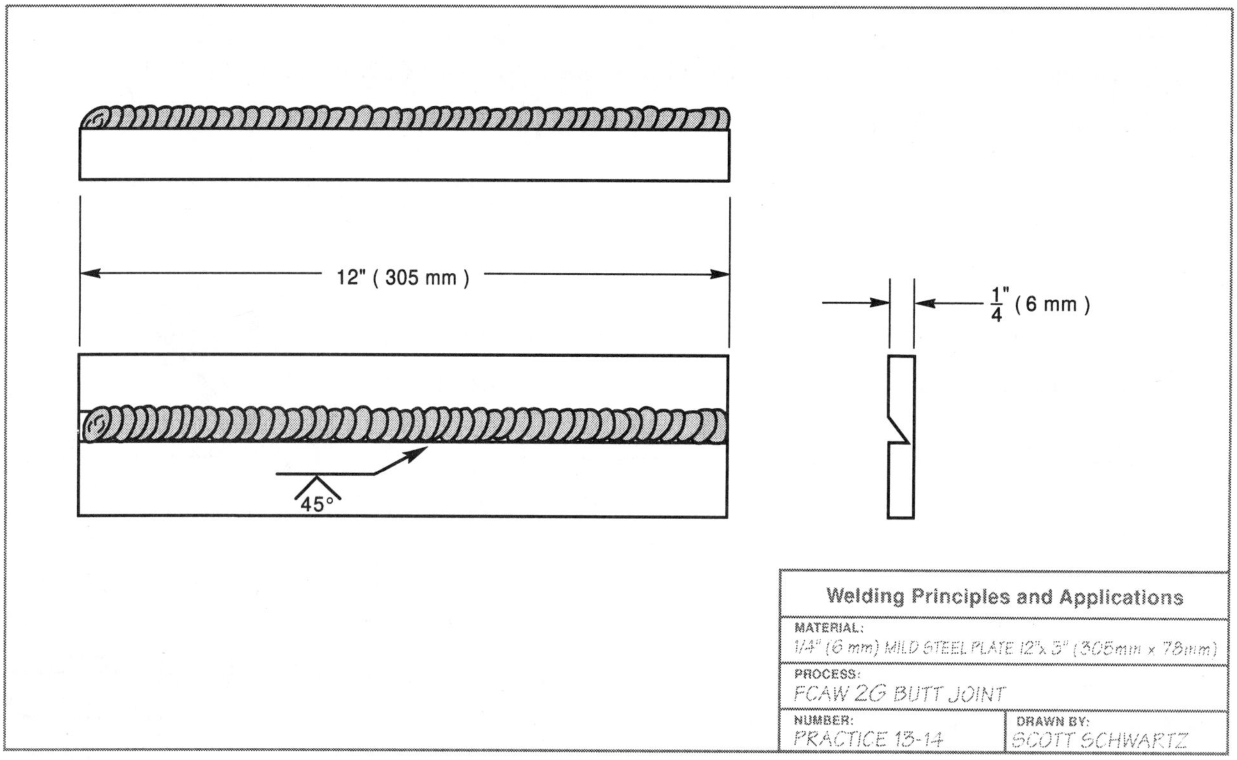

INSTRUCTIONS

1. Tack weld the plates into position.
2. Place the test plates in position at a comfortable height and location. Be sure that you will have complete and free movement along the full length of the weld joint. It's often a good idea to make a practice pass along the joint with the welding gun without power to make sure nothing will interfere with your making the weld. Be sure the welding cable is free and will not get caught on anything during the weld.
3. Start at one end and weld toward the other end. Keeping all of the weld beads small will help control their contour. Too large a root pass can trap slag under overlap which can occur along the lower edge of the weld.
4. Repeat with both classifications of electrodes as needed until beads can be made straight, uniform, and free from any visual defects.
5. Turn off the welding machine, shielding gas and clean up your work area when you are finished welding.

PRACTICE 13-15

Name____ Date ____________

Class ____________________ Instructor ____________________ Grade ____________

OBJECTIVE: After completing this practice, you should be able to make a groove butt weld in the horizontal position.

EQUIPMENT AND MATERIALS NEEDED FOR THIS PRACTICE

1. A properly set up and adjusted FCA welding machine
2. Table 13-1
3. Proper safety protection
4. 0.035-in. and/or 0.045-in. (0.9 mm and/or 1.2 mm) diameter E70T-1 and/or E70T-5 electrodes
5. One or more pieces of mild steel plate, 12 in. (305 mm) long and 3/8 in. (9.5 mm) thick beveled plate
6. One piece of mild steel strap 14 in. (355 mm) long 1 in. (25 mm) wide and 1/4 in. (6 mm) thick for a backing strip.

INSTRUCTIONS

1. Tack weld the backing strip to the plates. There should be approximately 1/8 in. (3 mm) root gap between the plates. The beveled surface can be made with or without a root face.
2. Place the test plates in position at a comfortable height and location. Be sure that you will have complete and free movement along the full length of the weld joint. It's often a good idea to make a practice pass along the joint with the welding gun without power to make sure nothing will interfere with your making the weld. Be sure the welding cable is free and will not get caught on anything during the weld.
3. Start the weld outside of the groove on the backing strip tab. This is done so that the arc is smooth and the molten weld pool size is established at the beginning of the groove. Continue the weld out on to the tab at the outer end of the groove. This is to insure that the end of the groove is completely filled with weld.
4. Repeat with both classifications of electrodes as needed until beads can be made straight, uniform, and free from any visual defects.
5. Turn off the welding machine, shielding gas and clean up your work area when you are finished welding.

PRACTICE 13-16

Name______________________________ Date ____________

Class ____________ Instructor ____________ Grade ____________

OBJECTIVE:

After completing this practice, you should be able to make a groove butt weld in the horizontal position.

EQUIPMENT AND MATERIALS NEEDED FOR THIS PRACTICE

1. A properly set up and adjusted FCA welding machine
2. Table 13-2
3. Proper safety protection
4. 0.035-in. and/or through 1/16 in. (0.9 mm and/or through 1.6 mm) diameter E70T-1 and/or E70T-5 electrodes
5. 7 in. (178 mm) long and 3/4 in. (19 mm) or thicker beveled plate
6. One piece of mild steel strap 14 in. (355 mm) long 1 in. (25 mm) wide and 1/4 in. (6 mm) thick for a backing strip.

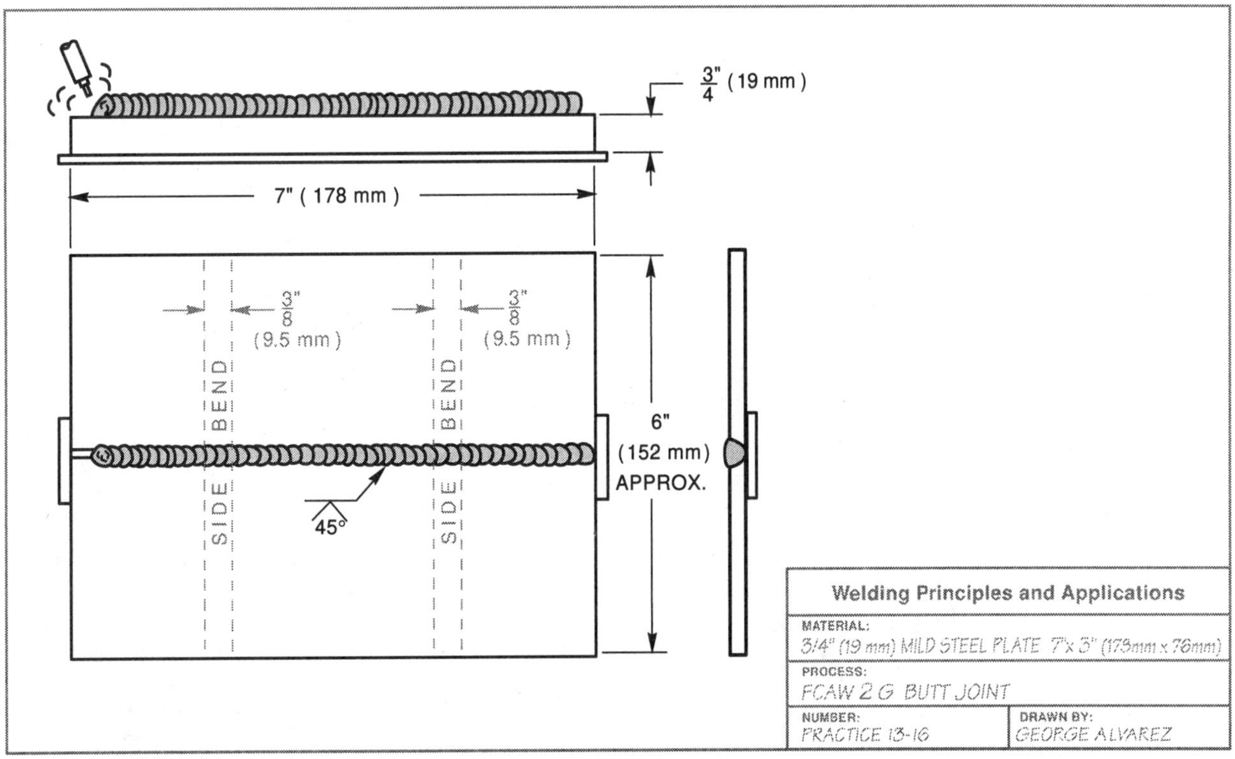

INSTRUCTIONS

1. Tack weld the backing strip to the plates. There should be approximately 1/8 in. (3 mm) root gap between the plates. The beveled surface can be made with or without a root face.
2. Place the test plates in position at a comfortable height and location. Be sure that you will have complete and free movement along the full length of the weld joint. It's often a good idea to make a practice pass along the joint with the welding gun without power to make sure nothing will interfere with your making the weld. Be sure the welding cable is free and will not get caught on anything during the weld.

3. Start the weld outside of the groove on the backing strip tab. This is done so that the arc is smooth and the molten weld pool size is established at the beginning of the groove. Continue the weld out on to the tab at the outer end of the groove. This is to insure that the end of the groove is completely filled with weld.
4. Repeat with both classifications of electrodes as needed until beads can be made straight, uniform, and free from any visual defects.
5. Turn off the welding machine, shielding gas and clean up your work area when you are finished welding.

PRACTICE 13-17

Name____ Date ______________

Class ______________________ Instructor ____________________ Grade ______________

OBJECTIVE: After completing this practice, you should be able to make a grooved butt weld in the overhead position.

EQUIPMENT AND MATERIALS NEEDED FOR THIS PRACTICE

1. A properly set up and adjusted FCA welding machine
2. Table 13-1
3. Proper safety protection including leather sleeves or leather jackets
4. 0.035-in. and/or 0.045-in. (0.9 mm and/or 1.2 mm) diameter E70T-1 and/or E70T-5 electrodes
5. One or more pieces of mild steel plate, 12 in. (305 mm) long and 1/4 in. (6 mm) Butt Joint 4G

INSTRUCTIONS

1. Tack weld the plates in position.
2. The molten weld pool should be kept as small as possible for easier control. Faster travel speeds allow the welder to maintain a high production rate even if multiple passes are required to complete the weld.
3. Weld penetration into the base metal at the start of the bead can be obtained by using a slow start or quickly reversing the weld direction.
4. Much of the spatter created during overhead welding falls into or on the nozzle and contact tube. The contact tube may short out to the gas nozzle. The shorted gas nozzle may arc to the work, causing damage both to the nozzle and to the plate. To control the amount of spatter, a longer stickout and/or a sharper gun-to-plate angle is required to allow most of the spatter to fall clear of the gun or nozzle.
5. Make several short weld beads using various techniques to establish the method that is most successful and most comfortable for you. After each weld, stop and evaluate it before making a change. When you have decided on the technique to be used, make a welded stringer bead that is 12 in. (305 mm) long.
6. Repeat with both classifications of electrodes as needed until consistently defect-free welds can be made in the 1/4 in. (6 mm) thick plate.
7. Turn off the welding machine, shielding gas and clean up your work area when you are finished welding.

PRACTICE 13-18

Name____ Date ____________

Class ____________________ Instructor ____________________ Grade ____________

OBJECTIVE:

After completing this practice, you should be able to make a grooved butt weld in the overhead position.

EQUIPMENT AND MATERIALS NEEDED FOR THIS PRACTICE

1. A properly set up and adjusted FCA welding machine
2. Table 13-1
3. Proper safety protection including leather sleeves or leather jackets
4. 0.035-in. and/or 0.045-in. (0.9 mm and/or 1.2 mm) diameter E70T-1 and/or E70T-5 electrodes
5. One or more pieces of mild steel plate, 12 in. (305 mm) long and 3/8 in. (9.5 mm) thick beveled plate
6. One piece of mild steel strap 14 in. (355 mm) long 1 in. (25 mm) wide and 1/4 in. (6 mm) thick for a backing strip.

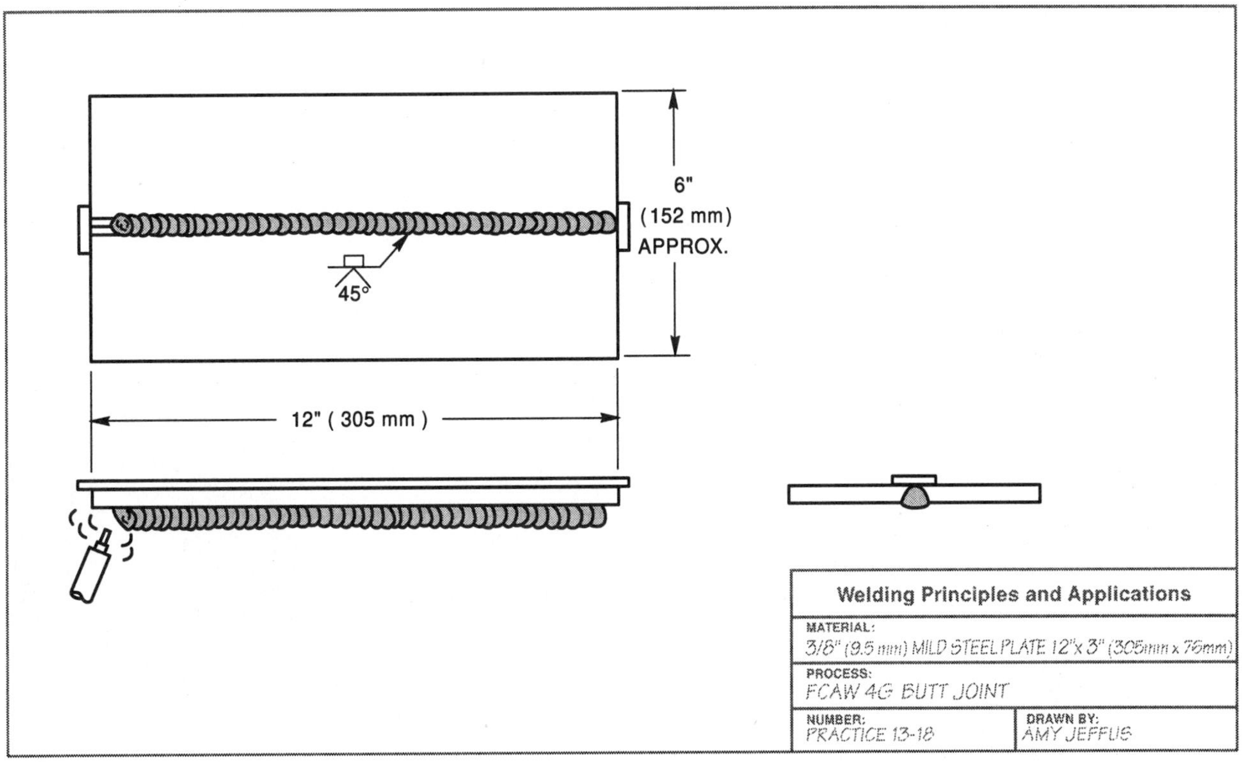

INSTRUCTIONS

1. Tack weld the backing strip to the plates. There should be approximately 1/8 in. (3 mm) root gap between the plates. The beveled surface can be made with or without a root face.
2. Place the test plates in position at a comfortable height and location. Be sure that you will have complete and free movement along the full length of the weld joint. It's often a good idea to make a practice pass along the joint with the welding gun without power to make sure nothing will interfere with your making the weld. Be sure the welding cable is free and will not get caught on anything during the weld.

3. Start the weld outside of the groove on the backing strip tab. This is done so that the arc is smooth and the molten weld pool size is established at the beginning of the groove. Continue the weld out on to the tab at the outer end of the groove. This is to insure that the end of the groove is completely filled with weld.
4. Repeat with both classifications of electrodes as needed until beads can be made straight, uniform, and free from any visual defects.
5. Turn off the welding machine, shielding gas and clean up your work area when you are finished welding.

PRACTICE 13-19

Name____ Date ______________

Class ________________________ Instructor ________________________ Grade ______________

OBJECTIVE: After completing this practice, you should be able to make butt welds in the vertical position.

EQUIPMENT AND MATERIALS NEEDED FOR THIS PRACTICE

1. A properly set up and adjusted FCA welding machine
2. Table 13-3
3. Proper safety protection
4. 0.030-in. and/or 0.035-in. (0.8 mm and/or 0.9 mm) diameter E70T-1 and/or E70T-5 electrodes
5. One or more pieces of mild steel plate, 12 in. (305 mm) long and 16-gauge to 18-gauge thick

INSTRUCTIONS

1. Tack weld the plates together. Do not leave a root opening for these welds. Even the slightest opening will result in a burnthrough. If a burnthrough occurs, the welder can be pulsed off and on so that the hole can be filled.
2. Place the test plates in position at a comfortable height and location. Be sure that you will have complete and free movement along the full length of the weld joint. It's often a good idea to make a practice pass along the joint with the welding gun without power to make sure nothing will interfere with your making the weld. Be sure the welding cable is free and will not get caught on anything during the weld.
3. Start at one end and weld toward the other end. Keeping all of the weld beads small will help control their contour.
4. Repeat with both classifications of electrodes as needed until beads can be made straight, uniform, and free from any visual defects.
5. Turn off the welding machine, shielding gas and clean up your work area when you are finished welding.

PRACTICE 13-20

OBJECTIVE: After completing this practice, you should be able to make fillet welds in both lap and tee joints in the vertical position.

EQUIPMENT AND MATERIALS NEEDED FOR THIS PRACTICE

1. A properly set up and adjusted FCA welding machine
2. Table 13-3
3. Proper safety protection
4. 0.030-in. and/or 0.035-in. (0.8 mm and/or 0.9 mm) diameter E70T-1 and/or E70T-5 electrodes
5. One or more pieces of mild steel plate, 12 in. (305 mm) long and 16-gauge to 18-gauge thick

INSTRUCTIONS

1. Tack weld the plates together. Do not leave a root opening for these welds. Even the slightest opening will result in a burnthrough. If a burnthrough occurs, the welder can be pulsed off and on so that the hole can be filled.
2. Place the test plates in position at a comfortable height and location. Be sure that you will have complete and free movement along the full length of the weld joint. It's often a good idea to make a practice pass along the joint with the welding gun without power to make sure nothing will interfere with your making the weld. Be sure the welding cable is free and will not get caught on anything during the weld.
3. Start at one end and weld toward the other end. Keeping all of the weld beads small will help control their contour.
4. Repeat with both classifications of electrodes as needed until beads can be made straight, uniform, and free from any visual defects.
5. Turn off the welding machine, shielding gas and clean up your work area when you are finished welding.

PRACTICE 13-21

OBJECTIVE: After completing this practice, you should be able to make butt welds in the overhead position.

EQUIPMENT AND MATERIALS NEEDED FOR THIS PRACTICE

1. A properly set up and adjusted FCA welding machine
2. Table 13-3
3. Proper safety protection including leather sleeves or leather jackets
4. 0.030-in. and/or 0.035-in. (0.8 mm and/or 0.9 mm) diameter E70T-1 and/or E70T-5 electrodes
5. One or more pieces of mild steel plate, 12 in. (305 mm) long and 16-gauge to 18-gauge thick

INSTRUCTIONS

1. Tack weld the plates together. Do not leave a root opening for these welds. Even the slightest opening will result in a burnthrough. If a burnthrough occurs, the welder can be pulsed off and on so that the hole can be filled.
2. Place the test plates in position at a comfortable height and location. Be sure that you will have complete and free movement along the full length of the weld joint. It's often a good idea to make a practice pass along the joint with the welding gun without power to make sure nothing will interfere with your making the weld. Be sure the welding cable is free and will not get caught on anything during the weld.
3. Start at one end and weld toward the other end. Keeping all of the weld beads small will help control their contour.
4. Repeat with both classifications of electrodes as needed until beads can be made straight, uniform, and free from any visual defects.
5. Turn off the welding machine, shielding gas and clean up your work area when you are finished welding.

PRACTICE 13-22

OBJECTIVE:

After completing this practice, you should be able to make fillet welds in both lap and tee joints in the overhead position.

EQUIPMENT AND MATERIALS NEEDED FOR THIS PRACTICE

1. A properly set up and adjusted FCA welding machine
2. Table 13-3
3. Proper safety protection including leather sleeves or leather jackets
4. 0.030-in. and/or 0.035-in. (0.8 mm and/or 0.9 mm) diameter E70T-1 and/or E70T-5 electrodes
5. One or more pieces of mild steel plate, 12 in. (305 mm) long and 16-gauge to 18-gauge thick

INSTRUCTIONS

1. Tack weld the plates together. Do not leave a root opening for these welds. Even the slightest opening will result in a burnthrough. If a burnthrough occurs, the welder can be pulsed off and on so that the hole can be filled.
2. Place the test plates in position at a comfortable height and location. Be sure that you will have complete and free movement along the full length of the weld joint. It's often a good idea to make a practice pass along the joint with the welding gun without power to make sure nothing will interfere with your making the weld. Be sure the welding cable is free and will not get caught on anything during the weld.
3. Start at one end and weld toward the other end. Keeping all of the weld beads small will help control their contour.
4. Repeat with both classifications of electrodes as needed until beads can be made straight, uniform, and free from any visual defects.
5. Turn off the welding machine, shielding gas and clean up your work area when you are finished welding.

CHAPTER 13: FLUX CORED ARC WELDING QUIZ

Name______________________________ Date __________

Class ______________ Instructor ______________ Grade __________

Instructions: Carefully read Chapter 13 in the text and complete the following questions.

A. SHORT ANSWER

1. How should a gas cylinder be secured before the cap is removed?

____

____

2. Why does FCA welding require greater protection than some other welding processes?

____

____

3. Why are larger pieces of metal used for most FCA welding?

____

____

4. What can cause bird's nesting?

____

____

5. How tight should the feed roller pressure be set?

____

____

6. Why can square groove welds be used for some FCA welding?

____

____

7. What is the purpose of the root pass?

____

____

8. What is the purpose of the filler pass?

____

____

9. What is the purpose of the cover pass?

____

____

10. When is it best to use stringer beads as opposed to weave beads?

____

____

11. Why are some welds started on the backing strip tab?

12. How large should a fillet weld be?

13. How can some tee joints be prepared for better weld penetration?

14. What would a notch at the leading edge of a fillet weld pool indicate?

15. Why should the electrode never be allowed to strike the metal ahead of the molten weld pool?

16. How can penetration at the beginning of a weld be obtained?

17. Why are vertical down FCA welds made in thin gauge metal?

18. How can burnthrough be repaired in thin gauged metals?

CHAPTER 14: OTHER CONSTANT POTENTIAL WELDING PROCESSES

CURRENT RANGES FOR VARIOUS WIRE SIZES USED IN SUBMERGED ARC WELDING

Wire Diameter, in. (mm)		Current Range, amp
3/32	(2.4 mm)	120 – 700
1/8	(3 mm)	220 – 1100
5/32	(4 mm)	340 – 1200
3/16	(4.8 mm)	400 – 1300
1/4	(6 mm)	600 – 1600
5/16	(8 mm)	1000 – 2500
3/8	(9.5 mm)	1500 – 4000
1/2	(13 mm)	2000 – 4800

ELECTROSLAG WELDING DEFECTS AND THEIR CAUSES

Location	Defects	Cause
Weld	Porosity	Gases, inadequate deoxidizers
	Non-metallic Inclusions	Excessive slag pool depth. High thermal conductivity base metal. Deep cuts in flame cut faces. Unfused non-metallics from plate laminations.
	Cracking	Carbon content. Form factor. Weld stopping.
Heat Affected Zone	Cracking	Rapid cooling of heat affected zone. Incomplete penetration at face. High restraint. Composition of base metal. Excessive slag pool depth.
	Undercutting	Excessive dwell time. Inadequate cooling of shoes. High voltage.
Fusion Line	Lack of Fusion	Low voltage. High wire feed rate. Excessive slag pool depth. Misalignment of electrodes. Excessive electrode-to-shoe distance. Inadequate dwell time. Excessive oscillation speed.

CHAPTER 14 OTHER CONSTANT POTENTIAL WELDING PROCESSES QUIZ

Name______________________________ Date ____________

Class ____________ Instructor ____________ Grade ____________

Instructions: Carefully read Chapter 14 in the text and answer the following questions.

A. IDENTIFICATION

In the space provided identify the items shown on the illustration.

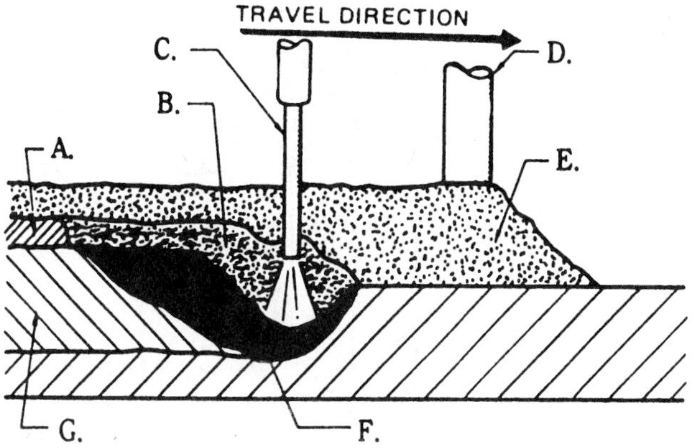

1. Identify the components of the submerged arc welding process.

a. ____________ e. ____________

b. ____________ f. ____________

c. ____________ g. ____________

d. ____________

B. TRUE-FALSE

Write the letter T in the space to the left if the statement is true and the letter F if the statement is false.

____ 2. Submerged arc welding (SAW) is a fusion welding process in which the molten weld pool is protected from the surrounding atmosphere by an external shielding gas.

____ 3. The drive rollers from the SAW process are usually the Smooth U-groove.

____ 4. Contact tips for the SAW process are normally made of aluminum-copper so they can withstand the heat of welding.

____ 5. If SAW flux becomes damp, it is permissible to dry it by using a cutting torch.

____ 6. One of the most significant advantages of SAW is that there is little if any fumes or smoke to exhaust.

____ 7. Electroslag welding produces a large grain size microstructure.

____ 8. Electroslag can only produce welds in the flat and horizontal positions.

____ 9. A major advantage of the electroslag welding process is that welds can be made having a thickness of several feet in only one pass.

____ 10. Electroslag is used to weld plates 3/8 in. (9.5 mm) thick or more.

C. SHORT ANSWER

Write a brief answer, in the space provided, that will answer the question or complete the statement.

11. The illustration below is a schematic drawing of what process?

____

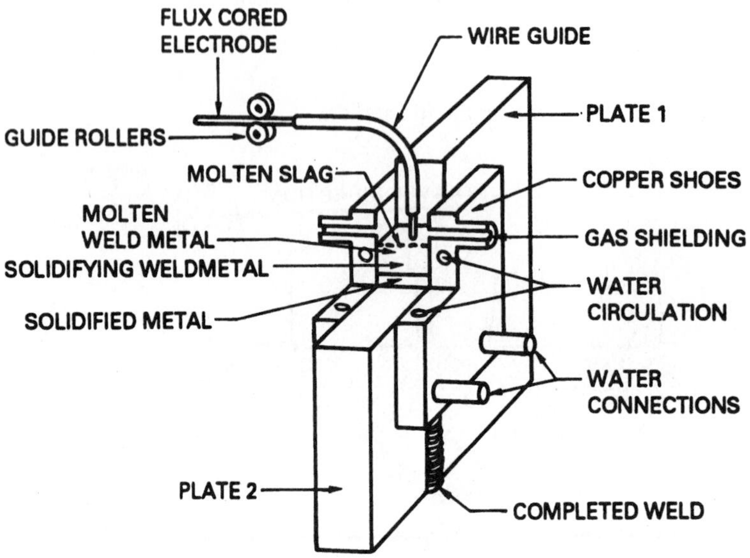

12. The following SAW electrodes and fluxes are made up of letters and numbers. Explain what each bracket in the electrode means using the American Welding Society (AWS) identification system.

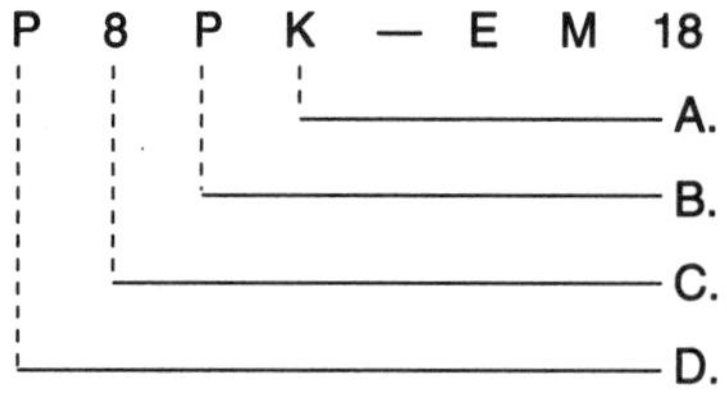

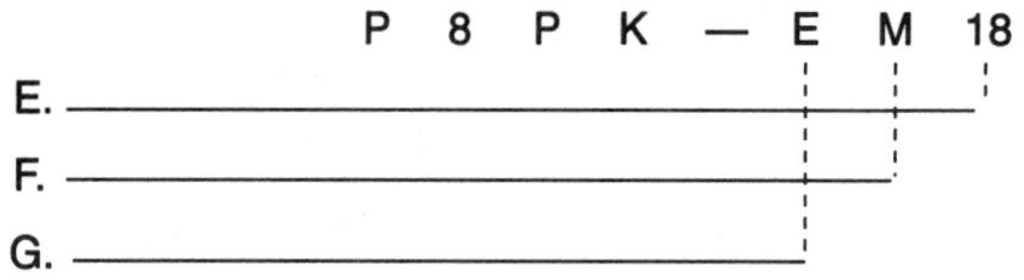

a. ______________ e. ______________

b. ______________ f. ______________

c. ______________ g. ______________

d. ______________

13. What are the three types of fluxes used with the SAW process?

a. ____

b. ____

c. ____

14. What is the recommended way of drying flux if it becomes damp?

____

15. List six advantages of the SAW process.

a.____

b. ____

c.____

d. ____

e.____

f.____

16. What are the six common methods of starting an arc for the SAW process?

a.____

b. ____

c.____

d. ____

e.____

f.____

D. ESSAY

Provide complete answers for all of the following questions.

17. What do SAW, ESW, and EGW have in common with GMAW and FCAW?

____

____

18. What produces the heat for welding in the SAW process?

____

____

19. Explain the electrode classification system used for SAW filler wire.

____

____

20. Explain the flux classification system used for SAW.

____

____

21. List five advantages of the submerged arc process.

____

____

22. List two disadvantages of the submerged arc process.

____

____

23. Why is it necessary to support the root face of a SAW?

24. Why is the SA process considered to be better for the atmosphere than other welding processes?

25. Why must you be careful when handling unfused SA welding fluxes following a weld?

26. List 4 disadvantages of using electroslag welding.

CHAPTER 15: GAS TUNGSTEN ARC WELDING EQUIPMENT, SETUP, OPERATION, AND FILLER METALS

CURRENT SELECTION FOR GAS TUNGSTEN-ARC WELDING

Material	Alternating Current			Direct Current						Tungsten Selection
	Stabilized			Straight Polarity			Reverse Polarity			
	Ex	Go	NR	Ex	Go	NR	Ex	Go	NR	
Magnesium up to 1/8 in. thick	X					X		X		Pure
Magnesium above 3/16 in. thick	X					X			X	Zirconium
Magnesium castings	X					X		X		Thoriated
Aluminum up to 3/32 in. thick	X					X		X		Pure
Aluminum over 3/32 in. thick	X					X			X	Zirconium
Aluminum castings	X				X				X	Thoriated
Stainless steel		X		X					X	Thoriated
Brass alloys		X		X					X	Thoriated Pure
Silicon copper			X						X	Zirconium
Silver		X		X					X	Thoriated
High-chromium, nickel-base, high-temperature alloys		X		X					X	Thoriated
Silver cladding	X					X			X	Thoriated
Hard facing	X			X					X	
Cast iron		X		X					X	
Low-carbon steel, 0.015 to 0.030 in.		X		X					X	
Low-carbon steel, 0.030 to 0.125 in.			X	X					X	Thoriated Pure Zirconium
High-carbon steel, 0.030 in.		X		X					X	
High-carbon steel, 0.030 in. and up		X		X					X	
Deoxidized copper			X	X					X	

GTAW TROUBLESHOOTING GUIDE

Problem	Remedy
Arc Blow	1. Make sure the ground is properly connected. 2. Changing the angle of the electrode relative to the work may stabilize the arc. 3. Make sure the base metal is clean. 4. Make sure tungsten electrode is clean. 5. Use a smaller tungsten. 6. Bring nozzle closer to work.
Brittle Welds	1. Check the type of filler metal being used. 2. Use pre & post heat while welding. 3. Check the welding procedure. A. Multilayer welds will tend to anneal hard heat affected zone.
Cracked Welds	1. Check for inferior welds. Make sure all welds are sound and the fusion is good. 2. Check the type of filler metal being used. 3. Check the welding procedure. A. Fill all craters at the end of the weld passes. B. Use pre & post heat. 4. Do not use too small a weld between heavy plates. 5. Check for proper preparation of joints. 6. Check for excessive rigidity of joints.
Inferior Weld Appearance	1. Change welding technique. 2. Use proper current. 3. Check for proper shielding gas. 4. Check for drafts blowing shielding gas away. 5. Check for proper filler metal. 6. Make sure base metal is clean.
Distortion	1. Make sure parts are properly tack welded together. 2. Clamp parts to resist shrinkage. 3. Removing of rolling or forming strains by stress reliev-ing before welding is sometimes helpful. 4. Distribute welding to prevent excessive local heating.
Porosity	1. Check shielding gas. 2. Check for drafts blowing shielding gas away. 3. Do not weld on wet metal. 4. Make sure base metal is clean. 5. Check shielding gas hoses; plastic hoses are best. 6. Check welding procedure and current settings.
Rapid Tungsten Electrode Consumption	1. Check polarity. 2. Decrease current. 3. Use a larger tungsten electrode. 4. Check shielding gas. A. Increase gas flow. 5. Check for good collet contact. A. Change collet. B. Use ground-finished tungsten.

Problem	Remedy
Tungsten Inclusions	1. Use a larger tungsten electrode or reduce current. 2. Do not allow the tungsten to come into contact with the molten weld pool while welding. 3. Use high-frequency starting device. 4. Do not weld with tungsten electrodes that have become cracked or split on the ends.
Lack of Penetration	1. Increase current. 2. Decrease welding speed. 3. Decrease the size of the filler metal. 4. Adjust root opening.
Undercutting	1. Decrease current. 2. Make smaller weld beads. 3. Use a closer tungsten-to-work distance. 4. Change welding technique.

CHAPTER 15: GAS TUNGSTEN ARC WELDING EQUIPMENT, SETUP, OPERATION, AND FILLER METALS QUIZ

Name____ Date ____________

Class ____________________ Instructor ____________________ Grade ____________

Instructions: Carefully read Chapter 15 in the text and answer the following questions.

A. SHORT ANSWER

Write a brief answer, in the space provided, that will answer the question or complete the statement.

1. List at least four methods of limiting tungsten erosion.

   a.____

   b. ____

   c.____

   d. ____

   e.____

   f.____

   g. ____

   h. ____

2. List seven classifications of tungsten electrodes that are commercially available.

   a.____

   b. ____

   c.____

   d. ____

   e.____

   f.____

   g. ____

3. List the two types of GTAW torches.

   a.____

   b. ____

4. Why are rubber hoses not recommended to be used for shielding gas hose from the GTAW process?

   ____

   ____

5. What are the advantages and disadvantages of using a small diameter nozzle versus a large diameter nozzle?

   ____

   ____

   ____

   ____

6. Select the advantages of the GTAW process from the following examples. (Place an "X" by the correct examples.)

_____ a. No flux used and no post cleaning required.

_____ b. Economical and preferred for welding sheet metal.

_____ c. Slag is easily removed.

_____ d. Welds can be as corrosion resistant as the base metal.

_____ e. The GTAW process is used on heavy plates where rapid production is necessary.

_____ f. The arc and weld puddle are clearly visible to the welder.

B. IDENTIFICATION

In the space provided identify the items shown on the illustration.

7. Identify the following GTAW equipment by placing the correct number in the space provided from the drawing below.

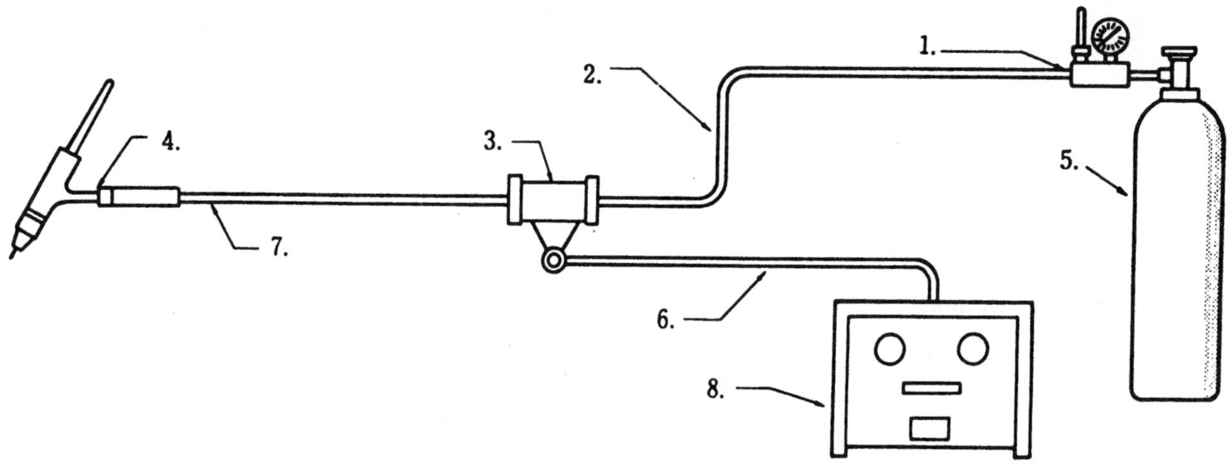

_____ a. argon gas

_____ b. argon hose

_____ c. welding cable

_____ d. cable and hose

_____ e. power supply

_____ f. flowmeter regulator

_____ g. torch

_____ h. cable adapter

8. From the illustration below, identify the following GTAW torch parts by placing the correct number in the space provided.

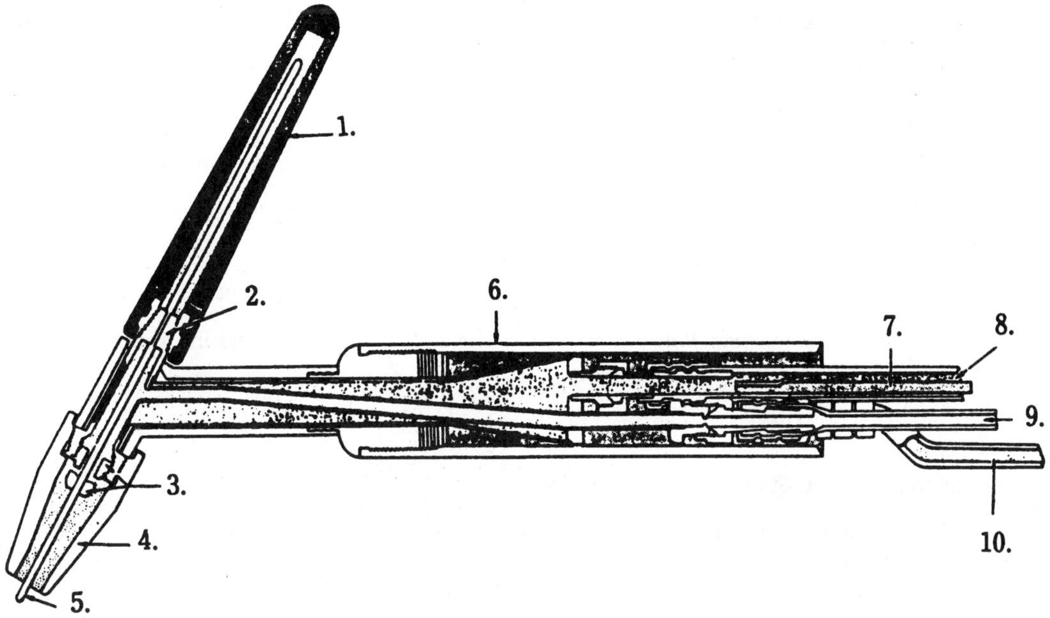

____ a. Gas hose

____ b. Collet

____ c. Torch handle

____ d. Tungsten electrode

____ e. Water inlet hose

____ f. Cap

____ g. Gas nozzle

____ h. Water outlet

____ i. Gas orifice nut

____ j. Electrode cable

C. MATCHING

In the space provided to the left, write the letter from column B that best answers the question or completes the statement in column A.

column A

____ 9. The high melting temperature and good electrical conductivity make ________ the best choice for a consumable electrode.

____ 10. A chucking device used to hold the tungsten in the torch.

____ 11. A calibrated metering device used to regulate the flow of gases to the torch and measured in cubic feet per hour (cfh).

____ 12. A gas which will not combine with other gases used to surround the weldzone and prevent contamination of the weld by oxygen and nitrogen in the air.

____ 13. An attachment that fits on the end of the GTAW torch to direct the flow of shielding gas to the tungsten and weld zone.

column B

a. collet
b. gas nozzle
c. tungsten
d. flowmeter
e. inert shielding gas

D. TRUE-FALSE

Write the letter T in the space to the left if the statement is true and the letter F if the statement is false.

____ 14. The eye-hand coordination required to make GTA welds is very similar to the coordination required for oxy-fuel gas welding.

____ 15. Fluxes are used to produce sound and corrosion resistant welds in the GTAW process.

______ 16. The GTAW process has proved to be very tedious and expensive for joining sections much thicker than 1/4 inch (6 mm).

______ 17. The tungsten is very sensitive to oxygen in the air so good shielding with oxygen-free gases is mandatory.

______ 18. The water-cooled GTA welding torch is less efficient than the air-cooled torch for removing the waste heat.

______ 19. Helium is a by-product of the natural gas industry.

______ 20. Nitrogen can be used as an additive to argon to increase penetration when welding copper.

______ 21. On a GTA welder the water hoses should have right-hand threads to prevent incorrectly connecting them to a shielding gas hose.

______ 22. When GTAW, adjust the tungsten length so that it does not stick out more then the diameter of the cup.

______ 23. Adding thoria or zirconia in small quantities will improve the electrode arc starting ability, resistance to contamination, and decrease current carrying capacity.

E. ESSAY

Provide complete answers to each of the following questions

24. Sketch the three basic tungsten electrode end shapes and name them.

25. Describe the process for producing tungsten electrodes.

____

____

26. What type of equipment is recommended for grinding tungsten electrodes?

____

____

27. How should a tungsten electrode be held while shaping the end with a grinder?

____

____

28. Why is argon the most commonly used shielding gas for GTA welding?

____

____

29. What effect does the addition of thoria have on the tungsten electrode?

____

____

30. What effect does the addition of zirconia have on the tungsten electrode?

____

____

31. What effect does the end shape of the tungsten have on its welding performance?

____

____

32. Why must tungsten be hot in order to have a stable arc?

____

____

33. What factor leads to increased tungsten erosion?

____

____

34. What are the different heat distributions between the work and tungsten for each of the following types of current?

    a. DCEP ____

    b. DCEN ____

    c. AC ____

35. Why is high frequency used for some GTA welding?

____

____

36. What is the hot start used by welders?

____

____

37. The postpurge time should be how long?

____

____

38. Define the term inert gas.

____

____

CHAPTER 16: GAS TUNGSTEN ARC WELDING OF PLATE

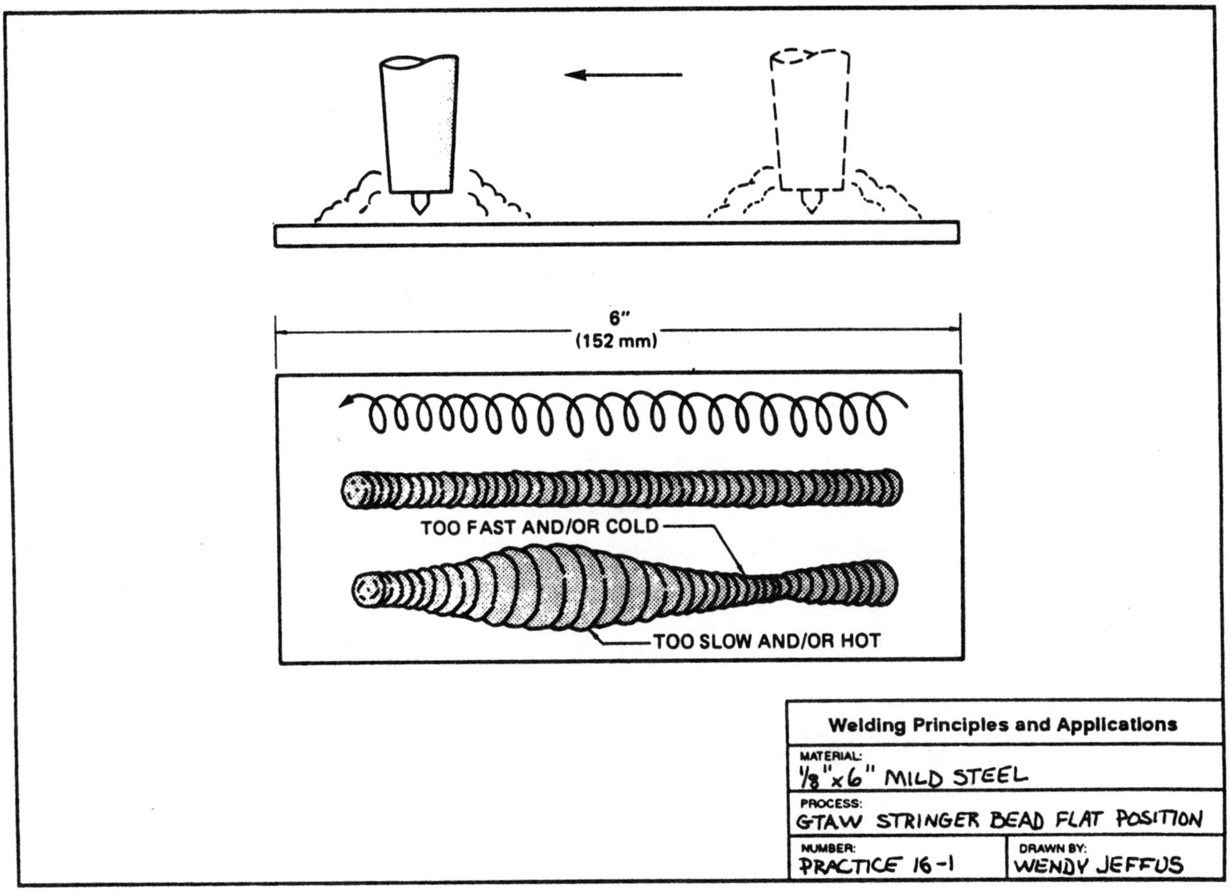

OPERATING INSTRUCTIONS FOR THE GTAW PROCESS

1. With the power off, switch the machine to the GTA welding mode.
2. Select the desired type of current and amperage range

Electrode Diameter		DCSP	DCRP	AC
in	(mm)			
.04	(1)	15-60	Not recommended	10-50
1/16	(2)	70-100	10-20	50-90
3/32	(2.4)	90-200	15-30	80-130
1/8	(3)	150-350	25-40	100-200
5/32	(4)	300-450	40-55	160-300

3. Set the fine current adjustment to the proper range, depending upon the size of the tungsten being used.
4. Place the high-frequency switch in the appropriate position, auto for DC or continuous for AC.
5. The remote control can be plugged in and selector switch set if you are using the remote.
6. The collet and collet body should be installed and match the tungsten size being used.
7. Install the tungsten into the torch and tighten the backcap to hold the tungsten in place.
8. Select and install the desired nozzle size. Adjust the tungsten length so that it does not stick out more than the inside diameter of the nozzle.

9. Check the manufacturer's operating manual for the machine to ensure that all connections and settings are correct.
10. Turn on the power, depress the remote control, and check for water or gas leaks.
11. While postpurge is still engaged, set the gas flow by adjusting the valve on the flowmeter.
12. Position yourself so that you are comfortable and can see the torch, tungsten, and plate while the tungsten tip is held about 1/4 in. (6 mm) above the metal. Try to hold the torch at a vertical angle ranging from 0° to 15°. Too steep an angle will not give adequate gas coverage.

    CAUTION Avoid touching the metal table with any unprotected skin or jewelry. The high frequency can cause an uncomfortable shock.

13. Lower your arc welding helmet and depress the remote control. A high-pitched, erratic arc should be immediately jumping across the gap between the tungsten and the plate. If the high-frequency arc is not established, lower the torch until it appears.
14. Slowly increase the current until the main welding arc appears.
15. Observe the color change of the tungsten as the arc appears.
16. Move the tungsten around in a small circle until a weld pool appears on the metal.
17. Slowly decrease the current and observe the change in the weld pool.
18. Reduce the current until the arc is extinguished.
19. Hold the torch in place over the weld until the postpurge stops.
20. Raise your hood and inspect the weld.
21. Turn off the welding machine, shielding gas and clean up your work area when you are finished welding.

PRACTICE 16-1

Name____ Date _____________

Base Metal Type _______________ Thickness _______ Filler Di. ________ Joint _____________

Class ______________________ Instructor ______________________ Grade _____________

OBJECTIVE: After completing this practice, you should be able to make stringer beads in the flat position on 16 gauge and 1/8-inch (3 mm) thick carbon steel without filler metal.

EQUIPMENT AND MATERIAL NEEDED FOR THIS PRACTICE

1. A properly set up and adjusted GTA welding machine
2. Proper safety protection (welding hood, safety glasses, pliers, gloves, long sleeve shirt, long pants and leather boots or shoes). Refer to Chapter 2 in the text for more specific safety information.
3. Two or more pieces of mild steel, 6 in. (152 mm) long and 16 gauge and 1/8 in. (3 mm) thick.

INSTRUCTIONS

1. Starting at one end of the piece of metal that is 1/8 in. (3 mm) thick, hold the torch as close as possible to a 90° angle.
2. Lower your hood, strike an arc, and establish a weld pool.
3. Move the torch in a circular oscillation pattern down the plate toward the other end.
4. If the size of the weld pool changes, speed up or slow down the travel rate to keep the weld pool the same size for the entire length of the plate.
5. Repeat the process using both thicknesses of metal until you can consistently make the weld visually defect-free.
6. Turn off the welding machine, shielding gas and clean up your work area when you are finished welding.

Comments

____

PRACTICE 16-2

OBJECTIVE: After completing this practice, you should be able to make stringer beads in the flat position on 16 gauge and 1/8-inch (3 mm) thick stainless steel without filler metal.

EQUIPMENT AND MATERIAL NEEDED FOR THIS PRACTICE

1. A properly set up and adjusted GTA welding machine
2. Proper safety protection (welding hood, safety glasses, pliers, gloves, long sleeve shirt, long pants and leather boots or shoes). Refer to Chapter 2 in the text for more specific safety information.
3. Two or more pieces of mild steel, 6 in. (152 mm) long and 16 gauge and 1/8 in. (3 mm) thick.

INSTRUCTIONS

1. Starting at one end of the piece of metal that is 1/8 in. (3 mm) thick, hold the torch as close as possible to a 90° angle.
2. Lower your hood, strike an arc, and establish a weld pool.
3. Move the torch in a circular oscillation pattern down the plate toward the other end.
4. If the size of the weld pool changes, speed up or slow down the travel rate to keep the weld pool the same size for the entire length of the plate.

To keep the formation of oxides on the bead to a minimum, a chill plate (a thick piece of metal used to absorb heat) may be required. Another method is to make the bead using as low a heat input as possible. When the weld is finished, the weld bead should be no darker than dark blue.

5. Repeat the process using both thicknesses of metal until you can consistently make the weld visually defect-free.
6. Turn off the welding machine, shielding gas and clean up your work area when you are finished welding.

Comments

PRACTICE 16-3

OBJECTIVE: After completing this practice, you should be able to make stringer beads in the flat position on 16 gauge and 1/8 inch (3 mm) thick aluminum without the filler metal.

EQUIPMENT AND MATERIAL NEEDED FOR THIS PRACTICE

1. A properly set up and adjusted GTA welding machine
2. Proper safety protection (welding hood, safety glasses, pliers, gloves, long sleeve shirt, long pants and leather boots or shoes). Refer to Chapter 2 in the text for more specific safety information.
3. Two or more pieces of mild steel, 6 in. (152 mm) long and 16 gauge and 1/8 in. (3 mm) thick.

INSTRUCTIONS

1. Starting at one end of the piece of metal that is 1/8 in. (3 mm) thick, hold the torch as close as possible to a 90° angle.
2. Lower your hood, strike an arc, and establish a weld pool.
3. Move the torch in a circular oscillation pattern down the plate toward the other end.
4. If the size of the weld pool changes, speed up or slow down the travel rate to keep the weld pool the same size for the entire length of the plate.

   A high current setting will allow faster travel speeds. The faster speed helps to control excessive penetration. Hot cracking may occur on some types of aluminum after a surfacing weld. This is not normally a problem when filler metal is added. If hot cracking should occur during this practice, do not be concerned.
5. Repeat the process using all thicknesses of metal until you can consistently make the weld visually defect-free.
6. Turn off the welding machine, shielding gas and clean up your work area when you are finished welding.

Comments

PRACTICE 16-4

Name______________________________ Date ____________

Base Metal Type ____________ Thickness ________ Filler Di. ________ Joint ____________

Class ____________ Instructor ____________ Grade ____________

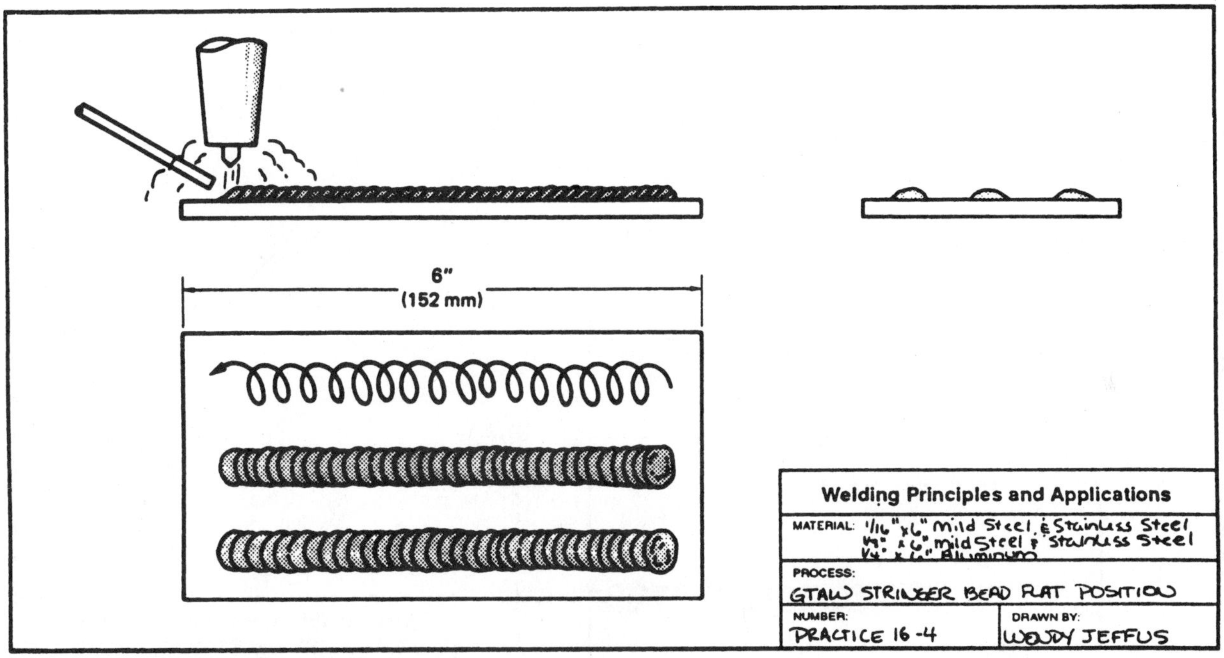

OBJECTIVE: After completing this practice, you should be able to weld stringer beads on carbon steel, stainless steel, and aluminum in the flat position using the correct filler metal.

EQUIPMENT AND MATERIAL NEEDED FOR THIS PRACTICE

1. A properly set up and adjusted GTA welding machine
2. Proper safety protection
3. Filler rods 36 in. (0.9 m) long x 1/16 in. (1.6 mm), 3/32 in. (2.4 mm), and 1/8 in. (3 mm) in diameter
4. One or more pieces of mild steel, stainless steel, and aluminum, 6 in. (152 mm) long x 1/16 in. (2 mm) and 1/8 in. (3 mm) thick, and aluminum plate 1/4 in. (6 mm) thick.

INSTRUCTIONS

1. Starting with the metal that is 1/8 in. (3 mm) thick and the filler rod having a 3/32-in. (2.4 mm) diameter, strike an arc and establish a weld pool.
2. Move the torch in a circle as in the practice beading. When the torch is on one side, add filler rod to the other side of the molten weld pool. The end of the rod should be dipped into the weld pool but should not be allowed to melt and drip into the weld pool.
3. Change to another size filler rod and determine its effect on the weld pool.
4. Maintain a smooth and uniform rhythm as filler metal is added. This will help to keep the bead uniform.
5. Vary the rhythms to determine which one is easiest for you. If the rod sticks, move the torch toward the rod until it melts free.
6. When the full 6-in. (152 mm) long weld bead is completed, cool and inspect it for uniformity and defects.

7. Repeat the process using all thicknesses of metal until you can consistently make the weld visually defect-free.
8. Turn off the welding machine, shielding gas and clean up your work area when you are finished welding.

Comments

PRACTICE 16-5

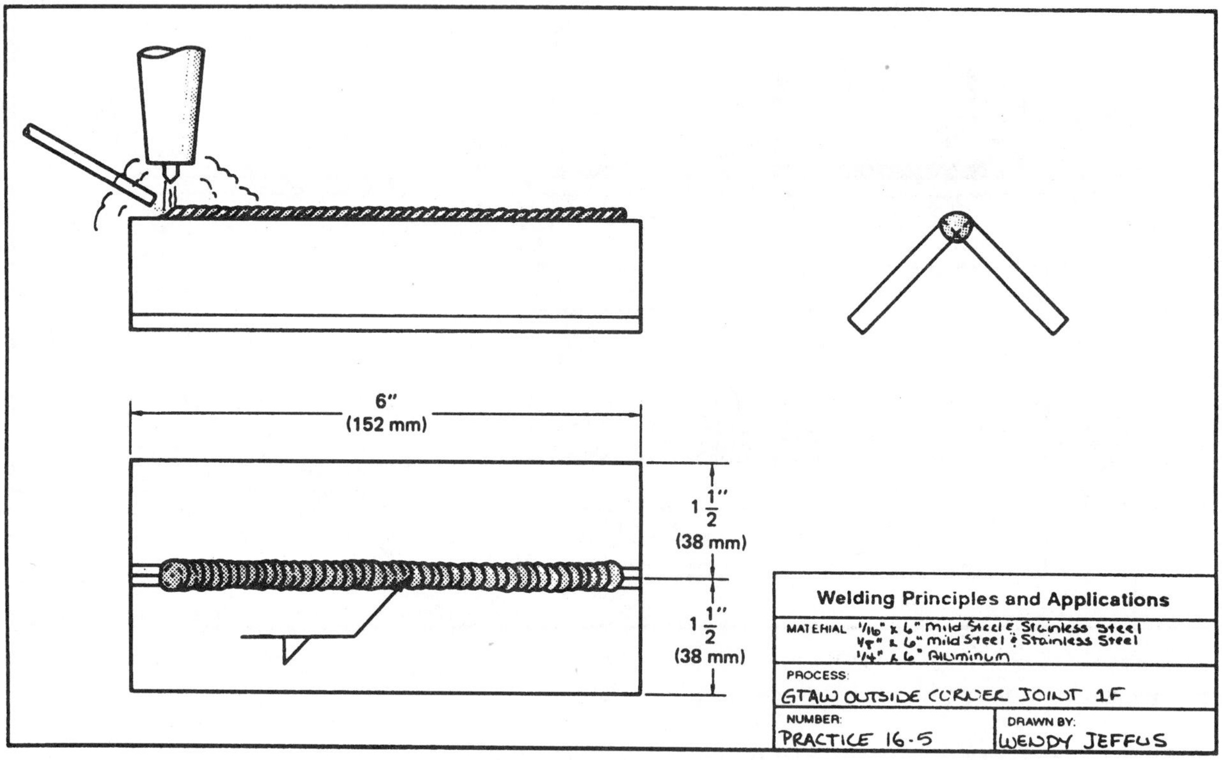

OBJECTIVE: After completing this practice, you should be able to weld an outside corner joint on carbon steel, stainless steel and aluminum in the flat position.

EQUIPMENT AND MATERIAL NEEDED FOR THIS PRACTICE

1. A properly set up and adjusted GTA welding machine
2. Proper safety protection
3. Filler rods 36 in. (0.9 m) long x 1/16 in. (1.6 mm), 3/32 in. (2.4 mm), and 1/8 in. (3 mm) in diameter
4. One or more pieces of mild steel, stainless steel, and aluminum, 6 in. (152 mm) long x 1/16 in. (2 mm) and 1/8 in. (3 mm) thick, and aluminum plate 1/4 in. (6 mm) thick.

INSTRUCTIONS

1. Place one of the pieces of metal flat on the table and hold or brace the other piece of metal vertically on it.
2. Tack weld both ends of the plates together.
3. Set the plates up and add two or three more tack welds on the joint as required.
4. Starting at one end, make a uniform weld, adding filler metal as needed. The metal areas should be precleaned before the weld is made.
5. Repeat each weld as needed until all are mastered.

6. Turn off the welding machine, shielding gas and clean up your work area when you are finished welding.

Comments

PRACTICE 16-6

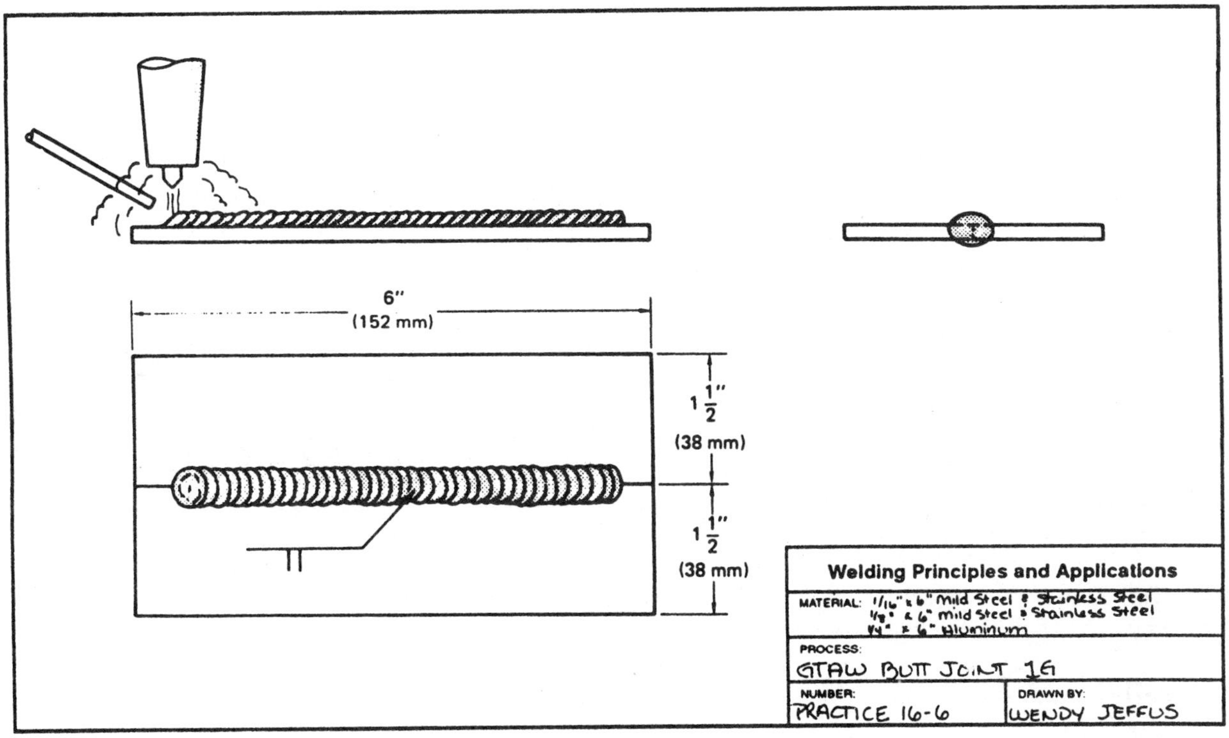

OBJECTIVE: After completing this practice, you should be able to weld a butt joint on carbon steel, stainless steel, and aluminum in the 1G position using the GTAW process.

EQUIPMENT AND MATERIAL NEEDED FOR THIS PRACTICE

1. A properly set up and adjusted GTA welding machine
2. Proper safety protection
3. Filler rods 36 in. (0.9 m) long x 1/16 in. (1.6 mm), 3/32 in. (2.4 mm), and 1/8 in. (3 mm) in diameter
4. One or more pieces of mild steel, stainless steel, and aluminum, 6 in. (152 mm) long x 1/16 in. (2 mm) and 1/8 in. (3 mm) thick, and aluminum plate 1/4 in. (6 mm) thick.

INSTRUCTIONS

1. Place the metal flat on the table and tack weld both ends together.
2. Two or three additional tack welds can be made along the joint as needed.
3. Starting at one end, make a uniform weld along the joint. Add filler metal as required to make a uniform weld.
4. Repeat the process using all thicknesses of metal until you can consistently make the weld visually defect-free.
5. Turn off the welding machine, shielding gas and clean up your work area when you are finished welding.

Comments

PRACTICE 16-7

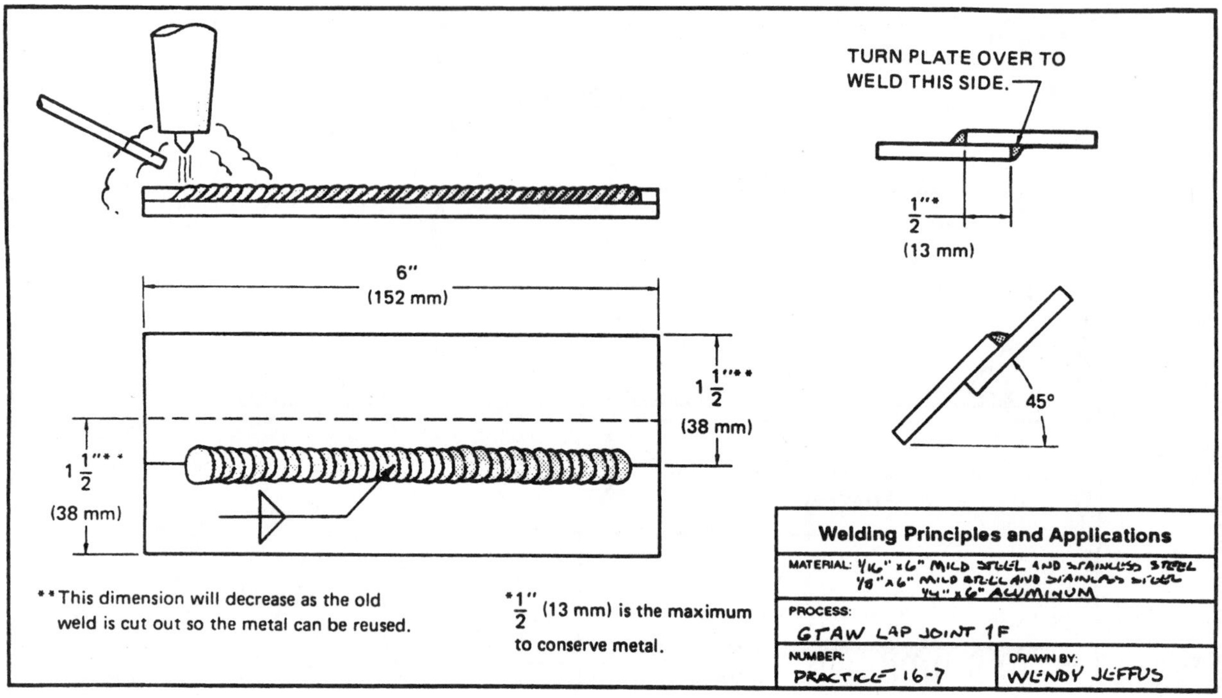

OBJECTIVE: After completing this practice, you should be able to weld lap joints on carbon steel, stainless steel, and aluminum in the 1F position using the GTAW process.

EQUIPMENT AND MATERIAL NEEDED FOR THIS PRACTICE

1. A properly set up and adjusted GTA welding machine
2. Proper safety protection
3. Filler rods 36 in. (0.9 m) long x 1/16 in. (1.6 mm), 3/32 in. (2.4 mm), and 1/8 in. (3 mm) in diameter
4. One or more pieces of mild steel, stainless steel, and aluminum, 6 in. (152 mm) long x 1/16 in. (2 mm) and 1/8 in. (3 mm) thick, and aluminum plate 1/4 in. (6 mm) thick.

INSTRUCTIONS

1. Place the two pieces of metal flat on the table with an overlap of 1/4 in. (6 mm) to 3/8 in. (10 mm).
2. Hold the pieces of metal tightly together and tack weld them.
3. Starting at one end, make a uniform fillet weld along the joint.
4. Both sides of the joint should be welded.
5. Repeat the process using all thicknesses of metal until you can consistently make the weld visually defect-free.
6. Turn off the welding machine, shielding gas and clean up your work area when you are finished welding.

Comment

____

PRACTICE 16-8

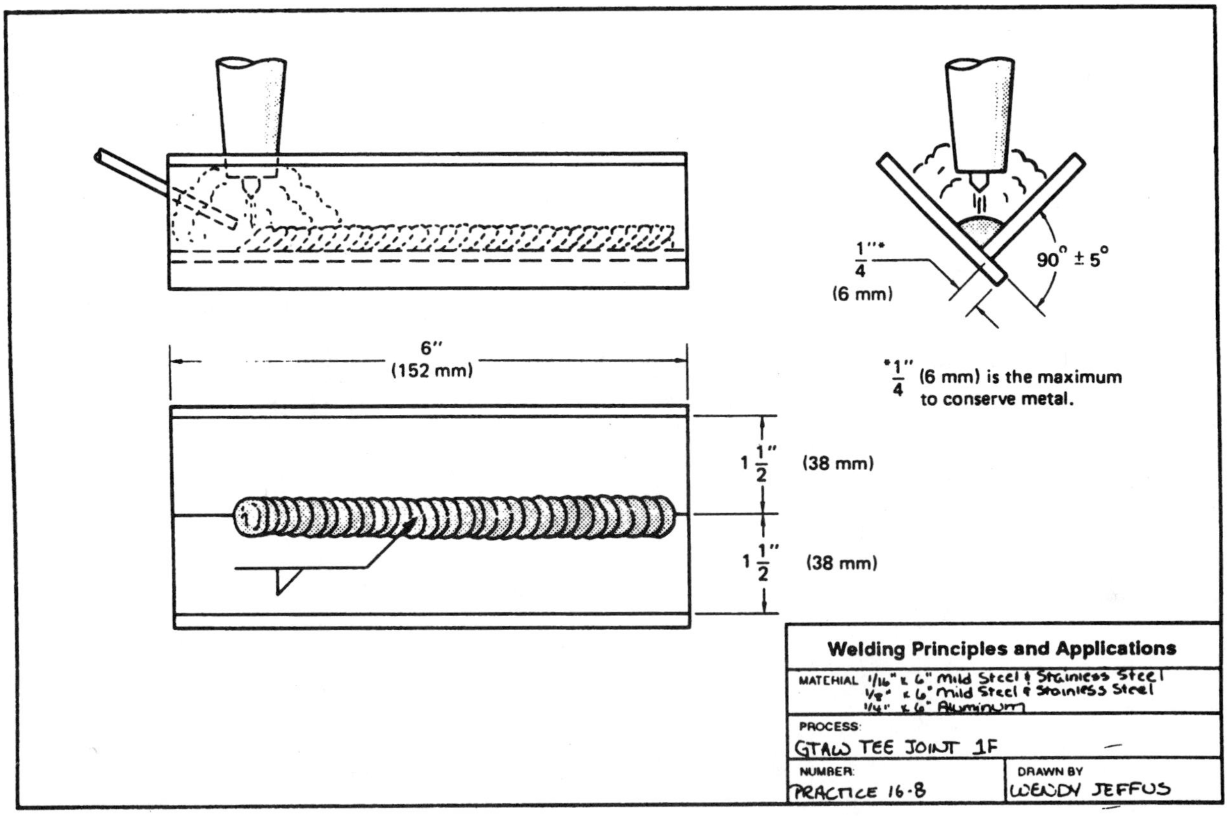

OBJECTIVE: After completing this practice, you should be able to weld tee joints on carbon steel, stainless steel, and aluminum in the 1F position using the GTAW process.

EQUIPMENT AND MATERIAL NEEDED FOR THIS PRACTICE

1. A properly set up and adjusted GTA welding machine
2. Proper safety protection
3. Filler rods 36 in. (0.9 m) long x 1/16 in. (1.6 mm), 3/32 in. (2.4 mm), and 1/8 in. (3 mm) in diameter
4. One or more pieces of mild steel, stainless steel, and aluminum, 6 in. (152 mm) long x 1/16 in. (2 mm) and 1/8 in. (3 mm) thick, and aluminum plate 1/4 in. (6 mm) thick.

INSTRUCTIONS

1. Place one of the pieces of metal flat on the table and hold or brace the other piece of metal vertically on it.
2. Tack weld both ends of the plates together.
3. Set up the plates in the flat position and add two or three more tack welds to the joint as required.
4. On the metal that is 1/16 in. (1.5 mm) thick, it may not be possible to weld both sides, but on the thicker material a fillet weld can usually be made on both sides. The exception to this is if carbide precipitation occurs on the stainless steel during welding.
5. Starting at one end, make a uniform weld, adding filler metal as needed.
6. Repeat the process using all thicknesses of metal until you can consistently make the weld visually defect-free.

7. Turn off the welding machine, shielding gas and clean up your work area when you are finished welding.

Comments

PRACTICE 16-9

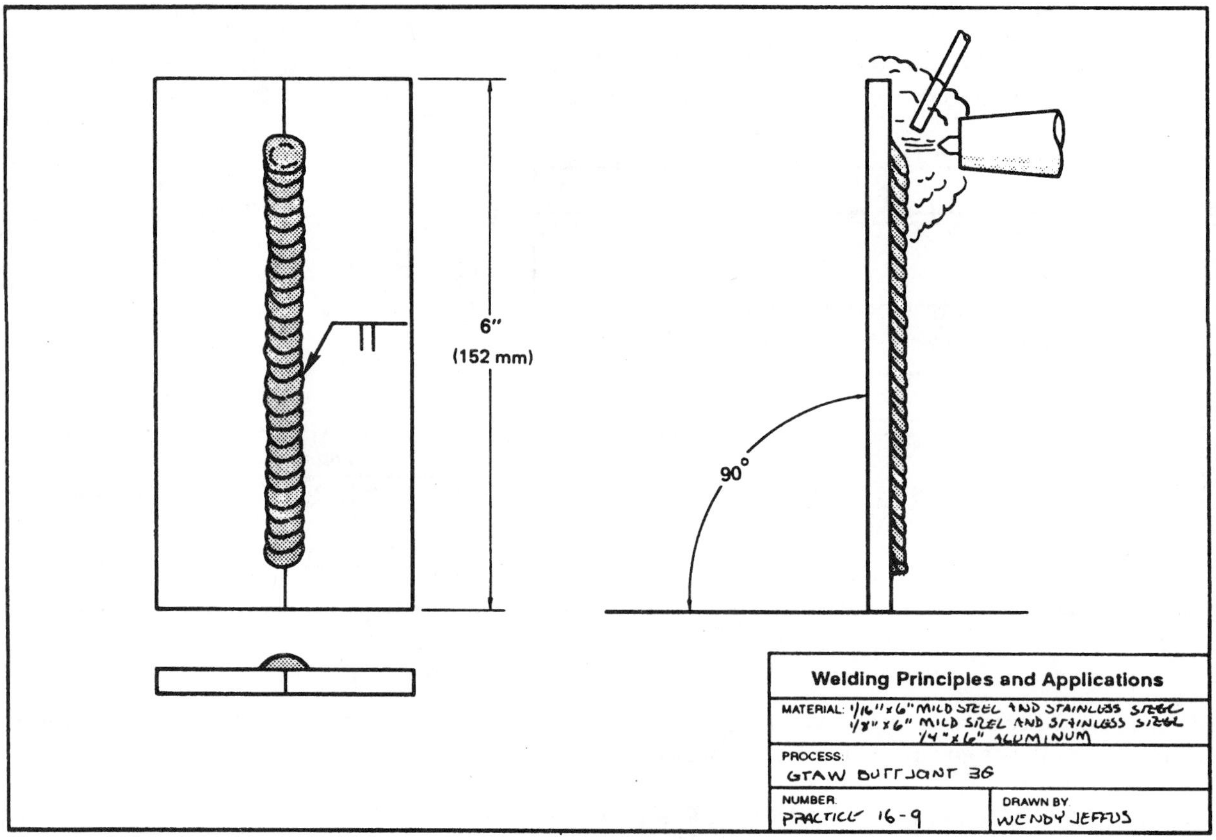

OBJECTIVE: After completing this practice, you should be able to make stringer beads on carbon steel, stainless steel, and aluminum in the 3G position using the GTAW process.

EQUIPMENT AND MATERIAL NEEDED FOR THIS PRACTICE

1. A properly set up and adjusted GTA welding machine
2. Proper safety protection
3. Filler rods 36 in. (0.9 m) long x 1/16 in. (1.6 mm), 3/32 in. (2.4 mm), and 1/8 in. (3 mm) in diameter
4. One or more pieces of mild steel, stainless steel, and aluminum, 6 in. (152 mm) long x 1/16 in. (2 mm) and 1/8 in. (3 mm) thick, and aluminum plate 1/4 in. (6 mm) thick.

INSTRUCTIONS

1. Starting at the bottom and welding in an upward direction, add the filler metal at the top edge of the weld pool and move the torch in a circle or "C" pattern.
2. If the weld pool size starts to increase, the "C" pattern can be increased in length or the power can be decreased.
3. Watch the weld pool and establish a rhythm of torch movement and addition of rod to keep the weld uniform.

4. Gradually increase the angle as you develop skill until the weld is being made in the vertical up position.
5. Repeat the process using all thicknesses of metal until you can consistently make the weld visually defect-free.
6. Turn off the welding machine, shielding gas and clean up your work area when you are finished welding.

Comments

PRACTICE 16-10

OBJECTIVE: After completing this practice, you should be able to make butt joints on carbon steel, stainless steel, and aluminum in a 45° vertical angle position using the GTAW process.

EQUIPMENT AND MATERIAL NEEDED FOR THIS PRACTICE

1. A properly set up and adjusted GTA welding machine
2. Proper safety protection
3. Filler rods 36 in. (0.9 m) long x 1/16 in. (1.6 mm), 3/32 in. (2.4 mm), and 1/8 in. (3 mm) in diameter
4. One or more pieces of mild steel, stainless steel, and aluminum, 6 in. (152 mm) long x 1/16 in. (2 mm) and 1/8 in. (3 mm) thick, and aluminum plate 1/4 in. (6 mm) thick.

INSTRUCTIONS

1. Tack weld the plates together and then place the plates on the welding table at a 45° vertical angle. Start the weld at the bottom and weld in an upward direction.
2. If the weld pool size starts to increase, the "C" pattern can be increased in length or the power can be decreased.
3. Watch the weld pool and establish a rhythm of torch movement and addition of rod to keep the weld uniform.
4. Repeat the process using all thicknesses of metal until you can consistently make the weld visually defect-free.
5. Turn off the welding machine, shielding gas and clean up your work area when you are finished welding.

Comments

PRACTICE 16-11

OBJECTIVE: After completing this practice, you should be able to make butt joints on carbon steel, stainless steel, and aluminum in the 3G position using GTAW process.

EQUIPMENT AND MATERIAL NEEDED FOR THIS PRACTICE

1. A properly set up and adjusted GTA welding machine
2. Proper safety protection
3. Filler rods 36 in. (0.9 m) long x 1/16 in. (1.6 mm), 3/32 in. (2.4 mm), and 1/8 in. (3 mm) in diameter
4. One or more pieces of mild steel, stainless steel, and aluminum, 6 in. (152 mm) long x 1/16 in. (2 mm) and 1/8 in. (3 mm) thick, and aluminum plate 1/4 in. (6 mm) thick.

INSTRUCTIONS

1. Tack weld the plates together and then place the plates on the welding table at a 45° vertical angle. Start the weld at the bottom and weld in an upward direction.
2. If the weld pool size starts to increase, the "C" pattern can be increased in length or the power can be decreased.

3. Watch the weld pool and establish a rhythm of torch movement and addition of rod to keep the weld uniform.
4. As you develop skill, continue increasing the angle until the weld is being made in the vertical up position.
5. Repeat the process using all thicknesses of metal until you can consistently make the weld visually defect-free.
6. Turn off the welding machine, shielding gas and clean up your work area when you are finished welding.

Comments

PRACTICE 16-12

Name______________________________ Date ____________

Base Metal Type ______________ Thickness ______ Filler Di. ________ Joint ____________

Class ____________________ Instructor ____________________ Grade ____________

OBJECTIVE: After completing this practice, you should be able to make tee joints on carbon steel, stainless steel, and aluminum in the 3F position using the GTAW process.

EQUIPMENT AND MATERIAL NEEDED FOR THIS PRACTICE

1. A properly set up and adjusted GTA welding machine
2. Proper safety protection (welding hood, safety glasses, pliers, gloves, long sleeve shirt, long pants and leather boots or shoes). Refer to Chapter 2 in the text for more specific safety information.
3. Two or more pieces of mild steel, 6 in. (152 mm) long and 16 gauge and 1/8 in. (3 mm) thick.

INSTRUCTIONS

1. After tack welding the plates together, start the weld at the bottom and weld in an upward direction. The edge of the side plate will heat up more quickly than the back plate. This rapid heating often leads to undercutting along this edge of the weld. Gradually increase the plate angle after each weld as you develop your skill. Increase the angle until the weld is being made in the vertical up position.
2. To control undercutting, keep the arc on the back plate and add the filler metal to the weld pool near the side plate.
3. Repeat the process using all thicknesses of metal until you can consistently make the weld visually defect-free.
4. Turn off the welding machine, shielding gas and clean up your work area when you are finished welding.

Comments

____

PRACTICE 16-13

OBJECTIVE: After completing this practice, you should be able to make stringer beads on carbon steel, stainless steel, and aluminum in the 2G position using the GTAW process.

EQUIPMENT AND MATERIAL NEEDED FOR THIS PRACTICE

1. A properly set up and adjusted GTA welding machine
2. Proper safety protection (welding hood, safety glasses, pliers, gloves, long sleeve shirt, long pants and leather boots or shoes). Refer to Chapter 2 in the text for more specific safety information.
3. Two or more pieces of mild steel, 6 in. (152 mm) long and 16 gauge and 1/8 in. (3 mm) thick.

INSTRUCTIONS

1. Gradually increase the plate angle as you develop your skill until the weld is being made in the horizontal position on a vertical plate.
2. Add the filler metal along the top leading edge of the weld pool. Surface tension will help hold the weld pool on the top if the bead is not too large. The weld should be uniform in width and reinforcement.
3. Repeat the process using all thicknesses of metal until you can consistently make the weld visually defect-free.
4. Turn off the welding machine, shielding gas and clean up your work area when you are finished welding.

Comments

PRACTICE 16-14

OBJECTIVE: After completing this practice, you should be able to weld butt joints on carbon steel, stainless steel and aluminum in the 2G position using the GTAW process.

EQUIPMENT AND MATERIAL NEEDED FOR THIS PRACTICE

1. A properly set up and adjusted GTA welding machine
2. Proper safety protection (welding hood, safety glasses, pliers, gloves, long sleeve shirt, long pants and leather boots or shoes). Refer to Chapter 2 in the text for more specific safety information.
3. Two or more pieces of mild steel, 6 in. (152 mm) long and 16 gauge and 1/8 in. (3 mm) thick.

INSTRUCTIONS

1. Tack weld the plates together, then place them in the 2G position on the welding table.
2. Add the filler metal to the top plate and keep the bead size small so it will be uniform.
3. Repeat the process using all thicknesses of metal until you can consistently make the weld visually defect-free.
4. Turn off the welding machine, shielding gas and clean up your work area when you are finished welding.

Comments

PRACTICE 16-15

OBJECTIVE: After completing this practice, you should be able to weld lap joints on carbon steel, stainless steel, and aluminum in the 2F position using the GTAW process.

EQUIPMENT AND MATERIAL NEEDED FOR THIS PRACTICE

1. A properly set up and adjusted GTA welding machine
2. Proper safety protection (welding hood, safety glasses, pliers, gloves, long sleeve shirt, long pants and leather boots or shoes). Refer to Chapter 2 in the text for more specific safety information.
3. Two or more pieces of mild steel, 6 in. (152 mm) long and 16 gauge and 1/8 in. (3 mm) thick.

INSTRUCTIONS

1. After tack welding the plates together, place them on the welding table in the 2F position.
2. Start the weld at one end. The bottom plate will act as a shelf to support the molten weld pool.
3. Add the filler metal along the top edge of the weld pool to help control undercutting.
4. Repeat the process using all thicknesses of metal until you can consistently make the weld visually defect-free.
5. Turn off the welding machine, shielding gas and clean up your work area when you are finished welding.

Comments

PRACTICE 16-16

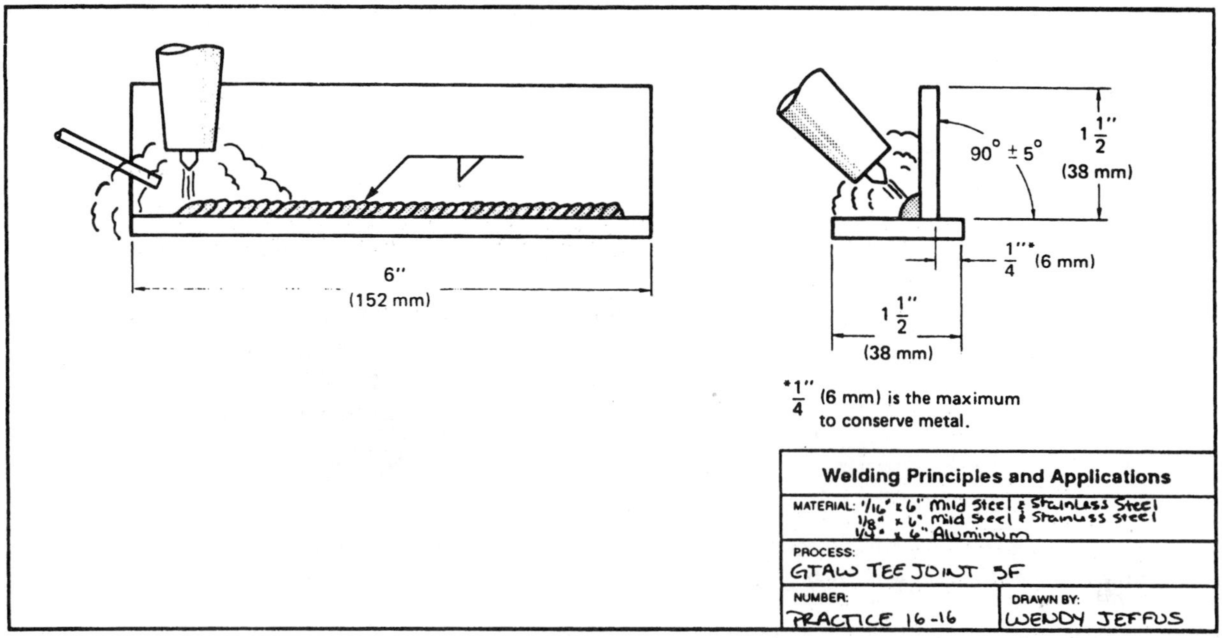

OBJECTIVE: After completing this practice, you should be able to weld tee joints on carbon steel, stainless steel, and aluminum in the 2F position using the GTAW process.

EQUIPMENT AND MATERIAL NEEDED FOR THIS PRACTICE

1. A properly set up and adjusted GTA welding machine
2. Proper safety protection (welding hood, safety glasses, pliers, gloves, long sleeve shirt, long pants and leather boots or shoes). Refer to Chapter 2 in the text for more specific safety information.
3. Two or more pieces of mild steel, 6 in. (152 mm) long and 16 gauge and 1/8 in. (3 mm) thick.

INSTRUCTIONS

1. After tack welding the plates together, place the plates in the 2F position on the welding table.
2. Start the weld at one end; the bottom plate will act as a shelf to support the molten weld pool.
3. Add the filler metal along the top leading edge of the weld pool. This will help control undercut.
4. Repeat the process using all thicknesses of metal until you can consistently make the weld visually defect-free.
5. Turn off the welding machine, shielding gas and clean up your work area when you are finished welding.

Comments

____

PRACTICE 16-17

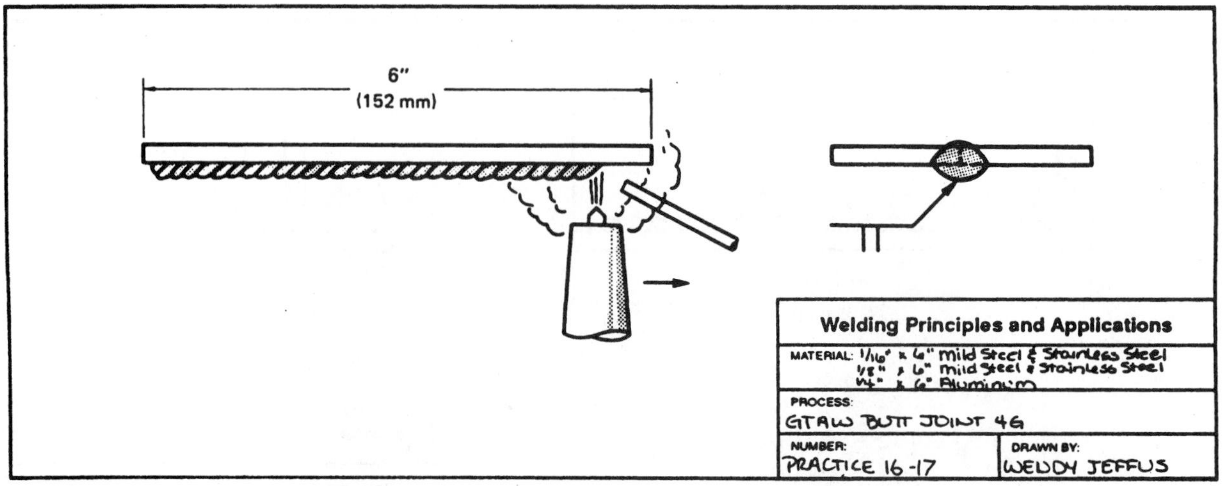

OBJECTIVE: After completing this practice, you should be able to make stringer beads on carbon steel, stainless steel, and aluminum in the 4G position using the GTAW process.

EQUIPMENT AND MATERIAL NEEDED FOR THIS PRACTICE

1. A properly set up and adjusted GTA welding machine
2. Proper safety protection (welding hood, safety glasses, pliers, gloves, long sleeve shirt, long pants and leather boots or shoes). Refer to Chapter 2 in the text for more specific safety information.
3. Two or more pieces of mild steel, 6 in. (152 mm) long and 16 gauge and 1/8 in. (3 mm) thick.

INSTRUCTIONS

1. Secure the plates in the 4G position. The surface tension on the molten metal will hold the welding bead on the plate providing that it is not too large.
2. Add the filler metal along the leading edge of the weld pool. A wide weld with little buildup will be easier to control and less likely to undercut along the edge.
3. Repeat the process using all thicknesses of metal until you can consistently make the weld visually defect-free.
4. Turn off the welding machine, shielding gas and clean up your work area when you are finished welding.

Comments

PRACTICE 16-18

OBJECTIVE: After completing this practice, you should be able to weld lap joints on carbon steel, stainless steel, and aluminum in the 4F position using the GTAW process

EQUIPMENT AND MATERIAL NEEDED FOR THIS PRACTICE

1. A properly set up and adjusted GTA welding machine
2. Proper safety protection (welding hood, safety glasses, pliers, gloves, long sleeve shirt, long pants and leather boots or shoes). Refer to Chapter 2 in the text for more specific safety information.
3. Two or more pieces of mild steel, 6 in. (152 mm) long and 16 gauge and 1/8 in. (3 mm) thick.

INSTRUCTIONS

1. Tack weld the plates together and secure them in the 4F position.
2. The major concentration of heat and filler metal should be on the top plate. Gravity and an occasional sweep of the torch along the bottom plate will pull the weld pool down. Undercutting along the top edge of the weld can be controlled by putting most of the filler metal along the top edge. The completed weld should be uniform and free from defects.
3. Repeat the process using all thicknesses of metal until you can consistently make the weld visually defect-free.
4. Turn off the welding machine, shielding gas and clean up your work area when you are finished welding.

Comments

____

CHAPTER 16: GAS TUNGSTEN ARC WELDING OF PLATE QUIZ

Name____ Date ____________

Class ________________ Instructor ________________ Grade ____________

A. MATCHING

In the space provided to the left, write the letter from column B that best answers the question or completes the statement in column A.

1. Match the following filler metals to the correct base metals.

	BASE METAL	FILLER ROD
____	a. 316	1. ER309
____	b. 1030	2. ER316L
____	c. 304	3. RG60
____	d. 1010	4. ER70S-3
____	e. 309	5. ER308

2. Match the following.

____	a. The current used to weld aluminum	1. chill plate
____	b. The current used to weld stainless steel	2. tan
____	c. A thick piece of metal used to absorb heat	3. AC-HF
____	d. The surface color of steel at 450°F	4. purple
____	e. The surface color of steel at 575°F	5. DCSP

B. SHORT ANSWER

Write a brief answer, in the space provided, that will answer the question or complete the statement.

3. List seven factors that determine the proper preflow and postflow times required to protect the tungsten and the weld.

   a.____

   b. ____

   c.____

   d. ____

   e.____

   f.____

   g. ____

4. Name four chemicals that can be used for chemical cleaning of metal for the GTAW process.

   a.____

   b. ____

   c.____

   d. ____

5. List five methods of mechanically cleaning metal for the GTAW process.

   a. ______

   b. ______

   c. ______

   d. ______

   e. ______

C. TRUE-FALSE

Write the letter T in the space to the left if the statement is true and the letter F if the statement is false.

_____ 6. The maximum flow rates of a shielding gas must never be exceeded.

_____ 7. The tungsten will become contaminated if the cup is rested against the plate.

_____ 8. The lowest possible gas flow rates and the shortest preflow or postflow time can help reduce the cost of welding by saving the expensive shielding gas.

_____ 9. If the welder's hands or gloves are not clean, the metal or filler rod may become contaminated when GTA welding aluminum.

_____ 10. Steel will turn the color blue at 600°F.

_____ 11. When GTA welding aluminum, cleanliness is no more of a problem than any other metal.

_____ 12. DCRP is used to GTA weld mild steel and stainless steel.

_____ 13. The most common sign that there is a problem with a stainless steel weld is the bead is dark in color after welding.

_____ 14. The high-frequency switch must be in the off position when GTA welding aluminum.

_____ 15. Excessive flow rates can cause contamination when GTA welding.

D. ESSAY

Provide complete answers for all of the following questions.

16. Why is it necessary for the welder to experiment in order to find the minimum machine amperage settings?

______

______

17. What effect does torch angle have on the shielding gas coverage?

______

______

18. What factor affects the shielding gas coverage of a weld?

______

______

19. When should the tungsten be cleaned?

______

______

20. What purpose does a prepurge time serve?

______

______

21. From the experiments performed in this chapter, what effect did the cup size have on gas coverage?

____

____

22. How are mild steel, stainless steel, and aluminum cleaned before GTA welding?

____

____

23. Why must metals be cleaned before GTA welding?

____

____

24. How can weld uniformity be maintained by the welder?

____

____

25. Where is the heat and metal concentrated when making a vertical (3F) tee joint?

____

____

26. Define the following terms: gas coverage pattern, oxide colors, and chill plate.

____

____

CHAPTER 17: GAS TUNGSTEN ARC WELDING OF PIPE

PRACTICE 17-1

Name____________________________________ Date ____________

Pipe Diameter______________ Filler Metal Type ______________ Diameter____________

Class __________________ Instructor __________________ Grade ____________

OBJECTIVE: After completing this practice, you should be able to properly tack weld 3-inch (76 mm) to 10-inch (254 mm) diameter schedule 40 carbon steel pipe using the GTAW process.

EQUIPMENT AND MATERIALS NEEDED FOR THIS PRACTICE

1. A properly set up and adjusted GTA welding machine
2. Proper safety protection (welding hood, safety glasses, wire brush, leather gloves, pliers, long sleeve shirt, long pants and leather boots or shoes). Refer to Chapter 2 in the text for more specific safety information.
3. Two or more pieces of 3-in. (76 mm) to 10-in. (254 mm) diameter schedule 40 mild steel pipe, prepared with single V-grooved joints
4. Several filler rods having 1/16-in. (1.6 mm), 3/32-in. (2.4 mm), and 1/8-in. (3 mm) diameters

INSTRUCTIONS

1. Bend the rods with the 1/16-in. (1.6 mm) and 3/32-in. (2.4 mm) diameters into a U-shape. These rods will be used to set the desired root opening.
2. Lay the pipe in an angle iron cradle. Slide the ends together so that the desired diameter wire is held between the ends.
3. Hold the torch nozzle against the beveled sides of the groove. The torch should be nearly parallel with the pipe.
4. Bring the filler rod end in close and rest it on the joint just ahead of the torch.
5. Lower your helmet and switch on the welding current by using the foot or hand control. Slowly straighten the torch so that the tungsten electrode is brought closer to the groove. This pivoting of the torch around the nozzle will keep the torch aligned with the joint and help prevent arc starts outside of the joint. When the tungsten electrode is close enough, an arc will be established.
6. Increase the current by depressing the foot or hand control until a molten weld pool is established on both root faces.
7. Dip the welding rod into the molten weld pool as the torch is pivoted from side to side.
8. Slowly move ahead and repeat this step until you have made a tack weld approximately 1/2 in. (13 mm) long. At the end of the tack weld, slowly reduce the current and fill the weld crater. If the tack weld crater is properly filled and it does not crack, grinding may not be required.
9. Roll the pipe 180° to the opposite side. Check the root opening and adjust the opening if needed. Make a tack weld 1/2 in. (13 mm) long.
10. Roll the pipe 90° to a spot halfway between the first two tack welds. Check and adjust the root opening if needed. Make a tack weld.
11. Roll the pipe 180° to the opposite side and make a tack weld halfway between the first two tack welds.
12. The completed joint should have four tack welds evenly spaced around the pipe (at 90° intervals). The root surfaces of the tack welds should be flat or slightly convex. The tack welds should have complete fusion into the base metal with no overlap at the start.
13. Continue making tack welds until this procedure is mastered.

14. Turn off the welding machine, shielding gas and clean up your work area when you are finished welding.

Comments

PRACTICE 17-2

OBJECTIVE: After completing this practice, you should be able to weld root welds on carbon steel pipe with single V-groove joints using the GTAW process in the 1G position.

EQUIPMENT AND MATERIALS NEEDED FOR THIS PRACTICE

1. A properly set up and adjusted GTA welding machine
2. Proper safety protection (welding hood, safety glasses, wire brush, leather gloves, pliers, long sleeve shirt, long pants and leather boots or shoes). Refer to Chapter 2 in the text for more specific safety information.
3. Two or more pieces of 3-in. (76 mm) to 10-in. (254 mm) diameter schedule 40 mild steel pipe, prepared with single V-grooved joints
4. Several filler rods having 1/16-in. (1.6 mm), 3/32-in. (2.4 mm), and 1/8-in. (3 mm) diameters

INSTRUCTIONS

1. Place the pipe securely in an angle iron vee block. Using the same procedure as practiced for the tack welds, place the nozzle against the beveled sides of the joint with the torch at a steep angle.
2. Start the weld near the 3 o'clock position and weld toward the 12 o'clock position. Stop welding just past the 12 o'clock position and roll the pipe. Starting the weld above the 3 o'clock position is easier and starting the weld below this position is harder. Brace yourself against the pipe and try moving through the length of the weld to determine if you have full freedom of movement.
3. Hold the welding rod close to the pipe so it is protected by the shielding gas, thus preventing air from being drawn into the inert gas around the weld. The end of the rod must be far enough away from the starting point so it will not be melted immediately by the arc. However, it must be close enough so that it can be seen by the light of the arc.
4. When you are comfortable and ready to start, lower your helmet. Switch on the welding current by depressing the foot or hand control. Slowly pivot the torch until the arc starts. Increase the current to establish molten weld pools on both sides of the root face. Add the welding rod to the molten weld pool as the torch is rocked from side to side and moved slowly ahead. The side-to-side motion can be used to walk the nozzle along the groove. The walking of the nozzle will ensure complete fusion in both root faces and help make a very uniform weld. When walking the nozzle along the groove, the tip of the torch cap will make a figure-8 motion.

   NOTE: **For the best results with nozzle walking you should use a high temperature ceramic nozzle such as silicon nitride.**

   Nozzle walking the torch along a groove can be practiced without welding power so you can see how to move the torch. This technique can be used on most GTA groove welds in pipe or plate.
5. Watch the molten weld pool to make sure that it is balanced between both sides. If the molten weld pool is not balanced, then one side is probably not as hot nor is it penetrating as well.
6. Stop adding filler metal to the molten weld pool when it is within 1/16 in. (2 mm) of the tack weld. At this time the keyhole will be much smaller or completely closed. Continue to rock the torch from side to side as you move ahead. Watch the molten weld pool. It should settle down or sink in when the weld has completely tied itself to the tack weld. Failure to do this will cause incomplete fusion or overlap at the root. If you are crossing a tack weld, carry the molten weld pool across the tack weld without adding filler metal and start adding welding rod at the other end. If you are at the closing end of the weld, slowly decrease the welding current as you add more welding rod to fill the weld crater.

7. After the weld is complete around the pipe, visually check the root for any defects. Repeat this practice as needed until it is mastered.
8. Turn off the welding machine, shielding gas and clean up your work area when you are finished welding.

Comments

PRACTICE 17-3

OBJECTIVE: After completing this practice, you should be able to weld stringer beads on 3-inch (76 mm) to 10-inch (254 mm) diameter schedule 40 carbon steel pipe using the GTAW process in the 1G position.

EQUIPMENT AND MATERIALS NEEDED FOR THIS PRACTICE

1. A properly set up and adjusted GTA welding machine
2. Proper safety protection (welding hood, safety glasses, wire brush, leather gloves, pliers, long sleeve shirt, long pants and leather boots or shoes). Refer to Chapter 2 in the text for more specific safety information.
3. Two or more pieces of 3-in. (76 mm) to 10-in. (254 mm) diameter schedule 40 mild steel pipe, prepared with single V-grooved joints
4. Several filler rods having 1/16-in. (1.6 mm), 3/32-in. (2.4 mm), and 1/8-in. (3 mm) diameters

INSTRUCTIONS

1. Start by cleaning a strip 1 in. (25 mm) wide around the pipe.
2. Brace yourself against the pipe so that you will not sway during the weld. The torch should have a slight upward slope, about 5° to 10° from perpendicular to the pipe. The welding rod should be held so that it enters the molten weld pool from the top center at a right angle to the torch.
3. Start the weld near the 6 o'clock position and weld upward to a point just past the 12 o'clock position. In order to minimize stops and starts, try to make the complete weld without stopping.
4. With the power off and your helmet up, move the torch through the weld to be sure you have full freedom of movement.
5. With the torch held in position so that the electrode is just above the desired starting spot, lower your helmet. Start the welding current by depressing the foot or hand control switch. Establish a weld pool and dip the welding rod in it. Use a straight forward and backward movement with both the torch and rod. Never move farther ahead than the leading edge of the weld pool. Too large a movement will lead to inadequate weld pool coverage by the shielding gas. The short motion is to allow the rod to be dipped into the weld pool without the heat from the arc melting the rod back.

   As the weld progresses from a vertical position to a flat position, the frequency of movement and pause times will change. Generally, the more vertical the weld, the faster the movement and the shorter the pause times. As the weld becomes flatter, the movement is slower and the pause times are longer. In the vertical position, gravity tends to pull the weld toward the back center of the bead. This makes a high crown on the weld with the possibility of undercutting along the edge. Flatter positions cause the weld to be pulled out, resulting in a thinner weld with less apparent root reinforcement.
6. When the weld reaches the 12 o'clock position, stop and roll the pipe. To stop slowly, decrease the current and add welding rod to fill the weld crater. Keep the torch held over the weld until the postpurge stops. This precaution will prevent the air from forming oxides on the hot weld bead.
7. After the weld is complete around the pipe, it should be visually inspected for straightness, uniformity, and defects. Repeat the process until you can consistently make the weld visually defect-free.
8. Turn off the welding machine, shielding gas and clean up your work area when you are finished welding.

Comments

PRACTICE 17-4

OBJECTIVE: After completing this practice, you should be able to make stringer beads on 3-inch (76 mm) to 10-inch (254 mm) diameter schedule 40 carbon steel pipe using the GTAW process in the 2G position.

EQUIPMENT AND MATERIALS NEEDED FOR THIS PRACTICE

1. A properly set up and adjusted GTA welding machine
2. Proper safety protection (welding hood, safety glasses, wire brush, leather gloves, pliers, long sleeve shirt, long pants and leather boots or shoes). Refer to Chapter 2 in the text for more specific safety information.
3. Two or more pieces of 3-in. (76 mm) to 10-in. (254 mm) diameter schedule 40 mild steel pipe, prepared with single V-grooved joints
4. Several filler rods having 1/16-in. (1.6 mm), 3/32-in. (2.4 mm), and 1/8-in. (3 mm) diameters

INSTRUCTIONS

1. You are to make straight stringer beads around an ungrooved pipe in the 2G position.
2. Hold the torch at a 5° angle from horizontal and 5° to 10° from perpendicular to the pipe. This will allow good visibility and simplify the process of adding the rod at the top of the bead.
3. Establish a small weld pool and add filler along the top front edge. Gravity will tend to pull the metal down, especially if the weld pool becomes too large. When the weld pool sags, undercut appears along the top edge of the bead. A slight "J" pattern may help to control weld bead sag by making a small shelf to support the weld pool while it cools.
4. When the weld is completed, visually inspect (VT) it for uniformity and straightness, and for any defects.
5. Repeat the process until you can consistently make the weld visually defect-free.
6. Turn off the welding machine, shielding gas and clean up your work area when you are finished welding.

Comments

CHAPTER 17: GAS TUNGSTEN ARC WELDING OF PIPE QUIZ

Name____ Date ____________

Class ____________________ Instructor ____________________ Grade ____________

Instructions: Carefully read Chapter 17 of the text and answer the following questions.

A. IDENTIFICATION

In the space provided identify the items shown on the illustration.

1. From the illustrations below, which of them is testing the root of the weld?

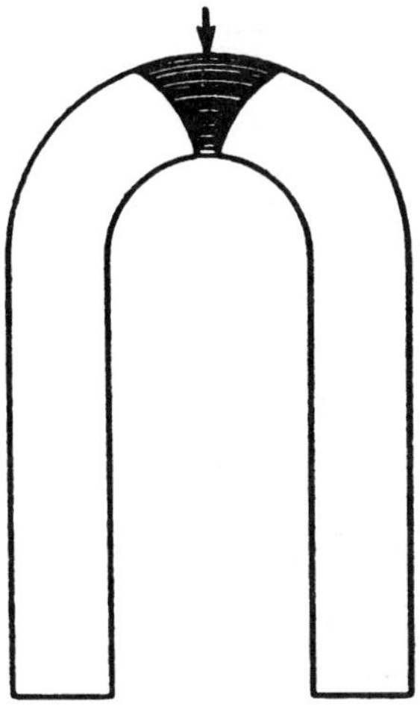

A

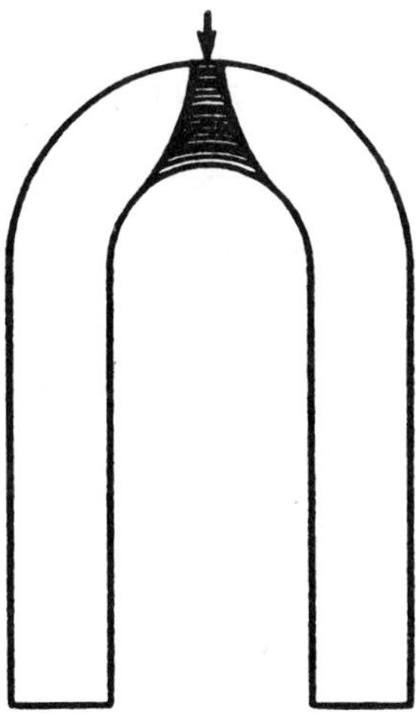

B

A. is testing the root of the weld.
B. is testing the root of the weld.

B. MATCHING

In the space provided to the left, write the letter from column B that best answers the question or completes the statement in column A.

	column A	column B
____	2. What is another name for excessive reinforcement, the excessive buildup of metal on the back side of a weld?	a. class 2
		b. weld root
____	3. What occurs when the back side of the root weld is concave in shape?	c. class 5
____	4. What are preplaced filler metals which are used for the root pass when consistent, high-quality welds are required?	d. class 4
		e. class 1
____	5. What is the distance measured between the original surface of the joint and the deepest point of fusion?	f. root penetration
		g. consumable inserts
____	6. What amount of metal is deposited on the back side of a welded joint?	h. root penetration
____	7. What is the deepest point into the joint of a weld that fusion between the base metal and filler metal occurs?	i. grapes
		j. suck back

_____ 8. What class is a Y-shaped consumable insert?

_____ 9. What class is an A-shaped consumable insert?

_____ 10. What class is a rectangular shaped consumable insert (contoured edges)?

_____ 11. What class is a J-shaped consumable insert?

C. SHORT ANSWER

Write a brief answer, in the space provided, that will answer the question or complete the statement.

12. List three ways of determining excessive reinforcement of a weld.

a. ______________________________

b. ______________________________

c. ______________________________

13. List the four most common root defects.

a. ______________________________

b. ______________________________

c. ______________________________

d. ______________________________

14. List three ways of determining the concavity of a weld.

a. ______________________________

b. ______________________________

c. ______________________________

D. ESSAY

Provide complete answers for all of the following questions.

15. What are the steps in assembling a pipe joint?

____

____

16. Identify each of the following parts of a single-V pipe groove.

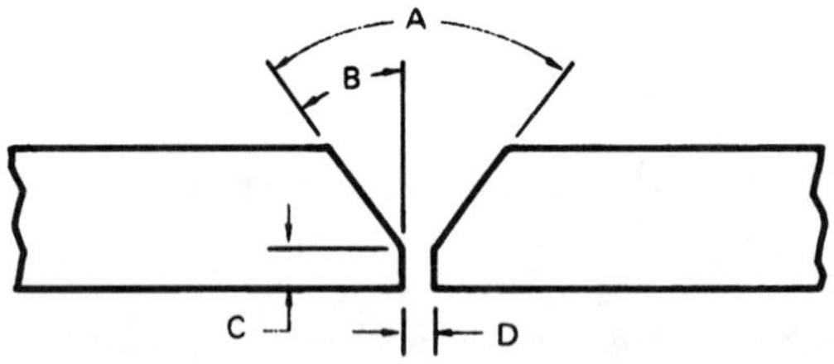

A. ______________________ C. ______________________

B. ______________________ D. ______________________

17. Why are the sizes of both the root and face reinforcements limited?

18. Why does a pipe bevel have a root face?

19. Why are strips cleaned on both sides of a pipe joint?

20. What is incomplete fusion?

21. Explain how to use a backing gas on both large- and small-diameter pipe.

22. Explain the technique of preplacing filler metal.

23. For what purpose are consumable inserts used?

24. Why is the GTA process used to weld pipe?

25. Describe how to use the single V-groove as a guide for the torch.

26. How should a weld bead be ended to prevent problems with weld craters?

27. List the two root defects that can be corrected by using a hot pass.

28. Why should a filler pass not penetrate deeply?

29. Describe three methods of making the cover pass (weld reinforcement).

____

____

30. Define the following terms: consumable inserts, backing gas, keyhole, and penetration.

____

____

CHAPTER 18: WELDING JOINT DESIGN, WELDING SYMBOLS AND FABRICATIONS

PRACTICE 18-1

Name______________________________ Date ______________

Class ______________ Instructor ______________ Grade ______________

OBJECTIVE: After completing this practice, you should be able to lay out square, rectangular and triangular parts to within ±1/16" tolerance in both standard units and S.I. units.

EQUIPMENT AND MATERIALS NEEDED FOR THIS PRACTICE

Piece of metal or paper, soapstone or pencil, tape measure, square.

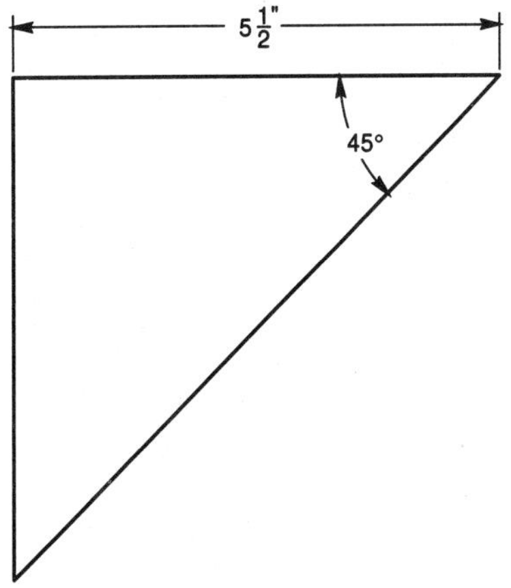

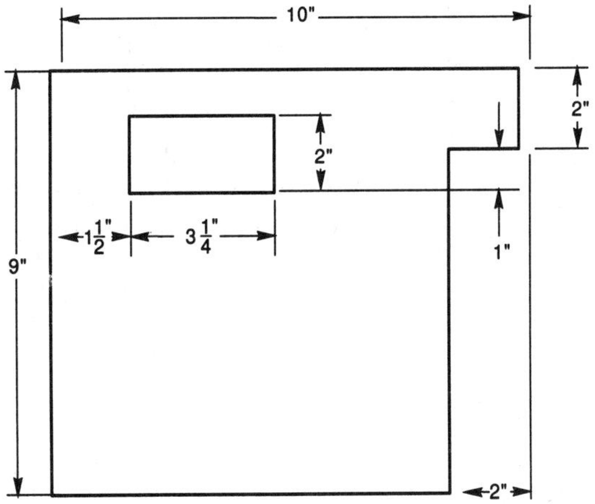

INSTRUCTIONS

1. If you are using a piece of paper draw two lines to form a 90° (right) angle near one corner of the paper, this will be your baseline.
2. Measure along the baseline or edge of the metal and lay out the lengths of each part.
3. Use the square or squared edge of the metal and lay out the widths of each part.
4. Connect the marks you made for each part by drawing a line between the laid out points.
5. Convert the dimensions into S.I. units and repeat the layout process.

PRACTICE 18-2

Name________________________________ Date ____________

Class ______________ Instructor ______________ Grade ____________

OBJECTIVE: After completing this practice, you should be able to lay out circles, arcs and curves to within ±1/16" tolerance in both standard units and S.I. units.

EQUIPMENT AND MATERIALS NEEDED FOR THIS PRACTICE

Piece of metal or paper, soapstone or pencil, tape measure, compass or circle template, square.

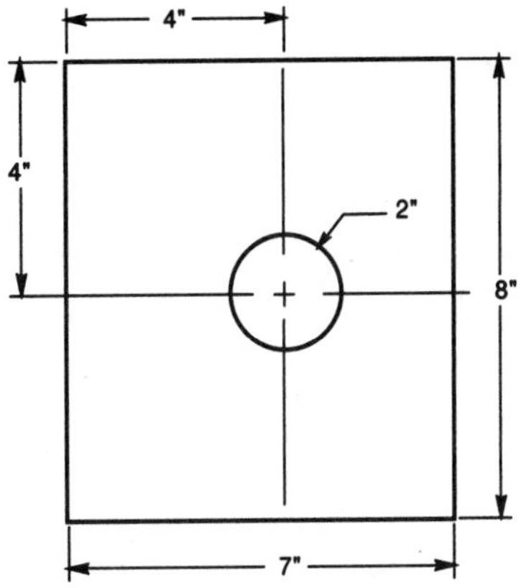

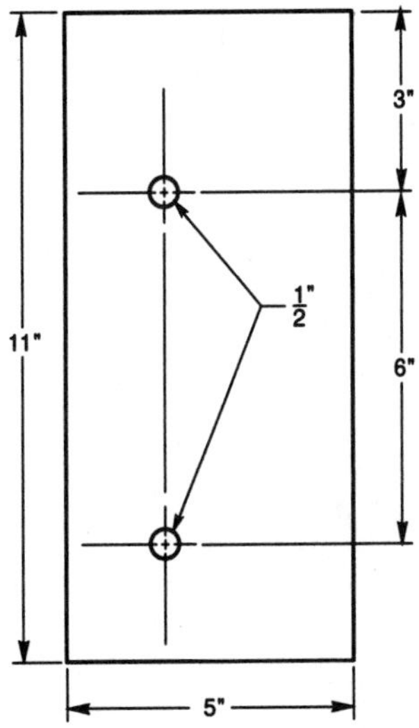

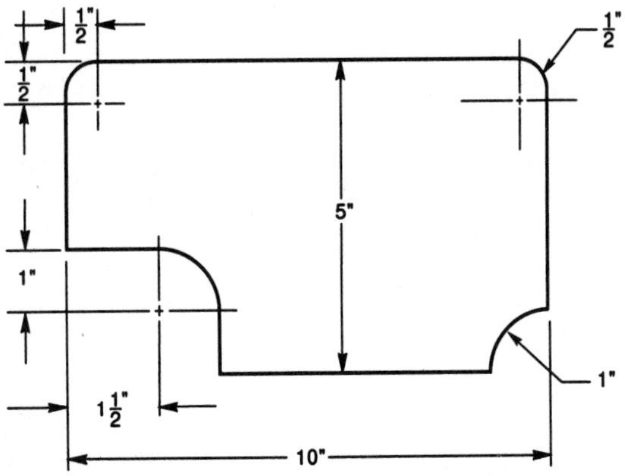

INSTRUCTIONS

1. If you are using a piece of paper draw two lines to form a 90° (right) angle near one corner of the paper, this will be your baseline.
2. Measure along the baseline or edge of the metal and lay out the lengths and centerline for each part.
3. Use the square or squared edge of the metal and lay out the widths and centerline for each part.
4. Connect the marks you made for each part by drawing a line between the laid out points.
5. Use a compass or circle template to lay out the circles and arcs. Be sure that the arcs meet the straight object lines so that they form a smooth tangent.
6. Convert the dimensions into S.I. units and repeat the layout process.

PRACTICE 18-3

Name________________________________ Date ____________

Class ______________ Instructor ______________ Grade ____________

OBJECTIVE: After completing this practice, you should be able to lay out parts so that they are nested together so that the least amount of material will be wasted.

EQUIPMENT AND MATERIALS NEEDED FOR THIS PRACTICE

Metal or paper that is 8 1/2" x 11", soapstone or pencil, tape measure, square.

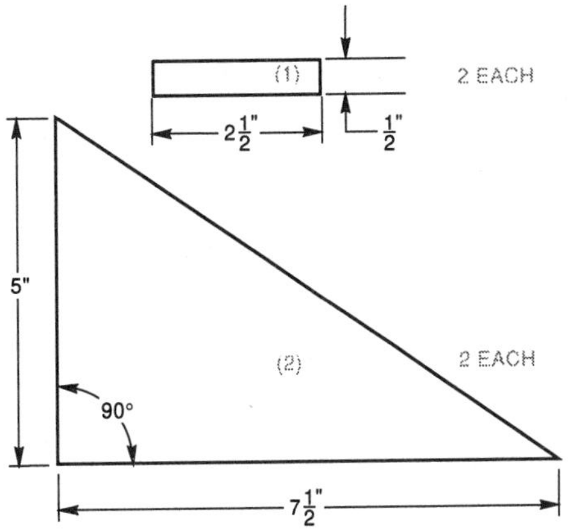

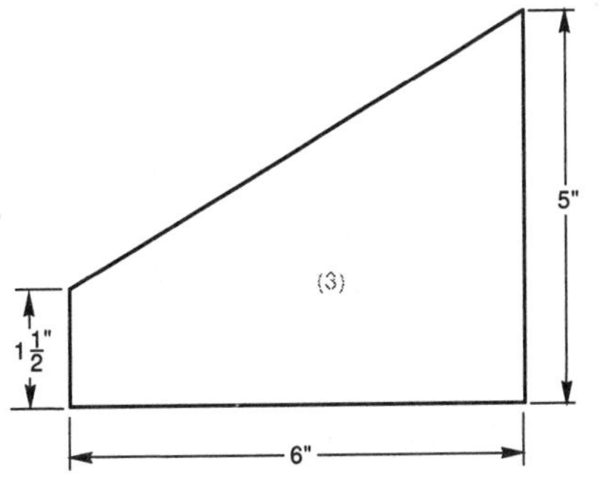

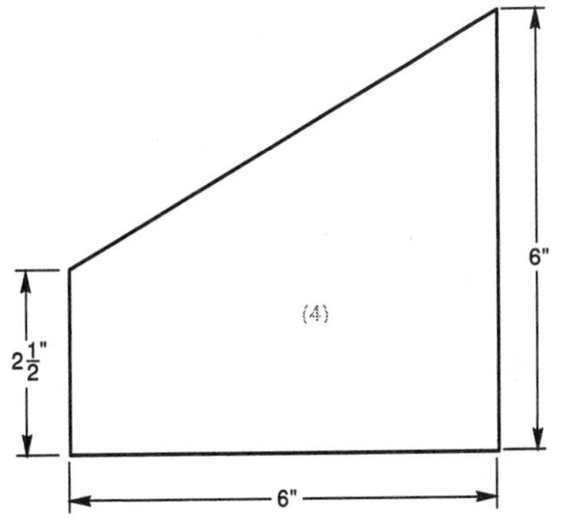

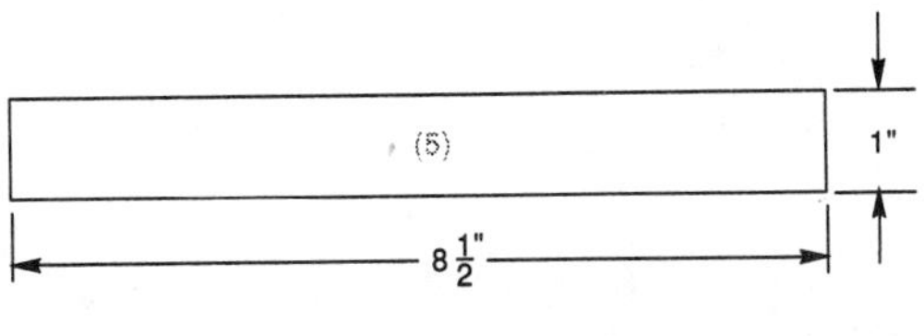

INSTRUCTIONS

1. Sketch the parts using different arrangements until you can arrive at the layout that requires the least space, assume a 0" kerf width.
2. If you are using a piece of paper draw two lines to form a 90° (right) angle near one corner of the paper, this will be your baseline.
3. Measure along the baseline or edge of the metal and lay out the lengths of each part.
4. Use the square or squared edge of the metal and lay out the widths of each part.
5. Connect the marks you made for each part by drawing a line between the laid out points.
6. Convert the dimensions into S.I. units and repeat the layout process.

PRACTICE 18-4

Name____ Date ____________

Class __________________ Instructor __________________ Grade ____________

OBJECTIVE: After completing this practice, you should be able to fill out a bill-of-materials.

EQUIPMENT AND MATERIALS NEEDED FOR THIS PRACTICE

Paper, pencil.

BILL OF MATERIALS				
Part	Number Required	Type of Material	Size Standard Units	SI Units

INSTRUCTIONS

1. Assume that all of the parts are made out of 1/2" (13 mm) low-carbon steel plate and that 1 set is needed.
2. Write the part number in the first left hand column.
3. Write the number of units required in the second column.
4. Write the type of material in the center column.
5. Write the overall dimension of the material in the next column.
6. Convert the standard units into S.I. units and write this in the right hand column.
7. Total the amount of each type of material.

PRACTICE 18-5

OBJECTIVE: After completing this practice, you should be able to lay out a shape allowing space for the material that will be removed in the cut's kerfs.

EQUIPMENT AND MATERIALS NEEDED FOR THIS PRACTICE

Pencil, paper 8 1/2" x 11", measuring tape or rule, square.

INSTRUCTIONS

1. If you are using a piece of paper draw two lines to form a 90° (right) angle near one corner of the paper, this will be your baseline.
2. Measure along the baseline or edge of the metal and lay out the lengths of each part, adding 3/32" to each part for the kerf.
3. Use the square or squared edge of the metal and lay out the widths of each part, adding 3/32" to each part for the kerf.
4. Connect the marks you made for each part by drawing a line between the laid out points.

CHAPTER 18: WELDING JOINT DESIGN, WELDING SYMBOLS AND FABRICATIONS QUIZ

Name______________________________ Date __________

Class ______________ Instructor ______________ Grade __________

Instructions: Carefully read Chapter 18 in the text and complete the following questions.

A. IDENTIFICATION

In the space provided identify the items shown on the illustration.

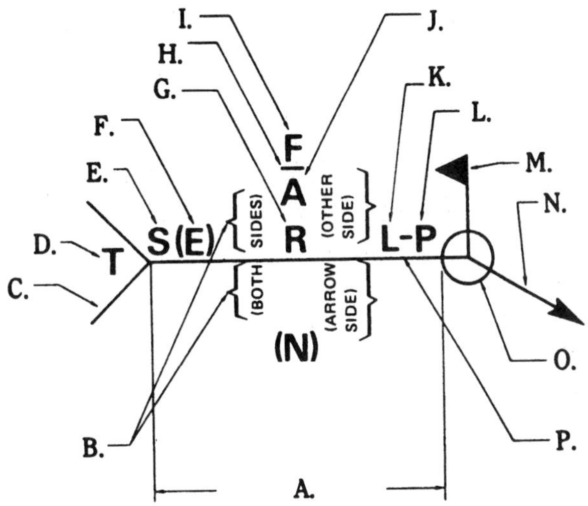

____ 1. Field weld symbol

____ 2. Groove angle; included angle of countersink for plug welds

____ 3. Reference line

____ 4. Basic weld symbol or detail reference

____ 5. Pitch (center to center spacing) of welds

____ 6. Specification, process, or other reference

____ 7. Finish symbol

____ 8. Tail

____ 9. Length of weld

____ 10. Arrow connecting reference line to arrow side member of joint

____ 11. Weld all around symbol

____ 12. Depth of preparation; size or strength for certain welds

____ 13. Elements in this area remain as shown when tail and arrow are reversed

____ 14. Root opening; depth of filling for plug and slot welds

____ 15. Contour symbol

____ 16. Effective throat

B. SHORT ANSWER

Write a brief answer, in the space provided, that will answer the question or complete the statement.

17. Identify the following abbreviations.

    a. MT ______________________________

    b. PT ______________________________

    c. VT ______________________________

    d. NRT ______________________________

    e. PRT ______________________________

    f. UT ______________________________

    g. ET ______________________________

    h. RT ______________________________

    i. RB ______________________________

    j. AU ______________________________

    k. MA ______________________________

    l. TB ______________________________

18. List eight classifications of welds.

    a. ______________________________

    b. ______________________________

    c. ______________________________

    d. ______________________________

    e. ______________________________

    f. ______________________________

    g. ______________________________

    h. ______________________________

19. Pipe welding positions are divided into two groups. What are they?

    a. ______________________________

    b. ______________________________

C. DRAW

In the space provided make a pencil drawing to illustrate the question.

20. From the following weld symbols, draw the welds in their appropriate locations by making a sketch of the joint.

a.

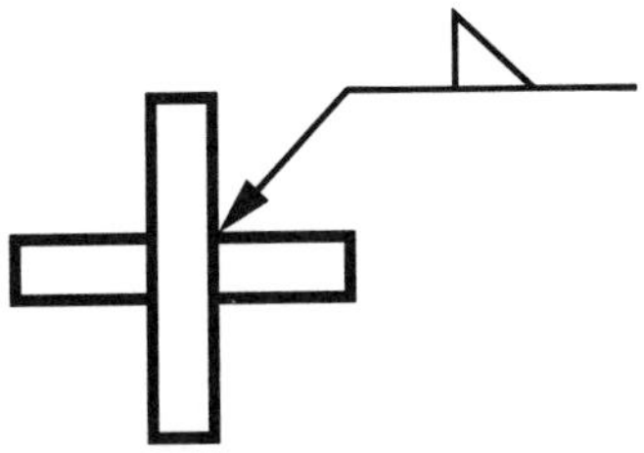

b.

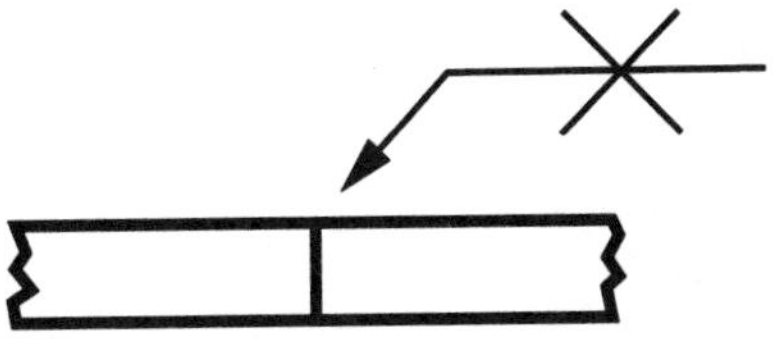

c.

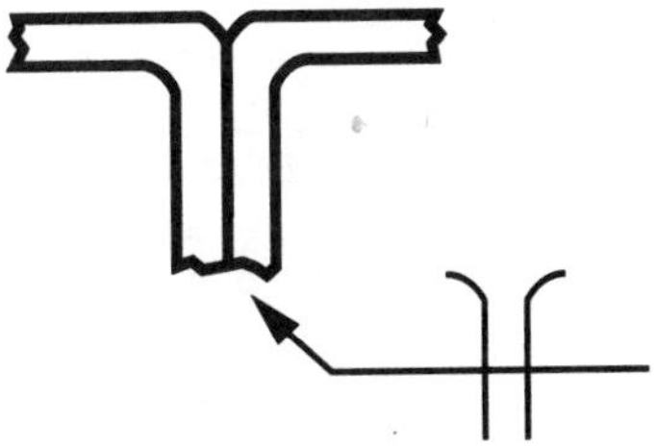

d.

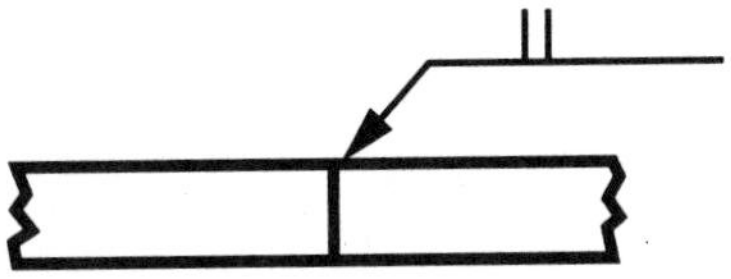

e.

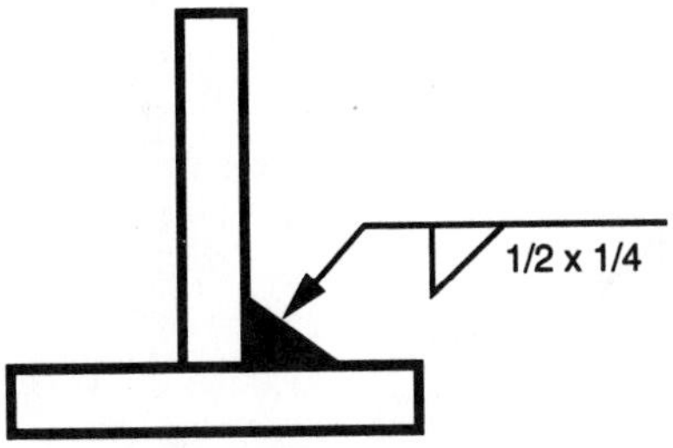

f.

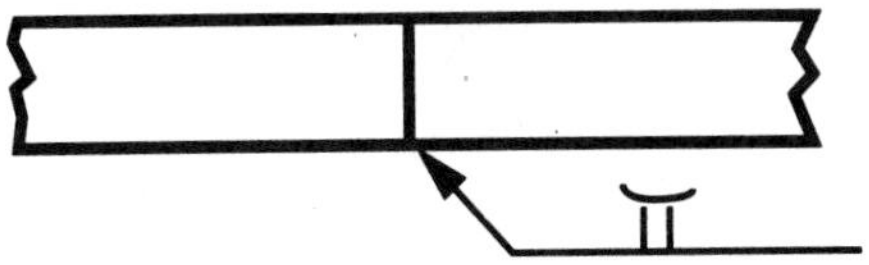

g.

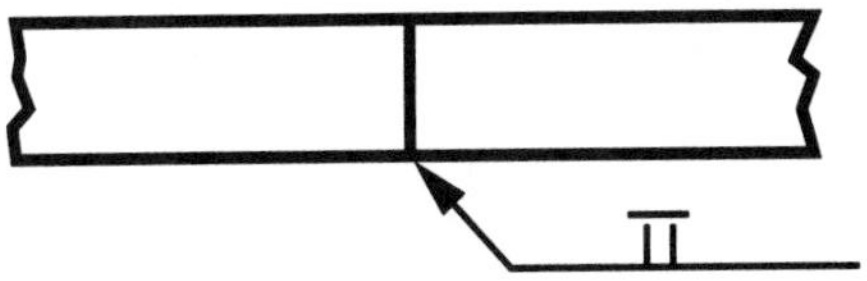

h.

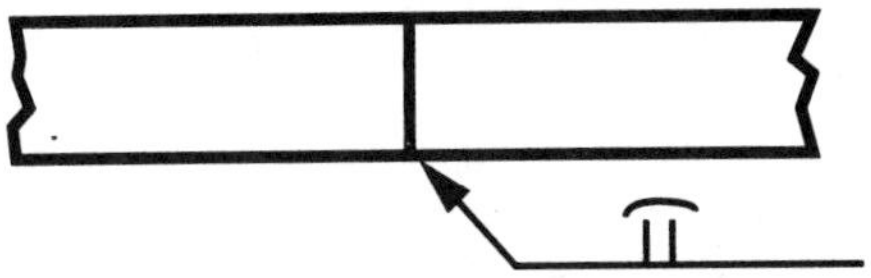

i.

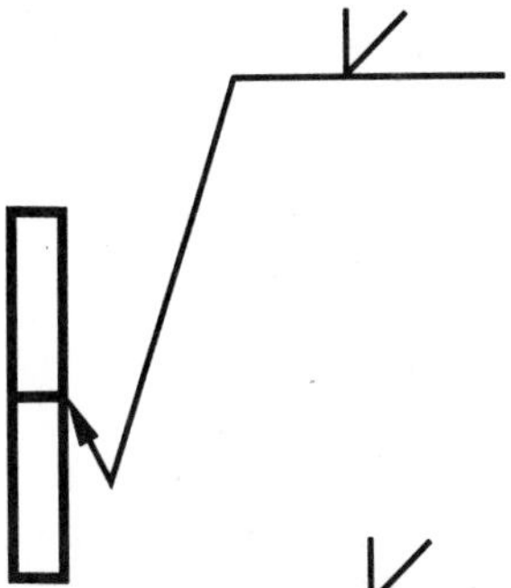

j.

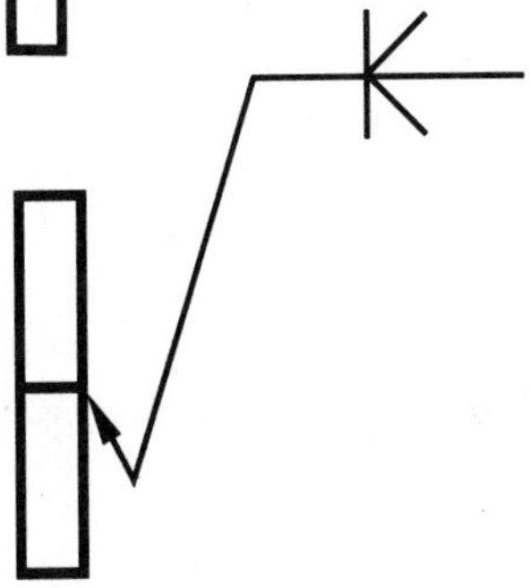

21. Sketch a V-grooved butt joint and label all of the joint's dimensions.

22. Sketch a weld on plates in the 1G and 1F positions.

23. Sketch a weld on plates in the 2G and 2F positions.

24. Sketch a weld on plates in the 3G and 3F positions.

25. Sketch a weld on plates in the 4G and 4F positions.

26. Sketch a weld on a pipe in the 1G position.

27. Sketch a weld on a pipe in the 5G position.

28. Sketch a weld on a pipe in the 2G position.

29. Sketch a weld on a pipe in the 6G position.

30. Sketch a weld on a pipe in the 6GR position

D. LAYOUT

Lay out the following parts on a 8 1/2" x 11" piece of paper. All layouts must be nested and assume a 0" kerf width unless otherwise noted.

31.

PART	NUMBER REQUIRED
1	4
2	1

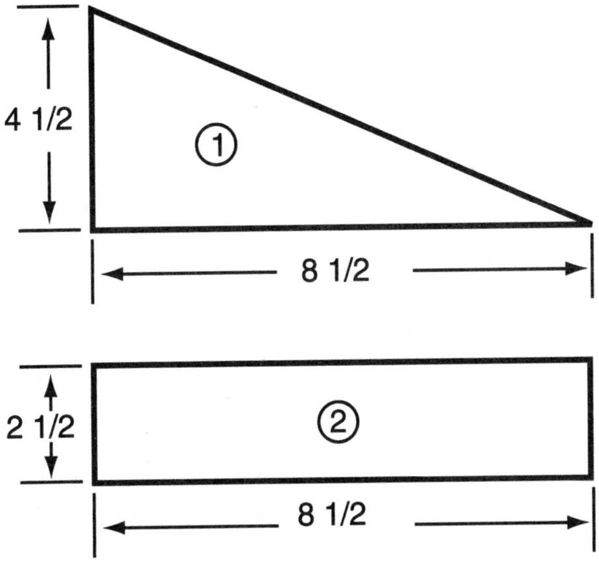

32.

PART	NUMBER REQUIRED
1	1
2	2
3	1
4	1

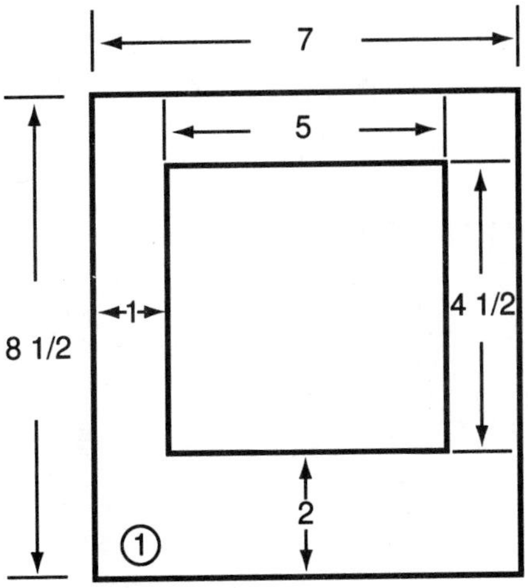

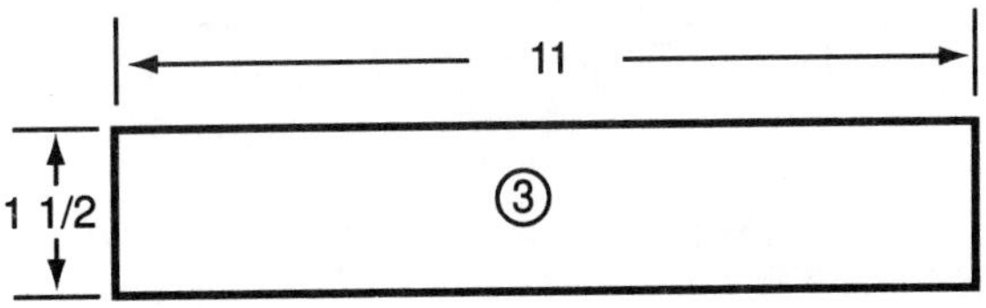

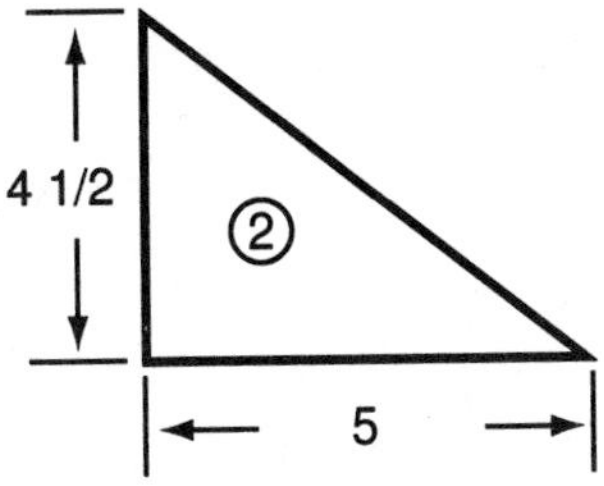

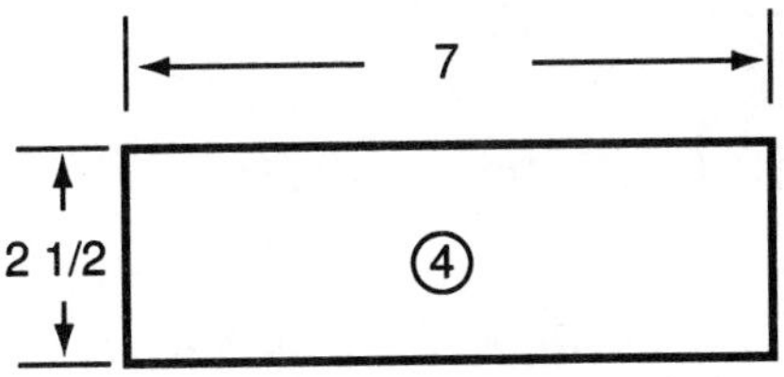

33.

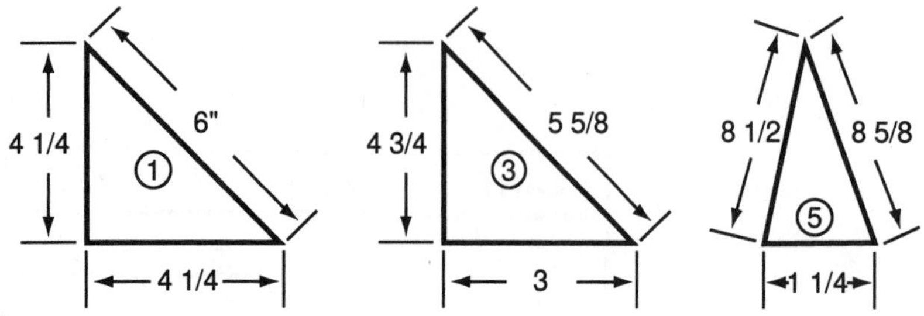

PART	NUMBER REQUIRED
1	2
2	2
3	1
4	1
5	1
6	1

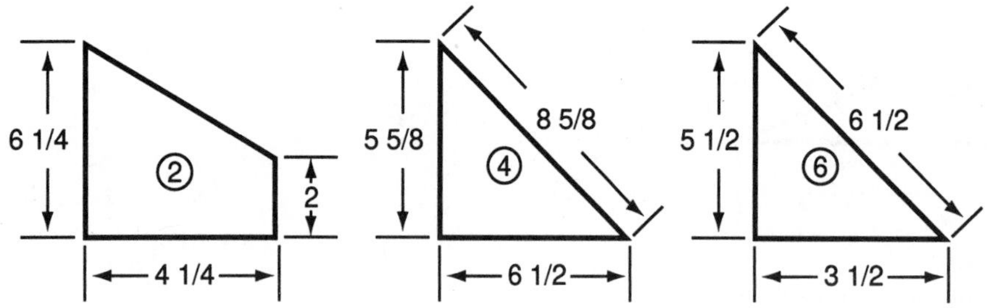

34.

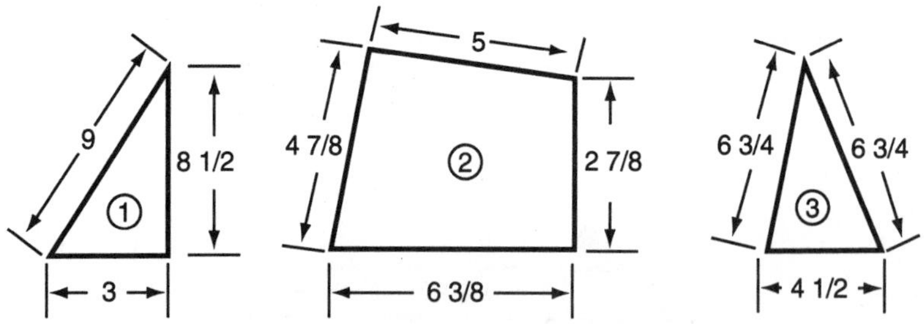

PART	NUMBER REQUIRED
1	1
2	1
3	1
4	1
5	1
6	1
7	2

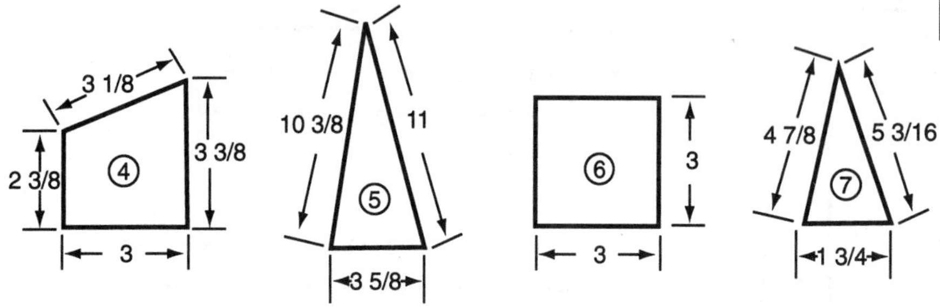

E. SHOP MATH

Calculate the following answers to the following math questions.

35. add 1/2 + 5/8 =______, 7/16 + 1 1/8 =______, 2 9/16 + 1 15/16 =______
36. add 2.5 + 6.4 =______, 0.3 + 8.5 =______, 0.6 + 0.84 =______
37. subtract 7/8 - 3/8 =______, 7 5/16 - 3 7/16 =______, 5 3/8 - 2 3/4 =______
38. subtract 6.8 - 3.4 =______, 5.5 - 3.7 =______, 5.8 - 4.75 =______
39. reduction 11/8 =______, 1 15/4 =______, 8 19/16 =______
40. rounding (2 decimal places) 3.789 =______, 4.3514 =______, 7.958 =______
41. fraction to decimals 3/4 =______, 5/8 =______, 11/16 =______

42. decimal to fractions .25 = ______ , .375 = ______ , .76 =______

43. inch to mm 1" = ______ mm, 1.5" = ______ mm, 1 3/4" = ______ mm

44. mm to inch 13 mm = ______ ", 8 mm = ______ ", 300 mm = ______ "

F. ESSAY

Provide complete answers for all of the following questions.

45. What are two effects that joint design has on the completed weld?

____

____

46. Why do joint designs require compromises?

____

____

47. How are welding symbols like a language for welders?

____

____

48. What are 3 basic parts of a weld joint design that can be changed?

____

____

49. What are some of the specific problems metals can have that would require careful weld joint selection?

____

____

50. What effect will oversized welds have on a joint?

____

____

51. List 5 things in addition to welding that a welder must do that are also charged to the welding cost.

____

____

52. When is the tail omitted from a welding symbol?

____

____

53. What information could be provided in the tail of a welding symbol?

____

____

54. How is the size of a fillet weld shown on a welding symbol?

____

____

55. What is an intermittent fillet weld?

56. Why are some welding joints grooved before welding?

57. List 4 ways that a plate edge can be grooved for welding.

58. What is the main purpose of the root face?

59. What types of metal might use a flange weld?

CHAPTER 19: WELDING CODES, STANDARDS AND WELDING COST

WELDER AND WELDING OPERATOR QUALIFICATION TEST RECORD (WQR)

Welder or welding operator's name ________________Identification no. _________

Welding process _________Manual _________ Semiautomatic _________Machine _________
Position ____

(Flat, horizonal, overhead, or vertical – if vertical, state whether up or down
In accordance with welding procedure specification no. ________________________

Material specification ____

Diameter and wall thickness (if pipe) – otherwise, joint thickness _____________________

Thickness range this qualifies ____

FILLER METAL

Specification No. _____________ Classification _____________ F-number _____________

Describe filler metal (if not covered by AWS specification) _________________________
____

Is backing strip used? ____

Filler metal diameter and trade name _____________________ Flux for submerged arc or gas for gas metal arc or flux-cored arc welding ______________________________________

Guided Bend Test Results

Appearance ___________________________ Weld Size ___________________________

Type	Result	Type	Result

Test conducted by ______________________ Laboratory test no. ______________________

Fillet Test Results

Appearance ___________________________ Fillet Size ___________________________

Fracture test root penetration ______________________ Macroetch ______________________

(Describe the location, nature, and size of any crack or tearing of the specimen.)
Test conducted by ______________________ Laboratory test no. ______________________

Radiographic Test Results

Film identification	Results	Remarks	Film identification	Results	Remarks

Test conducted by ______________________ Laboratory test no. ______________________

We, the undersigned, certify that the statements in this record are correct and that the welds were prepared and tested in accordance to these requirements.

Manufacturer or contractor ______________________

Authorized by ______________________

Date ______________________

PRACTICE 19-1

Name____ Date ____________

Class __________________ Instructor __________________ Grade ____________

OBJECTIVE: After completing this practice, you should be able to write a Welding Procedure Specification (WPS).

EQUIPMENT AND MATERIALS NEEDED FOR THIS PRACTICE

1. You will need the WPS form which can be found on the previous page.

INSTRUCTIONS

Using the form provided and following the example, you are going to write a welding procedure specification. Most of the unique information is provided in this short outline. You will need to refer to some of the chapters on welding and to your notes to establish the actual limits of the welding variables (voltage, amperage, gas flow rates, nozzle size, etc.)

1. The joint tolerances will be almost the same as the ones in the practice welds in this text, or you can use a code book to select a prequalified joint design. In either case, sketch the joint and include the dimension tolerances.
2. This information is included in each chapter where weld testing is required on practice welds.
3. Most of the preheat statement will be the same for all the WPSs you will be writing. You can copy the one on the sample or write your own.
4. This will require some of your knowledge and information found in chapters dealing with welding process.
5. The same statement will fit almost all of the practices in the text. Copy the example or develop your own.
6. Follow the recommendations in the chapters covering the material you are welding and the process you are using.
7. Follow the procedures outlined in this chapter.
8. For most WPSs there are no repairs or defects allowed.
9. Sketch a finished weld as it should look.

Comments

____

PRACTICE 19-2

Name______________________________ Date ____________

Class ______________ Instructor ______________ Grade ____________

PROCEDURE QUALIFICATION RECORD (PQR)

Welding Qualification Record No: ____________ WPS No: ____________ Date: ____________
Material specification ______________________ to ______________________
P-No. ______ Grade No. ______ to P-No. ______ Grade No. ______ Thickness and O.D. ______
Welding process: Manual ______________________ Automatic ______________________
Thickness Range ____

Filler Metal

Specification No. ____________ Classification ____________ F-number ____________
A-number ____________ Filler Metal Size ____________ Trade Name ____________
Describe filler metal (if not covered by AWS specification) ______________________
____

Flux or Atmosphere

Shielding Gas ____________ Flow Rate ____________ Purge ____________
Flux Classification ______________________ Trade Name ____________

Welding Variables

Joint Type ______________________ Position ______________________
Backing ______________________ Preheat ______________________
Passes and Size ______________________ Bead Type ______________________
No. of Arcs ______________________ Current ______________________
Ampere ______________________ Volts ______________________
Travel Speed ______________________ Oscillation ______________________
Interpass Temperature Range ____

Weld Results

Appearance ______________________ Weld Size ______________________

Guided Bend Test

Type	Result	Type	Result

Tensile Test

Specimen No.	Dimensions Width | Thickness	Area	Ultimate Total Load, lb.	Ultimate Unit Stress, psi.	Character of Failure and Location

Welder's Name ____________ Identification No.________ Laboratory Test No.________
By virtue of these test meets welder performance requirements.
Test Conducted by ______________________ Address ______________________
per______________________ Date ______________________
We certify that the statements in this record are correct and that the test welds performed and tested in accordance to the WPS.

Manufacture ______________________
Signed by ______________________
Date ______________________

OBJECTIVE: After completing this practice, you should be able to use a Procedure Qualification Record (PQR).

EQUIPMENT AND MATERIALS NEEDED FOR THIS PRACTICE

1. You will need the PQR form which can be found on the previous page.

INSTRUCTIONS

Following the procedure you wrote in practice 19-2, you are going to make the weld to see if your tentative welding procedure and specification can be certified.

Comments

PRACTICE 19-3

Name____ Date _______________

Class _______________________ Instructor _______________________ Grade _______________

OBJECTIVE: After completing this practice, you should be able to find the volume of a groove weld.

EQUIPMENT AND MATERIALS NEEDED FOR THIS PRACTICE

Pencil, paper, calculator.

INSTRUCTIONS

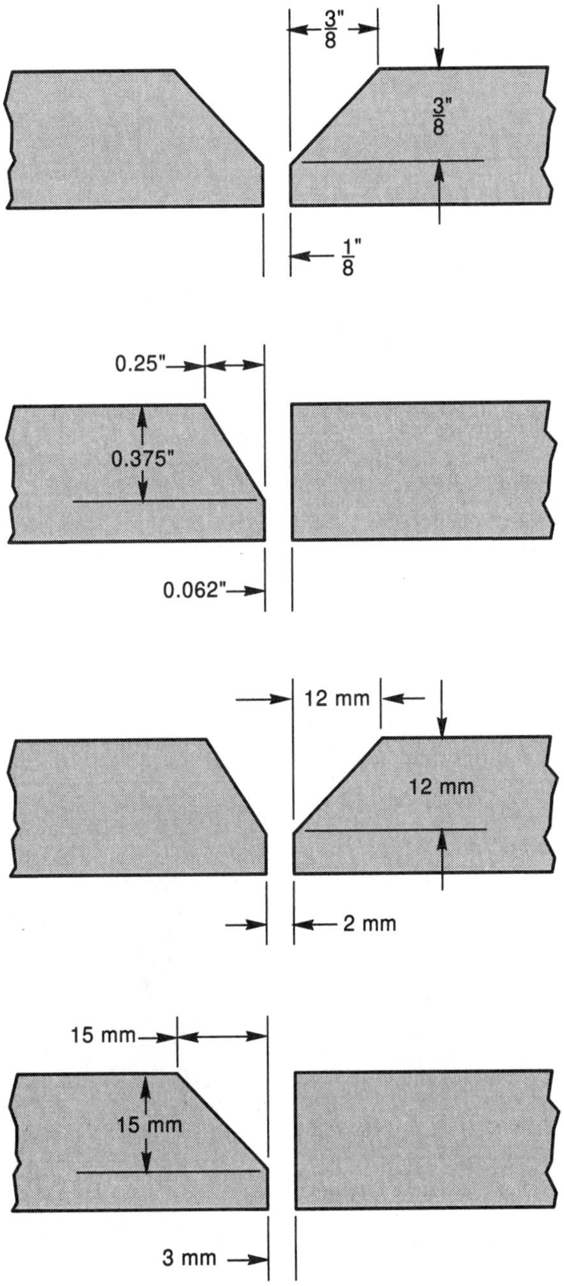

Use the dimensions given below and this illustration to determine the weld volume of the following sized grooved welds.

1. V-Groove joint with the following dimensions

   Width 3/8 in.

   Depth 3/8 in.

   Root Opening 1/8 in.

   Thickness 1/2 in.

   Weld Length 144 in.

2. Bevel joint with the following dimensions

   Width 0.25 in.

   Depth 0.375 in.

   Root Opening 0.062 in.

   Thickness 0.5 in.

   Weld Length 96 in.

3. V-Groove joint with the following dimensions

   Width 12 mm

   Depth 12 mm

   Root Opening 2 mm

   Thickness 15 mm

   Weld Length 3600 mm

4. Bevel joint with the following dimensions

   Width 15 mm

   Depth 15 mm

   Root Opening 3 mm

   Thickness 18 mm

   Weld Length 3 M

PRACTICE 19-4

Name____ Date ____________

Class ____________________ Instructor ____________________ Grade ____________

OBJECTIVE: After completing this practice, you should be able to find the weight of the filler metal required for each of the weld volumes calculated in PRACTICE 19-3.

EQUIPMENT AND MATERIALS NEEDED FOR THIS PRACTICE

Pencil, paper, calculator.

INSTRUCTIONS

1. Calculate the filler metal weight using steel standard units of 0.283 pounds per cubic inch (0.283 lb per cu/in.) and S.I. units of 7.66 grams per cubic centimeter (7.66 g per cu/cm).
2. Calculate the filler metal weight using steel standard units of 0.098 pounds per cubic inch (0.098 lb per cu/in.) and S.I. units of 2.51 grams per cubic centimeter (2.51 g per cu/cm).

CHAPTER 19: WELDING CODES, STANDARDS, AND CERTIFICATION QUIZ

Name______________________________ Date ____________

Class ______________ Instructor ______________ Grade ____________

Instructions: Carefully read Chapter 19 in the text and complete the following questions.

A. MATCHING

In the space provided to the left, write the letter from column B that best answers the question or completes the statement in column A.

	column A		column B
____	1. The code most commonly used for buildings and other structural steel.	a.	Local, state or federal government regulations
____	2. The code most commonly used for pipe lines.	b.	ASME Section IX
____	3. The code most commonly used for pressure vessels.	c.	AWS D1.1
____	4. Many governing agencies require that a specific code or standard be followed.	d.	API 1104
____	5. Lists all of the parameters required to produce a sound weld to the specific code, specification, or definition.	e.	Welding Procedure Specification

B. COST PER POUND OF METAL DEPOSITED

Welding Process: ______________________________
Filler Metal: AWS Number ______________ Diameter ______________
Welding Current: Amperage ______________ Voltage ______________

LABOR and OVERHEAD	(Labor & Overhead Cost/hr) / (Deposition Rate [lb/hr]) X (Operating Factor)	=	________
ELECTRODE	(Electrode Cost/lb) / (Deposition Efficiency)	=	________
GAS	(Gas Flow Rate [cfh]) X (Gas Cost/cu. ft.) / (Deposition Rate [lb/hr])	=	________
	Total Cost/lb of Weld Metal Deposited (Sum of the Above)		________

6. Use the above table and information supplied below to determine the Total Cost per pound of Weld Metal Deposited.

FCAW

Electrode Type	.045" dia. E71T-2
Labor & Overhead	$25.00/hr
Welding current	200 amperes
Deposition Rate	5.5 lbs/hr
Operation Factor	45%
Electrode Cost	$1.55/lb.
Deposition Efficiency	85%

Gas Flow Rate	35 cfh
Gas Cost Per Cu. Ft	\$.04 CO_2

7. Use the above table and information supplied below to determine the Total Cost per pound of Weld Metal Deposited.

SMAW	
Electrode Type	1/8" dia. E7018
Labor & Overhead	\$23.00/hr
Welding current	120 amperes
Deposition Rate	2.58 lbs/hr
Operation Factor	30%
Electrode Cost	\$0.97/lb.
Deposition Efficiency	71.6%
Gas Flow Rate	Not Applicable
Gas Cost Per Cu. Ft.	Not Applicable

C. ESSAY

Provide complete answers for all of the following questions.

8. What is meant by the term "qualifying a specification"?

____

____

9. List 5 requirements that will result in a code or standard being followed.

____

____

10. What is a major area that the following codes are used for?

A. API 1104______________________________

B. ASME Section IX______________________________

C. AWS D1.1 ______________________________

11. Explain the differences between the following terms:

A. Welding Procedure Specification and Welding Schedule ______________________________

____

B. Welding Schedule and Welding Procedure ______________________________

____

12. List 8 specific parameters found in WPSs.

____

____

____

13. How does a welder become "qualified"?

____

____

14. When can a welder be "certified"?

15. Who should supervise the testing of weld samples?

16. How long is a WPS in effect before it must be retested?

17. Why should supplementary information be included in the WPS?

18. What are some of the essential variables of WPSs?

19. What is a Nick Break Test?

CHAPTER 20: TESTING AND INSPECTION OF WELDS

ETCHING SOLUTIONS FOR MICROSCOPIC EXAMINATION OF METALS	
Metal to be Etched	**Etchant Mixture**
Aluminum	45cc hydrochloric acid 15cc nitric acid 15cc hydrofluoric acid 25cc water
Brass & copper alloys	25cc ammonium hydroxide 25cc hydrogen peroxide 25cc water
Iron & steel	5cc nitric acid 100cc ethyl alcohol
Nickel & its alloys	50cc of 70% nitric acid 50cc of 50% acetic acid
Stainless steels	30cc hydrochloric acid 10cc nitric acid 80cc glycerol

Mixing chemicals may be hazardous. Do not attempt to mix these solutions without proper supervision and instructions by someone trained to handle these materials such as a chemist.

SAFETY PRECAUTIONS

When working with etchants, use extreme caution. Protective clothing is required (safety glasses, face shield, gloves, and an apron). Any mixing, handling or use of an etchant is to be done in a well-ventilated area.

CAUTION **Always start the mixture by pouring the water and/or other acid solutions into the mixing container first. Add the acid slowly while constantly stirring the mixture.**

CHAPTER 20: TESTING AND INSPECTION OF WELDS QUIZ

Name____ Date _____________

Class ____________________ Instructor ____________________ Grade _____________

Instructions: Carefully read Chapter 20 in the text and answer the following questions.

A. MATCHING

In the space provided to the left, write the letter from column B that best answers the question or completes the statement in column A.

column A	column B
____ 1. What is the resistance of metal to penetration and is an index to wear resistance and strength of the metals?	a. worm hole
____ 2. What is the name of a weld that has a flaw within the tolerance?	b. defect
____ 3. What is the interruption of the typical structure of a weldment?	c. incomplete fusion
____ 4. A cylindrical porosity.	d. hardness
____ 5. What is the lack of coalescence between the molten filler metal and the base metal?	e. tolerance
____ 6. What is a discontinuity that will render a product unable to meet the minimum applicable acceptance standard or specification?	f. disontinuity
____ 7. What is the difference between acceptable and perfection?	g. overlap
____ 8. What is weld metal that flows over a surface without fusing to it?	h. inclusions
____ 9. What is the lack of coalescence between molten filler metal and the base metal?	i. incomplete fusion
____ 10. What can be expected if prior welds were improperly cleaned?	j. tolerance

B. SHORT ANSWER

Write a brief answer, in the space provided, that will answer the question or complete the statement.

11. What are the two classifications of methods used in product quality control?

a.____

b. ____

12. List three factors that you should consider when evaluating a weld with discontinuities.

a.____

b. ____

c.____

13. List four factors that can affect the selection of radiographic equipment.

a.____

b. ____

c.____

d. ____

14. What are the two types of ultrasonic equipment used in the welding industry?

a. ______________________________

b. ______________________________

C. TRUE-FALSE

Write the letter T, in the space to the left, if the statement is true and the letter F if the statement if false.

_____ 15. All discontinuities are defects.

_____ 16. The E7018 electrode should not be used on open root welds.

_____ 17. Arc strikes are created by the electrode, never by the ground clamp.

_____ 18. As the hardness of a metal is increased, the brittleness is also increased.

_____ 19. Ductility in tensile tests is usually measured as a percentage of elongation.

_____ 20. Toughness is measured most often by the Rockwell hardness tester.

_____ 21. When preparing a guided bend test, caution must be taken to ensure that all grinding marks run longitudinally to the specimen so that they do not cause stress cracking.

_____ 22. Magnetic particle inspection is the most frequently used nondestructive testing method.

_____ 23. Penetrant inspection is used to locate any crack or porosity in a welded product.

_____ 24. Magnetic particle inspection uses finely divided ferromagnetic particles to indicate defects on any material.

E. ESSAY

Provide complete answers for all of the following questions.

25. What is the difference between destructive testing and nondestructive testing?

____

____

26. What is the maximum strength of a weld having a maximum load of 50,000 lb (22,679 kg) and a cross-sectional area of .0125 in. (0.3 mm)?

____

____

27. What is fatigue testing?

____

____

28. List two methods of testing shear strength.

____

____

29. What is the difference between a guided bend and a free bend test?

____

____

30. What is longitudinal cracking?

____

____

31. Why are the corners rounded on the guided bend test specimens?

32. What is the purpose of testing welds by the etching method?

33. Explain the difference between Charpy and Izod impact tests.

34. Define the following terms: fitness for service, discontinuity, defect, weld layer, weld pass, NDT, transverse, and etching.

CHAPTER 21: WELDING CERTIFICATION

PRACTICE 21-1

Name____ Date ____________

Class ____________________ Instructor ____________________ Grade ____________

WELDING PROCEDURE SPECIFICATION (WPS)

Welding Procedures Specifications No: PRACTICE 21-1 Date: ___________

TITLE:

Welding SMAW of plate to plate .

SCOPE:

This procedure is applicable for V-groove plate with a backing strip

within the range of 3/16 in. (4.7 mm) through 3/4 in. (19 mm)

Welding may be performed in the following positions 2G .

BASE METAL:

The base metal shall conform to Carbon Steel M-1 or P-1, Group 1 or 2

Backing material specification Carbon Steel M-1 or P-1, Group 1, 2 or 3 .

FILLER METAL:

The filler metal shall conform to AWS specification No. E7018 from AWS specification A5.1 . This filler metal falls into F-number F-4 and A-number A-1 .

SHIELDING GAS:

The shielding gas, or gases, shall conform to the following compositions and purity:

N/A .

JOINT DESIGN AND TOLERANCES:

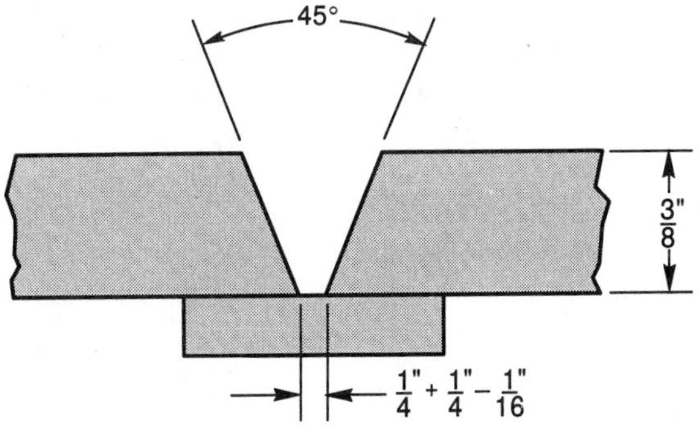

PREPARATION OF BASE METAL:

The bevel is to be flame cut on the edge of the plate before the parts are assembled. The beveled surface must be smooth and free of notches. Any roughness or notches that are deeper than 1/64 in. (0.4 mm) must be ground smooth.

All hydrocarbons and other contaminations, such as cutting fluids, grease, oil and primers, must be cleaned off of all parts and filler metals before welding. This cleaning can be done with any suitable solvents or detergents. The backing strip, groove face, inside and outside plate surface within 1 in. (25 mm) of the joint must be mechanically cleaned of slag, rust and mill scale. Cleaning must be done with a wire brush or grinder down to bright metal.

ELECTRICAL CHARACTERISTICS:

The current shall be Direct Current Electrode Positive (DCEP). The base metal shall be on the negative side of the line.

WELDS	FILLER METAL DIA.	CURRENT	AMPERAGE RANGE
Tack	3/32 in. (2.4 mm)	DCEP	70 to 115
Root	1/8 in. (3.2 mm)	DCEP	115 to 165
Filler	5/32 in. (4 mm)	DCEP	150 to 220

PREHEAT:

The parts must be heated to a temperature higher than 50°F (10°C) before any welding is started.

BACKING GAS:

N/A

SAFETY:

Proper protective clothing and equipment must be used. The area must be free of all hazards which may affect the welder or others in the area. The welding machine, welding leads, work clamp, electrode holder and other equipment must be in safe working order.

WELDING TECHNIQUE:

Tack weld the plates together with the backing strip. There should be about a 1/4-in. (6-mm) root gap between the plates. Use the E7018 arc welding electrodes to make a root pass to fuse the plates and backing strip together. Clean the slag from the root pass being sure to remove any trapped slag along the sides of the weld.

Using the E7018 arc welding electrodes, make a series of stringer or weave filler welds, no thicker than 1/4 in. (6.4 mm), in the groove until the joint is filled.

INTERPASS TEMPERATURE:

The plate should not be heated to a temperature higher than 350°F (175°C) during the welding process. After each weld pass is completed, allow it to cool but never to a temperature below 50°F (10°C). The weldment must not be quenched in water.

CLEANING:

The slag must cleaned off between passes. The weld beads may be cleaned by a hand wire brush, a hand chipping, punch and hammer or a needle-scaler. All weld cleaning must be performed with the test plate in the welding position. A grinder may not be used to remove weld control problems such as undercut, overlap, trapped slag, etc.

INSPECTION:

Visually inspect the weld for uniformity and discontinuities. There shall be no cracks, no incomplete fusion and no overlap. Undercut shall not exceed the lesser of 10% of the base metal thickness or 1/32 in. (0.8 mm). The frequency of porosity shall not exceed one in each 4 in. (100 mm) of weld length and the maximum diameter shall not exceed 3/32 in. (2.4 mm).

REPAIR:

No repairs of defects are allowed.

SKETCHES:

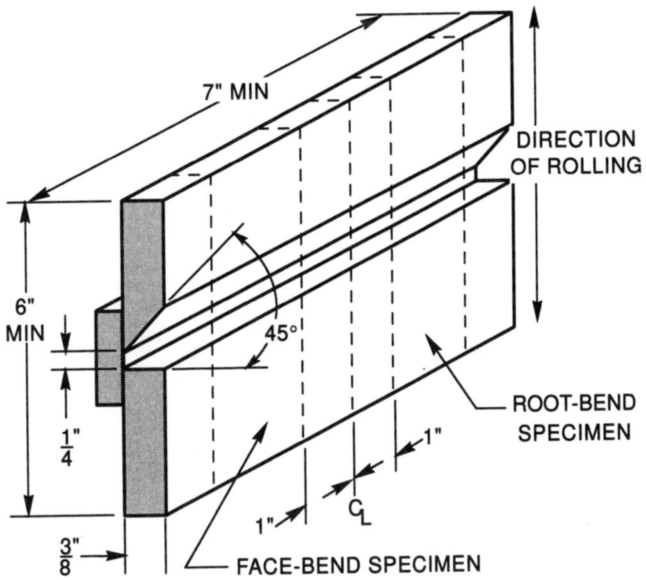

BEND TEST:

Transverse Face-Bend. The weld is perpendicular to the longitudinal axis of the specimen and is bent so that the weld face becomes the tension surface of the specimen.

Transverse Root-Bend. The weld is perpendicular to the longitudinal axis of the specimen and is bent so that the weld root becomes the tension surface of the specimen.

ACCEPTANCE CRITERIA FOR BEND TEST:

No single surface indication shall exceed 1/8 in. (3.2 mm) measured in any direction.

The sum of the greatest dimensions of all indications on the surface which exceed 1/32 in. (0.8 mm) but are less than or equal to 1/8 in (3.2 mm) shall not exceed 3/8 in. (9.6 mm).

PRACTICE 21-2

Name________________________________ Date ____________

Class ______________ Instructor ______________ Grade ____________

WELDING PROCEDURE SPECIFICATION (WPS)

Welding Procedures Specifications No: PRACTICE 21-2 Date: ____________

TITLE:

Welding SMAW of plate to plate .

SCOPE:

This procedure is applicable for V-groove plate with a backing strip

within the range of 3/16 in. (4.7 mm) through 3/4 in. (19 mm)

Welding may be performed in the following positions 3G .

BASE METAL:

The base metal shall conform to Carbon Steel M-1 or P-1, Group 1 or 2

Backing material specification Carbon Steel M-1 or P-1, Group 1, 2 or 3.

FILLER METAL:

The filler metal shall conform to AWS specification No. E7018 from AWS specification A5.1 . This filler metal falls into F-number F-4 and A-number A-1 .

SHIELDING GAS:

The shielding gas, or gases, shall conform to the following compositions and purity:

N/A .

JOINT DESIGN AND TOLERANCES:

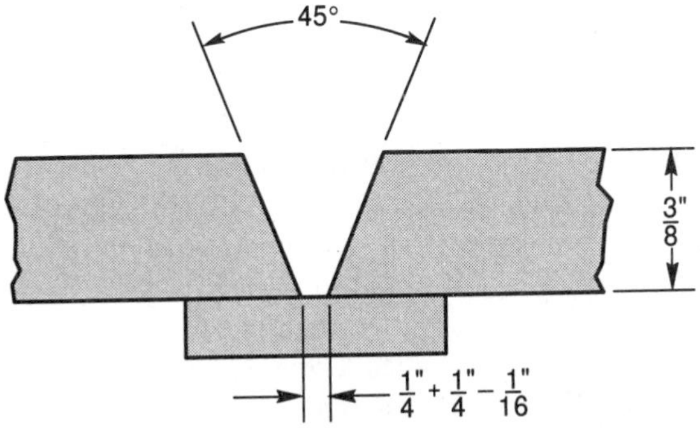

PREPARATION OF BASE METAL:

The bevel is to be flame cut on the edge of the plate before the parts are assembled. The beveled surface must be smooth and free of notches. Any roughness or notches that are deeper than 1/64 in. (0.4 mm) must be ground smooth.

All hydrocarbons and other contaminations, such as cutting fluids, grease, oil and primers, must be cleaned off of all parts and filler metals before welding. This cleaning can be done with any suitable solvents or detergents. The backing strip, groove face, inside and outside plate surface within 1 in. (25 mm) of the joint must be mechanically cleaned of slag, rust and mill scale. Cleaning must be done with a wire brush or grinder down to bright metal.

ELECTRICAL CHARACTERISTICS:

The current shall be Direct Current Electrode Positive (DCEP). The base metal shall be on the negative side of the line.

WELDS	FILLER METAL DIA.	CURRENT	AMPERAGE RANGE
Tack	3/32 in. (2.4 mm)	DCEP	70 to 115
Root	1/8 in. (3.2 mm)	DCEP	115 to 165
Filler	5/32 in. (4 mm)	DCEP	150 to 220

PREHEAT:

The parts must be heated to a temperature higher than 50°F (10°C) before any welding is started.

BACKING GAS:

N/A

SAFETY:

Proper protective clothing and equipment must be used. The area must be free of all hazards which may affect the welder or others in the area. The welding machine, welding leads, work clamp, electrode holder and other equipment must be in safe working order.

WELDING TECHNIQUE:

Tack weld the plates together with the backing strip. There should be about a 1/4-in. (6-mm) root gap between the plates. Use the E7018 arc welding electrodes to make a root pass to fuse the plates and backing strip together. Clean the slag from the root pass being sure to remove any trapped slag along the sides of the weld.

Using the E7018 arc welding electrodes, make a series of stringer or weave filler welds, no thicker than 1/4 in. (6.4 mm), in the groove until the joint is filled.

INTERPASS TEMPERATURE:

The plate should not be heated to a temperature higher than 350°F (175°C) during the welding process. After each weld pass is completed, allow it to cool but never to a temperature below 50°F (10°C). The weldment must not be quenched in water.

CLEANING:

The slag must cleaned off between passes. The weld beads may be cleaned by a hand wire brush, a hand chipping, punch and hammer or a needle-scaler. All weld cleaning must be performed with the test plate in the welding position. A grinder may not be used to remove weld control problems such as undercut, overlap, trapped slag, etc.

INSPECTION:

Visually inspect the weld for uniformity and discontinuities. There shall be no cracks, no incomplete fusion and no overlap. Undercut shall not exceed the lesser of 10% of the base metal thickness or 1/32 in. (0.8 mm). The frequency of porosity shall not exceed one in each 4 in. (100 mm) of weld length and the maximum diameter shall not exceed 3/32 in. (2.4 mm).

REPAIR:

No repairs of defects are allowed.

SKETCHES:

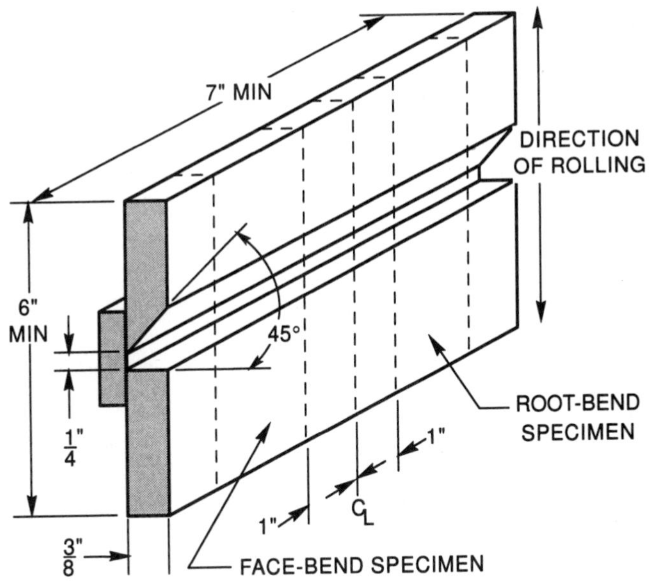

BEND TEST:

Transverse Face-Bend. The weld is perpendicular to the longitudinal axis of the specimen and is bent so that the weld face becomes the tension surface of the specimen.

Transverse Root-Bend. The weld is perpendicular to the longitudinal axis of the specimen and is bent so that the weld root becomes the tension surface of the specimen.

ACCEPTANCE CRITERIA FOR BEND TEST:

No single surface indication shall exceed 1/8 in. (3.2 mm) measured in any direction.

The sum of the greatest dimensions of all indications on the surface which exceed 1/32 in. (0.8 mm) but are less than or equal to 1/8 in. (3.2 mm) shall not exceed 3/8 in. (9.6 mm).

PRACTICE 21-3

Name______________________________ Date ____________

Class ______________ Instructor ______________ Grade ____________

WELDING PROCEDURE SPECIFICATION (WPS)

Welding Procedures Specifications No: PRACTICE 21-3 Date:____________

TITLE:

Welding GMAW-S of plate to plate.

SCOPE:

This procedure is applicable for V-groove, bevel and fillet welds

within the range of 1/8 in. (3.2 mm) through 1 1/2 in. (38 mm)

Welding may be performed in the following positions ALL .

BASE METAL:

The base metal shall conform to Carbon Steel M-1, P-1 and S-1 Group 1 or 2

Backing material specification NONE .

FILLER METAL:

The filler metal shall conform to AWS specification No. E70S-3 from AWS specification A5.18 . This filler metal falls into F-number F-6 and A-number A-1 .

SHIELDING GAS:

The shielding gas, or gases, shall conform to the following compositions and purity:

CO_2 at 30 to 50 CFH or 75% Ar/CO_2 25% at 30 to 50 CFH .

JOINT DESIGN AND TOLERANCES:

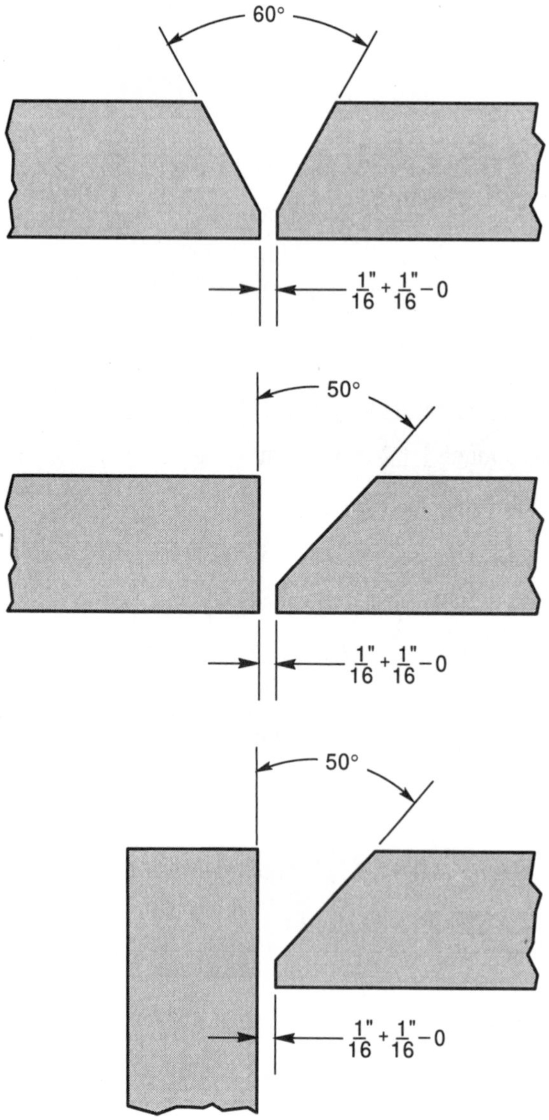

PREPARATION OF BASE METAL:

The bevels are to be flame cut on the edges of the plate before the parts are assembled. The beveled surface must be smooth and free of notches. Any roughness or notches that are deeper than 1/64 in. (0.4 mm) must be ground smooth.

All hydrocarbons and other contaminations, such as cutting fluids, grease, oil and primers, must be cleaned off of all parts and filler metals before welding. This cleaning can be done with any suitable solvents or detergents. The groove face and inside and outside plate surface within 1 in. (25 mm) of the joint must be mechanically cleaned of slag, rust and mill scale. Cleaning must be done with a wire brush or grinder down to bright metal.

ELECTRICAL CHARACTERISTICS:

The current shall be Direct Current Electrode Positive (DCEP) . The base metal shall be on the negative side of the line.

ELECTRODE		WELDING POWER			SHIELDING GAS		BASE METAL	
Type	Size	Amps	Wire Feed Speed IPM (cm/min)	Volts	Type	Flow	Type	Thickness
E70S-3	0.035 in. (0.9 mm)	90 to 120	180 to 300 (457 to 762)	15 to 19	CO_2 or 75%Ar/$CO_2$25%	30 to 50	Low-Carbon Steel	1/4 in. to 1/2 in. (6 mm to 13 mm)
E70S-3	0.045 in. (1.2 mm)	130 to 200	125 to 200 (318 to 508)	17 to 20	CO_2 or 75%Ar/$CO_2$25%	30 to 50	Low-Carbon Steel	1/4 in. to 1/2 in. (6 mm to 13 mm)

PREHEAT:

The parts must be heated to a temperature higher than 50°F (10°C) before any welding is started.

BACKING GAS:

N/A

SAFETY:

Proper protective clothing and equipment must be used. The area must be free of all hazards which may affect the welder or others in the area. The welding machine, welding leads, work clamp, electrode holder and other equipment must be in safe working order.

WELDING TECHNIQUE:

Using a 1/2 in. (13 mm) or larger gas nozzle for all welding, first tack weld the plates together according to the drawing. There should be about a 1/16-in. (1.6-mm) root gap between the plates with V-grooved or beveled edges. Use the E70S-3 arc welding electrodes to make a root pass to fuse the plates together. Clean any silicon slag from the root pass being sure to remove any trapped silicon slag along the sides of the weld.

Using the E70S-3 arc welding electrodes, make a series of stringer or weave filler welds, no thicker than 1/4 in. (6.4 mm), in the groove until the joint is filled. The 1/4 in. (6.4 mm) fillet welds are to be made with one pass.

INTERPASS TEMPERATURE:

The plate should not be heated to a temperature higher than 350°F (175°C) during the welding process. After each weld pass is completed, allow it to cool but never to a temperature below 50°F (10°C). The weldment must not be quenched in water.

CLEANING:

Any slag must be cleaned off between passes. The weld beads may be cleaned by a hand wire brush, a hand chipping, punch and hammer or a needle-scaler. All weld cleaning must be performed with the test plate in the welding position. A grinder may not be used to remove weld control problems such as undercut, overlap, trapped slag, etc.

INSPECTION:

Visually inspect the weld for uniformity and discontinuities. There shall be no cracks, no incomplete fusion and no overlap. Undercut shall not exceed the lesser of 10% of the base metal thickness or 1/32 in. (0.8 mm). The frequency of porosity shall not exceed one in each 4 in. (100 mm) of weld length and the maximum diameter shall not exceed 3/32 in. (2.4 mm).

REPAIR:

No repairs of defects are allowed.

SKETCHES:

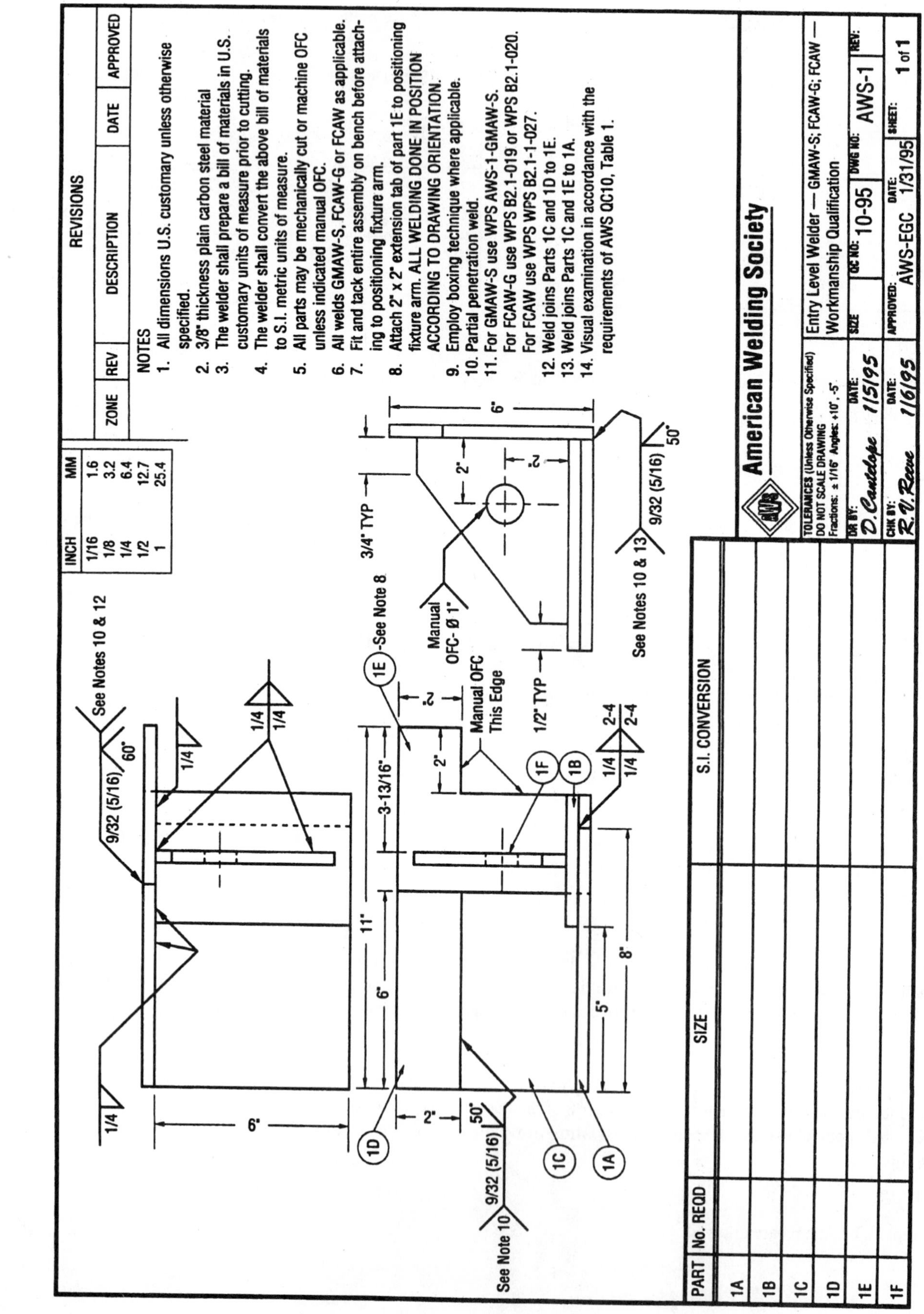
REVISIONS
ZONE
REV
DESCRIPTION
DATE
APPROVED
INCH MM
1/16 1.6
1/8 3.2
1/4 6.4
1/2 12.7
1 25.4
NOTES
1. All dimensions U.S. customary unless otherwise specified.
2. 3/8" thickness plain carbon steel material
3. The welder shall prepare a bill of materials in U.S. customary units of measure prior to cutting.
4. The welder shall convert the above bill of materials to S.I. metric units of measure.
5. All parts may be mechanically cut or machine OFC unless indicated manual OFC.
6. All welds GMAW-S, FCAW-G or FCAW as applicable.
7. Fit and tack entire assembly on bench before attaching to positioning fixture arm.
8. Attach 2" x 2" extension tab of part 1E to positioning fixture arm. ALL WELDING DONE IN POSITION ACCORDING TO DRAWING ORIENTATION.
9. Employ boxing technique where applicable.
10. Partial penetration weld.
11. For GMAW-S use WPS AWS-1-GMAW-S.
For FCAW-G use WPS B2.1-019 or WPS B2.1-020.
For FCAW use WPS WPS B2.1-1-027.
12. Weld joins Parts 1C and 1D to 1E.
13. Weld joins Parts 1C and 1E to 1A.
14. Visual examination in accordance with the requirements of AWS QC10, Table 1.
See Notes 10 & 12
9/32 (5/16)
60°
1/4
1/4
1/4
1/4
1/4
2-4
2-4
1E
-See Note 8
Manual OFC- Ø 1"
Manual OFC This Edge
1F
1B
1D
1C
1A
3/4" TYP
1/2" TYP
2"
2"
6"
3-13/16"
11"
5"
8"
6"
See Notes 10 & 13
9/32 (5/16)
50°
See Note 10
9/32 (5/16)
50°
PART
No. REQD
SIZE
S.I. CONVERSION
1A
1B
1C
1D
1E
1F
American Welding Society
TOLERANCES (Unless Otherwise Specified)
DO NOT SCALE DRAWING
Fractions: ± 1/16" Angles: +10°, -5°
Entry Level Welder — GMAW-S; FCAW-G; FCAW — Workmanship Qualification
DR BY: D. Cantelope
DATE: 1/5/95
SIZE
QC NO: 10-95
DWG NO: AWS-1
REV:
CHK BY: R.V. Reeve
DATE: 1/6/95
APPROVED: AWS-EGC
DATE: 1/31/95
SHEET: 1 of 1

PRACTICE 21-4

Name____ Date ____________

Class ____________________ Instructor ____________________ Grade ____________

WELDING PROCEDURE SPECIFICATION (WPS)

Welding Procedures Specifications No: PRACTICE 21-4 Date: ____________

TITLE:

Welding FCAW of plate to plate .

SCOPE:

This procedure is applicable for V-groove, bevel and fillet welds

within the range of 1/8 in. (3.2 mm) through 1 1/2 in. (38 mm)

Welding may be performed in the following positions ALL .

BASE METAL:

The base metal shall conform to Carbon Steel M-1, P-1 and S-1 Group 1 or 2

Backing material specification NONE .

FILLER METAL:

The filler metal shall conform to AWS specification No. E71T-1 from AWS specification A5.20 . This filler metal falls into F-number F-6 and A-number A-1 .

SHIELDING GAS:

The shielding gas, or gases, shall conform to the following compositions and purity:

CO_2 at 30 to 50 CFH or 75% Ar/CO_2 25% at 30 to 50 CFH .

JOINT DESIGN AND TOLERANCES:

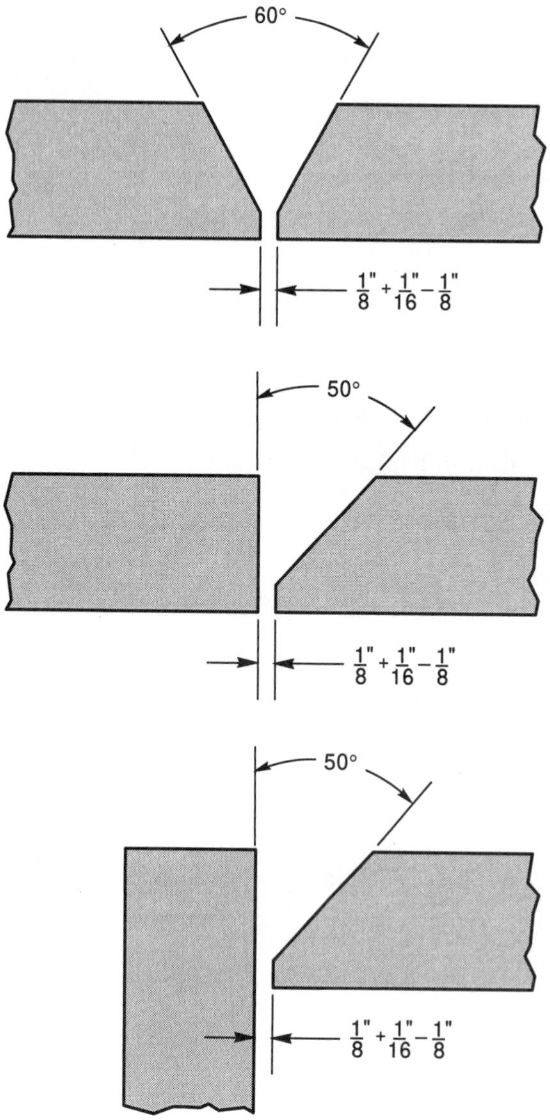

PREPARATION OF BASE METAL:

The bevels are to be flame cut on the edges of the plate before the parts are assembled. The beveled surface must be smooth and free of notches. Any roughness or notches that are deeper than 1/64 in. (0.4 mm) must be ground smooth.

All hydrocarbons and other contaminations, such as cutting fluids, grease, oil and primers, must be cleaned off of all parts and filler metals before welding. This cleaning can be done with any suitable solvents or detergents. The groove face and inside and outside plate surface within 1 in. (25 mm) of the joint must be mechanically cleaned of slag, rust and mill scale. Cleaning must be done with a wire brush or grinder down to bright metal.

ELECTRICAL CHARACTERISTICS:

The current shall be Direct Current Electrode Positive (DCEP) . The base metal shall be on the negative side of the line.

ELECTRODE		WELDING POWER			SHIELDING GAS		BASE METAL	
Type	Size	Amps	Wire Feed Speed IPM (cm/min)	Volts	Type	Flow	Type	Thickness
E71T-1	0.035 in. (0.9 mm)	130 to 150	288 to 380 (732 to 975)	22 to 25	CO_2 or 75%Ar/$CO_2$25%	30 to 50	Low-Carbon Steel	1/4 in. to 1/2 in. (6 mm to 13 mm)
E71T-1	0.045 in. (1.2 mm)	150 to 210	200 to 300 (508 to 762)	28 to 29	CO_2 or 75%Ar/$CO_2$25%	30 to 50	Low-Carbon Steel	1/4 in. to 1/2 in. (6 mm to 13 mm)

PREHEAT:

The parts must be heated to a temperature higher than 50°F (10°C) before any welding is started.

BACKING GAS:

N/A

SAFETY:

Proper protective clothing and equipment must be used. The area must be free of all hazards which may affect the welder or others in the area. The welding machine, welding leads, work clamp, electrode holder and other equipment must be in safe working order.

WELDING TECHNIQUE:

Using a 1/2 in. (13 mm) or larger gas nozzle and an approximately 3/4 in. (19 mm) contact tube to work distance for all welding, first tack weld the plates together according to the drawing. There should be about a 1/8-in. (3.2-mm) root gap between the plates with V-grooved or beveled edges. Use the E71T-1 arc welding electrodes to make a root pass to fuse the plates together. Clean the slag from the root pass being sure to remove any trapped slag along the sides of the weld.

Using the E71T-1 arc welding electrodes, make a series of stringer or weave filler welds, no thicker than 1/4 in. (6.4 mm), in the groove until the joint is filled. The 1/4 in. (6.4 mm) fillet welds are to be made with one pass.

INTERPASS TEMPERATURE:

The plate should not be heated to a temperature higher than 350°F (175°C) during the welding process. After each weld pass is completed, allow it to cool but never to a temperature below 50°F (10°C). The weldment must not be quenched in water.

CLEANING:

The slag must cleaned off between passes. The weld beads may be cleaned by a hand wire brush, a hand chipping, punch and hammer or a needle-scaler. All weld cleaning must be performed with the test plate in the welding position. A grinder may not be used to remove weld control problems such as undercut, overlap, trapped slag, etc.

INSPECTION:

Visually inspect the weld for uniformity and discontinuities. There shall be no cracks, no incomplete fusion and no overlap. Undercut shall not exceed the lesser of 10% of the base metal thickness or 1/32 in. (0.8 mm). The frequency of porosity shall not exceed one in each 4 in. (100 mm) of weld length and the maximum diameter shall not exceed 3/32 in. (2.4 mm).

REPAIR:

No repairs of defects are allowed.

SKETCHES:

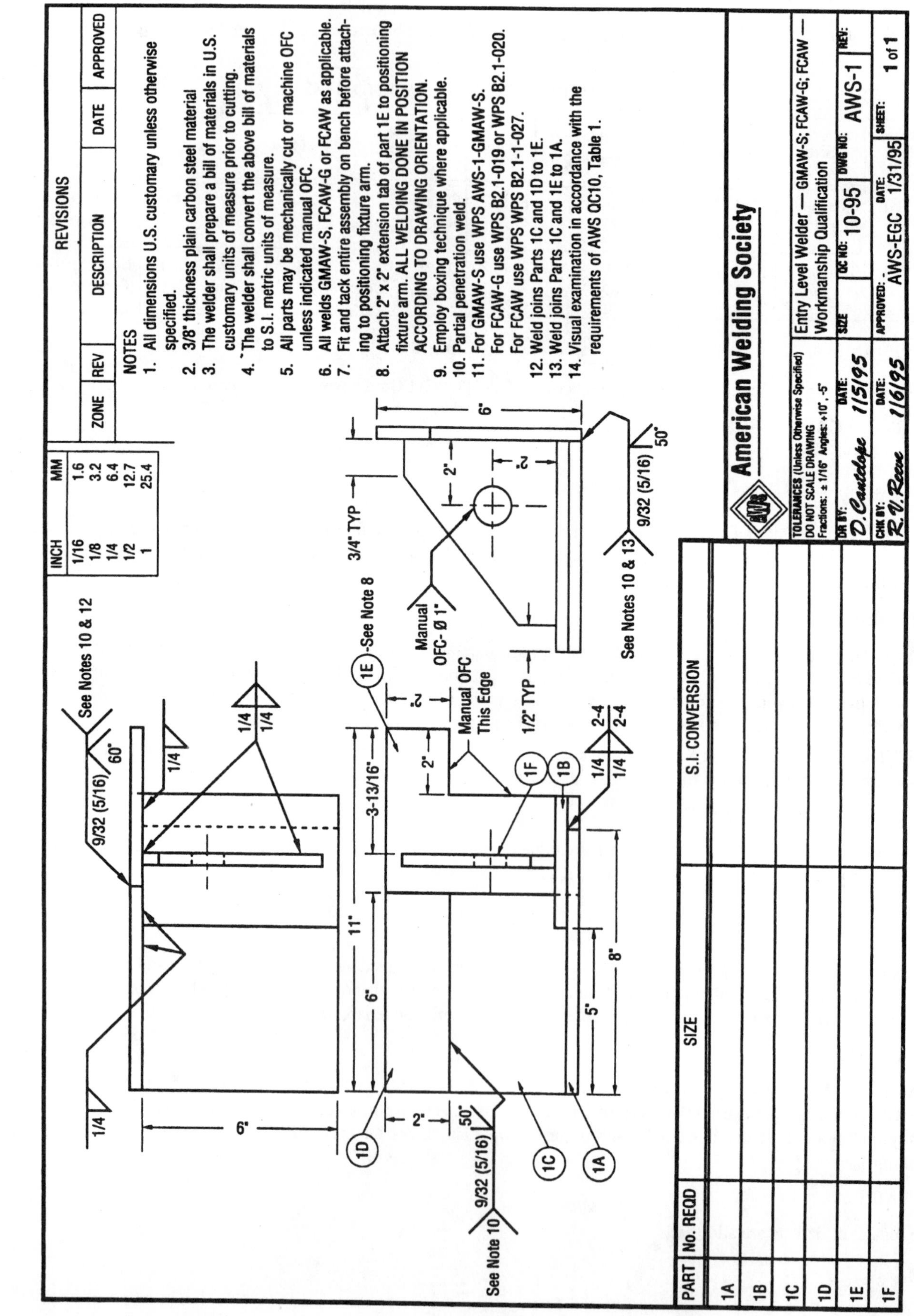
REVISIONS
ZONE
REV
DESCRIPTION
DATE
APPROVED
INCH MM
1/16 1.6
1/8 3.2
1/4 6.4
1/2 12.7
1 25.4
NOTES
1. All dimensions U.S. customary unless otherwise specified.
2. 3/8" thickness plain carbon steel material
3. The welder shall prepare a bill of materials in U.S. customary units of measure prior to cutting.
4. The welder shall convert the above bill of materials to S.I. metric units of measure.
5. All parts may be mechanically cut or machine OFC unless indicated manual OFC.
6. All welds GMAW-S, FCAW-G or FCAW as applicable.
7. Fit and tack entire assembly on bench before attaching to positioning fixture arm.
8. Attach 2" x 2" extension tab of part 1E to positioning fixture arm. ALL WELDING DONE IN POSITION ACCORDING TO DRAWING ORIENTATION.
9. Employ boxing technique where applicable.
10. Partial penetration weld.
11. For GMAW-S use WPS AWS-1-GMAW-S.
For FCAW-G use WPS B2.1-019 or WPS B2.1-020.
For FCAW use WPS B2.1-1-027.
12. Weld joins Parts 1C and 1D to 1E.
13. Weld joins Parts 1C and 1E to 1A.
14. Visual examination in accordance with the requirements of AWS QC10, Table 1.
See Notes 10 & 12
9/32 (5/16)
60°
1/4
2-4
1E
-See Note 8
3/4" TYP
Manual OFC- Ø 1"
Manual OFC This Edge
1/2" TYP
See Notes 10 & 13
50°
1F
1B
1D
1C
1A
See Note 10
6"
2"
11"
3-13/16"
5"
8"
PART
No. REQD
SIZE
S.I. CONVERSION
1A
1B
1C
1D
1E
1F
American Welding Society
TOLERANCES (Unless Otherwise Specified)
DO NOT SCALE DRAWING
Fractions: ± 1/16" Angles: +10°, -5°
Entry Level Welder — GMAW-S; FCAW-G; FCAW — Workmanship Qualification
DR BY: D. Cantelope
DATE: 1/5/95
SIZE
QC NO: 10-95
DWG NO: AWS-1
REV:
CHK BY: R.V. Reeve
DATE: 1/6/95
APPROVED: AWS-EGC
DATE: 1/31/95
SHEET: 1 of 1

PRACTICE 21-5

Name____ Date ______________

Class ______________________ Instructor ______________________ Grade ______________

WELDING PROCEDURE SPECIFICATION (WPS)

Welding Procedures Specifications No: PRACTICE 21-5 Date: ___________

TITLE:

Welding FCAW of plate to plate .

SCOPE:

This procedure is applicable for V-groove, bevel and fillet welds

within the range of 1/8 in. (3.2 mm) through 1 1/2 in. (38 mm)

Welding may be performed in the following positions ALL .

BASE METAL:

The base metal shall conform to Carbon Steel M-1, P-1 and S-1 Group 1 or 2

Backing material specification NONE .

FILLER METAL:

The filler metal shall conform to AWS specification No. E71T-11 from AWS specification A5.20 . This filler metal falls into F-number F-6 and A-number A-1 .

SHIELDING GAS:

The shielding gas, or gases, shall conform to the following compositions and purity:

N/A.

JOINT DESIGN AND TOLERANCES:

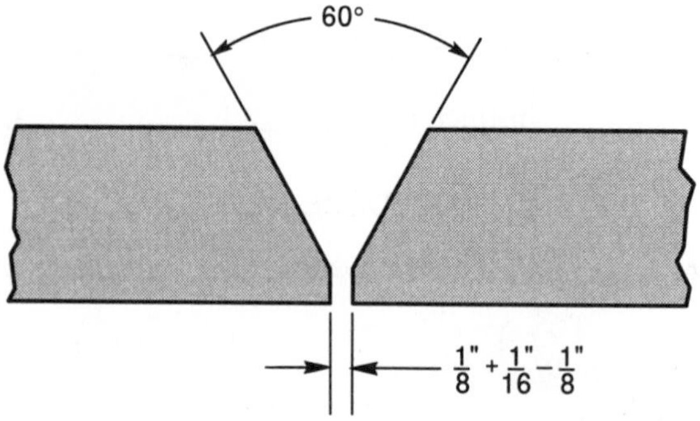

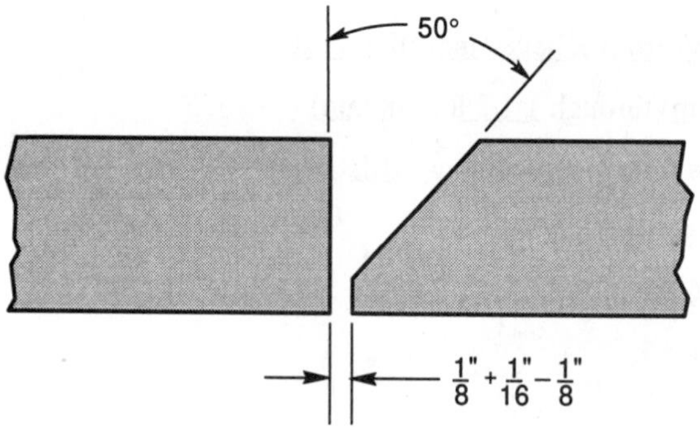

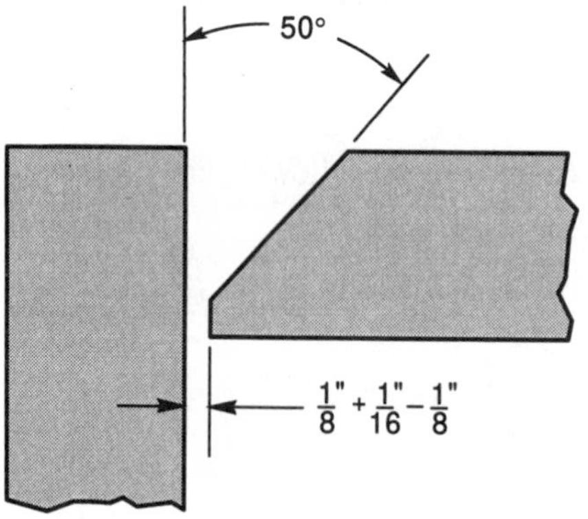

PREPARATION OF BASE METAL:

The bevels are to be flame cut on the edges of the plate before the parts are assembled. The beveled surface must be smooth and free of notches. Any roughness or notches that are deeper than 1/64 in. (0.4 mm) must be ground smooth.

All hydrocarbons and other contaminations, such as cutting fluids, grease, oil and primers, must be cleaned off of all parts and filler metals before welding. This cleaning can be done with any suitable solvents or detergents. The groove face and inside and outside plate surface within 1 in. (25 mm) of the joint must be mechanically cleaned of slag, rust and mill scale. Cleaning must be done with a wire brush or grinder down to bright metal.

ELECTRICAL CHARACTERISTICS:

The current shall be Direct Current Electrode Positive (DCEP) . The base metal shall be on the negative side of the line.

ELECTRODE		WELDING POWER			SHIELDING GAS		BASE METAL	
Type	Size	Amps	Wire Feed Speed IPM (cm/min)	Volts	Type	Flow	Type	Thickness
E71T-1	0.035 in. (0.9 mm)	130 to 150	288 to 380 (732 to 975)	22 to 25	CO_2 or 75%Ar/$CO_2$25%	30 to 50	Low-Carbon Steel	1/4 in. to 1/2 in. (6 mm to 13 mm)
E71T-1	0.045 in. (1.2 mm)	150 to 210	200 to 300 (508 to 762)	28 to 29	CO_2 or 75%Ar/$CO_2$25%	30 to 50	Low-Carbon Steel	1/4 in. to 1/2 in. (6 mm to 13 mm)

PREHEAT:

The parts must be heated to a temperature higher than 50°F (10°C) before any welding is started.

BACKING GAS:

N/A

SAFETY:

Proper protective clothing and equipment must be used. The area must be free of all hazards which may affect the welder or others in the area. The welding machine, welding leads, work clamp, electrode holder and other equipment must be in safe working order.

WELDING TECHNIQUE:

Using a 1/2 in. (13 mm) or larger gas nozzle and an approximately 3/4 in. (19 mm) contact tube-to-work distance for all welding, first tack weld the plates together according to the drawing. There should be about a 1/8-in. (3.2-mm) root gap between the plates with V-grooved or beveled edges. Use the E71T-1 arc welding electrodes to make a root pass to fuse the plates together. Clean the slag from the root pass being sure to remove any trapped slag along the sides of the weld.

Using the E71T-1 arc welding electrodes, make a series of stringer or weave filler welds, no thicker than 1/4 in. (6.4 mm), in the groove until the joint is filled. The 1/4 in. (6.4 mm) fillet welds are to be made with one pass.

INTERPASS TEMPERATURE:

The plate should not be heated to a temperature higher than 350°F (175°C) during the welding process. After each weld pass is completed, allow it to cool but never to a temperature below 50°F (10°C). The weldment must not be quenched in water.

CLEANING:

The slag must cleaned off between passes. The weld beads may be cleaned by a hand wire brush, a hand chipping, punch and hammer or a needle-scaler. All weld cleaning must be performed with the test plate in the welding position. A grinder may not be used to remove weld control problems such as undercut, overlap, trapped slag, etc.

INSPECTION:

Visually inspect the weld for uniformity and discontinuities. There shall be no cracks, no incomplete fusion and no overlap. Undercut shall not exceed the lesser of 10% of the base metal thickness or 1/32 in. (0.8 mm). The frequency of porosity shall not exceed one in each 4 in. (100 mm) of weld length and the maximum diameter shall not exceed 3/32 in. (2.4 mm).

REPAIR:

No repairs of defects are allowed.

SKETCHES:

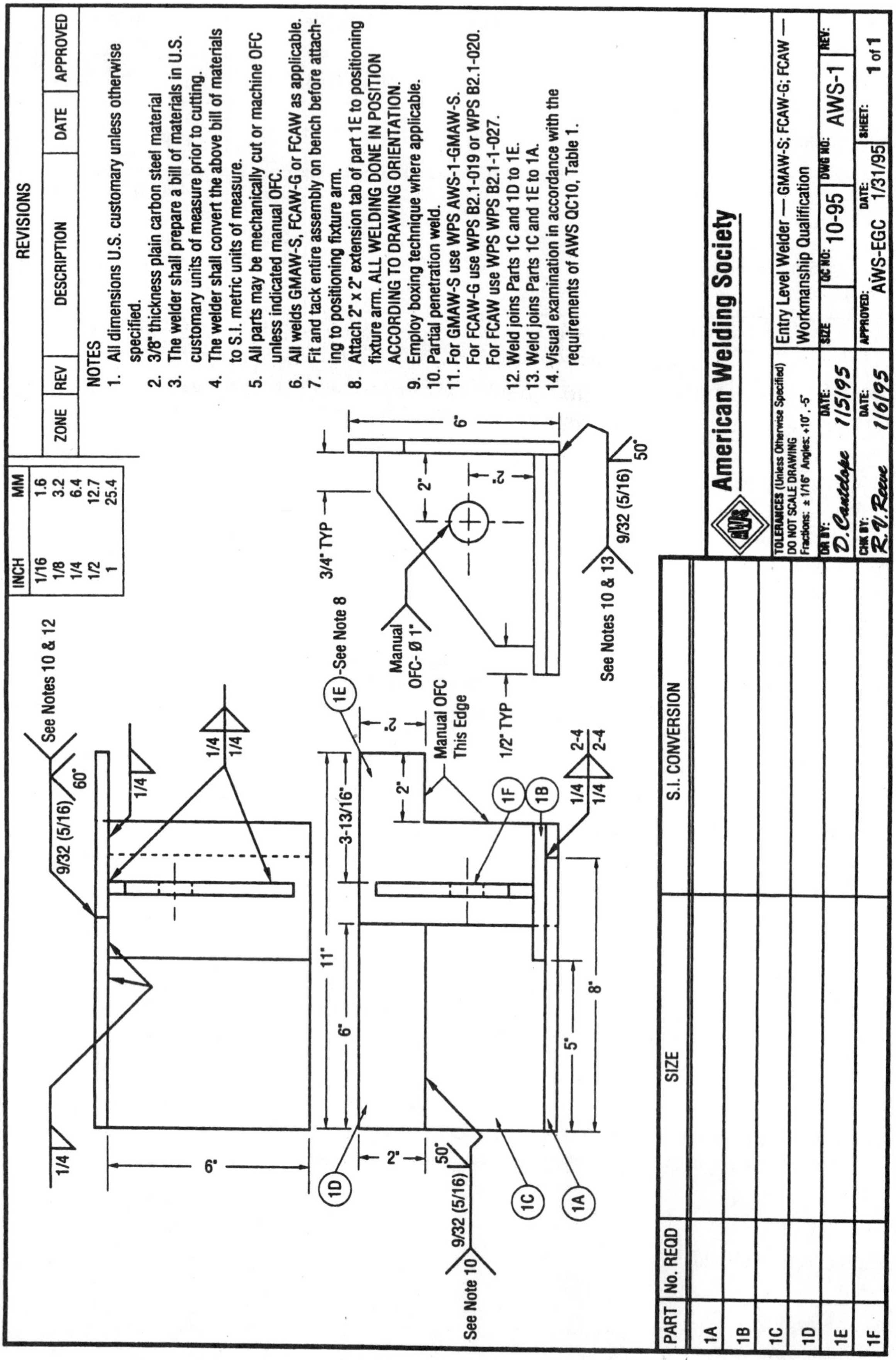
REVISIONS
ZONE
REV
DESCRIPTION
DATE
APPROVED
NOTES
1. All dimensions U.S. customary unless otherwise specified.
2. 3/8" thickness plain carbon steel material
3. The welder shall prepare a bill of materials in U.S. customary units of measure prior to cutting.
4. The welder shall convert the above bill of materials to S.I. metric units of measure.
5. All parts may be mechanically cut or machine OFC unless indicated manual OFC.
6. All welds GMAW-S, FCAW-G or FCAW as applicable.
7. Fit and tack entire assembly on bench before attaching to positioning fixture arm.
8. Attach 2" x 2" extension tab of part 1E to positioning fixture arm. ALL WELDING DONE IN POSITION ACCORDING TO DRAWING ORIENTATION.
9. Employ boxing technique where applicable.
10. Partial penetration weld.
11. For GMAW-S use WPS AWS-1-GMAW-S.
For FCAW-G use WPS B2.1-019 or WPS B2.1-020.
For FCAW use WPS B2.1-1-027.
12. Weld joins Parts 1C and 1D to 1E.
13. Weld joins Parts 1C and 1E to 1A.
14. Visual examination in accordance with the requirements of AWS QC10, Table 1.
INCH MM
1/16 1.6
1/8 3.2
1/4 6.4
1/2 12.7
1 25.4
See Notes 10 & 12
9/32 (5/16)
60°
1/4
1/4
1/4
1E
-See Note 8
Manual OFC- Ø 1"
3/4" TYP
2"
2"
6"
Manual OFC This Edge
1/2" TYP
1F
1B
1/4 2-4
1/4 2-4
3-13/16"
11"
6"
8"
5"
6"
2"
50°
9/32 (5/16)
See Note 10
1D
1C
1A
See Notes 10 & 13
9/32 (5/16)
50°
PART
No. REQD
SIZE
S.I. CONVERSION
1A
1B
1C
1D
1E
1F
American Welding Society
TOLERANCES (Unless Otherwise Specified)
DO NOT SCALE DRAWING
Fractions: ± 1/16" Angles: +10°, -5°
Entry Level Welder — GMAW-S; FCAW-G; FCAW — Workmanship Qualification
DR BY: D. Cantelupe DATE: 1/5/95
SIZE
QC NO: 10-95
DWG NO: AWS-1
REV:
CHK BY: R.V. Reeve DATE: 1/6/95
APPROVED: AWS-EGC DATE: 1/31/95
SHEET: 1 of 1

PRACTICE 21-6

Name______________________________ Date __________

Class __________ Instructor __________ Grade __________

WELDING PROCEDURE SPECIFICATION (WPS)

Welding Procedures Specifications No: PRACTICE 21-6 Date: __________

TITLE:

Welding GMAW of plate to plate .

SCOPE:

This procedure is applicable for V-groove and fillet welds

within the range of 1/8 in. (3.2 mm) through 1 1/2 in. (38 mm)

Welding may be performed in the following positions 1G and 2F .

BASE METAL:

The base metal shall conform to Carbon Steel M-1, P-1 and S-1 Group 1 or 2

Backing material specification NONE .

FILLER METAL:

The filler metal shall conform to AWS specification No. E70S-3 from AWS specification A5.18 . This filler metal falls into F-number F-6 and A-number A-1 .

SHIELDING GAS:

The shielding gas, or gases, shall conform to the following compositions and purity:

CO_2 at 30 to 50 CFH or 75% Ar/CO_2 25% at 30 to 50 CFH .

JOINT DESIGN AND TOLERANCES:

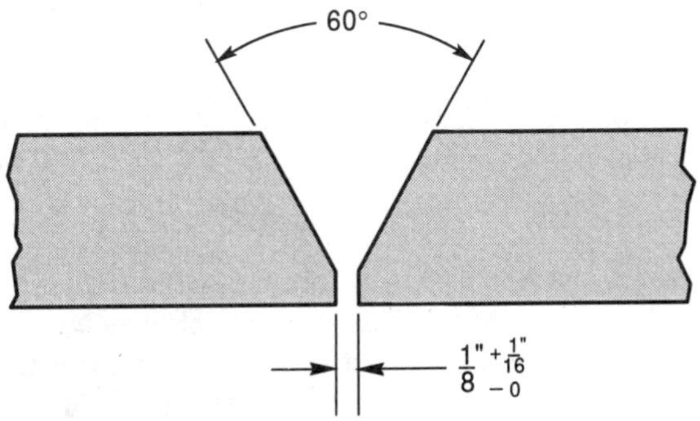

PREPARATION OF BASE METAL:

The bevels are to be flame cut on the edges of the plate before the parts are assembled. The beveled surface must be smooth and free of notches. Any roughness or notches that are deeper than 1/64 in. (0.4 mm) must be ground smooth.

All hydrocarbons and other contaminations, such as cutting fluids, grease, oil and primers, must be cleaned off of all parts and filler metals before welding. This cleaning can be done with any suitable solvents or detergents. The groove face and inside and outside plate surface within 1 in. (25 mm) of the joint must be mechanically cleaned of slag, rust and mill scale. Cleaning must be done with a wire brush or grinder down to bright metal.

ELECTRICAL CHARACTERISTICS:

The current shall be Direct Current Electrode Positive (DCEP) . The base metal shall be on the negative side of the line.

ELECTRODE		WELDING POWER			SHIELDING GAS		BASE METAL	
Type	Size	Amps	Wire Feed Speed IPM (cm/min)	Volts	Type	Flow	Type	Thickness
E70S-3	0.035 in. (0.9 mm)	180 to 230	400 to 550 (1016 to 1397)	25 to 27	Ar plus 2 % to 5% O_2	30 to 50	Low-Carbon Steel	1/4 in. to 1/2 in. (6 mm to 13 mm)
E70S-3	0.045 in. (1.2 mm)	260 to 340	300 to 500 (762 to 1270)	25 to 30	Ar plus 2 % to 5% O_2	30 to 50	Low-Carbon Steel	1/4 in. to 1/2 in. (6 mm to 13 mm)

PREHEAT:

The parts must be heated to a temperature higher than 50°F (10°C) before any welding is started.

BACKING GAS:

N/A

SAFETY:

Proper protective clothing and equipment must be used. The area must be free of all hazards which may affect the welder or others in the area. The welding machine, welding leads, work clamp, electrode holder and other equipment must be in safe working order.

WELDING TECHNIQUE:

Using a 3/4 in. (19 mm) or larger gas nozzle for all welding, first tack weld the plates together according to the drawing. There should be about a 1/16-in. (1.6-mm) root gap between the plates with V-grooved or beveled edges. Use the E70S-3 arc welding electrodes to make a root pass to fuse the plates together. Clean any silicon slag from the root pass being sure to remove any trapped silicon slag along the sides of the weld.

Using the E70S-3 arc welding electrodes, make a series of stringer or weave filler welds, no thicker than 1/4 in. (6.4 mm), in the groove until the joint is filled. The 1/4 in. (6.4 mm) fillet welds are to be made with one pass.

INTERPASS TEMPERATURE:

The plate should not be heated to a temperature higher than 350°F (175°C) during the welding process. After each weld pass is completed, allow it to cool but never to a temperature below 50°F (10°C). The weldment must not be quenched in water.

CLEANING:

Any slag must be cleaned off between passes. The weld beads may be cleaned by a hand wire brush, a hand chipping, punch and hammer or a needle-scaler. All weld cleaning must be performed with the test plate in the welding position. A grinder may not be used to remove weld control problems such as undercut, overlap, trapped slag, etc.

INSPECTION:

Visually inspect the weld for uniformity and discontinuities. There shall be no cracks, no incomplete fusion and no overlap. Undercut shall not exceed the lesser of 10% of the base metal thickness or 1/32 in. (0.8 mm). The frequency of porosity shall not exceed one in each 4 in. (100 mm) of weld length and the maximum diameter shall not exceed 3/32 in. (2.4 mm).

REPAIR:

No repairs of defects are allowed.

SKETCHES:

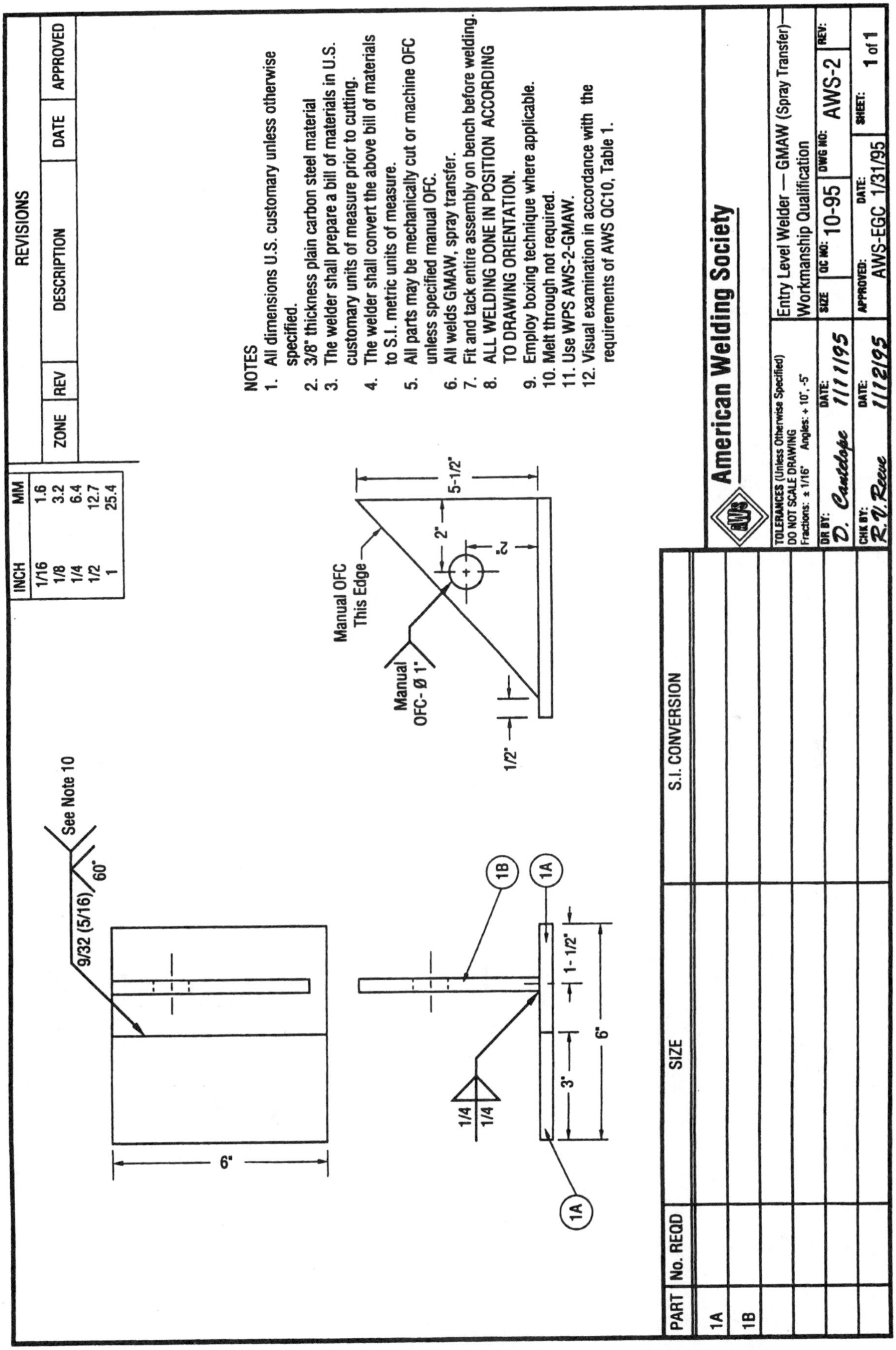
9/32 (5/16)
60°
See Note 10
6"
1/4
1/4
1B
1A
1A
3"
1- 1/2"
6"
Manual OFC
This Edge
Manual
OFC- Ø 1"
2"
2"
5-1/2"
1/2"
INCH MM
1/16 1.6
1/8 3.2
1/4 6.4
1/2 12.7
1 25.4
REVISIONS
ZONE REV DESCRIPTION DATE APPROVED
NOTES
1. All dimensions U.S. customary unless otherwise specified.
2. 3/8" thickness plain carbon steel material
3. The welder shall prepare a bill of materials in U.S. customary units of measure prior to cutting.
4. The welder shall convert the above bill of materials to S.I. metric units of measure.
5. All parts may be mechanically cut or machine OFC unless specified manual OFC.
6. All welds GMAW, spray transfer.
7. Fit and tack entire assembly on bench before welding.
8. ALL WELDING DONE IN POSITION ACCORDING TO DRAWING ORIENTATION.
9. Employ boxing technique where applicable.
10. Melt through not required.
11. Use WPS AWS-2-GMAW.
12. Visual examination in accordance with the requirements of AWS QC10, Table 1.
PART No. REQD SIZE S.I. CONVERSION
1A
1B
American Welding Society
TOLERANCES (Unless Otherwise Specified)
DO NOT SCALE DRAWING
Fractions: ± 1/16" Angles: + 10°, -5°
Entry Level Welder — GMAW (Spray Transfer)—
Workmanship Qualification
DR BY: D. Cantelope DATE: 1/11/95
CHK BY: R.V. Reeve DATE: 1/12/95
SIZE QC NO: 10-95 DWG NO: AWS-2 REV:
APPROVED: AWS-EGC DATE: 1/31/95 SHEET: 1 of 1

PRACTICE 21-7

Name________________________________ Date ____________

Class ______________ Instructor ______________ Grade ____________

WELDING PROCEDURE SPECIFICATION (WPS)

Welding Procedures Specifications No: PRACTICE 21-7 Date: ____________

TITLE:

Welding GTAW of sheet to sheet.

SCOPE:

This procedure is applicable for square groove and fillet welds

within the range of 18 gauge through 10 gauge

Welding may be performed in the following positions 1G and 2F.

BASE METAL:

The base metal shall conform to Carbon Steel M-1 Group 1

Backing material specification NONE.

FILLER METAL:

The filler metal shall conform to AWS specification No. E70S-3 from AWS specification A5.18. This filler metal falls into F-number F-6 and A-number A-1.

ELECTRODE:

The tungsten electrode shall conform to AWS specification No. EWTh-2 from AWS specification A5.12. The tungsten diameter shall be 1/8 in. (3.2 mm) maximum. The tungsten end shape shall be Tapered at 2 to 3 times in length to its diameter.

SHIELDING GAS:

The shielding gas, or gases, shall conform to the following compositions and purity:

Welding Grade Argon.

JOINT DESIGN AND TOLERANCES:

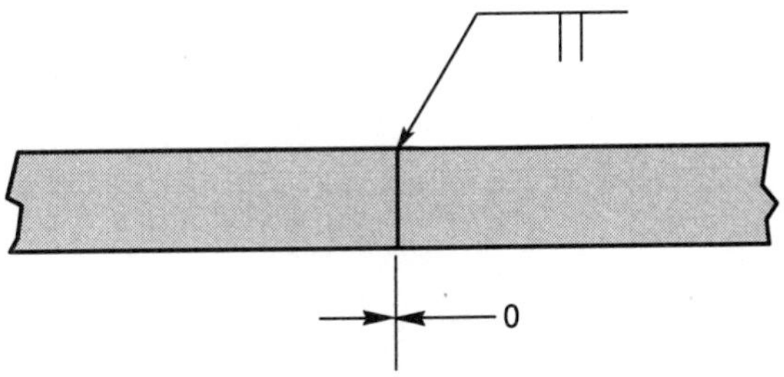

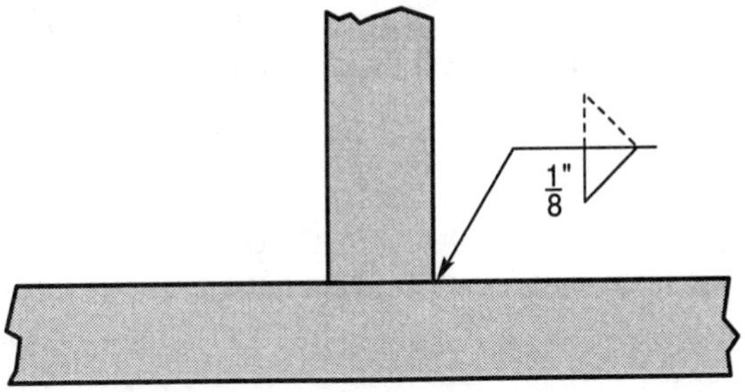

PREPARATION OF BASE METAL:

All hydrocarbons and other contaminations, such as cutting fluids, grease, oil and primers, must be cleaned off of all parts and filler metals before welding. This cleaning can be done with any suitable solvents or detergents. The joint face, inside and outside plate surface within 1 in. (25 mm) of the joint must be mechanically cleaned of slag, rust and mill scale. Cleaning must be done with a wire brush or grinder down to bright metal.

ELECTRICAL CHARACTERISTICS:

The current shall be Direct Current Electrode Negative (DCEN) . The base metal shall be on the positive side of the line.

METAL SPECIFICATIONS		GAS FLOW			NOZZLE SIZE in. (mm)	AMPERAGE Min. Max.
THICKNESS	DIA. of E70S-3*	RATES CFM (L/min)	PURGING TIMES PREPURGING	POSTPURGING		
18 ga.	1/16" (1.6 mm)	15 to 20 (7 to 9)	10 to 15 sec.	10 to 25 sec.	1/4 to 3/8 (6 to 10)	45 to 65
17 ga.	1/16" (1.6 mm)	15 to 20 (7 to 9)	10 to 15 sec.	10 to 25 sec.	1/4 to 3/8 (6 to 10)	45 to 70
16 ga.	1/16" (1.6 mm)	15 to 20 (7 to 9)	10 to 15 sec.	10 to 25 sec.	1/4 to 3/8 (6 to 10)	50 to 75
15 ga.	1/16" (1.6 mm)	15 to 20 (7 to 9)	10 to 15 sec.	10 to 25 sec.	1/4 to 3/8 (6 to 10)	55 to 80
14 ga.	3/32" (2.4 mm)	20 to 25 (9 to 12)	10 to 20 sec.	10 to 30 sec.	3/8 to 5/8 (10 to 16)	60 to 90
13 ga.	3/32" (2.4 mm)	20 to 25 (9 to 12)	10 to 20 sec.	10 to 30 sec.	3/8 to 5/8 (10 to 16)	60 to 100
12 ga.	3/32" (2.4 mm)	20 to 25 (9 to 12)	10 to 20 sec.	10 to 30 sec.	3/8 to 5/8 (10 to 16)	60 to 110
11 ga.	3/32" (2.4 mm)	20 to 25 (9 to 12)	10 to 20 sec.	10 to 30 sec.	3/8 to 5/8 (10 to 16)	60 to 120
10 ga.	3/32" (2.4 mm)	20 to 25 (9 to 12)	10 to 20 sec.	10 to 30 sec.	3/8 to 5/8 (10 to 16)	70 to 130

*Other E70S-X filler metal may be used.

PREHEAT:

The parts must be heated to a temperature higher than 50°F (10°C) before any welding is started.

BACKING GAS:

N/A

SAFETY:

Proper protective clothing and equipment must be used. The area must be free of all hazards which may affect the welder or others in the area. The welding machine, welding leads, work clamp, electrode holder and other equipment must be in safe working order.

WELDING TECHNIQUE:

TACK WELDS: With the parts securely clamped in place with the correct root gap, the tack welds are to be performed. Holding the electrode so that it is very close to the root face but not touching, slowly increase the current until the arc starts and a molten weld pool is formed. Add filler metal as required to maintain a slight convex weld face and a flat or slightly concave root face. When it's time to end the tack weld, lower the current slowly so that the molten weld pool can be tapered down in size. When all tack welds are complete, allow the parts to cool as needed before assembling the remaining parts. Repeat the tack welding procedure until the entire part is assembled.

SQUARE GROOVE AND FILLET WELDS: Holding the electrode so that it is very close to the metal surface but not touching, slowly increase the current until the arc starts and a molten weld pool is formed. As the weld progresses, add filler metal as required to maintain a flat or slightly convex weld face. If it's necessary to stop the weld, to reposition yourself, or the weld is completed, the current must be lowered slowly so that the molten weld pool can be tapered down in size.

INTERPASS TEMPERATURE:

The plate should not be heated to a temperature higher than 120°F (49°C) during the welding process. After each weld pass is completed, allow it to cool but never to a temperature below 50°F (10°C). The weldment must not be quenched in water.

CLEANING:

Recleaning may be required if the parts or filler metal become contaminated or reoxidize to a degree that the weld quality will be affected. Reclean using the same procedure used for the original metal preparation. Any slag must cleaned off between passes.

INSPECTION:

Visually inspect the weld for uniformity and discontinuities. There shall be no cracks, no incomplete fusion and no overlap. Undercut shall not exceed the lesser of 10% of the base metal thickness or 1/32 in. (0.8 mm). The frequency of porosity shall not exceed one in each 4 in. (100 mm) of weld length and the maximum diameter shall not exceed 3/32 in. (2.4 mm).

REPAIR:

No repairs of defects are allowed.

SKETCHES:

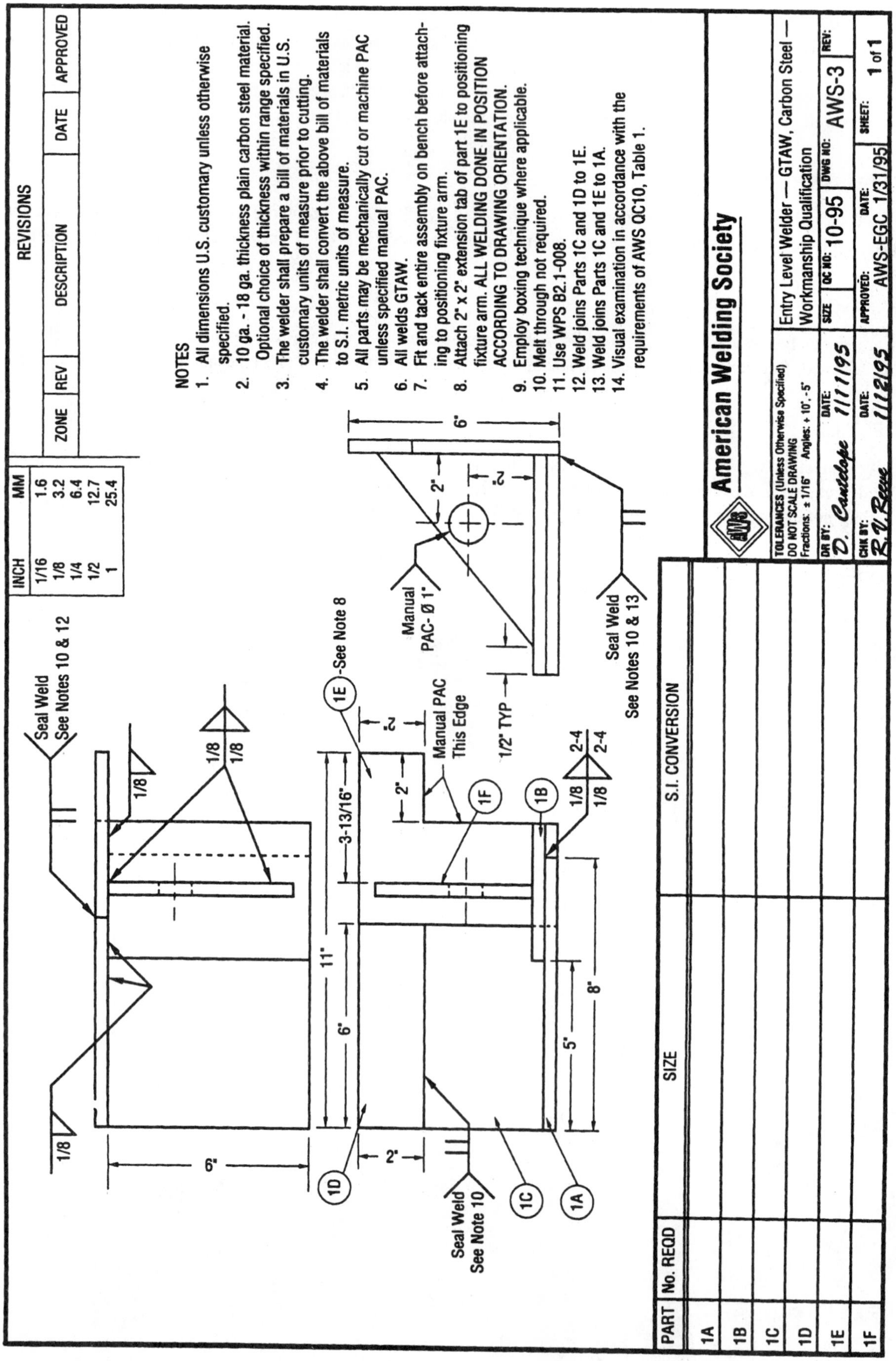
REVISIONS
ZONE
REV
DESCRIPTION
DATE
APPROVED
INCH MM
1/16 1.6
1/8 3.2
1/4 6.4
1/2 12.7
1 25.4
Seal Weld
See Notes 10 & 12
1/8
1/8
1/8
1/8
6"
2"
1D
1C
1A
Seal Weld
See Note 10
6"
11"
3-13/16"
5"
8"
2"
2"
2-4
2-4
1/8
1/8
1B
1F
1E
-See Note 8
Manual PAC
This Edge
1/2" TYP
Manual
PAC- Ø 1"
2"
6"
Seal Weld
See Notes 10 & 13
NOTES
1. All dimensions U.S. customary unless otherwise specified.
2. 10 ga. - 18 ga. thickness plain carbon steel material. Optional choice of thickness within range specified.
3. The welder shall prepare a bill of materials in U.S. customary units of measure prior to cutting.
4. The welder shall convert the above bill of materials to S.I. metric units of measure.
5. All parts may be mechanically cut or machine PAC unless specified manual PAC.
6. All welds GTAW.
7. Fit and tack entire assembly on bench before attaching to positioning fixture arm.
8. Attach 2" x 2" extension tab of part 1E to positioning fixture arm. ALL WELDING DONE IN POSITION ACCORDING TO DRAWING ORIENTATION.
9. Employ boxing technique where applicable.
10. Melt through not required.
11. Use WPS B2.1-008.
12. Weld joins Parts 1C and 1D to 1E.
13. Weld joins Parts 1C and 1E to 1A.
14. Visual examination in accordance with the requirements of AWS QC10, Table 1.
PART
No. REQD
SIZE
S.I. CONVERSION
1A
1B
1C
1D
1E
1F
American Welding Society
TOLERANCES (Unless Otherwise Specified)
DO NOT SCALE DRAWING
Fractions: ± 1/16" Angles: + 10°, -5°
Entry Level Welder — GTAW, Carbon Steel — Workmanship Qualification
DR BY: D. Cantelope
DATE: 1/1/95
SIZE
QC NO: 10-95
DWG NO: AWS-3
REV:
CHK BY: R.V. Reeve
DATE: 1/12/95
APPROVED: AWS-EGC
DATE: 1/31/95
SHEET: 1 of 1

PRACTICE 21-8

Name____ Date ____________

Class ____________________ Instructor ____________________ Grade ____________

WELDING PROCEDURE SPECIFICATION (WPS)

Welding Procedures Specifications No: PRACTICE 21-8 Date: ___________

TITLE:

Welding GTAW of sheet to sheet .

SCOPE:

This procedure is applicable for square groove and fillet welds

within the range of 18 gauge through 10 gauge

Welding may be performed in the following positions 1G and 2F .

BASE METAL:

The base metal shall conform to Austenitic Stainless Steel M-8 or P-8

Backing material specification NONE .

FILLER METAL:

The filler metal shall conform to AWS specification No. ER3XX from AWS specification A5.9 . This filler metal falls into F-number F-6 and A-number A-8 .

ELECTRODE:

The tungsten electrode shall conform to AWS specification No. EWTh-2 from AWS specification A5.12 . The tungsten diameter shall be 1/8 in. (3.2 mm) maximum . The tungsten end shape shall be Tapered at 2 to 3 times in length to its diameter .

SHIELDING GAS:

The shielding gas, or gases, shall conform to the following compositions and purity:

Welding Grade Argon .

JOINT DESIGN AND TOLERANCES:

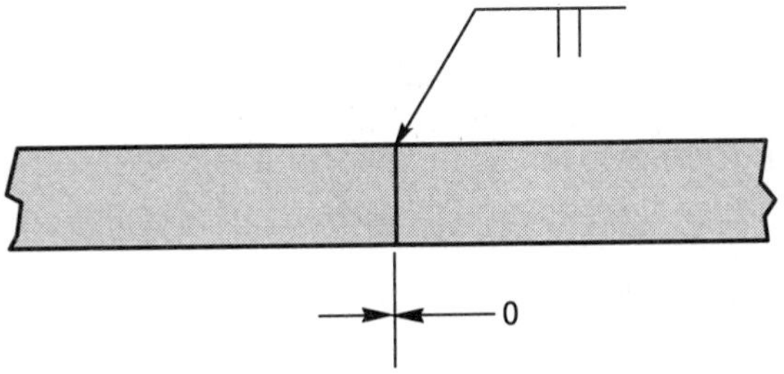

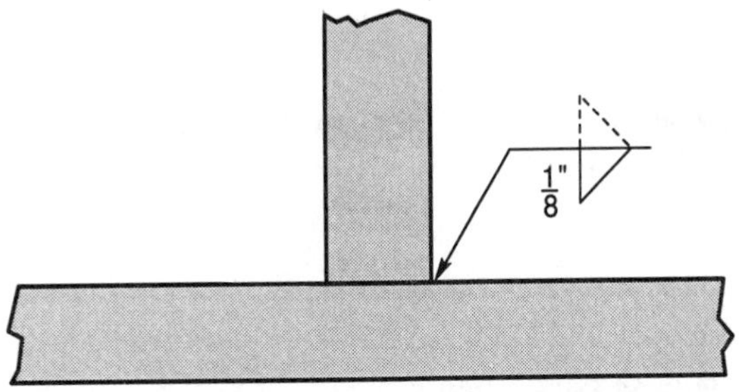

PREPARATION OF BASE METAL:

All hydrocarbons and other contaminations, such as cutting fluids, grease, oil and primers, must be cleaned off of all parts and filler metals before welding. This cleaning can be done with any suitable solvents or detergents. The joint face and inside and outside plate surface within 1 in. (25 mm) of the joint must be cleaned of slag, oxide and scale. Cleaning can be mechanical or chemical. Mechanical metal cleaning may be done by grinding, stainless steel wire brushing, scraping, machining, or filing. Chemical cleaning may be done by using acids, alkalies, solvents, or detergents. Cleaning must be done down to bright metal.

ELECTRICAL CHARACTERISTICS:

The current shall be Direct Current Electrode Negative (DCEN) . The base metal shall be on the positive side of the line.

METAL SPECIFICATIONS		GAS FLOW			NOZZLE SIZE in. (mm)	AMPERAGE Min. Max.
THICKNESS	DIA. of ER3XX*	RATES CFM (L/min)	PURGING TIMES PREPURGING	POSTPURGING		
18 ga.	1/16" (1.6 mm)	15 to 20 (7 to 9)	10 to 15 sec.	10 to 25 sec.	1/4 to 3/8 (6 to 10)	35 to 60
17 ga.	1/16" (1.6 mm)	15 to 20 (7 to 9)	10 to 15 sec.	10 to 25 sec.	1/4 to 3/8 (6 to 10)	40 to 65
16 ga.	1/16" (1.6 mm)	15 to 20 (7 to 9)	10 to 15 sec.	10 to 25 sec.	1/4 to 3/8 (6 to 10)	40 to 75
15 ga.	1/16" (1.6 mm)	15 to 20 (7 to 9)	10 to 15 sec.	10 to 25 sec.	1/4 to 3/8 (6 to 10)	50 to 80
14 ga.	3/32" (2.4 mm)	20 to 25 (9 to 12)	10 to 20 sec.	10 to 30 sec.	3/8 to 5/8 (10 to 16)	50 to 90
13 ga.	3/32" (2.4 mm)	20 to 25 (9 to 12)	10 to 20 sec.	10 to 30 sec.	3/8 to 5/8 (10 to 16)	55 to 100
12 ga.	3/32" (2.4 mm)	20 to 25 (9 to 12)	10 to 20 sec.	10 to 30 sec.	3/8 to 5/8 (10 to 16)	60 to 110
11 ga.	3/32" (2.4 mm)	20 to 25 (9 to 12)	10 to 20 sec.	10 to 30 sec.	3/8 to 5/8 (10 to 16)	65 to 120
10 ga.	3/32" (2.4 mm)	20 to 25 (9 to 12)	10 to 20 sec.	10 to 30 sec.	3/8 to 5/8 (10 to 16)	70 to 130

*Any RE3XX stainless steel A5.9 filler metal may be used.

PREHEAT:

The parts must be heated to a temperature higher than 50°F (10°C) before any welding is started.

BACKING GAS:

N/A

SAFETY:

Proper protective clothing and equipment must be used. The area must be free of all hazards which may affect the welder or others in the area. The welding machine, welding leads, work clamp, electrode holder and other equipment must be in safe working order.

WELDING TECHNIQUE:

TACK WELDS: With the parts securely clamped in place with the correct root gap, the tack welds are to be performed. Holding the electrode so that it is very close to the root face but not touching, slowly increase the current until the arc starts and a molten weld pool is formed. Add filler metal as required to maintain a slight convex weld face and a flat or slightly concave root face. When it's time to end the tack weld, lower the current slowly so that the molten weld pool can be tapered down in size. When all tack welds are complete, allow the parts to cool as needed before assembling the remaining parts. Repeat the tack welding procedure until the entire part is assembled.

SQUARE GROOVE AND FILLET WELDS: Holding the electrode so that it is very close to the metal surface but not touching, slowly increase the current until the arc starts and a molten weld pool is formed. As the weld progresses, add filler metal as required to maintain a flat or slightly convex weld face. If it's necessary to stop the weld, to reposition yourself, or the weld is completed, the current must be lowered slowly so that the molten weld pool can be tapered down in size.

INTERPASS TEMPERATURE:

The plate should not be heated to a temperature higher than 350°F (180°C) during the welding process. After each weld pass is completed, allow it to cool but never to a temperature below 50°F (10°C). The weldment must not be quenched in water.

CLEANING:

Recleaning may be required if the parts or filler metal become contaminated or reoxidize to a degree that the weld quality will be affected. Reclean using the same procedure used for the original metal preparation.

INSPECTION:

Visually inspect the weld for uniformity and discontinuities. There shall be no cracks, no incomplete fusion and no overlap. Undercut shall not exceed the lesser of 10% of the base metal thickness or 1/32 in. (0.8 mm). The frequency of porosity shall not exceed one in each 4 in. (100 mm) of weld length and the maximum diameter shall not exceed 3/32 in. (2.4 mm).

REPAIR:

No repairs of defects are allowed.

SKETCHES:

INCH	MM
1/16	1.6
1/8	3.2
1/4	6.4
1/2	12.7
1	25.4

REVISIONS				
ZONE	REV	DESCRIPTION	DATE	APPROVED

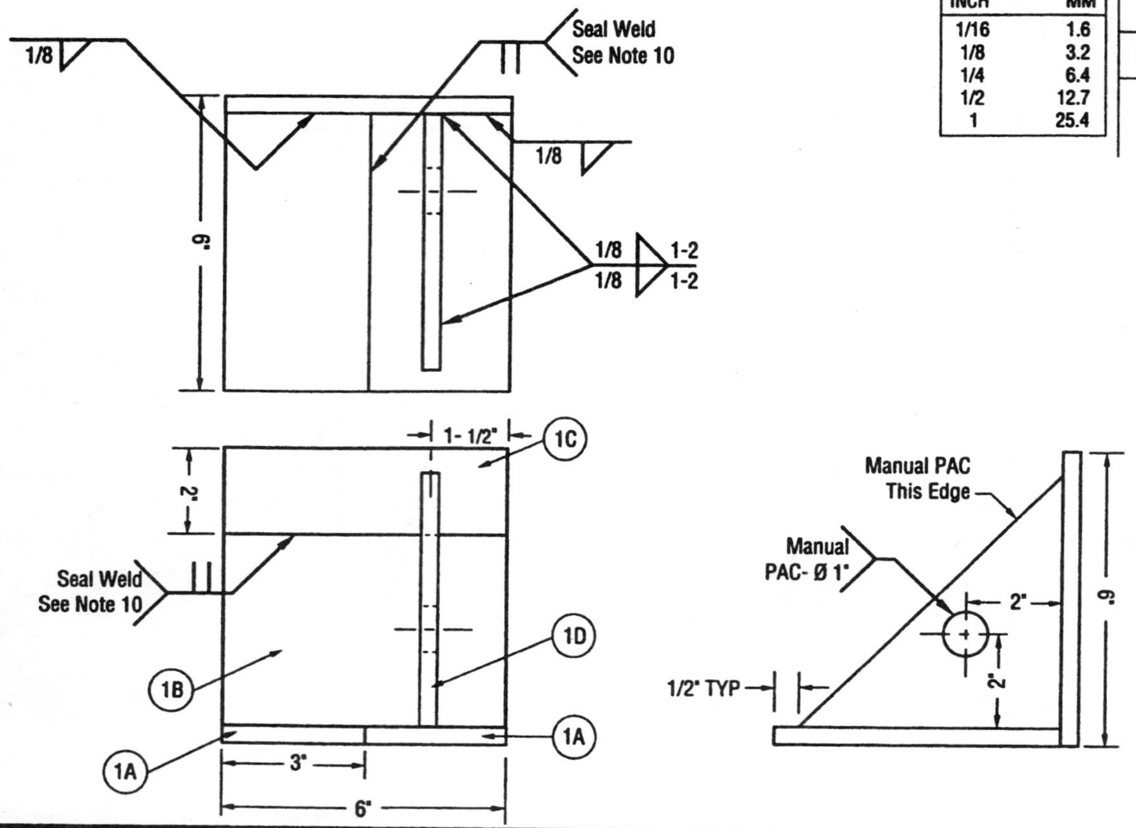

NOTES
1. All dimensions U.S. customary unless otherwise specified.
2. 10 ga. - 18 ga. thickness stainless steel material. Optional choice of thickness within range specified.
3. The welder shall prepare a bill of materials in U.S. customary units of measure prior to cutting.
4. The welder shall convert the above bill of materials to S.I. metric units of measure.
5. All parts may be mechanically cut or machine PAC unless specified manual PAC.
6. All welds GTAW.
7. Fit and tack entire assembly on bench before welding.
8. ALL WELDING DONE IN POSITION ACCORDING TO DRAWING ORIENTATION.
9. Employ boxing technique where applicable.
10. Melt through not required.
11. Use WPS B2.1.009.
12. Visual examination in accordance with the requirements of AWS QC10, Table 1.

PART	No. REQD	SIZE	S.I. CONVERSION
1A			
1B			

American Welding Society

TOLERANCES (Unless Otherwise Specified)
DO NOT SCALE DRAWING
Fractions: ± 1/16" Angles: + 10°, -5°

Entry Level Welder — GTAW, Stainless Steel — Workmanship Qualification

DR BY: D. Cantelope	DATE: 1/11/95	SIZE	QC NO: 10-95	DWG NO: AWS-4	REV:
CHK BY: R.V. Reeve	DATE: 1/12/95	APPROVED: AWS-EGC	DATE: 1/31/95	SHEET: 1 of 1	

PRACTICE 21-9

Name________________________________ Date ____________

Class ________________ Instructor ________________ Grade ____________

WELDING PROCEDURE SPECIFICATION (WPS)

Welding Procedures Specifications No: PRACTICE 21-9 Date: ___________

TITLE:

Welding GTAW of sheet to sheet.

SCOPE:

This procedure is applicable for square groove and fillet welds

within the range of 18 gauge through 10 gauge

Welding may be performed in the following positions 1G and 2F.

BASE METAL:

The base metal shall conform to Aluminum M-22 or P-22

Backing material specification NONE.

FILLER METAL:

The filler metal shall conform to AWS specification No. ER4043 from AWS specification A5.10. This filler metal falls into F-number F-23 and A-number __________.

ELECTRODE:

The tungsten electrode shall conform to AWS specification No. EWP from AWS specification A5.12. The tungsten diameter shall be 1/8 in. (3.2 mm) maximum. The tungsten end shape shall be Rounded.

SHIELDING GAS:

The shielding gas, or gases, shall conform to the following compositions and purity:

Welding Grade Argon.

JOINT DESIGN AND TOLERANCES:

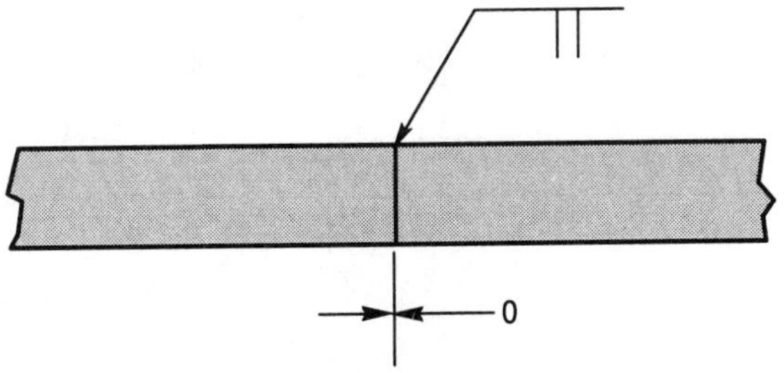

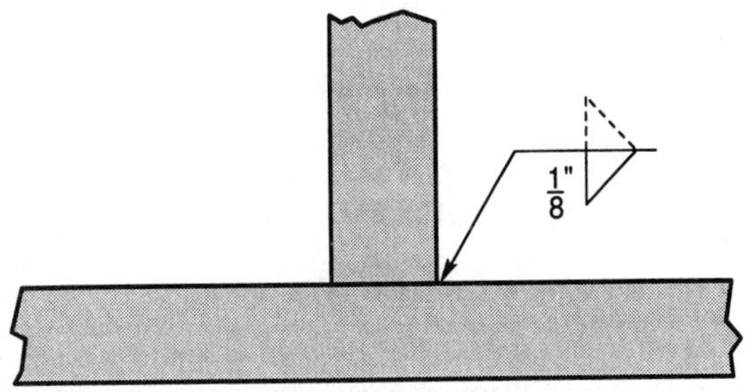

PREPARATION OF BASE METAL:

All hydrocarbons and other contaminations, such as cutting fluids, grease, oil and primers, must be cleaned off of all parts and filler metals before welding. This cleaning can be done with any suitable solvents or detergents. The joint face, inside and outside plate surface within 1 in. (25 mm) of the joint must be mechanically or chemically cleaned of oxides. Mechanical cleaning may be done by stainless steel wire brushing, scraping, machining, or filing. Chemical cleaning may be done by using acids, alkalies, solvents, or detergents. Because the oxide layer may reform quickly and affect the weld, welding should be started within 10 minutes of cleaning.

ELECTRICAL CHARACTERISTICS:

The current shall be Alternating Current High Frequency Stabilized (balanced wave preferably). The base metal shall be on the N/A side of the line.

METAL SPECIFICATIONS		GAS FLOW			NOZZLE SIZE in. (mm)	AMPERAGE Min. Max.
THICKNESS	DIA. of ER3XX*	RATES CFM (L/min)	PURGING TIMES PREPURGING	POSTPURGING		
18 ga.	1/16" (1.6 mm)	20 to 30 (9 to 14)	10 to 15 sec.	10 to 25 sec.	1/4 to 3/8 (6 to 10)	40 to 60
17 ga.	1/16" (1.6 mm)	20 to 30 (9 to 14)	10 to 15 sec.	10 to 25 sec.	1/4 to 3/8 (6 to 10)	50 to 70
16 ga.	1/16" (1.6 mm)	20 to 30 (9 to 14)	10 to 15 sec.	10 to 25 sec.	1/4 to 3/8 (6 to 10)	60 to 75
15 ga.	1/16" (1.6 mm)	20 to 30 (9 to 14)	10 to 15 sec.	10 to 25 sec.	1/4 to 3/8 (6 to 10)	65 to 85
14 ga.	3/32" (2.4 mm)	20 to 30 (9 to 14)	10 to 20 sec.	10 to 30 sec.	3/8 to 5/8 (10 to 16)	75 to 90
13 ga.	3/32" (2.4 mm)	25 to 40 (12 to 19)	10 to 20 sec.	10 to 30 sec.	3/8 to 5/8 (10 to 16)	85 to 100
12 ga.	3/32" (2.4 mm)	25 to 40 (12 to 19)	10 to 20 sec.	10 to 30 sec.	3/8 to 5/8 (10 to 16)	90 to 110
11 ga.	3/32" (2.4 mm)	25 to 40 (12 to 19)	10 to 20 sec.	10 to 30 sec.	3/8 to 5/8 (10 to 16)	100 to 115
10 ga.	3/32" (2.4 mm)	25 to 40 (12 to 19)	10 to 20 sec.	10 to 30 sec.	3/8 to 5/8 (10 to 16)	110 to 125

*Other aluminum A5.10 filler metal may be used if needed.

PREHEAT:

The parts must be heated to a temperature higher than 50°F (10°C) before any welding is started.

BACKING GAS:

N/A

SAFETY:

Proper protective clothing and equipment must be used. The area must be free of all hazards which may affect the welder or others in the area. The welding machine, welding leads, work clamp, electrode holder and other equipment must be in safe working order.

WELDING TECHNIQUE:

The welder's hands or gloves must be clean and oil-free to prevent recontaminating the metal or filler rods.

TACK WELDS: With the parts securely clamped in place with the correct root gap, the tack welds are to be performed. Holding the electrode so that it is very close to the root face but not touching, slowly increase the current until the arc starts and a molten weld pool is formed. Add filler metal as required to maintain a slight convex weld face and a flat or slightly concave root face. When it's time to end the tack weld, lower the current slowly so that the molten weld pool can be tapered down in size. When all tack welds are complete, allow the parts to cool as needed before assembling the remaining parts. Repeat the tack welding procedure until the entire part is assembled.

SQUARE GROOVE AND FILLET WELDS: Holding the electrode so that it is very close to the metal surface but not touching, slowly increase the current until the arc starts and a molten weld pool is formed. As the weld progresses, add filler metal as required to maintain a flat or slightly convex weld face. If it's necessary to stop the weld, to reposition yourself, or the weld is completed, the current must be lowered slowly so that the molten weld pool can be tapered down in size.

INTERPASS TEMPERATURE:

The plate should not be heated to a temperature higher than 120°F (49°C) during the welding process. After each weld pass is completed, allow it to cool but never to a temperature below 50°F (10°C). The weldment must not be quenched in water.

CLEANING:

Recleaning may be required if the parts or filler metal become contaminated or reoxidize to a degree that the weld quality will be affected. Reclean using the same procedure used for the original metal preparation.

INSPECTION:

Visually inspect the weld for uniformity and discontinuities. There shall be no cracks, no incomplete fusion and no overlap. Undercut shall not exceed the lesser of 10% of the base metal thickness or 1/32 in. (0.8 mm). The frequency of porosity shall not exceed one in each 4 in. (100 mm) of weld length and the maximum diameter shall not exceed 3/32 in. (2.4 mm).

REPAIR:

No repairs of defects are allowed.

SKETCHES:

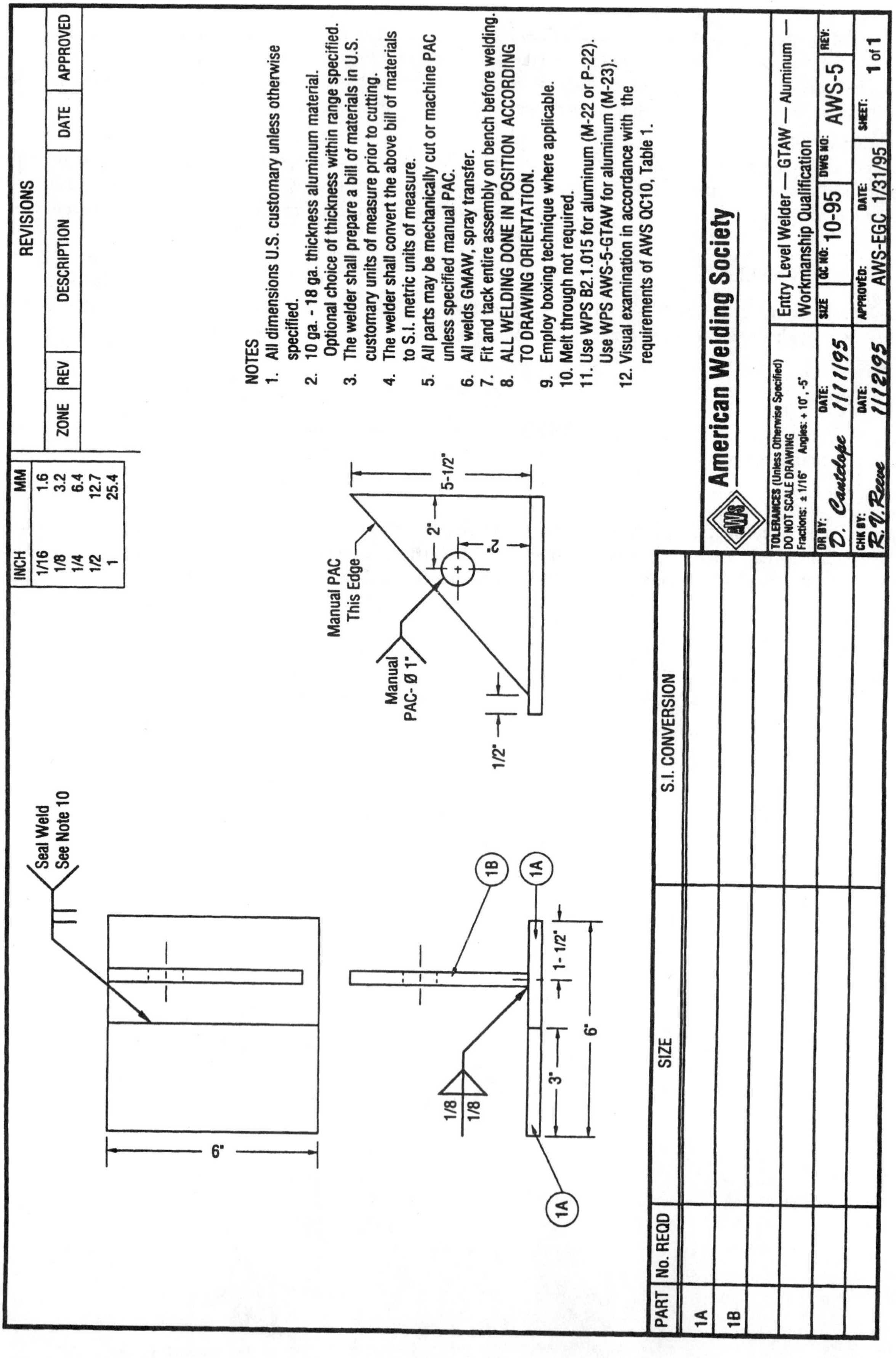
REVISIONS
ZONE
REV
DESCRIPTION
DATE
APPROVED
INCH MM
1/16 1.6
1/8 3.2
1/4 6.4
1/2 12.7
1 25.4
NOTES
1. All dimensions U.S. customary unless otherwise specified.
2. 10 ga. - 18 ga. thickness aluminum material. Optional choice of thickness within range specified.
3. The welder shall prepare a bill of materials in U.S. customary units of measure prior to cutting.
4. The welder shall convert the above bill of materials to S.I. metric units of measure.
5. All parts may be mechanically cut or machine PAC unless specified manual PAC.
6. All welds GMAW, spray transfer.
7. Fit and tack entire assembly on bench before welding.
8. ALL WELDING DONE IN POSITION ACCORDING TO DRAWING ORIENTATION.
9. Employ boxing technique where applicable.
10. Melt through not required.
11. Use WPS B2.1.015 for aluminum (M-22 or P-22). Use WPS AWS-5-GTAW for aluminum (M-23).
12. Visual examination in accordance with the requirements of AWS QC10, Table 1.
Seal Weld
See Note 10
6"
1B
1A
1A
1/8
1/8
3"
1- 1/2"
6"
Manual PAC
This Edge
Manual
PAC- Ø 1"
2"
2"
5-1/2"
1/2"
PART
No. REQD
SIZE
S.I. CONVERSION
1A
1B
American Welding Society
TOLERANCES (Unless Otherwise Specified)
DO NOT SCALE DRAWING
Fractions: ± 1/16" Angles: + 10°, -5°
Entry Level Welder — GTAW — Aluminum — Workmanship Qualification
DR BY: D. Cantelope
DATE: 1/11/95
SIZE
QC NO: 10-95
DWG NO: AWS-5
REV:
CHK BY: R.V. Reeve
DATE: 1/12/95
APPROVED: AWS-EGC
DATE: 1/31/95
SHEET: 1 of 1

PRACTICE 21-10

Name______________________________ Date ____________

Class ____________________ Instructor ____________________ Grade ____________

WELDER AND WELDER OPERATOR QUALIFICATION TEST RECORD (WPS)

Using a completed weld such as the ones from PRACTICE 21-1 or 21-2, you will follow the steps listed below and complete the test record shown in **Figure 21-34**. This form is a composite of sample test recording forms provided by AWS, ASME, and API codes. You may want to obtain a copy of one of the codes or standards and compare a weld you made to the standard. This is a good form to use when you are testing one of the practice welds in this text.

NOTE: Not all of the blanks will be filled in on the forms. The forms are designed to be used with a large variety of weld procedures, so they have spaces that will not be used each time.

1. Welder's name: The person who performed the weld.
2. Identification no.: On a welding job, every person has an identification number that is used on the time card and paycheck. In this space, you can write the class number or section number since you do not have a clock number.
3. Welding process(es): Was the weld performed with SMAW, GMAW, or GTAW?
4. How was the weld accomplished: manually, semiautomatically, or automatically?
5. Test position: 1G, 2G, 3G, 4G, 1F, 2F, 3F, 4F, 5G, 6G, 6GR, Figure 21-35.
6. What WPS was used for this test?
7. Base metal specification: This is the ASTM specification number, Table 21-4.
8. Test material thickness (or) test pipe diameter (and) wall thickness: The actual thickness of the welded material or pipe diameter and wall thickness.
9. Thickness range qualified (or) diameter range qualified: For both plate and pipe, a weld performed successfully on one thickness qualifies a welder to weld on material within that range. See Table 21-5 for a list of thickness ranges.
10. Filler metal specification number: The AWS has specifications for chemical composition and physical properties for electrodes. Some of these specifications are listed in Table 21-6.
11. Classification number: This is the standard number found on the electrode or electrode box, such as E6010, E7018, E316-15, ER1100, etc.
12. F number: A specific grouping number for several classifications of electrodes having similar composition and welding characteristics. See Table 21-7 for the F number corresponding to the electrode used.
13. Give the manufacturer's chemical composition and physical properties as provided.
14. Backing strip material specification: This is the ASTM specification number.
15. Give the diameter of electrode used and the manufacturer's identification name or number.
16. Flux for SAW or shielding gas(es) and flow rate for GMAW, FCAW, or GTAW.

If the weld is a groove weld, follow steps 17 through 22 and then skip to step 27. If the weld test was a fillet weld, skip to step 22.

17. Visually inspect the weld and record any flaws.
18. Record the weld face, root face, and reinforcement dimensions.
19. Four (4) test specimens are used for 3/8 in. or thinner metal. Two (2) will be root bent and two (2) face bent. For thicker metal all four (4) will be side bent.
20. Visually inspect the specimens after testing and record any discontinuities.
21. Who witnessed the welding for verification that the WPS was followed?

22. The identification number assigned by the testing.

If the weld is a filler weld, follow steps 23 through 28.

23. Visually inspect the weld and record any flaws.
24. Record the legs and reinforcement dimensions.
25. Measure and record the depth of the root penetration.
26. Polish the side of the specimens and apply an acid to show the complete outline of the weld.
27. Who witnessed the welding for verification that the WPS was followed?
28. The identification number assigned by the testing.

If a radiographic test is used, follow steps 29 through 33. If this test is not used, go to step 34.

29. The number the lab placed on the x-ray film before it was exposed on the weld.
30. Record the results of the reading of the film.
31. Whether the test passed or failed the specific code.
32. Who witnessed the welding for verification that the WPS was followed?
33. The number assigned by the testing.
34. The name of the company who requested the test.
35. The name of the person who interpreted the results. This is usually a Certified Welding Inspector or other qualified person.
36. Date the results of the test were completed.

PERFORMANCE QUALIFICATION TEST RECORD

Identification No. ______________________ Weld Stamp No. ______________

Name ______________________ Social Security No. ______________

Eye correction required Yes ☐ No ☐

Type of eye correction Eye glasses ☐
Contact lenses ☐
Magnifiers ☐

Qualified with WPS No. ________ Process ________ Manual ☐ Semi-automatic ☐

Position Flat (1G, 1F ☐) Horizontal (2G, 2F ☐) Viatica (3G, 3F ☐) Overhead (4G, 4F ☐)

Test base metal specification ______________________ Thickness ______________

AWS filler metal specification ______________________ Size ______________

Shielding gas ______________________ Flow Rate ______________

GUIDED BEND TEST RESULTS

Visual Test results Pass ☐ Fail ☐ Weld size ________

Type of Bend	Result
Face ☐ Root ☐ Side ☐	Pass ☐ Fail ☐
Face ☐ Root ☐ Side ☐	Pass ☐ Fail ☐

The above named person is qualified for the welding process used in this test within the limits of essential variables including materials and filler metal as provided by the AWS D1.1_____ Code. We, the undersigned, certify that the statements in this record are correct and that the test welds were prepared, welded, and tested in accordance with the requirements of the AWS D1.1 _____ Code.

Date Tested ____________ Signed by ______________________

Test Supervisor

Signed by ______________________ ______________

Corporate Representative Title

CHAPTER 21: WELDING CERTIFICATION QUIZ

Name____ Date ______________

Class ______________________ Instructor ______________________ Grade ______________

1. How do many companies verify a welder's skills before they are hired?

____

____

2. What are the three different levels the AWS Certified Welder Program is divided into?

____

____

3. What does the term certified mean relative to a welder's skills?

____

____

4. What affect on a certification does the thickness have?

____

____

5. What affect on certification does the position of the weld test plates have?

____

____

6. How does the WQR relate to the WPQ and the WQP?

____

____

7. What is a Welder Certification?

____

____

8. What advantages other than just their welding skills does an AWS certified welder bring to a company?

____

____

9. What does it take to pass a welding performance test?

____

____

10. What layout skills does an AWS Certified Entry Level Welder need?

____

____

11. What types of written records of the welding may be required of the welder as part of the AWS Certified Entry Level Welder?

____

____

12. What types of verbal instructions may a AWS Certified Entry Level Welder be given?

13. What types of information may be included on a welding safety test?

14. Why is having good housekeeping skills an important part of a welder's job?

15. What are some of the items that a welder may need to service as part of routine repairs?

16. How can parts that have distorted during the cutting process be fitted together accurately?

17. Where must arc strikes be made and why must they be made there?

18. How are weld beads on test specimens to be cleaned?

19. List the acceptance guidelines for welds inspected to the AWS Entry Level Welder certification program.

20. How are transverse face and root-bends prepared and tested?

CHAPTER 22: RAILROAD WELDING QUIZ

Name____ Date ____________

Class ____________________ Instructor ____________________ Grade ____________

A. SHORT ANSWER

1. How did the development of the rail industry affect the country's growth?

____

____

2. List things to build for railroads where welding is used.

____

____

3. What is the difference between a metal's yield strength and ultiment strength?

____

____

4. What happens to a metal after it has passed the yield point?

____

____

5. How is a metal's hardness affected by cold working?

____

____

6. What forces does a metal's toughness help it withstand?

____

____

7. Why is the term soft carbon rails misleading?

____

____

8. What is a third rail?

____

____

9. What effect on tops of austenitic manganese steels does its plasmic deformation from use have?

____

____

10. How are large components such as frogs made?

____

____

11. Outline the steps that might be included in a typical WPS for repairing high strength steels such as austenitic manganese.

12. List the advantages that welded rail can provide.

13. How does austenitic manganese steel's expansion rate affect welding repairs?

14. What effect does making short narrow welds have on distortion?

15. Who sets the standard or controls the length and angle of the taper resulting from the offset when joining old rails to new?

16. How large an area should be preheated for welding?

17. What causes carbide precipitation in steels?

18. How does the formation of carbide precipitation affect steels?

19. Under what temperature conditions should high strength steels, such as austenitic manganese, be welded?

20. How does hydrogen affect welds?

21. List the ways of controlling hydrogen-caused cracking.

22. What problem does oxyfuel gouging have that is not present with air arc gouging?

23. What type of cuts should be made when air arc gouging?

____

____

24. Why do rail ends become damaged?

____

____

25. Why must all filler metal fluxes be kept dry?

____

____

26. What is the recommended procedure for starting any SMAW bead on high strength steels?

____

____

27. How should any SMA welding bead be ended?

____

____

28. What are the advantages of using FCAW on rails?

____

____

29. What type of process is FW?

____

____

30. Why is thermite welding used for joining rails?

____

____

CHAPTER 23: WELDING METALLURGY

MELTING POINTS OF METALS AND ALLOYS

Metal or alloy	Melting Point °F	°C
Aluminum, cast (8% copper)	1175	635
Aluminum, pure	1220	660
Aluminum (5% silicon)	1118	603
Brass, naval	1625	885
Brass, yellow	1660	904
Bronze, aluminum	1905	1041
Bronze, manganese	1600	871
Bronze, phosphor	1830 to 1922	999 to 1050
Bronze, tobin	1625	885
Chromium	2740	1504
Copper	1981	1083
Iron, cast	2300	1260
Iron, malleable	2300	1260
Iron, pure	2786	1530
Iron, wrought	2750	1510
Lead	620	327
Magnesium	1200	649
Manganese	2246	1230
Molybdenum	4532	2500
Monel metal	2480	1360
Nickel	2686	1452
Nickel silver (18% nickel)	2030	1110
Silver, pure	1762	961
Silver solders (50% silver)	1160 to 1275	627 to 690
Solder (50–50)	420	216
Stainless steel (18–8)	2550	1399
Stainless steel, low carbon (18–8)	2640	1449
Steel, high carbon (0.55–0.83% carbon)	2500 to 2550	1371 to 1399
Steel, low carbon (maximum 0.30% carbon)	2600 to 2750	1427 to 1510
Steel, medium carbon (0.30–0.55% carbon)	2550 to 2600	1399 to 1427
Steel, cast	2600 to 2750	1427 to 1510
Steel, manganese	2450	1343
Steel, nickel (3.5% nickel)	2600	1427
Tantalum	5160	2849
Tin	420	232
Titanium	3270	1799
Tungsten	6152	3400
Vanadium	3182	1750
White metal	725	385
Zinc	786	419

HEAT COLORS AT GIVEN TEMPERATURES OF FERROUS MATERIALS		
Temper Color	**Temperature**	
	°F	**°C**
Faint straw	400	204
Straw	440	227
Dark straw	460	238
Very deep straw	480	249
Brown yellow	500	260
Bronze or brown purple	520	271
Peacock or full people	540	282
Bluish purple	550	288
Blue	570	299
Full blue	590	310
Very dark blue	600	316
Light blue	640	338
Faint red (visible in dark)	750	399
Faint red	900	482
Blood red	1050	565
Dark cherry	1175	635
Medium cherry	1250	677
Cherry or full red	1375	746
Bright cherry	1450	788
Bright red	1550	843
Salmon	1650	899
Orange	1725	940
Lemon	1825	996
Light yellow	1975	1079
White	2200	1204

SURFACE COLOR OF SOME COMMON METALS			
Metals	**Color of Unfinished, Unbroken Surface**	**Color and Structure of Newly Fractured Surface**	**Color of Freshly Filed Surface**
White cast iron	Dull gray	Silvery white; crystalline	Silvery white
Gray cast iron	Dull gray	Dark silvery; crystalline	Light silvery gray
Malleable iron	Dull gray	Dark gray; finely crystalline	Light silvery gray
Wrought iron	Light gray	Bright gray	Light silvery gray
Low-carbon and cast steel	Dark gray	Bright gray	Bright silvery gray
High-carbon steel	Dark gray	Light gray	Bright silvery gray
Stainless steel	Dark gray	Medium gray	Bright silvery gray
Copper	Reddish brown to green	Bright red	Bright copper color
Brass and bronze	Reddish yellow, yellow-green, or brown	Red to yellow	Reddish yellow to yellowish white
Aluminum	Light gray	White; finely crystalline	White
Monel metal	Dark gray	Light gray	Light gray
Nickel	Dark gray	Off-white	Bright silvery white
Lead	White to gray	Light gray; crystalline	White
Copper-Nickel (70–30)	Gray	Light gray	Bright silvery white

IDENTIFICATION OF METALS BY CHIP TEST	
Metals	**Chip Characteristics**
White cast iron	Chips are small, brittle fragments. Chipped surfaces not smooth.
Gray cast iron	Chips are about 1/8 inch in length. Metal not easily chipped, so chips break off and prevent smooth cut.
Malleable iron	Chips are 1/4 to 3/8 inch in length (larger than chips from cast iron). Metal is tough and hard to chip.
Wrought iron	Chips have smooth edges. Metal is easily cut or chipped; chip can be made as a continuous strip.
Low-carbon and cast steel	Chips have smooth edges. Metal is easily cut or chipped; chip can be made as a continuous strip.
High-carbon steel	Chips show a fine grain structure. Edges of chips are lighter in color than chips of low-carbon steel. Metal is hard, but can be chipped in a continuous strip.
Copper	Chips are smooth, with sawtooth edges where cut. Metal is easily cut; chip can be cut as a continuous strip.
Brass and bronze	Chips are smooth, with sawtooth edges. These metals are easily cut, but chips are more brittle than chips of copper. Continuous strip is not easily cut.
Aluminum and aluminum alloys	Chips are smooth, with sawtooth edges. Chip can be cut as a continuous strip.
Monel	Chips have smooth edges. Continuous strip can be cut. Metal chips easily.
Nickel	Chips have smooth edges. Continuous strip can be cut. Metal chips easily.
Lead	Chips of any shape may be obtained because the metal is so soft that it can be cut with a knife.

IDENTIFICATION OF METALS BY OXYACETYLENE TORCH TEST

Metals	Reactions when heated by oxyacetylene torch
White cast iron	Metal becomes dull red before melting. Melts at moderate rate. A medium tough film of slag develops. Molten metal is watery, reddish white in color, and does not show sparks. When flame is removed, depression in surface of metal under flame disappears.
Gray cast iron	Pool of molten metal is quiet, rather watery, but with heavy, tough film forming on surface. When torch flame is raised, depression in surface of metal disappears instantly. Molten pool takes time to solidify, and gives off no sparks.
Malleable iron	Metal becomes red before melting; melts at moderate rate. A medium tough film of slag develops, but can be broken up. Molten pool is straw-colored, watery, and leaves blow holes when it boils. Center of pool does not give off sparks, but the bright outside portion does.
Wrought iron	Metal becomes bright red before it melts. Melting occurs quietly and rapidly, without sparking. There is a characteristic slag coating, greasy or oily in appearance, with white lines. The straw-colored molten pool is not viscous, is usually quiet but may have a tendency to spark; is easily broken up.
Low-carbon and Cast Steel	Melts quickly under the torch, becoming bright red before it melts. Molten pool is liquid, straw-colored, gives off sparks when melted, and solidifies almost instantly. Slag is similar to the molten metal and is quiet.
High-carbon steel	Metal becomes bright red before melting, melts rapidly. Melting surface has cellular appearance, and is brighter than molten metal of low-carbon steel; sparks more freely, and sparks are whiter. Slag is similar to the molten metal and is quiet.
Stainless steels	Reactions vary depending upon the composition.
Copper	Metal has high heat conductivity; therefore, larger flame is required to produce fusion than would be required for the same size piece of steel. Copper color may become intense before metal melts; metal metals slowly, and may turn black and then red. There is little slag. Molten pool shows mirrorlike surface directly under flame, and tends to bubble. Copper that contains small amounts of other metals melts more easily, solidifies more slowly than pure copper.
Brass and bronze	These metals melt very rapidly, becoming noticeably red before melting. True brass gives off white fumes when melting. Bronze flows very freely when melting, and may fume slightly.
Aluminum and aluminum alloys	Melting is very rapid, with no apparent change in color of metal. Molten pool is same color as unheated metal and is fluid; stiff black scum forms on surface, tends to mix with the metal, and is difficult to remove.
Monel	Melts more slowly than steel, becoming red before melting. Slag is gray scum, quiet, and hard to break up. Under the scum, molten pool is fluid and quiet.
Nickel	Melts slowly (about like Monel), becoming red before melting. Slag is gray scum, quiet, and hard to break up. Under the scum, molten pool is fluid and quiet.
Lead	Melts at very low temperature, with no apparent change in color. Molten metal is white and fluid under a thin coat of dull gray slag. At higher temperature, pool boils and gives off poisonous fumes.

CHAPTER 23: WELDING METALLURGY QUIZ

Name____ Date ____________

Class ____________________ Instructor ____________________ Grade ____________

INSTRUCTIONS: Carefully read Chapter 23 in the text and answer the following questions.

A. MATCHING

In the space provided to the left, write the letter from column B that best answers the question or completes the statement in column A.

	column A		column B
____	1. the SI unit of heat	a.	Tempering
____	2. the heat required to change matter from one state to another	b.	Allotropic
____	3. the SI unit of degrees	c.	Solid Solution
____	4. have no orderly arrangement in the crystalline structure	d.	Joule
____	5. the fundamental building blocks of all metals	e.	Cementite
____	6. two or more metals dissolved into each other	f.	Celcius
____	7. the abrupt change of microstructure from a liquid to a solid	g.	Amorphic
____	8. a metal that can exist in two or more crystalline structures	h.	Lattices
____	9. a compound of iron and carbon, Iron Carbide	i.	Eutective reaction
____	10. the process of reheating a part that has been hardened through heating and quenched for the purpose of increasing toughness	j.	Latent heat

B. SHORT ANSWER

Write a brief answer, in the space provided, that will answer the question or complete the statement.

11. ______________ is the property of a material to withstand a twisting force.

12. ______________ is the ability of a material to return to its original form after the removal of a load.

13. ______________ is the measure of how well a part can withstand forces acting to cut or slice it apart.

14. ______________ is the property that allows a metal to withstand forces, sudden shock, or bends without fracturing.

15. ______________ is the resistance to penetration.

16. ______________ problems are avoidable by keeping organic materials away from weld joints, keeping the welding consumables dry, and preheating the components to be welded.

17. ______________ is used to reduce the rate at which welds cool.

18. When ______________ is viewed under a microscope, it has an acicular grain structure.

19. ______________ is a process of reheating a part after it has been heated and quenched for the purpose of increasing toughness and improving the tensile strength.

20. ______________ metals have the ability to exist in two or more different crystalline structures in their solid state.

21. Many of the problems and defects associated with welding are due to hydrogen.Place an "X" in the blanks provided by the following list of products that contain hydrogen.

____ a. Aluminum oxide

____ b. Moisture in electrode coatings

_____ c. Carbon

_____ d. Moisture in humid air or in weld joints

_____ e. Silicon

_____ f. Organic lubricants

_____ g. Rust in weld joints

_____ h. Organic particles such as paint

_____ i. Cloth fibers

22. What are the four most common methods of quenching metals?

    a. ______________________________

    b. ______________________________

    c. ______________________________

    d. ______________________________

23. What three conditions must be present to cause hydrogen induced cracking?

    a. ______________________________

    b. ______________________________

    c. ______________________________

24. What are the two methods with which ductility can be measured when performing a tensile test?

    a. ______________________________

    b. ______________________________

25. List four ways that strength can be measured in a material.

    a. ______________________________

    b. ______________________________

    c. ______________________________

    d. ______________________________

C. TRUE-FALSE

Write the letter T in the space to the left if the statement is true and the letter F if the statement is false.

_____ 26. Latent heat is the heat required to change matter from one state to another.

_____ 27. One BTU is defined as the amount of heat required to raise one gallon of water one degree fahrenheit.

_____ 28. It is possible to have a material at a high temperature but with very little heat.

_____ 29. Amorphic materials have no orderly arrangement of their atoms into crystals.

_____ 30. Pure iron exists in the hexagonal close-packed cubic unit cell at temperatures over 1333° fahrenheit.

_____ 31. When welding medium and high-carbon steels, the cooling rates can be fast enough to produce martensite.

_____ 32. When metals are heated, grain growth is expected.

_____ 33. The longer a metal is held at a high temperature, the smaller the grain size.

_____ 34. It is possible to make all steels non-magnetic by heating them to a temperature high enough to cause them to enter the austenitic grain structure.

_____ 35. The yield strength of steels increase as the temperature of the metal increases.

D. ESSAY

Provide complete answers to all of the following.

36. Explain why welders should have some understanding of metallurgy.

37. Describe the changes that occur in an alloy of 30% tin and 70% lead as it cools slowly from 600°F to 200°F (316°C to 93°C).

38. Explain four methods that can be used for strengthening metals.

39. Explain how the heat of welding reduces the strength obtained with the methods discussed in #12.

40. Explain the differences between preheat and stress relief anneal.

41. Describe some of the welding problems caused by air.

42. Explain how to avoid corrosion problems in the heat-affected zone of stainless steels.

43. Describe how poor welding techniques can produce defective welds.

44. How can the defects discussed in #17 be avoided?

45. Describe the weld defects that can be produced because of poor weld penetration.

CHAPTER 24: WELDABILITY OF METALS

STANDARD STEEL AND STEEL ALLOY NUMBERING SYSTEM

Class	Number
Plain carbon steels	10XX
Free-cutting carbon steels	11XX
Manganese steels	13XX
Nickel steels	20XX
Nickel-chromium steels	30XX
Molybdenum steels	40XX
Chrome-molybdenum steels	41XX
Nickel-chrome-molybdenum steels	43XX, 47XX
Nickel-molybdenum steels	46XX, 48XX
Chromium steels	50XX
Chromium-vanadium steels	60XX
Heat resisting casting alloys	70XX
Nickel-chrome-molybdenum steels	80XX, 93XX, 98XX
Silicon-manganese steels	90XX

STANDARD ALUMINUM AND ALUMINUM ALLOY NUMBER DESIGNATIONS

Major alloying element	Number
Aluminum (99% minimum)	1XXX
Copper	2XXX
Manganese	3XXX
Silicon	4XXX
Magnesium	5XXX
Magnesium-silicon	6XXX
Zinc	7XXX
Other element	8XXX
Unused class	9XXX

STANDARD WROUGHT ALUMINUM AND MAGNESIUM COMPOSITIONS TEMPER DESIGNATION	
Designation	**Temper**
F	As fabricated
O	Annealed
H	Strain hardened
H1	Strain hardened only
H2	Strain hardened, then partially annealed
H3	Strain hardened, then stabilized
W	Solution heat treated but with unstable temper
T	Thermally treated to produce stable tempers other than F, O, or H
T2	Annealed (for castings only)
T3	Solution heat treated, then cold worked
T4	Solution heat treated, then naturally aged
T5	Artificially aged
T6	Solution heat treated, then artificially aged
T7	Solution heat treated, then stabilized
T8	Solution heat treated, then cold worked, then artificially aged
T9	Solution heat treated, then artificially aged, then cold worked
T10	Artificially aged, then cold worked

STANDARD COPPER AND COPPER ALLOY SERIES DESIGNATIONS	
Series	**Alloying element**
100	None or very slight amount
200, 300, 400, and 665 to 699	Zinc
500	Tin
600 to 640	Aluminum
700 to 735	Nickel
735 to 799	Nickel and zinc

LETTERS USED TO IDENTIFY ALLOYING ELEMENTS IN MAGNESIUM ALLOYS	
Letter	**Alloying element**
A	Aluminum
B	Bismuth
C	Copper
D	Cadmium
E	Rare earth
F	Iron
H	Thorium
K	Zirconium
L	Beryllium
M	Manganese
N	Nickel
P	Lead
Q	Silver
R	Chromium
S	Silicon
T	Tin
Z	Zinc

STANDARD STAINLESS STEEL NUMBERING SYSTEM	
Austenitic	**Common Application and Characteristics**
301	A general utility stainless steel, easily worked
302	Readily fabricated, for decorative or corrosion resistance
304, 304LC	A general utility stainless steel, easily worked
308	Used where corrosion resistance better than 1800 is needed
309	High scaling resistance and good strength at high temperatures
310	More chromium and nickel for greater resistance to scaling in high heat
316, 316LC	Excellent resistance to chemical corrosion
317	Higher alloy than 316 for better corrosion resistance
321	Titanium stabilized to prevent carbide precipitation
347	Columbian stabilized to prevent carbide precipitation
Martensitic	
403	Used for forged turbine blades
410	General purpose, low priced, heat treatable
414	Nickel added; for knife blades, springs
416	Free machining
420	Higher carbon for cutlery and surgical instruments
431	High mechanical properties
440A	For instruments, cutlery, valves
440B	Higher carbon than 440A
440C	Higher carbon that 440A or B for high hardness
501	Less resistance to corrosion than chromium nickel types
502	Less resistance to corrosion than chromium nickel types
Ferritic	
405	Nonhardening when air cooled from high temperatures
406	For electrical resistances
430	Easily formed alloy, for automobile trim
430F	Free machining variety of 430 grade
446	High resistance to corrosion and scaling up to 215°F

CHAPTER 24: WELDABILITY OF METALS QUIZ

Name______________________________ Date ____________

Class ____________________ Instructor ____________________ Grade ____________

Instructions: Carefully read Chapter 24 in the text and answer the following questions.

A. MATCHING

In the space provided to the left, write the letter from column B that best answers the question or completes the statement in column A.

Using the SAW and AISI classification systems, match the following numbers with the proper type of steel.

column A	column B
____ 1. 1XXX	a. tungsten
____ 2. 2XXX	b. chromium
____ 3. 3XXX	c. molybdenum
____ 4. 4XXX	d. carbon
____ 5. 5XXX	e. silicomanganese
____ 6. 6XXX	f. nickel-chromium-vanadium
____ 7. 7XXX	g. nickel
____ 8. 8XXX	h. chromium-vanadium
____ 9. 9XXX	i. nickel-chrome

Match the following terms with their definitions.

____ 10. What is a silvery-gray metal weighing about half as much as steel, or about one and one-half times as much as aluminum?

____ 11. What is an extremely light metal having a silvery-white color? Its weight is one-fourth that of steel and approximately two-thirds that of aluminum.

____ 12. This type of steel is used for high-temperature service and for aircraft parts.

____ 13. What is gray cast iron that has been annealed to convert the brittle graphite flakes to nodules of carbon?

____ 14. What is basically an alloy of iron and carbon?

____ 15. What has from 0.30% to 0.50% carbon content?

____ 16. What has a carbon content from 0.8% to 1.50%?

____ 17. What has a carbon content from 0.50% to 0.90%?

____ 18. These steels are used to wear resistance in applications involving impact.

____ 19. All grades of what metal have a high carbon content, usually ranging from 2% to 4%?

a. tool steels
b. cast iron
c. carbon steel
d. titanium
e. malleable cast iron
f. high-manganese steels
g. magnesium
h. chromium-molybdenum
i. medium-carbon steels
j. high-carbon steels

B. TRUE-FALSE

Write the letter T, in the space to the left, if the statement is true and the letter F if the statement if false.

_____ 20. Steels containing less than 0.40% carbon normally require preheating to prevent cracking.

_____ 21. Low-carbon steels are more difficult to weld than high-carbon steels.

_____ 22. High-manganese steels are used in places where wear resistance and impact applications are involved.

_____ 23. Carbide precipitation occurs in steels with high carbon content.

_____ 24. Gray cast iron is practically not weldable.

_____ 25. Non-machinable cast iron SMAW electrodes are nothing but a mild steel cored electrode with a special flux.

_____ 26. If braze welding is performed on a broken casting, the part cannot be subjected to service temperatures higher than 260°C.

_____ 27. Spot welding is one process that is not recommended for magnesium parts.

_____ 28. The last two or three digits of the SAE classification system for steel indicates the exact carbon content.

_____ 29. Ferritic stainless steel's good weldability is due to the high nickel content.

_____ 30. The oxide that is on aluminum has a higher melting point than the aluminum itself.

C. SHORT ANSWER

Write a brief answer, in the space provided, that will answer the question or complete the statement.

31. _______________ occurs when alloys containing both chromium and carbon are heated.

32. The four groups of stainless steel are _______________, _______________, _______________, and _______________.

33. _______________ stainless steels are not hardenable by quenching.

34. The most common grades of cast iron contain _______________ to _______________ total carbon.

35. The two types of SMAW electrodes used for welding cast iron are _______________ and _______________.

36. Define the term *weldability*.

____

____

37. What effect does heating and cooling have on metals with poor weldability?

____

____

38. What do the abbreviations AISI and SAE stand for?

____

____

39. Explain the significance of each of the four digits in the steel number 2140.

____

____

40. What problems are encountered when welding high-carbon steels?

____

____

41. Why are tool steels difficult to weld?

____

____

42. Describe how to weld gray cast iron.

____

____

43. Why must titanium be kept clean during welding?

____

____

44. Define the following terms: oxide, 18-8 stainless, and ambient temperature.

____

____

CHAPTER 25: FILLER METAL SELECTION

American Welding Society and American Society for Testing and Materials Specifications

AWS Designation	ASTM Designation	Title
A5.1	A 233	Mild Steel Covered Arc Welding Electrodes
A5.2	A 251	Iron and Steel Gas Welding Rods
A5.3	B 184	Aluminum and Aluminum-Alloy Arc Welding Electrodes
A5.4	A 298	Corrosion-Resisting Chromium and Chromium-Nickel Steel Covered Welding Electrodes
A5.5	A 316	Low-Alloy Steel Covered Arc Welding Electrodes
A5.6	B 255	Copper and Copper-Alloy Arc Welding Electrodes
A5.7	B 259	Copper and Copper-Alloy Welding Rods
A5.8	B 260	Brazing Filler Metal
A5.9	A 371	Corrosion-Resisting Chromium and Chromium-Nickel Steel Welding Rods and Bare Electrodes
A5.10	B 285	Aluminum and Aluminum-Alloy Welding Rods and Bare Electrodes
A5.11	B 295	Nickel and Nickel-Alloy Covered Welding Electrodes
A5.12	B 297	Tungsten Arc Welding Electrodes
A5.13	A 399	Surfacing Welding Rods and Electrode
A5.14	B 304	Nickel and Nickel-Alloy Bare Welding Rods and Electrodes
A5.15	A 398	Welding Rods and Covered Electrodes for Welding Cast Iron
A5.16	B 232	Titanium and Titanium-Alloy Bare Welding Rods and Electrodes
A5.17	A 558	Bare Mild Steel Electrodes and Fluxes for Submerged Arc Welding
A5.18	A 559	Mild Steel Electrodes for Gas Metal Arc Welding

CHAPTER 25: FILLER METAL SELECTION QUIZ

Name____ Date ____________

Class __________________ Instructor __________________ Grade ____________

Instructions: Carefully read Chapter 25 in the text and answer the following questions.

A. TRUE-FALSE

Write the letter T in the space to the left if the statement is true and the letter F if the statement is false.

____ 1. The AWS electrode classifications are for the minimum requirements within a group.

____ 2. Welding fluxes on electrodes can affect the penetration of the weld bead.

____ 3. EW indicates the type of filler metal used for the GTAW process.

____ 4. E6010 electrodes are designed to be used with AC current.

____ 5. Nickel arc welding electrodes work well on cast iron because the carbon in cast iron does not migrate into the nickel weld metal.

____ 6. The E7018 electrode should never be used for an open root weld.

____ 7. The AWS identification system for covered electrodes is based on the numbering system for stainless steels developed by the American Iron and Steel Institute (AISI).

____ 8. The American Iron and Steel Institute (AISI) uses a three digit number to identify the type of stainless steel.

____ 9. The number 16 in the electrode E308-16 means that it is a low-hydrogen electrode.

____ 10. The suffix C1 in the electrode E9018-C1 means that it contains 1% carbon.

B. SHORT ANSWER

Write a brief answer, in the space provided, that will answer the question or complete the statement.

11. What welding currents can be used on the following electrodes?

a. EXXX0 ____________ e. EXXX4 ____________

b. EXXX1 ____________ f. EXXX5 ____________

c. EXXX2 ____________ g. EXXX6 ____________

d. EXXX3 ____________ h. EXXX8 ____________

12. List four organizations that have developed a number system for shielded metal arc welding electrodes.

a.____

b. ____

c.____

d. ____

13. The following electrodes are made up of letters and numbers. Explain what each bracket in the electrode means using the American Welding Society (AWS) numbering system.

A	B	C	D		E	F	G	H		I	J	K	L	M
E	60	1	2		E	70	S	3		E	7	1	T	2

a. ____________________

b. ____________________

c. ____________________

d. ____________________

e. ____________________

f. ____________________

g. ____________________

h. ____________________

i. ____________________

j. ____________________

k. ____________________

l. ____________________

m. ____________________

14. List five functions of the flux on a shielded metal arc welding electrode.

a. ____________________

b. ____________________

c. ____________________

d. ____________________

e. ____________________

15. List two functions of the core wire in a shielded metal arc welding electrode.

a. ____________________

b. ____________________

16. Place an X beside each of the following flux cored electrodes that can be used in all positions.

_____ a. E70T-1

_____ b. E70T-2

_____ c. E70T-4

_____ d. E71T-2

_____ e. E71T-10

C. MATCHING

In the space provied to the left, write the letter from column B that best answers the question or completes the statement in column A.

column A	column B
____ 17. As the percentage of this increases, tensile strength increases, and cracking may increase.	a. Ni b. Mn
____ 18. This is usually a contaminant and the percentage should be kept as low as possible. As the percentage of this increases, it can cause weld brittleness, reduced shock resistance, and increased cracking.	c. Cr d. Mo e. C
____ 19. As the percentage of this increases, the tensile strength, toughness, and corrosion resistance increases.	f. Si g. S
____ 20. As the percentage of this increases, tensile strength at elevated temperatures and corrosion resistance increase.	h. P
____ 21. This is usually a contaminant and the percentage should be kept as low as possible, below .04%. As the percentage of carbon increases, this element can cause hot shortness and porosity.	
____ 22. As the percentage of this increases, the tensile strength hardness, resistance to abrasion, and porosity all increase; hot shortness is reduced.	
____ 23. As the percentage of this increases, tensile strength, hardness, and corrosion resistance increase, with some decrease in ductility.	
____ 24. As the percentage of this increases, the tensile strength increases, the hardness increases, and the ductility is reduced.	

D. ESSAY

Provide complete answers to all of the following.

25. What are the names of the organizations the following abbreviations stand for?

    A. AWS ____________________

    B. ASTM ____________________

    C. AISI ____________________

26. Why do some manufacturers choose to add one type of element to an electrode and another manufacturer makes a different choice?

    ____

    ____

27. Why do some manufacturers choose to make more than one electrode within a single classification?

    ____

    ____

28. List 4 physical properties of a filler metal that might be listed in a manufacturer's technical description.

    ____

    ____

29. What does the Yield Point test demonstrate?

30. List 4 properties of iron that change when the percentage of carbon changes.

31. List 4 properties of iron that change when the percentage of manganese changes.

32. List 2 properties of iron that change when the percentage of phosphorus changes.

33. List 2 properties of iron that change when the percentage of silicon changes.

34. List 2 properties of iron that change when the percentage of nickel changes.

35. List 2 properties of iron that change when the percentage of molybdenum changes.

36. List 2 properties of iron that change when the percentage of copper changes.

37. What is meant by carbon equivalence (CE)?

38. List 3 functions of the core wire for stick electrodes.

39. List 5 functions of the flux covering for stick electrodes.

40. Why do some high-temperature slags solidify before the weld metal solidifies?

41. List 6 things that must be considered before selecting a SAW electrode.

____

____

42. Explain the meaning of the following AWS classifications.

1. E______________________________
2. R______________________________
3. ER ______________________________
4. EC ______________________________
5. B______________________________
6. BR ______________________________
7. RG ______________________________
8. IN______________________________
9. EW______________________________
10. F______________________________
11. S______________________________
12. T______________________________
13. L______________________________

43. Explain the "0" and "1" as they are used in the AWS numbering system for tubular wire.

____

____

44. Explain the AWS electrode identification system for stainless steel filler metals.

____

____

45. Explain this AWS electrode identification "ECuAl."

____

____

46. Explain the AWS electrode identification system for aluminum and aluminum alloy filler metals.

____

____

47. List 3 classifications or groups of hardfacing electrodes.

____

____

CHAPTER 26: WELDING AUTOMATION AND ROBOTICS QUIZ

Name________________________________ Date ____________

Class ________________ Instructor ________________ Grade ____________

Instructions: Carefully read Chapter 26 in the text and complete the following questions.

A. IDENTIFICATION

In the space provided identify the items shown on the illustration.

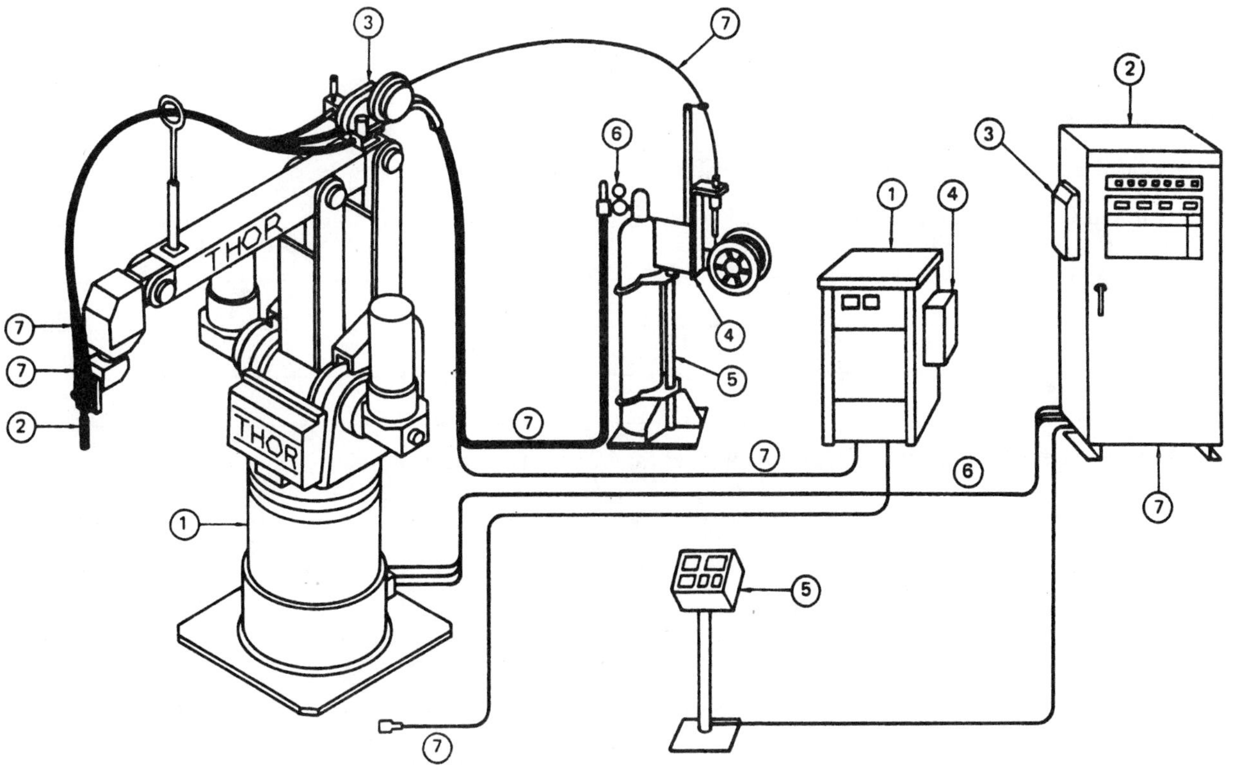

(Courtesy of Merrick Engineering, Inc.)

____ 1. arc welding robot

____ 2. robot control unit

____ 3. teaching box

____ 4. wire feeder

____ 5. welding power supply

____ 6. shielding gas cylinder

____ 7. welding torch

B. TRUE-FALSE

Write the letter T in the space to the left if the statement is true and the letter F if the statement is false.

____ 8. The manipulation of the electrode or torch in a straight line or oscillating pattern affects the size and shape of the weld.

_____ 9. The most commonly used semiautomatic arc welding process is GMAW.

_____ 10. The most commonly used manual arc welding process is SMAW.

_____ 11. The automatic joining process is a dedicated process (designed to do only one type of welding on a specific part) that does not require adjustments to be made by the operator during the actual welding cycle.

_____ 12. Most robots can perform movements in three basic directions.

_____ 13. The disc storage is not as fast as the cassette tape but both work well.

_____ 14. A system utilizing manual welders can be 80% more productive than a system using a robot.

_____ 15. Electronic noise can damage a program, interrupt input or output signals, and cause erratic operations.

_____ 16. It is much easier to train a welder to operate a robot than it is to train a computer technician to make good welds.

_____ 17. In the 1920s, American technology produced the first industrial robots.

C. SHORT ANSWER

Write a brief answer, in the space provided, that will answer the question or complete the statement.

18. List four factors to be considered for proper system planning.

    a. ______________________________

    b. ______________________________

    c. ______________________________

    d. ______________________________

19. List five safety precautions that are recommended for the use of automatic welding equipment and robots.

    a. ______________________________

    b. ______________________________

    c. ______________________________

    d. ______________________________

    e. ______________________________

D. ESSAY

Provide complete answers for all of the following questions.

20. What is meant by the abbreviation CAD/CAM?

    ____

    ____

21. What variables does the welder control during manual arc welding?

    ____

    ____

22. What variables does the welder control during semiautomatic arc welding?

    ____

    ____

23. What variables does the welder operator control during machine welding?

24. What is the direction of the X-axis?

25. What is the direction of the Y-axis?

26. What is the direction of the Z-axis?

27. How can a robot be programmed?

28. What are the advantages of paper tape program storage?

29. Why should the robotic arm be able to move at various speeds?

30. Explain why the robot should be interfaced with other equipment.

31. What is meant by the term work zone?

32. List five robot safety considerations.

33. Define the following terms: duty cycle, pick and place, work cell, axes, and teach pendant.

CHAPTER 27: OTHER WELDING PROCESSES QUIZ

Name____________________ Date ________

Class __________ Instructor __________ Grade ________

Instructions: Carefully read Chapter 27 in the text and complete the following questions.

A. SHORT ANSWER

Write a brief answer, in the space provided, that will answer the question or complete the statement.

The following abbreviations refer to welding processes. Give the full name for each process.

1. RSEW ________
2. LBW ________
3. FW ________
4. SAW ________
5. PEW ________
6. PAW ________
7. RPW ________
8. THSP ________
9. UW ________
10. USW ________
11. SW ________
12. RW ________
13. EBW ________
14. RSW ________
15. ESW ________
16. PAC ________

17. Identify the parts of the welding process indicated on the drawing below.

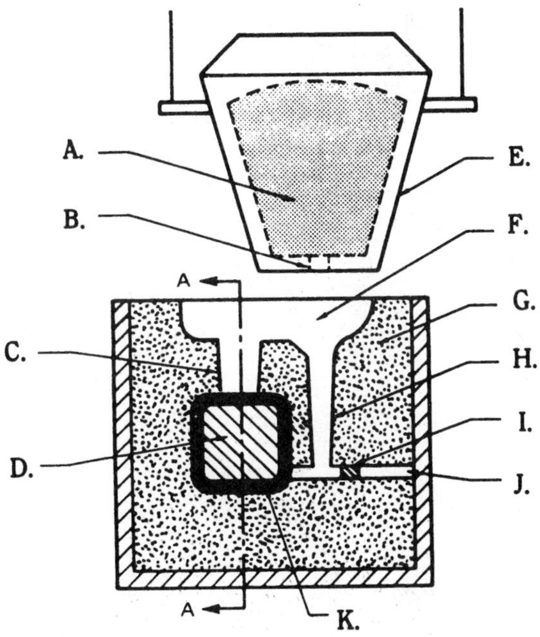

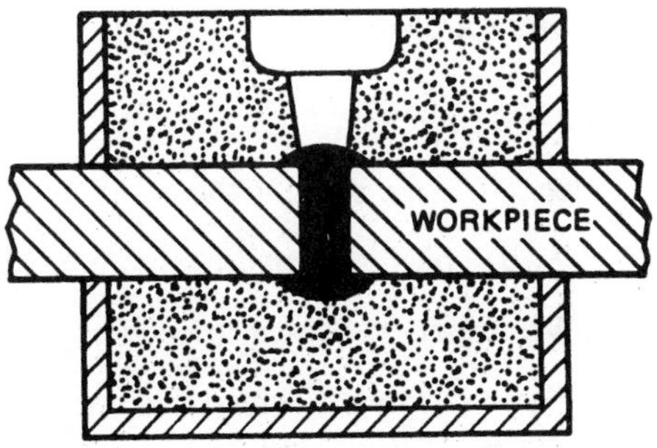

SECTION A-A

a. ________

b. ________

c. ________

d. ________

e. ________

f. ________

g. ________

h. ________

i. ________

j. ________

k. ________

18. List the seven materials that the AWS classifies as hardfacing metals.

a. ______________ e. ______________

b. ______________ f. ______________

c. ______________ g. ______________

d. ______________

19. What are the four functions that the timer controls on RW equipment?

a. ____

b. ____

c. ____

d. ____

20. From the illustration below, which of the diagrams would be classified as a transferred plasma arc?

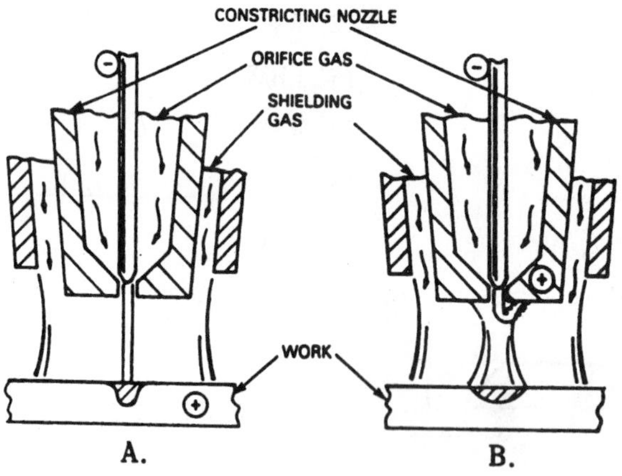

(Courtesy of American Welding Society.)

_____ a. Transferred plasma arc

_____ b. Transferred plasma arc

_____ c. Both A & B are classified as transferred plasma arcs

B. TRUE-FALSE

Write the letter T in the space to the left if the statement is true and the letter F if the statement is false.

_____21. Fluxes of filler metals are not needed for the RW process.

_____22. Projection welding is a specific type of laser welding.

_____23. Seam welding is similar in some ways to spot welding except that the spots are spaced so close together that they actually overlap one another to make a continuous seam weld.

_____24. Stainless steel cannot be joined using the projection welding process.

_____25. It is possible for heat-treated parts to be percussion welded without becoming annealed.

_____26. A laser beam is also called a sonotrode.

_____27. Plasma is considered as the fourth state of matter (the other three being solid, liquid, and gaseous).

_____28. The thermite welding process is similar to the investment casting method.

_____29. Melting of the base metal does not occur during the welding cycle when using the ultrasonic welding process.

_____30. Laser welds must be made in a vacuum.

C. ESSAY

Provide complete answers for all of the following questions.

31. What is resistance welding?

____

____

32. How is a seam weld produced?

____

____

33. Describe the flash welding process.

____

____

34. What is flash welding?

____

____

35. What is electron beam welding?

____

____

36. How does ultrasonic welding differ from resistance welding?

____

____

37. Explain how inertia welding is performed.

____

____

38. How is the concentrated coherent light beam produced in a laser?

____

____

39. How is plasma generated for plasma welding?

____

____

40. What is thermite welding?

____

____

41. What is hardfacing?

____

____

42. List four advantages of shielded metal arc hardfacing.

43. List four advantages of thermal spraying.

44. Thermal spraying forms what type of surface bonds?

45. In the electroslag welding process, how is the welding heat produced?

46. Define the following terms: plasma, fly-wheel, anode, optical, electrical resistance, and evacuated chamber.

CHAPTER 28: OXYFUEL WELDING EQUIPMENT, SETUP AND OPERATION

PRACTICE 28-1

Name_______________________________ Date ____________

Class ____________ Instructor ______________ Grade ____________

OBJECTIVE: After completing this practice, you will be able to safely set up an oxyfuel torch set.

EQUIPMENT AND MATERIAL NEEDED FOR THIS PRACTICE

1. Disassembled oxyfuel torch set, two regulators, two reverse flow valves, one set of hoses, a torch body, a welding tip, two cylinders, a portable cart or supporting wall with safety chain, and a wrench.

INSTRUCTIONS

1. Safety chain the cylinders in the cart or to a wall. Then remove the valve protection caps.
2. Crack the cylinder valve on each cylinder for a second to blow away dirt that may be in the valve.

   CAUTION **Always stand to one side. Point the valve away from anyone in the area and be sure there are no sources of ignition when cracking the valve.**

3. Attach the regulators to the cylinder valves. The nuts should be started by hand and then tightened with a wrench.
4. Attach a reverse flow valve or flashback arrestor, if the torch does not have them built in, to the hose connection on the regulator or to the hose connection on the torch body, depending on the type of reverse flow valve in the set. Occasionally, test each reverse flow valve by blowing through it to make sure it works properly.
5. Connect the hoses. The red hose has a left-hand nut and attaches to the fuel gas regulator. The green hose has a right-hand nut and attaches to the oxygen regulator.
6. Attach the torch to the hoses. Connect both hose nuts fingertight before using a wrench to tighten either one.
7. Check the tip seals for nicks or O rings, if used, for damage. Check the owner's manual, or a supplier, to determine if the torch tip should be tightened by hand only or should be tightened with a wrench.

   CAUTION **Tightening a tip the incorrect way may be dangerous and might damage the equipment. Check all connections to be sure they are tight. The oxyfuel equipment is now assembled and ready for use.**

   CAUTION **Connections should not be overtightened. If they do not seal properly, repair or replace them.**

   CAUTION **Leaking cylinder valve stems should not be repaired. Turn off the valve, disconnect the cylinder, mark the cylinder, and notify the supplier to come and pick up the bad cylinder. The assembled oxyfuel welding equipment is now tested and ready to be ignited and adjusted.**

Comments

____

PRACTICE 28-2

Name____ Date ____________

Class __________________ Instructor __________________ Grade ____________

OBJECTIVE: After completing this practice, you should be able to safely turn on and test oxyfuel equipment for gas leaks.

EQUIPMENT AND MATERIALS NEEDED FOR THIS PRACTICE

1. Use oxyfuel equipment that is properly assembled.
2. A nonadjustable tank wrench
3. A leak-detecting solution

INSTRUCTIONS

1. Back out the regulator pressure adjusting screws until they are loose.
2. Standing to one side of the regulator, open the cylinder valve SLOWLY so that the pressure rises on the gauge slowly.

   CAUTION **If the valve is opened quickly, the regulator or gauge may be damaged, or the gauge may explode.**

3. Open the oxygen valve all the way until it is sealed at the top.
4. Open the acetylene or other fuel gas valve 1/4 turn or just enough to get gas pressure. If the cylinder valve does not have a handwheel, use a nonadjustable wrench and leave it in place on the valve stem while the gas is on.

   CAUTION **The acetylene valve should never be opened more than 1 1/2 turns, so that in an emergency it can be turned off quickly.**

5. Open one torch valve and point the tip away from any source of ignition. Slowly turn in the pressure adjusting screw until gas can be heard escaping from the torch. The gas should flow long enough to allow the hose to be completely purged (emptied) of air and replaced by the gas before the torch valve is closed. Repeat this process with the other gas.
6. After purging is completed, and with both torch valves off, adjust both regulators to read 5 psig (35 kPag).
7. Spray a leak-detecting solution on each hose and regulator connection and on each valve stem on the torch and cylinders. Watch for bubbles which indicate a leak. Turn off the cylinder valve before tightening any leaking connections.

   CAUTION **Connections should not be overtightened. If they do not seal properly, repair or replace them.**

   CAUTION **Leaking cylinder valve stems should not be repaired. Turn off the valve, disconnect the cylinder, mark the cylinder, and notify the supplier to come and pick up the bad cylinder.**

The assembled oxyfuel welding equipment is now tested and ready to be ignited and adjusted.

Comments

____

PRACTICE 28-3

Name____ Date ____________

Class ____________________ Instructor ____________________ Grade ____________

OBJECTIVE: After completing this practice, you should be able to safely light and adjust an oxyacetylene flame.

EQUIPMENT AND MATERIAL NEEDED FOR THIS PRACTICE

1. Use oxyfuel welding equipment that is properly assembled and tested.
2. A sparklighter
3. Gas welding goggles
4. Gloves and proper protective clothing

INSTRUCTIONS

1. Wearing proper clothing, gloves and gas welding goggles, turn both regulator adjusting screws in until the working pressure gauges read 5 psig (35 kPag). If you mistakenly turn on more than 5 psig (35 kPag), open the torch valve to allow the pressure to drop as the adjusting screw is turned outward.
2. Turn on the torch fuel-gas valve just enough so that some gas escapes.

   CAUTION **Be sure the torch is pointed away from any sources of ignition or any object or person that might be damaged or harmed by the flame when it is lit.**

3. Using a sparklighter, light the torch. Hold the lighter near the end of the tip but not covering the end.

   CAUTION **A sparklighter is the only safe device to use when lighting any torch.**

4. With the torch lit, increase the flow of acetylene until the flame stops smoking.
5. Slowly turn on the oxygen and adjust the torch to a neutral flame.

This flame setting uses the minimum gas flow rate for this specific tip. The fuel flow should never be adjusted to a rate below the point where the smoke stops. This is the minimum flow rate at which the cool gases will pull the flame heat out of the tip. If excessive heat is allowed to build up in a tip, it can cause a backfire or flashback.

The maximum gas flow rate gives a flame which, when adjusted to the neutral setting, does not settle back on the tip.

Comments

____

PRACTICE 28-4

Name______________________________ Date ____________

Class ______________ Instructor ______________ Grade ____________

OBJECTIVE: After completing this practice, you should be able to turn off and disassemble oxyfuel equipment.

EQUIPMENT AND MATERIAL NEEDED FOR THIS PRACTICE

1. Use oxyfuel welding equipment that is properly assembled and tested.
2. A sparklighter
3. Gas welding goggles
4. Gloves and proper protective clothing

INSTRUCTIONS

1. First, quickly turn off the torch fuel-gas valve. This action blows the flame out and away from the tip, ensuring that the fire is out. In addition, it prevents the flame from burning back inside the torch. On large tips or hot tips, turning the fuel off first may cause the tip to pop. The pop is caused by a lean fuel mixture in the tip.

   If you find that the tip pops each time you turn the fuel off first, turn the oxygen off first to prevent the pop. Be sure that the flame is out before putting the torch down.
2. After the flame is out, turn off the oxygen valve.
3. Turn off the cylinder valves.
4. Open one torch valve at a time to bleed off the pressure.
5. When all of the pressure is released from the system, back both regulator adjusting screws out until they are loose.
6. Loosen both ends of both hoses and unscrew them.
7. Loosen both regulators and unscrew them from the cylinder valves.
8. Replace the valve protection caps.

Comments

____

CHAPTER 28: OXYFUEL WELDING EQUIPMENT, SETUP, AND OPERATION QUIZ

Name____ Date ____________

Class ________________ Instructor ________________ Grade ____________

Instructions: Carefully read Chapter 28 in the text and answer the following questions.

A. IDENTIFICATION

In the space provided identify the items shown on the illustration.

1. Name the parts of the regulator shown below.

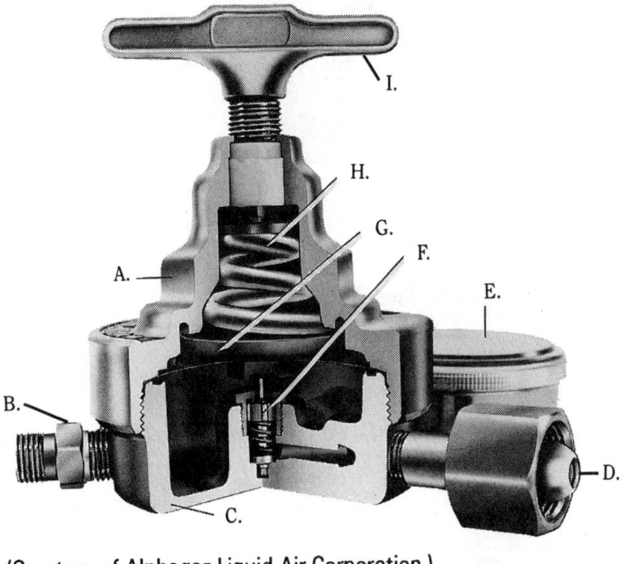

(Courtesy of Alphagaz Liquid Air Corporation.)

a. ____________ f. ____________

b. ____________ g. ____________

c. ____________ h. ____________

d. ____________ i. ____________

e. ____________

2. From the picture below, are the fittings designed for fuel gas or oxygen?

   a. Left **THESE TWO CAN'T BE RIGHT—SHOULD SAY GAS AND OXYGEN—WHICH WHERE?**
   b. Right

3. From the picture used for question 2, are the threads left- or right-hand threads?
   a. Left
   b. Right

4. Identify each of the parts of a torch by inserting the correct letter from the illustration in the space provided.

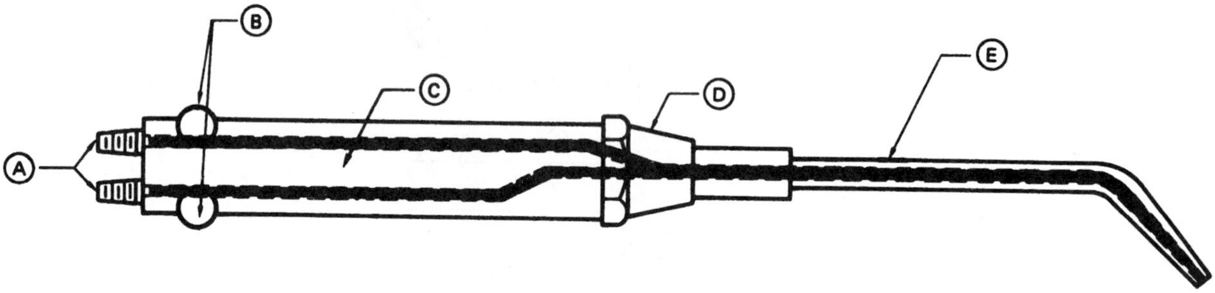

_____ a. tip

_____ b. mixer

_____ c. torch body

_____ d. control valve

_____ e. hose connection

5. Identify each of the parts of a torch by inserting the correct letter from the illustration in the space provided.

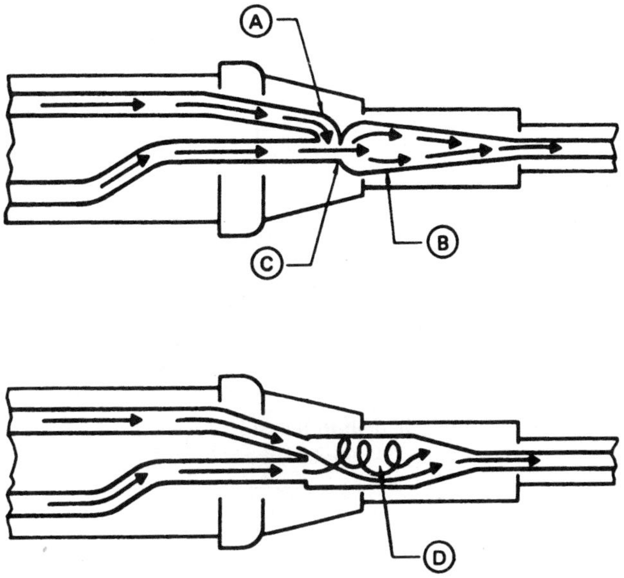

____ a. injector mixing chamber

____ b. equal-pressure mixing chamber

____ c. injector

____ d. venturi

B. SHORT ANSWER

Write a brief answer, in the space provided, that will answer the question or complete the statement.

6. Using the same illustration as in question 2 and 3, how can you tell if the fitting is left- or right-hand threads?

____

____

7. All _______________ processes use a high-heat and high-temperature flame produced by burning a fuel gas mixed with pure oxygen.

8. A _______________ threaded fitting has a notched nut.

9. _______________ a regulator may cause a fire or an explosion.

10. Oxygen hoses must be _______________ in color and have right-hand threaded fittings.

C. TRUE-FALSE

Write the letter T in the space to the left if the statement is true and the letter F if the statement is false.

____ 11. All oxygen cylinders have left-hand threads.

____ 12. If the adjustment screw is not loosened when the work is completed and the cylinder valve is turned off, it is possible that long-term damage to the diaphragm and springs may result.

____ 13. There are no internal or external moving parts on a regulator or a gauge that require oiling.

____ 14. The standards for tip size identification were developed by the American Welding Society (AWS).

____ 15. An injector-type torch must never be used on a low-pressure residential natural gas fuel supply.

____ 16. Oxygen hoses must be green in color and have left-hand threaded fittings.

_____ 17. If new hose is not available and your hoses become damaged, tape can be used to stop leaks.

_____ 18. A little oxygen flow should be turned on when cleaning a tip so that the dirt that is loosened will be blown away.

_____ 19. Broken tip cleaners cannot be removed from a welding tip.

_____ 20. Excessive use of a tip cleaner can cause damage to a tip.

D. SHORT ANSWER

Write a brief answer, in the space provided, that will answer the question or complete the statement.

21. What is the difference between a single-stage and a double-stage regulator?

____

____

22. Why should long hoses be larger in diameter than short hoses?

____

____

23. What is the difference between psi and psig (kg/cm^2 and kg/cm^{2}G)?

____

____

24. What does it mean if a regulator creeps?

____

____

25. How is a leaking regulator diaphragm tested?

____

____

26. What is a backfire?

____

____

27. What is a flashback?

____

____

28. Why can an injector torch system use low-pressure fuel gases?

____

____

29. How can a leak around a torch valve stem be stopped?

____

____

30. How is a leaking tip seat tested?

____

____

31. Why are hoses bled?

32. How is a flame turned off?

33. How far should oxygen and acetylene valves be turned on? Why?

34. How does a regulator control gas pressure?

35. What are the three different types of flames?

36. Define the following terms: line drop, Bourdon tube, safety release valve, safety disc, mixing chamber, injector, permeability, purge bleed, manifold, cylinder pressure, diaphragm, creep, Siamese hose, equal pressure, and leak-detecting solution.

CHAPTER 29: OXYFUEL AND FILLER METALS QUIZ

Name____ Date ____________

Class ____________________ Instructor ____________________ Grade ____________

Instructions: Carefully read Chapter 29 in the text and complete the following questions.

A. IDENTIFICATION

In the space provided identify the items shown on the illustration.

1. Identify the parts of an oxyfuel flame from the illustration below.

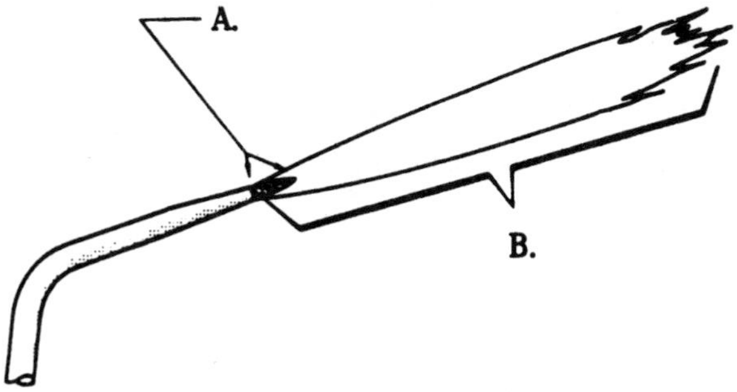

a. ____________

b. ____________

B. SHORT ANSWER

Write a brief answer, in the space provided, that will answer the question or complete the statement.

2. Place an "X" next to 5 considerations for making a selection of which gas to use for your oxyfuel processes.

____ a. molecular structure

____ b. availability of gas

____ c. color of cylinder

____ d. cost of gas

____ e. welder skills

____ f. inhomogeneity

____ g. safety

____ h. performance of gas

3. Classify the following filler rods as to be ferrous or non-ferrous metals by placing an "F" in front of ferrous and "N" in front of non-ferrous.

____ a. cast iron

____ b. nickel

____ c. copper

____ d. low-alloy steel

____ e. mild steel

____ f. aluminum

_____ g. stainless steel

_____ h. manganese bronze

4. What are the two major safety problems that exist when using hydrogen as a fuel gas?

   a. _____

   b. _____

5. What are the three major AWS specifications for ferrous filler metals?

   a. _____

   b. _____

   c. _____

C. TRUE-FALSE

Write the letter T in the space to the left if the statement is true and the letter F if the statement is false.

_____ 6. The data available for fuel gas flame characteristics is not gathered in a consistent manner.

_____ 7. It is possible for a hydrogen leak to be on fire and not be noticed because the hydrogen flame is almost invisible.

_____ 8. MPS gases have a neutral flame temperature much higher than that of acetylene.

_____ 9. The pressure in a cylinder containing a liquified gas is an accurate indication of how full or empty the tank is.

_____ 10. The withdrawal rate of acetylene from a cylinder should not exceed one-seventh of the total cylinder capacity per hour.

_____ 11. Acetylene has the fastest burning velocity of any of the fuel gases.

_____ 12. Stainless steel or aluminum cannot be oxyfuel welded.

_____ 13. Magnesium alloys cannot be joined by a torch because it is a fire hazard.

_____ 14. Flux is not needed with the copper-phosphorus filler rods when joining copper tubing because the phosphorus makes the rod self-fluxing on copper.

_____ 15. Naval brass and white brass are the same thing.

D. ESSAY

Provide complete answers for all of the following questions.

16. What was the first device to use high-pressure oxygen for cutting?

_____

_____

17. How is acetylene gas produced?

_____

_____

18. Why is the working pressure of acetylene restricted?

_____

_____

19. What factors determine the pressure in a liquified gas cylinder?

_____

_____

20. Explain each part of the following AWS rod classifications:

a. RG60

1. R____________________

2. G____________________

3. 60 ____________________

b. ER308

1. E____________________

2. R____________________

3. 308 ____________________

c. BRCuZn-A

1. B____________________

2. R ____________________

3. CuZn____________________

4. -A ____________________

21. When the percentage of the following elements is changed in steel, what is the effect of each on the steel?

a. carbon (C) ____________________

b. silicon (Si) ____________________

c. nickel (Ni) ____________________

d. manganese (Mn) ____________________

22. What makes the BCuP-2 rod self-fluxing on copper?

____

____

23. List two major flame characteristics for each of the following:

a. oxy MAPP® ____________________

b. oxypropane ____________________

c. oxyhydrogen __________ __________

d. oxyacetylene ____________________

24. Why is an accidental fire a limited problem when oxyfuel welding magnesium?

____

____

25. Why might the temperature of an oxyfuel flame given in one published source be different from that given in other sources?

____

____

26. Define each of the following terms: flashback, ferrous metal, neutral flame, oxidizing flame, carburizing flame, optical pyrometer, molecule, backfire, metallizing, regulator, reducing flame, and wetting.

____

____

CHAPTER 30: OXYACETYLENE WELDING

PRACTICE 30-1

Name____________________________________ Date ____________

Base Metal Thickness ____________ Filler Metal Diameter ________________________

Class __________________ Instructor __________________ Grade ____________

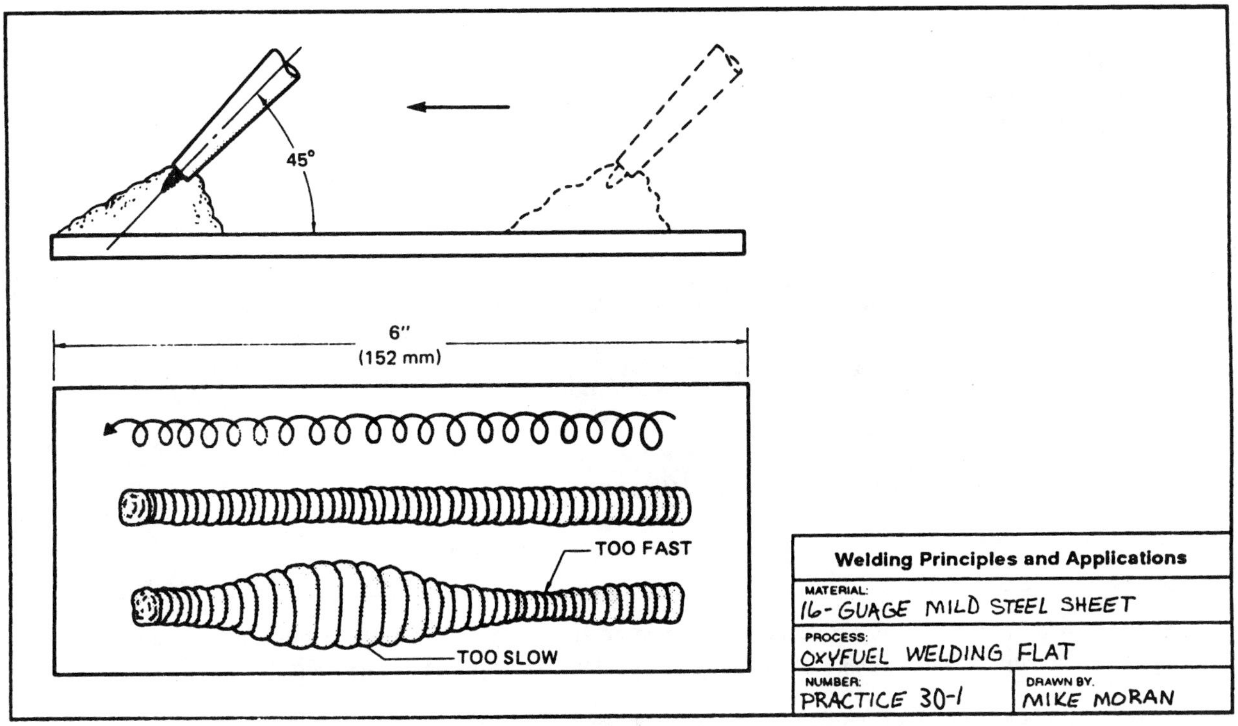

OBJECTIVE: After completing this practice, you should be able to push a pool on 16-gauge carbon steel sheet.

EQUIPMENT AND MATERIALS NEEDED FOR THIS PRACTICE

1. Properly set up oxyacetylene welding equipment.
2. Proper safety protection (welding goggles, safety glasses, spark lighter and pliers). Refer to Chapter 2 in the text for more specific safety information.
3. Two or more pieces of 16-gauge carbon steel sheet, approximately 6 in. (152 mm) long.

INSTRUCTIONS

1. Start at one end and hold the torch at a 45° angle in the direction of the weld.
2. When the metal starts to melt, move the torch in a circular pattern down the sheet toward the other end. If the size of the molten weld pool changes, speed up or slow down to keep it the same size all the way down the sheet.
3. Repeat this practice until you can keep the width of the molten weld pool uniform and the direction of travel in a straight line.

4. Turn off the gas cylinders, regulators and clean up your work area when you are finished welding.

Comments

EXPERIMENT 30-2

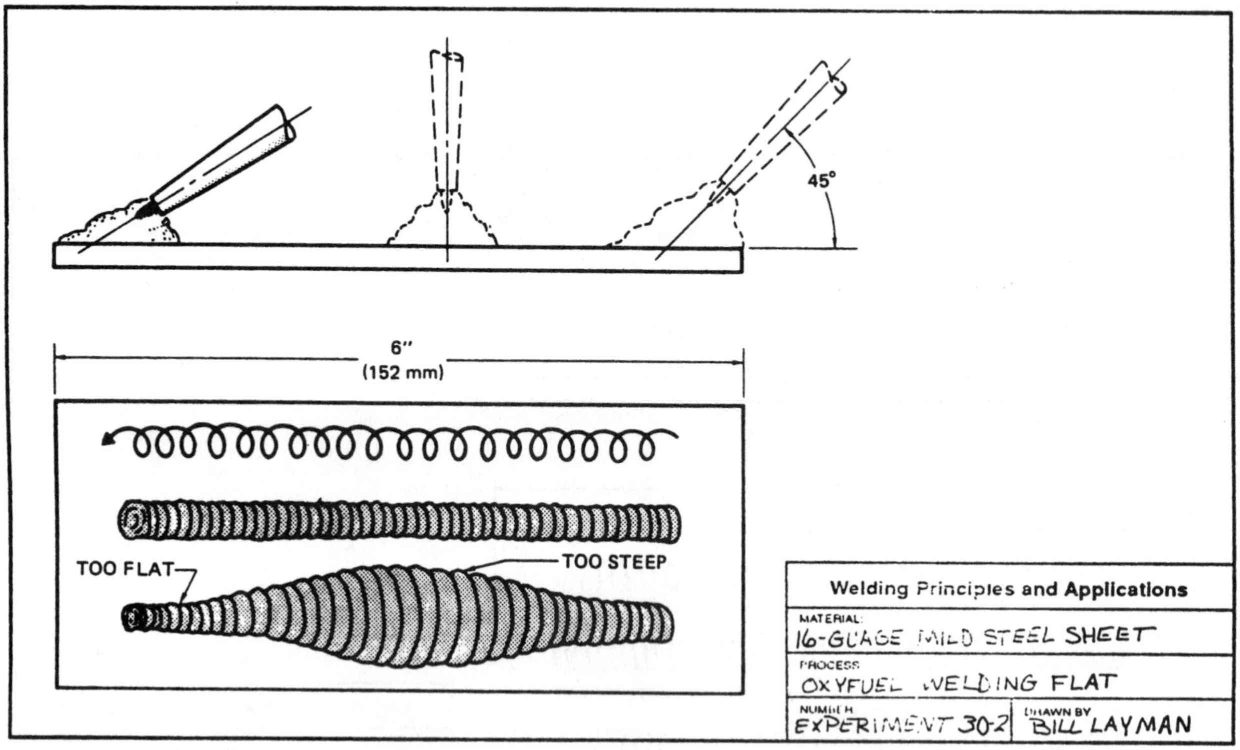

OBJECTIVE: After completing this practice, you should be able to demonstrate the controlling of the weld pool by changing the torch angle and torch height while pushing a pool on 16-gauge carbon steel sheet.

EQUIPMENT AND MATERIALS NEEDED FOR THIS PRACTICE

1. Properly set up oxyacetylene welding equipment.
2. Proper safety protection (welding goggles, safety glasses, spark lighter and pliers). Refer to Chapter 2 in the text for more specific safety information.
3. Two or more pieces of 16-gauge carbon steel sheet, approximately 6 in. (152 mm) long.

INSTRUCTIONS

CHANGING TORCH ANGLE

1. Start at one end and hold the torch at a 45° angle in the direction of the weld.
2. When the metal starts to melt, move the torch in a circular pattern down the sheet toward the other end. As the weld is moved toward the other end gradually change the torch angle from the starting 45° to an ending angle of 90°.
3. Repeat this part of the experiment until you can control the width of the molten weld pool by changing the torch angle.

Comments

INSTRUCTIONS

CHANGING TORCH HEIGHT

1. Start at one end and hold the torch with the inner cone about 1/8 in. (3 mm) above the metal surface at a 45° angle in the direction of the weld.
2. When the metal starts to melt, move the torch in a circular pattern down the sheet toward the other end. As the weld is moved toward the other end gradually change the torch height for the starting 1/8 in. (3 mm) to an ending height of 1/2 in. (13 mm).
3. Repeat this part of the experiment until you can control the width of the molten weld pool by changing the torch height.
4. Turn off the gas cylinders, regulators and clean up your work area when you are finished welding.

Comments

PRACTICE 30-3

Name____ Date ______________

Base Metal Thickness ______________ Filler Metal Diameter ____________________________

Class ________________________ Instructor ________________________ Grade ______________

OBJECTIVE: After completing this practice, you should be able to make stringer beads on sheet steel in the flat position.

EQUIPMENT AND MATERIALS NEEDED FOR THIS PRACTICE

1. Properly set up oxyacetylene welding equipment.
2. Proper safety protection (welding goggles, safety glasses, spark lighter and pliers). Refer to Chapter 2 in the text for more specific safety information.
3. Two or more pieces of 16-gauge carbon steel sheet, approximately 6 in. (152 mm) long.
4. 1/16 in., 3/32 in., and 1/8 in. (3 mm) diameter RG45 filler wire. The size of filler rod that you are most comfortable with.

INSTRUCTIONS

1. Use a clean piece of 16-gauge mild steel and a torch adjusted to a neutral flame.
2. Hold the torch at a 45° angle to the metal with the inner cone about 1/8 in. (3 mm) above the metal surface.
3. The end of the welding rod should always be kept inside the protective envelope of the flame. Experiment with the three different welding rods for your preference of filler wire.
4. The end of the welding rod should be dipped into the leading edge of the molten weld pool. If the rod touches the hot metal around the molten weld pool, it will stick. When this happens, move the flame directly to the end of the rod to melt and free it.
5. Move the torch in a circular pattern down the sheet toward the other end while adding filler rod.
6. The width and buildup of the welding bead should be uniform.
7. Repeat this practice until you can keep the width of the bead uniform and the direction of travel in a straight line.
8. Turn off the gas cylinders, regulators and clean up your work area when you are finished welding.

Comments

____

PRACTICE 30-4

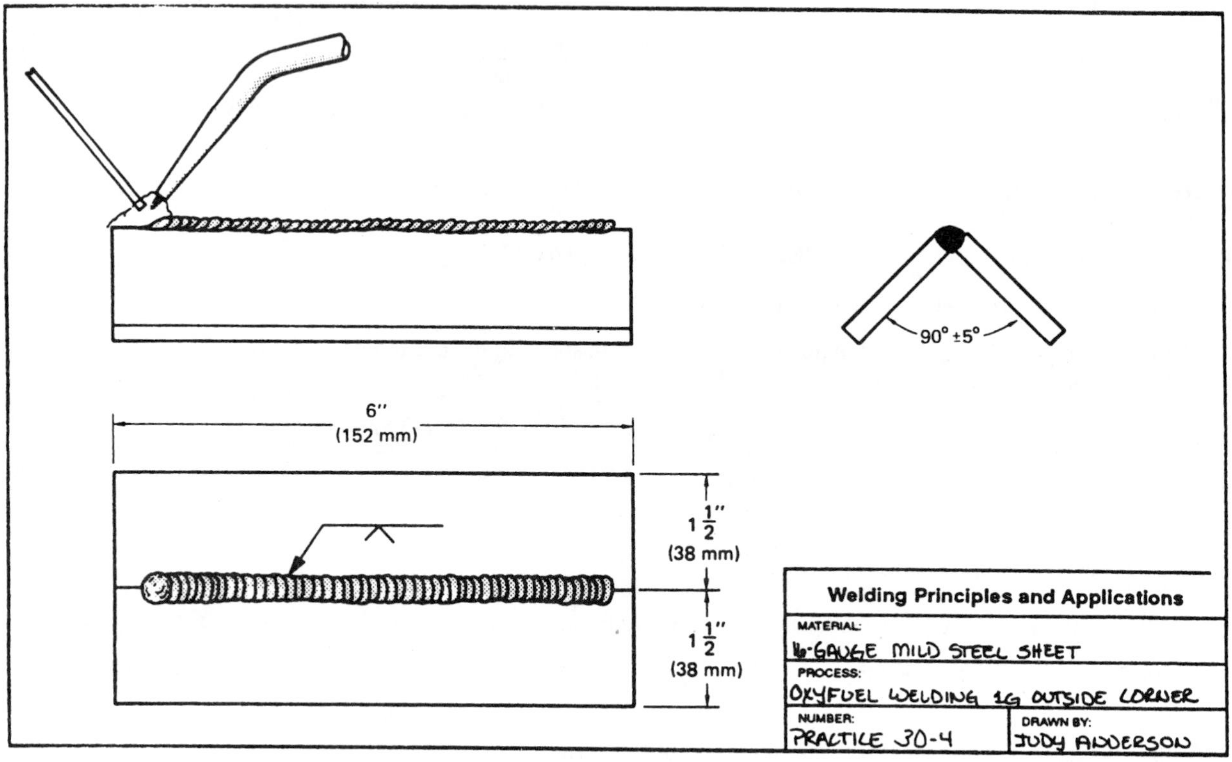

OBJECTIVE: After completing this practice, you should be able to weld outside corner joints in the flat position.

EQUIPMENT AND MATERIALS NEEDED FOR THIS PRACTICE

1. Properly set up oxyacetylene welding equipment.
2. Proper safety protection (welding goggles, safety glasses, spark lighter and pliers). Refer to Chapter 2 in the text for more specific safety information.
3. Two or more pieces of 16-gauge carbon steel sheet, approximately 6 in. (152 mm) long.
4. 1/16 in., 3/32 in., and 1/8 in. (3 mm) diameter RG45 filler wire. The size of filler rod that you are most comfortable with.

INSTRUCTIONS

1. Place one of the pieces of metal in a jig or on a fireback and hold or brace the other piece of metal horizontally on it.
2. Tack the ends of the two sheets together.
3. Then set it upright and put two or three more tacks on the joint.
4. Hold the torch at a 45° angle to the metal with the inner cone about 1/8 in. (3 mm) above the metal surface and make a uniform weld along the joint.
5. Repeat this weld until the weld can be made without defects.
6. Turn off the gas cylinders, regulators and clean up your work area when you are finished welding.

Comments

PRACTICE 30-5

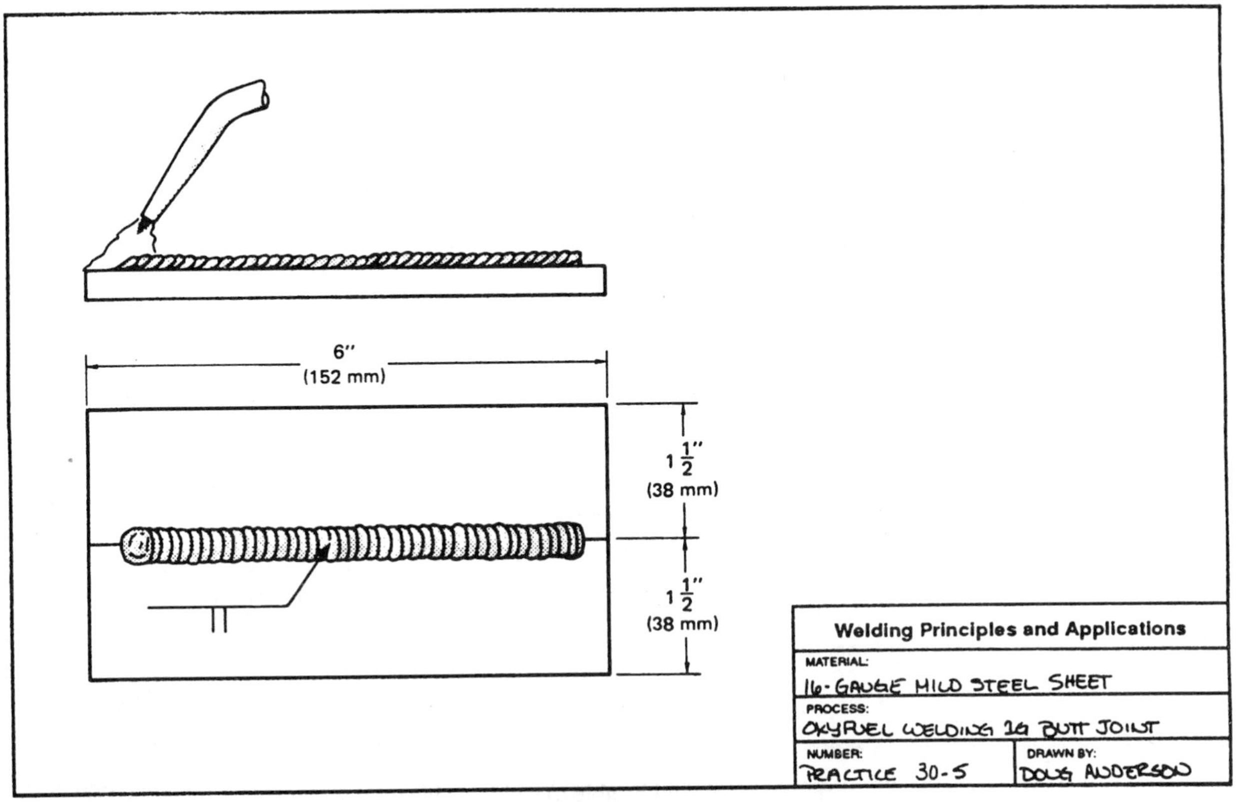

OBJECTIVE: After completing this practice, you should be able to weld butt joints in the flat position.

EQUIPMENT AND MATERIALS NEEDED FOR THIS PRACTICE

1. Properly set up oxyacetylene welding equipment.
2. Proper safety protection (welding goggles, safety glasses, spark lighter and pliers). Refer to Chapter 2 in the text for more specific safety information.
3. Two or more pieces of 16-gauge carbon steel sheet, approximately 6 in. (152 mm) long.
4. 1/16 in., 3/32 in., and 1/8 in. (3 mm) diameter RG45 filler wire. The size of filler rod that you are most comfortable with.

INSTRUCTIONS

1. Place the two pieces of metal in a jig or on a firebrick and tack weld both ends together.
2. The tack on the ends can be made by simply heating the ends and allowing them to fuse together or by placing a small drop of filler metal on the sheet and heating the filler metal until it fuses to the sheet. The latter way is especially convenient if you have to use one hand to hold the sheets together and the other to hold the torch.
3. After both ends are tacked together, place one or two small tacks along the joint to prevent warping during welding.
4. With the sheets tacked together, start welding from one end to the other.
5. Repeat this weld until you can make a welded butt joint that is uniform in width and reinforcement and has no visual defects. The penetration of this practice weld may vary.
6. Turn off the gas cylinders, regulators and clean up your work area when you are finished welding.

Comments

____

PRACTICE 30-6

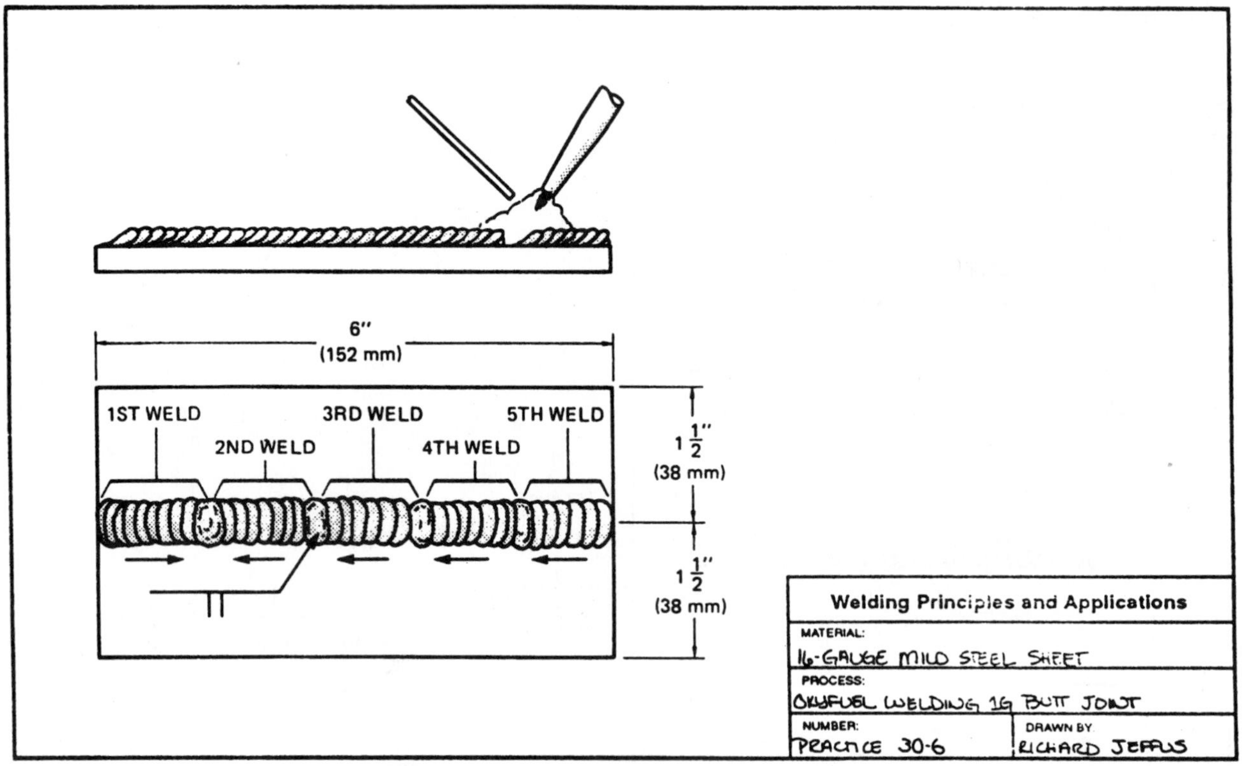

OBJECTIVE: After completing this practice, you should be able to weld butt joints on gauge material with minimum distortion.

EQUIPMENT AND MATERIALS NEEDED FOR THIS PRACTICE

1. Properly set up oxyacetylene welding equipment.
2. Proper safety protection (welding goggles, safety glasses, spark lighter and pliers). Refer to Chapter 2 in the text for more specific safety information.
3. Two or more pieces of 16-gauge carbon steel sheet, approximately 6 in. (152 mm) long.
4. 1/16 in., 3/32 in., and 1/8 in. (3 mm) diameter RG45 filler wire. The size of filler rod that you are most comfortable with.

INSTRUCTIONS

1. Tack weld the two plates together.
2. Use a back stepping technique. Distortion can be controlled by back stepping, proper tacking, and clamping.
3. Practice this weld until you can pass a visual inspection (VT) for distortion.
4. Turn off the gas cylinders, regulators and clean up your work area when you are finished welding.

Comments

____

PRACTICE 30-7

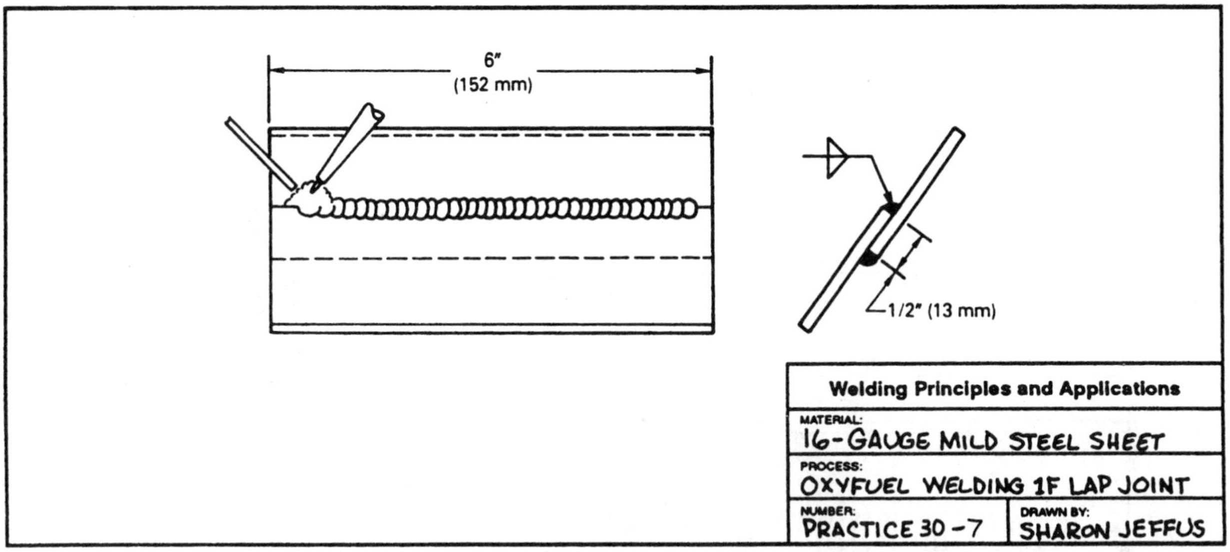

OBJECTIVE: After completing this practice, you should be able to weld lap joints on gauge material in the flat position.

EQUIPMENT AND MATERIALS NEEDED FOR THIS PRACTICE

1. Properly set up oxyacetylene welding equipment.
2. Proper safety protection (welding goggles, safety glasses, spark lighter and pliers). Refer to Chapter 2 in the text for more specific safety information.
3. Two or more pieces of 16-gauge carbon steel sheet, approximately 6 in. (152 mm) long.
4. 1/16 in., 3/32 in., and 1/8 in. (3 mm) diameter RG45 filler wire. The size of filler rod that you are most comfortable with.

INSTRUCTIONS

1. Place the two pieces of metal on a firebrick and tack both ends.
2. Starting at one end, make a uniform weld along the joint. Both sides of the joint can be welded.
3. Repeat this weld until the weld can be made without defects.
4. Turn off the gas cylinders, regulators and clean up your work area when you are finished welding.

Comments

PRACTICE 30-8

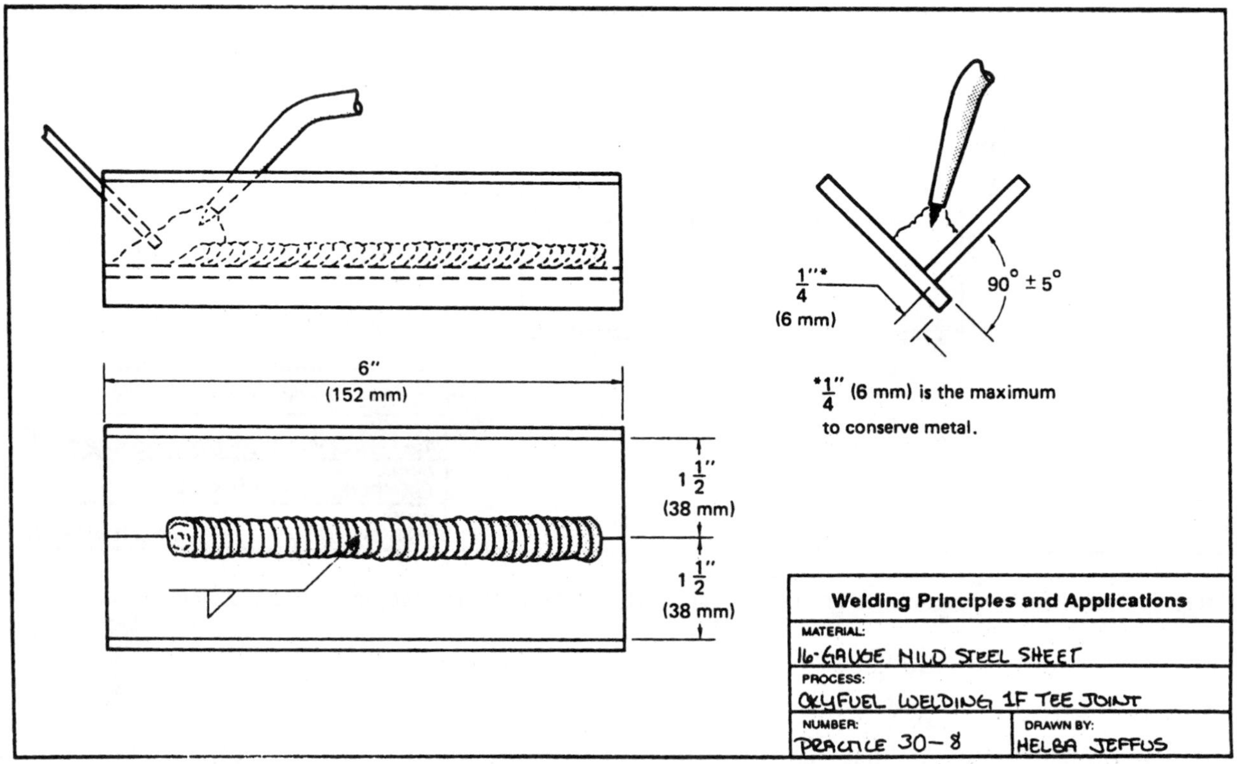

OBJECTIVE: After completing this practice, you should be able to weld tee joints on gauge materials in the flat position.

EQUIPMENT AND MATERIALS NEEDED FOR THIS PRACTICE

1. Properly set up oxyacetylene welding equipment.
2. Proper safety protection (welding goggles, safety glasses, spark lighter and pliers). Refer to Chapter 2 in the text for more specific safety information.
3. Two or more pieces of 16-gauge carbon steel sheet, approximately 6 in. (152 mm) long.
4. 1/16 in., 3/32 in., and 1/8 in. (3 mm) diameter RG45 filler wire. The size of filler rod that you are most comfortable with.

INSTRUCTIONS

1. Place the first piece of metal flat on a firebrick and hold or brace the second piece vertically on the first piece. The vertical piece should be within 5° of square to the bottom sheet.
2. Tack the two sheets at the ends.
3. Starting at one end, make a uniform weld along the joint.
4. Repeat this weld until the weld can be made without defects.
5. Turn off the gas cylinders, regulators and clean up your work area when you are finished welding.

Comments

PRACTICE 30-9, 30-10, 30-11, and 30-12

OBJECTIVE: After completing this practice, you should be able to make stringer beads as well as weld butt joints, lap joints and tee joints in the horizontal position on gauge material.

EQUIPMENT AND MATERIALS NEEDED FOR THIS PRACTICE

1. Properly set up oxyacetylene welding equipment.
2. Proper safety protection (welding goggles, safety glasses, spark lighter and pliers). Refer to Chapter 2 in the text for more specific safety information.
3. Two or more pieces of 16-gauge carbon steel sheet, approximately 6 in. (152 mm) long.
4. 1/16 in., 3/32 in., and 1/8 in. (3 mm) diameter RG45 filler wire. The size of filler rod that you are most comfortable with.

INSTRUCTIONS

1. Tack the sheets together and supporting them in the horizontal position, make a weld using the same technique as practiced in the horizontal beading.
2. The weld must be uniform in width and reinforcement and have no visual defects.
3. If you want to test your skill, shear out a strip 1 in. (25 mm) wide, and test it for 100% root penetration.
4. Repeat this weld until the weld can be made without defects.
5. Turn off the gas cylinders, regulators and clean up your work area when you are finished welding.

Comments

___

CHAPTER 30: OXYACETYLENE WELDING QUIZ

Name______________________________________ Date ____________

Class ____________________ Instructor ____________________ Grade ____________

Instructions: Carefully read Chapter 30 in the text and complete the following questions.

A. IDENTIFICATION

In the space provided identify the items shown on the illustration.

1. If the reinforcement on the following welds is removed, which would be the strongest weld?

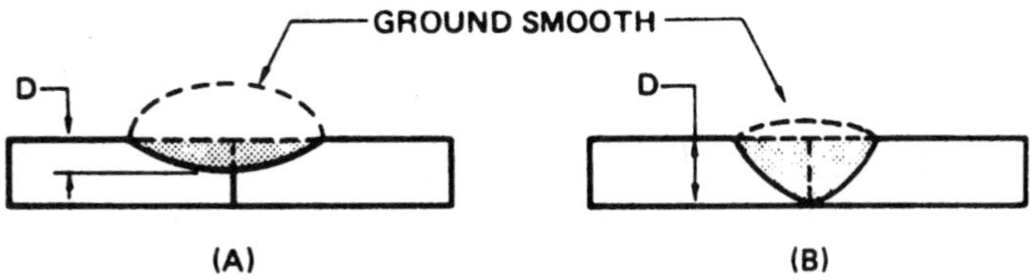

____ (a) weld is the strongest

____ (b) weld is the strongest

B. DRAW

In the space provided make a pencil drawing to illustrate the question.

2. Draw a picture of the following weld joints.
   a. corner joint
   b. butt joint
   c. tee joint
   d. lap joint

C. TRUE-FALSE

Write the letter T in the space to the left if the statement is true and the letter F if the statement is false.

____ 3. The outside corner joint is the most difficult joint to make.

____ 4. If different thicknesses of metal are being oxyacetylene welded the torch should be directed toward the thinnest piece so that it will melt first.

____ 5. Mild steel is the easiest metal to gas weld.

____ 6. A larger diameter welding rod will reduce penetration.

____ 7. Never reduce the torch flame when the correct tip size is unavailable.

____ 8. A large-diameter filler rod can be used as a heat sink to keep the weld pool wide.

____ 9. A lap joint never requires 100% penetration.

____ 10. Small pools are less likely than large ones to drip when welding in the vertical position.

____ 11. When a weld is performed in any position other than flat, it is considered to be an out-of-position weld.

____ 12. Surface tension in the pool of a tee joint enables a larger weld to be made than either the butt or lap joints without as severe a problem with dripping in the out-of-position welds.

____ 13. If the weld pool is cooled slowly, it will rapidly oxidize.

______ 14. Thin wall tubing does not require grooved preparation.

______ 15. Changes in the torch angle will affect the size of the pool.

______ 16. Excessive penetration or burnthrough is usually not a problem on tubing.

______ 17. It is impossible to make uniform stops and starts that are as strong as the surrounding weld bead.

D. MATCHING

In the space provided to the left, write the letter from column B that best answers the question or completes the statement in column A.

	column A	column B
______	18. Which position is the pipe held fixed at a 45° angle?	a. 1G
______	19. Which position is the pipe rolled horizontally and the weld is made flat by depositing it near the top?	b. 6G
______	20. Which position is the pipe fixed vertically and the weld made around the pipe horizontally?	c. 5G
______	21. Which position is the pipe fixed horizontally and may not be rotated while welding?	d. 2G

E. SHORT ANSWER

Write a brief answer, in the space provided, that will answer the question or complete the statement.

22. Put an "X" next to 3 reasons why filler metal is not added by melting the rod and dripping it into the pool.

______ a. the metal cannot always be added where it is needed.

______ b. the rod sticks to the base metal if it is added any other way.

______ c. the method works only in the flat position.

______ d. important alloys are burned out.

______ e. it takes more skill.

23. What holds the molten pool in place when welding in the overhead position?

____

____

24. Why is it suggested that you are not to cut the welding wire in two pieces for welding?

____

____

E. ESSAY

Provide complete answers for all of the following questions.

25. What is most gas welded pipe used for today?

____

____

26. What effect does the torch angle have on the size of the pool?

____

____

27. Why should the torch be flashed off the weld pool when making many out-of-position welds?

28. What will happen to the molten weld pool if the protecting outer flame is quickly moved away?

29. How do welders know when they are close to burning through when welding?

30. How can changes in the sizes of the filler metal affect the size of the weld?

31. How should the torch be manipulated when making a vertical down outside corner joint?

32. What is a shelf used for when welding vertically?

33. How is a vertical weld pool kept from dripping?

34. When practicing vertical welds, why should a welder start at a 45° angle before attempting a vertical sheet?

35. How is the torch flame adjusted differently for a tee joint?

36. Why should a horizontal bead be started small?

37. Why is only small-diameter pipe gas welded today?

38. How should the end of a bead be made so that it can be restarted correctly?

39. How should a weld bead be started to prevent a cold lap?

40. How is the end of thin-wall piping prepared for welding?

41. How is the size and shape of the bead controlled as the weld moves from the overhead to the vertical position on a pipe held in the 5G position?

42. How will the weld bead change in shape if the welding manipulation is not changed as the weld progresses from the vertical to the flat position on a pipe in the 5G position?

43. What is meant by the term *stepping the pool?*

44. Where should the welding rod be added to the weld pool on a pipe in the 2G position? Why?

45. How can a pipe in the 2G position be turned without invalidating the test?

46. Why is the 6G pipe welding position so difficult to do correctly?

47. What is a keyhole, and why is it used?

48. Why is burnthrough usually not a problem on tubing?

49. What is the purpose of each of the three weld passes used in welding some pipe?

50. Define the following terms: heat sink, shelf, root pass, filler pass, cover pass, and keyhole.

CHAPTER 31: SOLDERING, BRAZING, AND BRAZE WELDING

Brazing Troubleshooting	
Problem	**Correction**
Brazing Alloy will not melt & adhere to the base metal.	1. Braze on clean metal only. 2. Increase the heat of the base metal. 3. Use more flux. 4. Check brazing alloy to see if it is compatible with base metal. 5. Roughen work surface.
Brazing alloy flows away from joint.	1. Direct the heat into the joint. 2. Reduce heat directed at the joint. 3. Reposition the assembly so that gravity may help the flow of the brazing alloy into the joint. 4. Use more flux. 5. Make sure that the base metal is clean.
Capillary action will not occur.	1. Braze on clean metal only. 2. If the gap opening is not uniform, it may interrupt the capillary flow. 3. Assembly fit up may be too tight or too loose. 4. Too much heat can cause the flux to break down.

PRACTICE 31-1

Name____ Date ______________

Class ____________________ Instructor ____________________ Grade ______________

OBJECTIVE: After completing this practice, the student should be able to braze stringer beads on 16 gauge carbon steel.

EQUIPMENT AND MATERIAL NEEDED FOR THIS PRACTICE

1. A properly lit and adjusted torch.
2. Proper safety protection (welding goggles, safety glasses, pliers, long sleeve shirt, long pants, leather shoes or boots and a spark lighter).
3. 6 in. (152 mm) of clean 16 gauge mild steel.
4. Brazing flux, and BRCuZn brazing rod.

INSTRUCTIONS

1. Light and adjust the torch to a neutral flame.
2. If a prefluxed rod is not used, you must flux the brazing rod by heating the end, with the torch, and dipping the hot end into the flux.
3. Place the sheet flat on a firebrick and hold the flame at one end.
4. Touch the flux-covered rod to the sheet and allow a small amount of brazing rod to melt onto the hot sheet.
5. Once the molten brazing metal wets the sheet, start moving the torch in a circular pattern while dipping the rod into the molten braze pool as you move along the sheet. If the size of the molten pool increases, you can control it by reducing the torch angle, raising the torch, traveling at a faster rate, or flashing the flame off the molten braze pool. Flashing the torch off a braze joint will not cause oxidation problems as it does when welding, because the molten metal is protected by a layer of flux.
6. As the braze bead progresses across the sheet, dip the end of the rod back in the flux, if a powdered flux is used, as often as needed to keep a small molten pool of flux ahead of the bead.
7. Repeat this practice until you can consistently produce brazed stringer beads that are straight with uniform width and buildup.
8. Turn off the gas cylinders, regulators and clean up your work area when you are finished brazing.

Comments

____

PRACTICE 31-2

Name____ Date ______________

Class ________________________ Instructor ________________________ Grade ______________

OBJECTIVE: After completing this practice, you should be able to braze butt joints in the flat position on 16 gauge carbon steel.

EQUIPMENT AND MATERIAL NEEDED FOR THIS PRACTICE

1. A properly lit and adjusted torch.
2. Proper safety protection (welding goggles, safety glasses, pliers, long sleeve shirt, long pants, leather shoes or boots and a spark lighter).
3. 6 in. (152 mm) of clean 16 gauge mild steel.
4. Two or more pieces of 16 gauge carbon steel, 6 in. long.

INSTRUCTIONS

1. Place the metal flat on a firebrick, hold the plates tightly together, and make a tack braze at both ends of the joint. If the plates become distorted, they can be bent back into shape with a hammer before making another tack weld in the center.
2. Align the sheets so that you can comfortably make a braze bead along the joint.
3. Starting as you did in Practice 31-1, make a uniform braze along the joint.
4. Repeat this practice until a uniform braze can be made without defects.
5. Turn off the gas cylinders, regulators and clean up your work area when you are finished brazing.

Comments

____

PRACTICE 31-3 and 31-4

Name____ Date ____________

Class ____________________ Instructor ____________________ Grade ____________

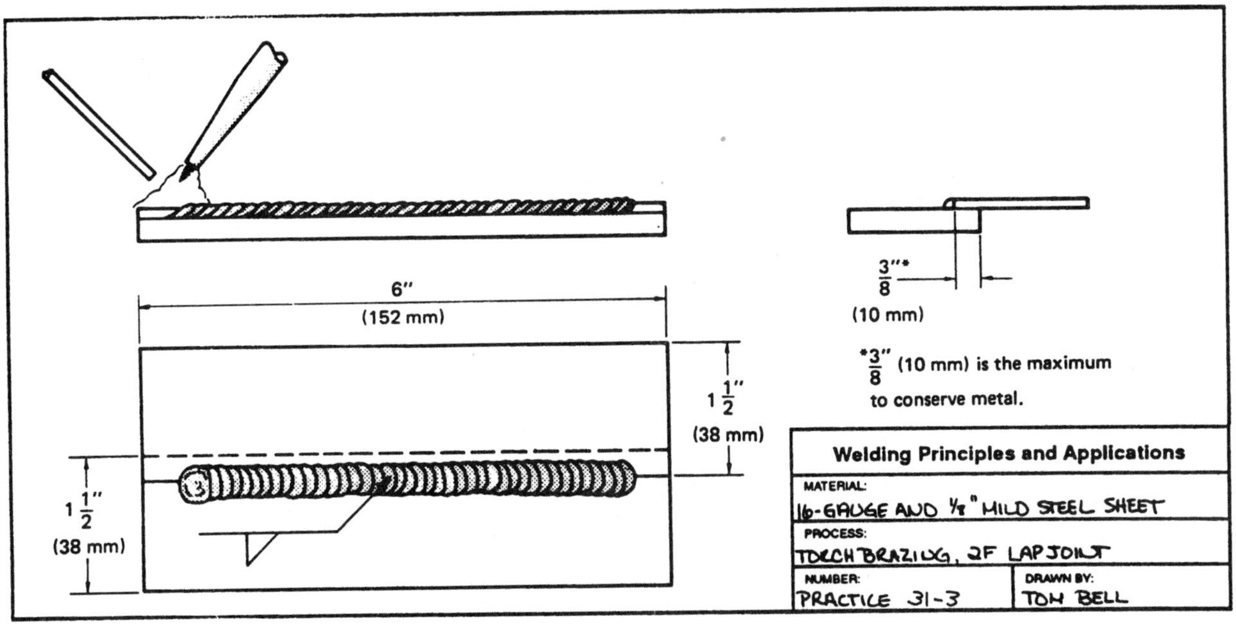

OBJECTIVE: After completing this practice, you should be able to braze tee and lap joints on two pieces of carbon steel of different thicknesses.

EQUIPMENT AND MATERIAL NEEDED FOR THIS PRACTICE

1. A properly lit and adjusted torch.
2. Proper safety protection (welding goggles, safety glasses, pliers, long sleeve shirt, long pants, leather shoes or boots and a spark lighter).
3. Two pieces of carbon steel 6 in. (152 mm) long, one 16 gauge and the other 1/4 in. (6 mm) thick.

INSTRUCTIONS

1. Tack braze the pieces together being sure that they are held tightly together.
2. Place the metal on a firebrick with the thin metal up.
3. Apply heat to the exposed thick metal and more slowly to the overlapping thin metal so that conduction from the thin metal will heat the thick metal at the lap. If the braze is started before the thick metal is sufficiently heated, the filler metal will be chilled and a bond will not occur.
4. After the joint is completed and cooled, tap the joint with a hammer to see if there is a good bonded joint.
5. Repeat this practice until the joint can be made without defects.
6. Turn off the gas cylinders, regulators and clean up your work area when you are finished brazing.

Comments

____

PRACTICE 31-5 and 31-6

Name____ Date ______________

Class ____________________ Instructor ____________________ Grade ______________

OBJECTIVE: After completing this practice, you should be able to braze a butt and tee joints on 1/4 in. (6mm) carbon steel.

EQUIPMENT AND MATERIAL NEEDED FOR THIS PRACTICE

1. A properly lit and adjusted torch.
2. Proper safety protection (welding goggles, safety glasses, pliers, long sleeve shirt, long pants, leather shoes or boots and a spark lighter).
3. Two or more pieces of 1/4 in. (6 mm) thick carbon steel 6 in. (152 mm) long.

INSTRUCTIONS

1. Grind the edges of the plate so that they are slightly rounded. The rounded edges are a better shape for brazing because they distribute the strain on the braze more uniformly.
2. After the plates have been prepared, tack braze both ends together.
3. Because of the mass of the plates, it may be necessary to preheat the plates. This helps the penetration and also eliminates cold lap at the root. The flame should be moved in a triangular motion so that the root is heated, as well as the top of the bead.
4. When the joint is complete and cool, bend the joint to check for complete root bonding.
5. Repeat this practice until the joint can be made without defects.
6. Turn off the gas cylinders, regulators and clean up your work area when you are finished brazing.

Comments

____

PRACTICE 31-7

Name____ Date ____________

Class __________________ Instructor __________________ Grade ____________

OBJECTIVE: After completing this practice, you should be able to build up a flat surface by brazing.

EQUIPMENT AND MATERIAL NEEDED FOR THIS PRACTICE

1. A properly lit and adjusted torch.
2. Proper safety protection (welding goggles, safety glasses, pliers, long sleeve shirt, long pants, leather shoes or boots and a spark lighter).
3. 1 or more pieces of 3 in. (76 mm) square carbon steel plate 1/4 in. (6 mm) thick.

INSTRUCTIONS

1. Place the square plate flat on a firebrick.
2. Start along one side of the plate and make a braze weld down that side. When you get to the end, turn the plate 180° and braze back alongside the first braze covering about one-half of the first braze bead.
3. Repeat this procedure until the side is covered with braze metal.
4. Turn the plate 90° and repeat the process. Be sure that you are getting good fusion with the first layer and that there are no slag deposits trapped under the braze. Be sure to build up the edges so that they could be cut back square.
5. This process should be repeated until there is at least 1/4 in. (6 mm) of buildup on the surface.
6. The surfacing can be checked visually or by machining the square to a 3 in. (76 mm) x 1/2 in. (13 mm) block and checking for slag inclusions. The plate will warp as a result of this; it should be clamped down to prevent distortion.
7. Turn off the gas cylinders, regulators and clean up your work area when you are finished brazing.

Comments

____

PRACTICE 31-8

Name________________________ Date __________

Class ______________ Instructor ______________ Grade __________

OBJECTIVE: After completing this practice, you should be able to solder lap joints on carbon steel in the horizontal position.

EQUIPMENT AND MATERIAL NEEDED FOR THIS PRACTICE

1. A properly lit and adjusted torch.
2. Proper safety protection (welding goggles, safety glasses, pliers, long sleeve shirt, long pants, leather shoes or boots and a spark lighter).
3. Tin-lead or tin-antimony solder and flux.
4. 2 or more pieces of 18 to 24 gauge carbon steel sheet, 6 in. (152 mm) long.

INSTRUCTIONS

1. Tack the pieces of metal together.
2. Apply the flux and heat the metal slowly, checking the temperature by touching the solder wire to the metal often.
3. When the work gets hot enough, flash the flame off frequently to prevent overheating and proceed along the joint.
4. When the joint is completed, the solder should be uniform.
5. Repeat this practice until it can be made without defects.
6. Turn off the gas cylinders, regulators and clean up your work area when you are finished soldering.

Comments

____

CHAPTER 31: SOLDERING, BRAZING, AND BRAZE WELDING QUIZ

Name______________________________ Date ____________

Class ____________ Instructor ____________ Grade ____________

Instructions: Carefully read Chapter 31 in the text. After reading, complete the following questions.

A. SHORT ANSWER

Write a brief answer, in the space provided, that will answer the question or complete the statement.

1. Select five of the following that are advantages of soldering and brazing. (Place an "x" by the correct examples.)

____ a. It is impossible to make inclusions by soldering or brazing.

____ b. Dissimilar materials can be joined.

____ c. Parts of varying thickness can be joined.

____ d. Parts can be temporarily joined without damaging them.

____ e. You do not have to worry about overheating the parts.

____ f. The internal stresses caused by rapid temperature changes can be reduced.

Define the following terms associated with soldering, brazing, and braze welding.

2. Liquid-solid phase bonding process.

____

____

____

3. Flux.

____

____

____

4. Paste range.

____

____

____

5. Capillary action.

____

____

____

B. MATCHING

In the space provided to the left, write the letter from column B that best answers the question or completes the statement in column A.

column A

_____ 6. What is the ability to withstand being pulled apart?

_____ 7. What is the ability to bend without failing?

_____ 8. What is the ability to be bent repeatedly without exceeding its elastic limit and without failure?

_____ 9. What removes light surface oxides, promotes wetting, and aids in capillary action?

_____ 10. What is a method of soldering or brazing that uses a high frequency electrical current to establish a corresponding current on the surface of the part?

_____ 11. What is the temperature range in which a metal is partly liquid and partly solid as it is heated and cooled?

_____ 12. What is the solder alloy that is often used on food-handling equipment and copper pipes?

_____ 13. Which solder or brazing alloy has a good wetting action and corrosion resistance on aluminum and aluminum alloys?

_____ 14. What has the ability to withstand a force parallel to the joint?

_____ 15. What has the ability to resist chemical attack?

column B

a. flux
b. cadmium-silver
c. induction
d. shear strength
e. cadmium-zinc
f. corrosion resistance
g. fatigue resistance
h. ductility
i. paste range
j. tensile strength

C. TRUE-FALSE

Write the letter T in the space to the left if the statement is true and the letter F if the statement if false.

_____ 16. Braze welding does not rely on capillary action to introduce filler metal into the joint.

_____ 17. Brazing is divided into two major categories, brazing and braze welding.

_____ 18. Fluxes are available in many forms, such as washers, rings, and solids.

_____ 19. The oxyacetylene flame is preferred over other fuel gases, such as butane, propane, or natural gas because it heats more uniformly.

_____ 20. One disadvantage about some of the processes of brazing is that if moisture is trapped in the joint an explosion could occur.

_____ 21. Tin-Antimony cannot be used around food-handling equipment.

_____ 22. If cadmium or zinc which is an alloy of some brazing and soldering filler materials is overheated, the fumes can be hazardous unless properly ventilated.

_____ 23. Copper-phos-silver braze alloys should be used to braze steel because of its high tensile strength.

_____ 24. Soldering and brazing differ only in that soldering takes place at a temperature below 800°F and brazing occurs at a temperature above 800°F.

_____ 25. Flux will remove oil, dirt or any other surface contaminant.

D. ESSAY

Provide complete answers for all of the following questions.

26. Soldering is performed below what temperature? Brazing is performed above what temperature?

27. What is capillary action?

28. List four advantages of soldering and brazing as compared to other methods of joining.

29. What are the three functions of a soldering or brazing flux in making a sound joint?

30. Why are MAPP®, propane, or natural gas better fuel gases than acetylene for brazing or soldering?

31. List three advantages of torch brazing.

32. How does an induction brazing machine work?

33. List four brazing alloys and the types of metals they will join. *(Use Table 31-5.)*

34. Why is it important that both pieces of metal being joined be heated at the same rate to the same temperature?

35. How are the edges of a plate shaped for braze welding? Why?

36. Define the following terms: liquid-solid phase bonding, tensile strength, shear strength, ductility, fatigue resistance, corrosion resistance, neutral, paste range, and eutectic.